10687582

COLLEGE OF MARIN LIBRARY
COLLEGE AVENUE
KENTFIELD, CA 94904

'Wedlock's the devil'

BYRON'S LETTERS AND JOURNALS

VOLUME 4

1814–1815

His [the Mussulman's] religion to please neither *party* is made;
On *husbands'* tis *hard*, to the wives most uncivil;
Still I can't contradict, what so oft has been said,
"Though women are angels, yet wedlock's the devil".

TO ELIZA. *Fugitive Pieces*

'Wedlock's the devil'

BYRON'S LETTERS AND JOURNALS

Edited by
LESLIE A. MARCHAND

VOLUME 4
1814–1815

*The complete and unexpurgated text of
all the letters available in manuscript and
the full printed version of all others*

THE BELKNAP PRESS OF
HARVARD UNIVERSITY PRESS
CAMBRIDGE, MASSACHUSETTS
1975

© Editorial, Leslie A. Marchand 1975
© Byron copyright material, John Murray 1975
© Hitherto unpublished letters or parts
of letters to Miss Milbanke before
her marriage, the Earl of Lytton 1975

All rights reserved. No part of this
publication may be reproduced, stored in
a retrieval system, or transmitted, in any
form or by any means, electronic, mechanical,
photocopying, recording or otherwise,
without the prior permission of
the publisher.

ISBN 0-674-08944-8

Library of Congress Catalog
Card Number 73-81853

Printed in the United States
of America

CONTENTS

EDITORIAL NOTE

Following the principle already established of making each volume in this edition as self-contained as possible, the editorial principles as set forth in the first volume are repeated at the end of this note. And the Byron chronology, the list of letters and sources, the list of forgeries, the bibliography, and the biographical sketches of chief correspondents and persons frequently mentioned in the text all pertain to the period and the letters contained in this volume. The index of proper names will serve the reader until the general index appears in the final volume.

* * * * * *

ACKNOWLEDGMENTS. (Volume 4). My debt increases to my publisher and friend John G. Murray, whose meticulous editing of my text and notes is only exceeded by his general enthusiasm for the project as a whole. Mrs. Doris Langley Moore is a constant source of detailed information concerning matters which might have escaped me. The encouragement I have received from my American publishers, the Harvard University Press, particularly from Mrs. E. T. Wilcox, the Editor-in-Chief, and Miss Mary Jane McKinven, of the Publicity Department, deserves special mention. I am grateful for the continued cooperation of the staff of the Carl H. Pforzheimer Library, and especially of Donald H. Reiman, editor of *Shelley and His Circle*, and Mrs. Doucet D. Fischer. And Mr. Carl H. Pforzheimer Jr. has been most kind and ready to render assistance.

For permission to get photocopies of letters in their possession and to use them in this volume I wish to thank the following libraries and individuals: Beinecke Rare Book and Manuscript Library, Yale University; Henry E. and Albert A. Berg Collection, New York Public Library; Biblioteca Nazionale Centrale, Florence; British Museum (Department of Manuscripts); Clark Library, University of California, Los Angeles; William L. Clements Library, University of Michigan; Dartmouth College Library; Greater London Record Office and Library; Harrow School Library; Haverford College Library; Historical Society of Pennsylvania; Houghton Library, Harvard University; Henry E. Huntington Library; the Earl of Jersey; Keats-Shelley Memorial Library, Rome; the Marquess of

Lansdowne; La Trobe Library, State Library of Victoria, Melbourne, Australia; University of Leeds Library; the Earl of Lytton; John S. Mayfield; Pierpont Morgan Library; Mr. John Murray; National Library of Scotland; University of Nottingham Library; Mr. H. F. Oppenheimer; Mrs. Aristotle Onassis; Carl H. Pforzheimer Library; Robert H. Taylor Collection, Princeton University Library; Francis Lewis Randolph; Roe-Byron Collection, Newstead Abbey; Rosenbach Museum; Royal Pavilion Brighton; John Rylands University Library, Manchester; Stark Library, University of Texas; Syracuse University Library; Trinity College Library, Cambridge; Victoria and Albert Museum (John Forster Collection); D. M. S. Watson Library, University College London.

For assistance of various kinds I am indebted to the following: Bernard Blackstone; Mrs. Edward E. Bostetter; John Buxton; Vera Cacciatore; John Clubbe; C. J. W. Eliot; David V. Erdman; Paul Fussell, Jr.; E. D. H. Johnson; Pericles Kollas; Jerome J. McGann; M. Byron Raizis; Gordon N. Ray; William St. Clair; Nassos Tzartzanos; Carl Woodring.

* * * * * *

EDITORIAL PRINCIPLES. With minor exceptions, herein noted, I have tried to reproduce Byron's letters as they were written. The letters are arranged consecutively in chronological order. The name of the addressee is given at the top left in brackets. The source of the text is indicated in the list of letters in the Appendix. If it is a printed text, it is taken from the first printed form of the letter known or presumed to be copied from the original manuscript, or from a more reliable editor, such as Prothero, when he also had access to the manuscript. In this case, as with handwritten or typed copies, or quotations in sale catalogues, the text of this source is given precisely.

When the text is taken from the autograph letter or a photo copy or facsimile of it, the present whereabouts or ownership is given, whether it is in a library or a private collection. When the manuscript is the source, no attempt is made to indicate previous publication, if any. Here I have been faithful to the manuscript with the following exceptions:

1. The place and date of writing is invariably placed at the top right in one line if possible to save space, and to follow Byron's general practice. Fortunately Byron dated most of his letters in this way, but

occasionally he put the date at the end. Byron's usual custom of putting no punctuation after the year is followed throughout.

2. Superior letters such as S^r or 30th have been lowered to Sr. and 30th. The & has been retained, but $\&^c$ has been printed &c.

3. Byron's spelling has been followed (and generally his spelling is good, though not always consistent), and *sic* has been avoided except in a few instances when an inadvertent misspelling might change the meaning or be ambiguous, as for instance when he spells *there* t-h-e-i-r.

4. Although, like many of his contemporaries, Byron was inconsistent and eccentric in his capitalization, I have felt it was better to let him have his way, to preserve the flavour of his personality and his times. With him the capital letter sometimes indicates the importance he gives to a word in a particular context; but in the very next line it might not be capitalized. If clarity has seemed to demand a modification, I have used square brackets to indicate any departure from the manuscript.

5. Obvious slips of the pen crossed out by the writer have been silently omitted. But crossed out words of any significance to the meaning or emphasis are enclosed in angled brackets $\langle\rangle$.

6. Letters undated, or dated with the day of the week only, have been dated, when possible, in square brackets. If the date is conjectural, it is given with a question mark in brackets. The same practice is followed for letters from printed sources. The post mark date is given, to indicate an approximate date, only when the letter itself is undated.

7. The salutation is put on the same line as the text, separated from it by a dash. The complimentary closing, often on several lines in the manuscript, is given in one line if possible. The P.S., wherever it may be written in the manuscript, follows the signature.

8. Byron's punctuation follows no rules of his own or others' making. He used dashes and commas freely, but for no apparent reason, other than possibly for natural pause between phrases, or sometimes for emphasis. He is guilty of the "comma splice", and one can seldom be sure where he intended to end a sentence, or whether he recognized the sentence as a unit of expression. He did at certain intervals place a period and a dash, beginning again with a capital letter. These larger divisions sometimes, though not always, represented what in other writers, particularly in writers of today, correspond to paragraphs. He sometimes used semicolons, but often where we would use commas. Byron himself recognized his lack of knowledge of the logic or the rules of punctuation. He wrote to his pub-

lisher John Murray on August 26, 1813: "Do you know anybody who can *stop*—I mean point—commas and so forth, for I am I fear a sad hand at your punctuation". It is not without reason then that most editors, including R. E. Prothero, have imposed sentences and paragraphs on him in line with their interpretation of his intended meaning. It is my feeling, however, that this detracts from the impression of Byronic spontaneity and the onrush of ideas in his letters, without a compensating gain in clarity. In fact, it may often arbitrarily impose a meaning or an emphasis not intended by the writer. I feel that there is less danger of distortion if the reader may see exactly how he punctuated and then determine whether a phrase between commas or dashes belongs to one sentence or another. Byron's punctuation seldom if ever makes the reading difficult or the meaning unclear. In rare instances I have inserted a period, a comma, or a semicolon, but have enclosed it in square brackets to indicate it was mine and not his.

9. Words missing but obvious from the context, such as those lacunae caused by holes in the manuscript, are supplied within square brackets. If they are wholly conjectural, they are followed by a question mark. The same is true of doubtful readings in the manuscript.

Undated letters have been placed within the chronological sequence when from internal or external evidence there are reasonable grounds for a conjectural date. This has seemed more useful than putting them together at the end of the volumes. Where a more precise date cannot be established from the context, these letters are placed at the beginning of the month or year in which they seem most likely to have been written.

ANNOTATION. I have tried to make the footnotes as brief and informative as possible, eschewing, sometimes with reluctance, the leisurely expansiveness of R. E. Prothero, who in his admirable edition of the *Letters and Journals* often gave pages of supplementary biographical information and whole letters *to* Byron, which was possible at a time when book publishing was less expensive, and when the extant and available Byron letters numbered scarcely more than a third of those in the present edition. Needless to say, I have found Prothero's notes of inestimable assistance in the identification of persons and quotations in the letters which he edited, though where possible I have double checked them. And I must say that while I have found some errors, they are rare. With this general acknowledgment I have left the reader to assume that where a source of information in the notes is not given, it comes from Prothero's edition, where additional details may be found.

The footnotes are numbered for each letter. Where the numbers are repeated on a page, the sequence of the letters will make the reference clear.

In an appendix in each volume I have given brief biographical sketches of Byron's principal correspondents first appearing in that volume. These are necessarily very short, and the stress is always on Byron's relations with the subject of the sketch. Identification of less frequent correspondents and other persons mentioned in the letters are given in footnotes as they appear, and the location of these, as well as the biographical sketches in the appendix, will be indicated by italic numbers in the index. Similarly italic indications will refer the reader to the principal biographical notes on persons mentioned in the text of the letters.

With respect to the annotation of literary allusions and quotations in the letters, I have tried to identify all quotations in the text, but have not always been successful in locating Byron's sources in obscure dramas whose phrases, serious or ridiculous, haunted his memory. When I have failed to identify either a quotation or a name, I have frankly said so, instead of letting the reader suppose that I merely passed it by as unimportant or overlooked it. No doubt readers with special knowledge in various fields may be able to enlighten me. If so, I shall try to make amends with notes in later volumes.

I have sometimes omitted the identification of familiar quotations. But since this work will be read on both sides of the Atlantic, I have explained some things that would be perfectly clear to a British reader but not to an American. I trust that English readers will make allowance for this. As Johnson said in the Preface to his edition of Shakespeare: "It is impossible for an expositor not to write too little for some, and too much for others . . . how long soever he may deliberate, [he] will at last explain many lines which the learned will think impossible to be mistaken, and omit many for which the ignorant will want his help. These are censures merely relative, and must be quietly endured".

I have occasionally given cross references, but in the main have left it to the reader to consult the index for names which have been identified in earlier notes.

BYRON CHRONOLOGY

1814 Jan. 17—Set out for Newstead with Augusta.
Feb. 1—*Corsair* sold 10,000 copies on first day of publication.
Feb. 6—Left Newstead for London.
   —Attacked in Tory press for "Lines to a Lady Weeping".
March—Sat to Phillips for portrait.
March 28—Took apartment in Albany.
April 2—With Augusta at Six-Mile-Bottom.
April—"Ode to Napoleon Buonaparte."
May 14—Began *Lara*.
July 1—At Duke of Wellington's Ball.
July 3—At Six-Mile-Bottom again.
July 20—At Hastings with Augusta.
Aug. 6—*Lara* published with Rogers' *Jacqueline*.
Aug. 11—Back in London.
Aug. 20—Left for Newstead with Augusta and her children.
Sept. 9—Tentative proposal to Annabella Milbanke.
Sept. 18—Received Annabella's acceptance.
Sept. 21—Left for London.
Oct.—Irritated by Hanson's delays in arranging marriage settlement.
   —Began *Hebrew Melodies*.
Oct. 29—Left for Seaham, near Durham, home of Annabella Milbanke.
Oct. 30–31—At Six-Mile-Bottom.
Nov. 2—Arrived at Seaham.
Nov. 16—Left for London.
Nov. 18—At Cambridge.
Nov. 19–22—At Six-Mile-Bottom.
Nov. 23—Applauded by students at Cambridge.
Nov. 24—Back to London.
Dec. 24—Left with Hobhouse for Seaham.
Dec. 25—Christmas at Six-Mile-Bottom.
Dec. 26—With Hobhouse en route—"The Bridegroom more and more *less* impatient."
Dec. 30—Arrived at Seaham.
1815 Jan. 2—Married at Seaham to Annabella Milbanke.

7

Jan. 2–21—"Treacle-moon" at Halnaby in Yorkshire.

Jan. 21–March 9—at Seaham, home of Sir Ralph and Lady Milbanke.

March 9—The Byrons left Seaham for Six-Mile-Bottom to visit Augusta Leigh, Byron's half-sister.

March 12–28—At Six-Mile-Bottom.

March 28—The Byrons set out for London.

March 29—Settled at 13 Piccadilly Terrace, in house leased from the Duchess of Devonshire.

March 31—Wrote his first letter to Coleridge.

April 7—Met Walter Scott at John Murray's.

April 17—Lord Wentworth died; the Milbankes took the name of Noel.

April—*Hebrew Melodies* published with musical score by Braham and Nathan.

April–June [25?]—Augusta with the Byrons in London.

May—Byron became a member of the Sub-Committee of Management of Drury Lane Theatre.

June–July—Visited Leigh Hunt at Maida Vale.

July 29—Byron signed new will, leaving residue of estate to Augusta Leigh.

Aug. 30–Sept. 4—Byron visited his sister at Six-Mile-Bottom.

Oct.—Wrote *Siege of Corinth*.

Nov.—Bailiffs entered 13 Piccadilly Terrace in behalf of creditors.

　—Wrote *Parisina*.

Nov. 15—Augusta arrived at 13 Piccadilly Terrace.

Nov.—Mrs. Clermont and George Anson Byron came to stay at Piccadilly Terrace.

Dec. 10—Byron's daughter Ada born.

BYRON'S LETTERS AND JOURNALS

[TO ROBERT CHARLES DALLAS]   [*1814?*]

Dear Sir/—Could you come here for a few minutes?

yrs. &c.

B

[TO ?]   [*1814?*]

P. S. I entreat you to be more regular, last week I wrote to you on
the same and on another subject.

[TO JOHN MURRAY]   [*1814?*]

Dear Sir—Will you get me *Chalmer's Edition of the Tatler* (I
believe) or Guardian or Adventurer published a few years ago—it
contains an *Editorial note* on Wortley Montague which I have in vain
searched for in this Edition—it is referred to in the [work?] & Letters
of Steele—Chalmer's Edition of the Tatler is a separate work—& I
must find if possible this passage on Montague—I am at my wit's end
about it—Colman is very *farouche*—Hogg excellent in many parts but
attempts too much.—

ever yrs.

[TO JOHN MURRAY (*a*)]   [*January*] 1814

When published let the *Notes* be at the *end* as in the other tales—
I shall send some mottoes from Dante for each Canto[1]—and one for
the title page tomorrow.

[TO JOHN MURRAY (*b*)]   [*January, 1814?*]

Dear Sir/—I send you one more *after thought*—if possible—(and
even in an *erratum* if too late for the *body corporate*) insert it—as it is
on a topic which it was almost inexcuseable to forget[1]

ever yrs.

B

P.S.—One line in answer with a pencil.—

[1] A motto from Dante headed each canto of *The Corsair*.
[1] This could refer to *The Corsair* which was in process of publication in January,
1814, but Byron was always sending in "after thoughts" for all his publications.

11

My dear Merivale—I have redde Roncesvaux[1] with very great pleasure and (if I were so disposed) see very little room for Criticism —there is a choice of two lines in one of ye. last C[ant]os I think "Live & protect["] better because "Oh who?["] implies a doubt of Roland's power or inclination.—I would allow ye.—but that point you yourself must determine on—I mean the doubt as to where to place a part of the poem—whether between the actions or no—only if you wish to have all the success you deserve—*never listen to friends*— and as I am not the least troublesome of the number—least of all to me.—I hope you will be out soon[.] *March* Sir—*March* is the month— the teeming time for the trade & they must be considered.—You have written a very noble poem & nothing but the detestable taste of the day can do you harm—but I think you will beat it—your measure is uncommonly well chosen & wielded.—[end of letter missing in MS.]

My dear Moore—I dedicate to you the last production with which I shall trespass on public patience, and your indulgence for some years—and I own that I feel anxious to avail myself of this latest & only opportunity of adorning my pages with a name consecrated by unshaken public principle & the most undoubted and various talents.— While Ireland ranks you among the firmest of her patriots—while you stand alone, the first of her bards in her estimation and Britain repeats and ratifies the decree—permit one whose only regret since our first acquaintance has been the years he had lost before it commenced—to add the humble but sincere suffrage of Friendship to the voice of more than one Nation.———It will at least prove to you that I have neither forgotten the gratification derived from your society nor abandoned the prospect of it's renewal when your leisure or inclination allow[s] you to atone to your friends for too long an absence.—It is said among those friends—I trust truly—that you are engaged in the composition of a poem whose scene will be laid in the East—none can do those scenes so much justice.———The wrongs of your own Country—the magnificent and fiery spirit of her sons—the beauty and feeling of her daughters may there be found—and Collins when he denominated his

---

[1] In 1814 Merivale published *Orlando in Roncesvalles*, a poem in ottava rima, suggested by his reading Pulci's *Morgante Maggiore* (the first canto of which Byron later translated, during his Italian years).

Oriental his Irish Eclogues was not aware how true at least [was] a part of his parallel.——Your Imagination will create a warmer Sun & less clouded sky—but wildness tenderness and originality are part of your national claim of Oriental descent to which you have already thus far proved your title more clearly than the most zealous of your Country's Antiquarians.—May I add a few words on a subject on which all men are said to be fluent and none agreeable?—Self.—I have written much & published more than enough to demand a longer silence than I now meditate—but for some years to come it is my intention to tempt no further the award of "Gods—men—nor columns".—In the present composition I have attempted not the most difficult but perhaps the best adapted measure to our language—the good old & now neglected heroic couplet—the Stanza of Spenser is perhaps too slow and dignified for narrative—though I confess it is the measure most after my own heart—and Scott alone (he will excuse the Mr. "we do not say Mr. Caesar") Scott alone of the present generation has hitherto completely triumphed over the fatal facility of the octosyllabic verse—and this is not the least victory of his varied & mighty Genius.—In Blank verse—Milton Thomson and our Dramatists are the beacons that shine along the deep but warn us from the rough & barren rock on which they are kindled.—The heroic couplet is not the most popular measure certainly—but as I did not deviate into the other from a wish to flatter what is called public opinion—I shall quit it without further apology & take my chance once more with that versification in which I have hitherto published nothing but compositions whose former circulation is part of my present & future regret.——With regard to my story—& stories in general, I should have been glad to have rendered my personages more perfect & amiable if possible—inasmuch as I have been some- times criticised & considered no less responsible for their deeds & qualities than if all had been personal. Be it so—if I *have* deviated into the gloomy vanity of "drawing from self" the pictures are probably like since they are unfavourable—and if not—those who know me are undeceived—and those who do not—I have little interest in un- deceiving.—I have no particular desire that any but my acquaintance should think the author better than the beings of his imagining—but I cannot help a little surprize & perhaps amusement at some odd exceptions in the present instance—when several (far more deserving I allow) poets in every good plight & quite exempted from all participation in the faults of those heroes who nevertheless might be found with little more morality than "The Giaour" and perhaps—but

13

No—I must admit Childe Harold to be a very repulsive personage—
and as to his identity—those who like it must give him whatever
"Alias" they please.——If however anything could remove the
impression it may be of some service to me—that the Man who is
alike the delight of his readers and his friends—the poet of all circles
—and the idol of his own—permits me here & elsewhere to subscribe
myself

most truly & affectionately his servant

Byron[1]

[TO JOHN MURRAY]   *1814 Jany. 2. Sunday*

Dear Sir/—Excuse this dirty paper—it is the *pen*ultimate half
sheet of a quire.——Thanks for your books & the L[on]d[o]n
Chron[icle][1] which I return—The Corsair is copied & now at Ld.
Hol[land]'s but I wish Mr. G[iffor]d to have it tonight.—Mr.
D[alla]s is very *perverse*—so that I have offended both him & you—
when I really meaned to do good at least to one—& certainly not to
annoy either.[2]—But I shall manage him I hope—I am pretty confident
of the *tale* itself—but one cannot be sure.—If I get it from Ld.
H[olland] it shall be sent

yrs. ever

B

[TO JOHN MURRAY]   *[January 3? 1814]*

Dear Sir—I will answer your letter this evening—in the mean time
it may be sufficient to say—that there was no intention on my part to
annoy you—but merely to *serve* Dallas—& also to rescue myself from
a possible imputation that *I* had other objects than fame in writing so
frequently—whenever I avail myself of any profit arising from my

---

[1] This dedicatory letter to Moore was prefixed to *The Corsair* when it was
published on the first of February, 1814. Murray had objected to Byron's references
to Irish politics in the letter, and Byron then wrote a shorter letter, but Moore
preferred the first one and Byron insisted on its being published with the poem.
Byron had laboured over the letter. There is an earlier draft among the Murray
MSS. with many changes and deletions.

[1] The *London Chronicle*, from 1757, had published much poetry and criticism of
older writers. Boswell contributed to it from 1766 to 1790.

[2] Byron had given the copyright of *The Corsair* to Dallas, with the liberty to
publish with any bookseller he pleased. This alarmed Murray who was then not on
good terms with Dallas. See Dec. 18, 1813, to Dallas (Vol. 3, pp. 202–203).

pen—depend upon it it is not for my own convenience—at least it never has been so—& I hope never will—

yrs. truly

B

P.S.—I shall answer this evening—& will set all right about D[alla]s————I thank you for your expressions of personal regard—which I can assure you I do not lightly value.——

[TO JOHN MURRAY]   *Tuesday [January 4, 1814]*

Dear Sir/—From Mr. G[ifford] every comma is an obligation for which thank him in my name & behalf—I am at a loss to guess to "what *remarks*" he alludes in the note which I [reta]in—*none* were on any of ye. proofs—and the *M.S. you* sent to ye. printers without shewing it to me *since.*—They are (if any) probably there—But pray explain this to Mr. G[ifford] & tell him that of course I should have attended to them—& will *now* if I can find them.—

yrs. ever

BN

[TO THOMAS ASHE]   *January 5th. 1814*

Sir/—When you accuse a stranger of neglect you forget that it is possible business or absence from London may have interfered to delay his answer—as has actually occurred in the present instance.— But—to the point—what is the sum you think will be of service to you—I am willing to do what I can to extricate you from your situation.—Your first scheme I was considering but your own impatience appears to have rendered it abortive—if not irretrievable— I will deposit in Mr. Murray's hands (with his consent) the sum you mentioned to be advanced for the time at ten pounds per month[1]—

yrs. truly

BYRON

P.S.—I write in the greatest hurry—which may make my letter a little abrupt—but as I said before I have no wish to distress your feelings.———

1 See Dec. 14, 1813, to Ashe, note 1 (Vol. 3, p. 197).

Dear Sir/—If you will look over the loose MSS. (*not* the "Corsair" M.S.) I think you will find there is another stanza in the song which I have inserted in Canto *1st*.[1]—if so copy & send it in it's right place to the press with the proof I am now correcting

yrs. truly

B

P.S.—You recollect *this* song was sent some time ago for C[hilde] H[arol]d. Correct the *punctuation* of this by Mr. G[ifford]'s proof— *this* must be for the press—because I have added—& altered—there were some *sad* printers' blunders *"lovely"* for *"lonely"*—*"lifeless"* for *"listness"* &c. &c. I wish one could find an *infallible* printer.—I shall send the *Deds* [Dedications] to Mr. Moore tomorrow—& if I do not insert one of them—depend upon it *you* shall have it in a *note*—I shall state my intentions—your exquisite tory reasons—& my gentle compliance.———

[TO THOMAS MOORE] *January 6, 1814*

I have got a devil of a long story in the press, entitled "The Corsair," in the regular heroic measure. It is a pirate's isle, peopled with my own creatures, and you may easily suppose they do a world of mischief through the three Cantos. Now for your Dedication—if you will accept it. This is positively my last experiment on public *literary* opinion, till I turn my thirtieth year,—if so be I flourish until that downhill period. I have a confidence for you—a perplexing one to me, and, just at present, in a state of abeyance in itself. * * *

* * * * * * * * * * * * * * *

However we shall see. In the mean time, you may amuse yourself with my suspense, and put all the justices of peace in requisition, in case I come into your county with "hack but bent."

Seriously, whether I am to hear from her or him, it is a *pause*, which I shall fill up with as few thoughts of my own as I can borrow from other people. Any thing is better than stagnation; and now, in the interregnum of my autumn and a strange summer adventure,[1]

1 This probably refers to the song 'Thou act not false' added at the end of the 7th edition of *Childe Harold*, [early 1814].
1 The summer adventure was with Augusta Leigh, the autumn one with Lady Frances Webster. The present perplexity, described no doubt in the omission indicated by the asterisks, must have concerned some eclaircissement with Lady Frances, and a possible duel with her husband.

which I don't like to think of (I don't mean * * [Caroline?]'s, however, which is laughable only), the antithetical state of my lucubrations makes me alive, and Macbeth can "sleep no more:"—he was lucky in getting rid of the drowsy sensation of waking again.

Pray write to me. I must send you a copy of the letter of Dedication.[2] When do you come out? I am sure we don't *clash* this time, for I am all at sea, and in action,—and a wife, and a mistress, &c. &c.

Thomas, thou art a happy fellow; but if you wish us to be so, you must come up to town, as you did last year; and we shall have a world to say, and to see, and to hear. Let me hear from you.

P.S.—Of course you will keep my secret, and don't even talk in your sleep of it. Happen what may, your Dedication is ensured, being already written; and I shall copy it out fair to-night, in case business or amusement—Amant alterna Camoenae.[3]

[TO AUGUSTA LEIGH]   [*January 7, 1814?*]

My dearest A.—I shall write tomorrow—but did *not* go to Ly M[elbourne]'s twelfth cake banquet.—M[ary Chaworth Musters] has written again—*all friendship*—& really very simple & pathetic—*bad usage—paleness—ill health*—old *friendship—once—good motive*—virtue —& so forth.———You shall hear from me tomorrow

ever dearest Augusta

yrs.

B

[TO JOHN MURRAY (*a*)]   [*January 7, 1814*]

Dear Sir/—You don't like the dedication—very well—there is another—but you will send the other to Mr. Moore—that he may know I *had* written it.——I send also mottos for the cantos—I think you will allow that an Elephant may be more sagacious but cannot be more docile.—

yrs.

Bn

The *name* is again altered to "*Medora*"[1]

[2] Byron's dedicatory letter to Moore for *The Corsair*.
[3] "singing by turns the Muse's love", Virgil, *Eclogue 3*.
[1] The name of the heroine of *The Corsair* was first Francesca, then changed to Genevra (or Ginevra), and finally to Medora. Byron had written two sonnets "To Genevra" in December, 1813, obviously addressed to Lady Frances Webster. Medora was the name given by Augusta Leigh to her daughter born in April, 1814. Apparently he shifted back and forth about the name. See *Poetry*, III, 239n.

17

[*January 7, 1814?*]

Dear M.—*Dont* send the dedications to Ld. H[olland] or Mr. G[ifford]—you will play the *devil*.

yrs.

B

[TO THOMAS MOORE]   *January 7th, 1814*

My dear Moore.—I had written to you a long letter of dedication, which I suppress, because, though it contained something relating to you which every one had been glad to hear, yet there was too much about politics, and poesy, and all things whatsoever, ending with that topic on which most men are fluent, and none very amusing—*one's self*.[1] It might have been re-written—but to what purpose? My praise could add nothing to your well-earned and firmly-established fame: and with my most hearty admiration of your talents, and delight in your conversation, you are already acquainted. In availing myself of your friendly permission to inscribe this Poem to you, I can only wish the offering were as worthy of your acceptance as your regard is dear to,

Yours, most affectionately and faithfully,

BYRON

[TO THOMAS MOORE]   *January 8th, 1814*

As it would not be fair to press you into a Dedication, without previous notice, I send you *two*, and I will tell you *why two*. The first, Mr. M[urray], who sometimes takes upon him the critic (and I bear it from *astonishment*), says, may do you *harm*—God forbid!—this alone makes me listen to him. The fact is, he is a damned Tory, and has, I dare swear, something of *self*, which I cannot divine, at the bottom of his objection, as it is the allusion to Ireland to which he objects. But he be d—d—though a good fellow enough (your sinner would not be worth a d—n).

Take your choice;—no one, save he and Mr. Dallas, has seen either, and D. is quite on my side, and for the first. If I can but testify

---

[1] Byron had written a long letter dedicating *The Corsair* to Moore, in which he made some allusions to the Irish question and other political matters, which Murray objected to. He then wrote a substitute dedication. He sent both to Moore asking him to choose between them. Moore chose the original letter which was finally published with the poem. See Jan. 8, 1814, to Moore.

to you and the world how truly I admire and esteem you, I shall be quite satisfied. As to *prose*, I don't know Addison's from Johnson's; but I will try to mend my cacology. Pray perpend, pronounce, and don't be offended with either.

My last epistle would probably put you in a fidget. But the devil, who *ought* to be civil on such occasions, proved so, and took my letter to the right place.

* * * * * * * * * * * * * * * *

Is it not odd?—the very fate I said she had escaped from * *, she has now undergone from the worthy * *. Like Mr. Fitzgerald,[1] shall I not lay claim to the character of "Vates?"—as he did in the Morning Herald for prophesying the fall of Buonaparte,—who, by the by, I don't think is yet fallen. I wish he would rally and rout your legitimate sovereigns, having a mortal hate to all royal entails.—But I am scrawling a treatise. Good night. Ever, &c.

[TO LADY MELBOURNE]   *January 8th. 1814*

My dear Ly. M[elbourn]e.—I have had too much in my head to write—but don't think my silence capricious.—C[aroline] is quite out—in ye. first place *she*[1] was not under the same roof—but first with my old friends the H[arrowby]'s in B[erke]l[e]y Square—and afterwards at her friends the V[illiers]'s nearer me.—The separation & the express are utterly false & without even a shadow of foundation so you see her spies are ill paid or badly informed.—But—if she had been in ye. same house—it is less singular than C[aroline]'s *coming* to it—the house was a very decent house till that illustrious person thought proper to render it otherwise.——As to Me. de Stael—I never go near her—her books are very delightful—but in society I see nothing but a very plain woman forcing one to listen & look at her with her pen behind her ear and her mouth full of *ink*.—So much for her.— Now for a confidence—my old love of all loves—Mrs.—[Chaworth- Musters] (whom somebody told you knew nothing about me) has written to me *twice*—no *love* but she wants to see me—and though it will be a melancholy interview I shall go—we have hardly met & never been on any intimate terms since her marriage—*he* has been playing the Devil—with all kinds of *vulgar* mistresses—& behaving

---

[1] This was the "hoarse Fitzgerald" mentioned in the first line of *English Bards and Scotch Reviewers*. William Thomas Fitzgerald (1759–1829) was a poetaster who considered himself a kind of unofficial poet laureate.
[1] Augusta Leigh.

ill enough in every respect.—I enclose you the *last* which pray return immediately with your *opinion*—whether I *ought* to see her or not—you see she is unhappy—she was a spoilt heiress—but has seen little or nothing of the world—very pretty—& once simple in character & clever—but with no peculiar accomplishments—but endeared to me by a thousand childish & singular recollections—you know her estate joined mine & we were as children very much together—but no matter—*this* was a love-match—they are *separated.*—I have heard from Ph. [Frances Webster]—who seems embarrassed with constancy—her *date* is the *Grampian* hills[2]—to be sure with that latitude & her precious epoux—it must be a shuddering kind of existence.— C[aroline] may do as she pleases—thanks to your goodnature rather than my merits or prudence—there is little to dread from her love & I forgive her hatred.——Ly. H[arrowby?]'s second son is in Notts & *she* has been guessing & asking about Mrs. C[haworth-Musters]—no matter—so that I keep her from *all other* conjectures.—I write to you in a tone which nothing but hurry can excuse—don't think me impatient or peevish but merely *confused—consider* one moment—*all things*—& do not wonder—by the bye—I lately passed my time very *happily.*——By the bye—this letter will prove to you that we were at least friends—& that the Mother in law—erred when she told you that it was quite a *dream*—will you believe me another time.— Adieu, ever yrs. pray write—& believe me

most affectly. yrs.

B

[TO JOHN MURRAY]   [*January 8, 1814*]

Dear Sir/—Correct ⟨Mr. G⟩ the present *proof* by *mine* as there are a few words & &cs—which require [annexing?] to this—or correct *mine* of last night by this—which you please.—And let me have all tomorrow—The 3 (2 of them sonnets) smaller pieces publish at the end of the notes or after them.—

yrs. truly

Bɴ

Mr. M[oor]e has decided most *decidedly* for ye. *first* dedication—so send it with ye. next proof.———

2 The Grampian Hills, Scotland.

My dear Ly. M[elbourn]e.—The "beloved friend" was always a *she Dogstar*—& had an ascendancy over her which I have felt to my cost—& depend upon it whatever point she has to carry will be carried—but I hear (not from *either*) that they are to be reconciled immediately—if so—I shall not journey 150 miles to be a witness of ye. reunion—and though I have no feelings beyond esteem &c. now to spare—& she still fewer for me—in *that case* her wishing to see me was rather premature—because evidently she does not desire *him* to know anything of the matter.—"Like C[aroline]?" no more than I am like *Wm.* and as far *her* superior—as I say most sincerely (with "*an air*" you will say) & believe Wm. is to me in every good and praiseworthy quality.—As for C[aroline] don't talk of her—for I am really advancing fast to an utter detestation—which I try to curb—and which I must curb—for it is most ungenerous to allow it to get the better of me—because there are sacrifices which once made—no provocation can quite cancel.————"My confusion" did not begin till I was *alone*—& has therefore nothing to do with the question of happiness—and as to "*abandon*"—none but the greatest of Sinners can have any idea of it—but *that* depends entirely on the persons themselves—however there is no *compassion*—and there is an end of my theoretical observations.————I cannot conceive why the D———l should angle with so many baits for one whom all the world will tell you belonged to him probably before he was born.—But when they give me a character for "Art" it is surely most mistaken—no one was ever more heedless.—Moore in a letter to me on a *different subject you may suppose*—says "the only chance of Salvation for you (I never look for any from *yourself*) is the ["] &c &c.—now—what he wishes me to avoid—*you* would call "my salvation"[1]—No matter—nothing can deprive me of the past—and as to the *future*—what promise did *it* ever keep to any human being?—Besides—"there is a world beyond Rome"[2] and though you will not believe me—nothing but this confounded delay of Newstead &c. could have prevented me from being long ago in my isles of the East. Why should I remain or care?—I am not— never was—nor can be popular—and you will own I do not deserve nor indeed strive to be so—I never *won* the world—& what it has awarded me has always been [wrung?] from it's caprice—my life here

---

[1] Lady Melbourne, Byron realized, hoped that his interest in Lady Frances Webster would distract him from his more dangerous incestuous relation with his half-sister, Augusta Leigh.

[2] Unidentified.

is frittered away—there I was always in action or at least in motion
— —and except during Night—always on or in the sea—& on horseback—I am sadly sick of my present sluggishness—and I hate
civilization.— —Pray why the *Parenthesis?*—do you not know that
shyness is really & truly ye. *family* appendage—it may look like
modesty (but few see the likeness) it is very often contempt of
others—& no great liking to one'self.— —As to *loud* talking &
shining as it is called I leave it to your wits—my only object in
society is to see some *one* person—to whom it is generally expedient
to talk rather in a low voice—and if they listen—and don't look uncomfortable (as *you* always do with me) it is all I hope—& when they
are gone—I look about me—and see what proselytes my Master is
making—and interrupt nobody.—Perhaps I shall go into Notts—but
if they are together—I do not see how even friendship (on such a
foundation as ours) would be much to the purpose

ever yrs.

B

P.S.—Lady Mount[norris][3] was seized with a sudden penchant
for— —[Augusta] and called on her at the Vil[li]er's and asked her to
some party—in gratitude I presume for the *Aston* Rumour[4] of which
I suppose the *elder* informed her—I am sure she could not refrain from
saying something of her S[iste]r Ph [Frances] as both she & I saw that
she was vigilant to plague us.—That business will never be renewed
or rather never completed—I *heard* from *Ph* the other day as usual—
but we shall not meet till Spring—by which time it is impossible she
should not be altered—and even if not [I] shall not fool away my time
on *theories*—and that stupid speculative reverie of Platonics—in
which I was obliged to humour her fears or her coquetry.—She will
fall eventually (probably soon) into some less indulgent instructor's
precepts—for whom I have been merely paving the way—it was not
my fault that this will be the case—but she—no—*I* was the fool of her
whimsical romance—

[TO JOHN MURRAY]   [*January 10 or 11, 1814?*]

Let the following lines be sent immediately, and form the *last
section* (number it) *but one* of the 3d. (last) Canto.

[3] Mother of Lady Frances Webster.
[4] The rumour of Byron's involvement with Lady Frances Webster.

My dear Lady M[elbourn]e.—I have heard from (what new initial shall we fix upon) *M*[ary Chaworth-Musters] again—and am at a loss.—You must advise me[.] I will tell you why.—It is impossible I should now feel anything beyond friendship for her or any *one* else in present circumstances—and the kind of feeling which has lately absorbed me has a mixture of the *terrible* which renders all other— even passion (pour les autres) insipid to a degree[1]—in short one of its effects has been like the habit of Mithridates who by using himself gradually to poison of the strongest kind at last rendered all others ineffectual when he sought them as a remedy for all evils & a release from existence.———In my answer to M. I touched very slightly on my *past* feelings towards her & explained what they *now* were—hers I conceive to be much the same—and she says as much—but I am not quite so sure that seeing her again—& being on the terms of intimacy we once were—would not bring on the *old attack* on *me*—and the recollection of the former is not sufficiently agreeable to make me wish to risk another.—She is much governed by "dear friend"[2] and "dear friend" and I for certain reasons are not very likely to agree on that subject if on any other—I only wonder how she came to allow her to write to me at all.—"Dear friend" is the elder by several years—was never handsome—but not unwilling to be thought so—I don't know how to manage her—even if I wish to preserve this same sickly friendship which is reviving between M. & Me——I must try my hand at dissimulation—& shall probably overact my part if I get interested in the business in the mean time it must take it's course.—— She talks of coming to town in Spring—in that case I might have at least turned her friendship to some account by playing it off against *Ph.* [Frances Webster] which from the disposition of the latter would have ensured *her*—but I have quite resigned my pretensions in that quarter and in every other.—I have just received ye. enclosed from C[aroline]—she seems to wish to alarm by some idea of my being *hated* by somebody I like—to whom or what she alludes I do not know nor much conjecture.—I shall not answer—and you will have ye. goodness to throw it C[aroline]'*s* into the fire.—You will read ye. other inclosure—favour me with your counsel—& return it.—We

---

[1] Lady Melbourne knew that Byron referred to his feeling for Augusta.
[2] The "dear friend" was a Miss Radford, whom Mary described as a "near and dear relative".

shall perhaps not correspond much longer[3] but as long as I can I shall
not cease occasionally to sign myself

ever yrs,

B

P.S.—If C[aroline] has taken *anything* into her head (which by the
bye she *would* probably have done—at all events) it is all over—she
will never rest till she has destroyed me in some way or other—when
it comes to that point—& through her (yet I hardly know how for I
have neither written nor held any conversation of any kind with
C[aroline] since our summer fracas) if it comes to that point—she
will regret it—I have neither weapon nor defence against herself—
but some of her instruments or connections (I mean *maternal* ones
with yours I can have nothing to do) will probably be involved by
her—and if but one it—will be good company in whatever journey I
may wish to set out upon.— —

[TO JOHN HANSON] [*January 11, 1814*]

Dear Sir/—I wish to know whether any or what news has been
heard of or from Mr. Claughton—and I wish also you or Charles
would see Howard in order to make some arrangement on ye. score
of those infernal annuities.—

yrs. truly

Bn

Pray send me one line & make my respects to ye. Ladies—you
can't mean to allow Claughton to go on *so forever*.— —

[TO JOHN MURRAY] [*January 11, 1814*]

Dear Sir/—Correct this proof by Mr. G[ifford]'s (and from the
M.S.S.) particularly as to the *pointing*—I have added a section for
Gulnare to fill up the parting—& dismiss her more ceremoniously—
if Mr. G[ifford] or you dislike—'tis but a *spunge* and another midnight
better employed than in yawning over Miss E[dgewort]h—who by
the bye may now return ye. compliment.—

ever yrs.

Bn

---

[3] This is Byron's hint, repeated several times in his letters to Lady Melbourne,
that if he did something desperate such as elope with Augusta, he would not
embarrass his confidante by continuing to correspond with her.

Wednesday—or Thursday—

P.S.—I have redde "Patronage"[1] it is full of praises of Lord
Ellenborough!!! from which I infer near & dear relations at the bar—
and has much of her heartlessness & little of her humour (wit she
has none) and she must live more than 3 weeks in London to describe
good (or if you will) *high* society—the *ton* of her book is as vulgar as
her father[2]—and no more attractive than her eyes—I do not love Me.
de Stael—but depend upon it—she beats all your Natives hollow as an
Authoress—in my opinion—and I would not say this if I could help
it.————

P.S.—Pray repeat my best acknowledgements to Mr. G[iffor]d—
in any words that may best express how truly his kindness obliges
me—I won't bore him with *lip* thanks or *notes*.——

[TO AUGUSTA LEIGH]   *Jany. 12th. 1814*

My dearest Augusta—On Sunday or Monday next with leave of
your lord and president—you will be *well* & ready to accompany me to
Newstead—which you *should* see & I will endeavour to render as
comfortable as I can for both our sakes—as to time of stay there—
suit your own convenience I am at your disposal.———Claughton is I
believe inclined to settle—if so—I shall be able to do something further for *yours* & *you*—which I need not say will give me ye. greatest
pleasure.—More news from Mrs.——[Chaworth-Musters]—*all
friendship*—you shall see her.——Excuse haste & evil penmanship

ever yrs.

B_N

[TO AUGUSTA LEIGH]   [*January 1814?*]

P.S.—Can you tell me—(but that may be done on meeting) *how
much* G[eorge] *owes*—I trust on C[laughto]n's paying the residue—I
shall be able to make some arrangement—for *him*—but at all events
you & the Children shall be properly taken care of.—what I did for

[1] In Maria Edgeworth's *Patronage*, the Lord Chief Justice, "Lord Oldborough",
is idealized as a benevolent judge.
[2] Byron later described Edgeworth as a fine old fellow but a bore. See Nov. 4,
1820, to Murray, and the Ravenna Diary, Jan. 19, 1821.

25

him might be *seized* &c. anything done for yourself would be safer & more advantageous to both.[1]—

[TO LADY MELBOURNE]   *January 12th. 1814*

My dear Ly. M[elbourn]e.—More letters one—two—three—from C[aroline] who wants pictures—forgiveness—praise for forbearance— promise of future confidence—and God knows what beside with leave to shew some elderly gentleman of wit and discretion the "Curse of Minerva."—She may shew him the "Curse of Car[olin]e L[am]b"— or whatever she pleases—and may tell him the same long story she did to Sheridan the other day—I really believe her shortest & best way would be to print it as her recitations are endless—and I think she never will rest till she or Me. de Stael have it circulated through regenerated Germany—where she may enjoy the honours of Suicide till a happy old age.——But a truce with these fooleries—I *must not*— & *can not* write—and as to pictures I have no time to sit for a Sign Post.—Just as I had got her quite out of my head—and she was quietly disposed with you and every one else—here she comes again— it is too late—and never was a more unlucky moment—as it happens that the least additional drop will make my cup run over—and any irritation—*revenge her* amply—but certainly at the same time separate her and you and me beyond ye. possibility of reunion—for the remain- der of our lives.[1]———I don't think mine will be a long one (this you will think *like her*—but I don't allude to Suicide—*that* is weak— and if I were inclined that way it would never be from the pressure of pain—but satiety of pleasure) because from mere common causes & effects it cannot last—I began very early & very violently—and alternate extremes of excess and abstinence have utterly destroyed— oh! unsentimental word!—my *stomach*—and as Lady Oxford used *seriously* to say a *broken heart* means nothing but *bad digestion*. I am one day in high health—and the next on fire or ice—in short I shall turn hypochon*driacal*—or drops*ical*—whim*sical* I am already—but don't let me get *tragical*.—The last dangerous illness I had was a fever in the Morea in 1811 [sic]—this very *month*—and what do you suppose was the effect?—I really *can't* tell you—but it is perfectly true—that at the time when I myself thought & everyone else thought I was

----

[1] This postscript, detached from the letter to which it belonged, is marked on the cover "Castle Eden Nov. fifteenth [1814?]". But the subject matter suggests that it belongs to, or was written soon after the letter of Jan. 12, 1814, to Augusta.
[1] See Jan. 11, 1814, to Lady Melbourne.

dying———I had very nearly made my exit like some "just man" whom a King of Poland envied.———You will not believe this—but pray confine your scepticism to any *good* you may hear of me—I think you have seen that in my statements to you—truth has been the basis—you do not know how uncomfortable the doubts (not yours) about M[*ary Chaworth-Musters*] had made me—you have now perceived that we were "inmates of the same house" and I think you may also see that she was not ignorant that I was attached to her, I never said that it was returned however in a boyish & girlish way I might fancy it.—Heigh ho!—well—it does not much [matter]— but if I could begin life again—there is much of it I would pass in the same manner.———I leave town on Sunday or Monday next—and will write to you from Newstead—if you can pacify C[arolin]e and keep her in her good resolutions you will do her a service—as for me I am not worth serving nor preserving.———By the bye—don't you pity poor Napoleon—and are these your heroes?—Commend me to the Romans—or Macbeth—or Richard 3d.—this man's spirit seems broken—it is but a bastard devil at last—and a sad whining example to your future Conquerors—it will work a moral revolution—he must *feel* doubtless—if he did not there would be little merit in insensibility —but why shew it to the world—a thorough mind would either rise from the rebound or at least go out "with harness on it's back."[2]———

ever yrs.
B

[TO LADY MELBOURNE]   *Jany. 13th. 1814*

My dear Ly. M[elbourn]e.—I do not see how you could well have said less—and that I am not angry may be proved by my saying a word more on ye. subject.—You are quite mistaken however as to *her*[1]— and it must be from some misrepresentation of mine that you throw the blame so completely on the side least deserving and least able to bear it—I dare say I made the best of my own story as one always does from natural selfishness without intending it—but it was not her fault—but my own *folly* (give it what name may suit it better) and her weakness—for—the intentions of both were very different and for some time adhered to—& when *not* it was entirely my own—

---

[2] *Macbeth*, Act V, sccoe 5, line 52.
[1] Augusta Leigh.

in short I know no name for my own conduct.—Pray do not speak so harshly of her to me—the cause of all————I wrote to you yesterday on other subjects and particularly C[aroline]——As to *manner*—mine is the same to anyone I know or like—and I am almost sure less marked to her than to *you*—besides any constraint or reserve would appear much more extraordinary than the reverse—until something more than manner is ascertainable.—Nevertheless I heartily wish Me. de Stael at the Devil—with her observations—I am certain I did not see her—and she might as well have had something else to do with her eyes than to observe people at so respectful a distance.————So "*Ph* [Frances Webster] is out of my thoughts"—in the first place if she were out of them—she had probably not found a place in my words—and in the next—she has no *claim*—if people will stop at the first tense of the verb "aimer" they must not be surprised if one finishes the conjugation with somebody else.—"How soon I get the better of"—in the name of St. Francis and his wife of Snow[2]—and Pygmalion & his statue what was there here to get the better of?—a few kisses for which she was no worse—and I no better.——Had the event been different—so would my subsequent resolutions & feelings —for I am neither ungrateful—nor at all disposed to be disappointed—on the contrary I do firmly believe—that I have often only begun to *love*—at the very time I have heard people say that some dispositions become indifferent.————Besides—her fool of a husband—and my own recent good resolutions—and a mixture of different piques and mental stimulants together with something not unlike encouragement on her part—led me into that foolish business—out of which the way is quite easy—and I really do not see that I have much to reproach myself with on her account—if you think differently pray say so.—As to Mrs. C[haworth-Musters] I will go—but I don't see any good that can result from it—certainly none to me—but I have no right to consider myself.—When I say this I merely allude to uncomfortable *feelings*—for there is neither chance nor fear of anything else—for she is a very good girl—and I am too much dispirited to rise even to admiration.—I do verily believe—*you* hope otherwise—as a means of *improving* me—but I am sunk in my own estimation—and care of course very little for that of others.———As to *Ph*—she will end as all women in her situation do—it is impossible she can *care* about a man

---

[2] The legend that St. Francis dampened his passions with a wife of snow was one which Byron referred to again in *Don Juan* (6:17). Byron may have picked up the "wife of snow" legend from Butler's *Hudibras* (Part 2, canto 1, 374), for he had been reading that poem (see May 24, 1813, to Lady Melbourne, Vol. 3, p. 52).

who acted so weakly as I did with regard to herself.——What a fool I am—I have been interrupted by a visitor who is just gone—& have been laughing this half hour at a thousand absurdities as if I had nothing serious to think about.—

yrs. ever

B

P.S.—Another epistle from M[ary Chaworth-Musters]—my answer must be under cover to "dear friend" who is doing or suffering a folly—what can *she Miss R[adford]* be about?[3]—the only thing that could make it look ill—is *mystery*—I wrote to her and *franked*— thinking there was no need of concealment—and indeed conceiving the affectation of it an impertinence.—but she desires me not—and I obey—I suspect R[adford] of wishing to make a scene between *him* & *me* out of dislike to both—but that shall not prevent me from going a moment—I shall leave town on Sunday.———

[page missing?] pantomime—I don't think I laughed once save in soliloquy for ten days—which *you* who know me won't believe (every one else thinks me the most gloomy of existences) we used to sit & look at one another—except in *duetto* & then even our serious nonsense was not fluent—to be sure our gestures were rather more sensible— the most amusing part was the interchange of notes—for we sat up all night scribbling to each other—& came down like Ghosts in the morning—I shall never forget the quiet manner in which she would pass her epistles in a music book—or any book—looking in——[Webster]'s face with great tranquillity the whole time—& taking mine in the same way—once she offered one as I was leading her to dinner at N[ewstead]—all the servants before—& W[ebster] & sister close behind—to take it was impossible—and how she was to retain it without *pockets*—was equally perplexing—I had the cover of a letter from Claughton in mine—and gave it to her saying "there is the Frank for Ly. Water[ford?][4] you asked for" she returned it with the note beneath with—"it is dated wrong—alter it tomorrow" and W[ebster] complaining that women did nothing but scribble— wondered how people could have the patience to frank & alter franks— and then happily digressed to the day of the month—fish sauce—good wine—& bad weather.——Your "matrimonial ladder" wants but one more descending step—*"d—nation"* I wonder how the *carpenter* omitted it—it amused me much.—I wish I were married—I don't

[3] See Jan. 11, 1814, to Lady Melbourne, note 2.
[4] Susanna Hussey, daughter and heir of the 2nd Earl of Tyrconnel (Irish), married in 1805 the 2nd Marquess of Waterford (Irish).

care about beauty nor *subsequent* virtue—nor much about fortune—I have made up my mind to share the decorations of my betters—but I should like—let me see—liveliness—gentleness—cleanliness—& something of comeliness—& *my own* first born—was ever man more moderate? what do you think of my "Bachelor's wife"? What a letter have I written"

[TO THOMAS MOORE]   *January 13, 1814*

I have but a moment to write, but all is as it should be. I have said really far short of my opinion, but if you think enough, I am content.[1] Will you return the proof by the post, as I leave town on Sunday, and have no other corrected copy. I put "servant," as being less familiar before the public; because I don't like presuming upon our friendship to infringe upon forms. As to the other *word*, you may be sure it is one I cannot hear or repeat too often.

I write in an agony of haste and confusion—Perdonate.

[TO JOHN HANSON]   *Jy. 13th. 1814*

Dear Sir/—I just write a line to state that in case of Mr. C[laughto]n's arrival in town you will probably leave a note or message for him stating when you return in order to discuss this business. —If Charles remains he can act as your deputy in the interim.—

ever yrs.

B_N

[TO ?]   *[January 14, 1814]*

Many thanks for Sadi,[1] yourself, and your harmonious namesake[2]— to the two last I am infinitely indebted as I mean to be to the former. Fogs, journeys, and business have hitherto prevented the due acknowledgments of your kindness which to me has been uniform, and deeply felt since our first acquaintance. C[hilde] H[arold] is at present out of print, but Mr. Murray talks of an illustrated edition, and in that case I should wish my friends to have Stothard's designs. . . . I preserve your

1 Byron's dedicatory letter to Moore prefaced to *The Corsair.*
1 Sadi was the 13th century Persion poet, author of *Gulistan.*
2 Unidentified.

seal [the Paphian] with great care. It is a most agreeable impression and confirmation of my text, for I was rather afraid that passage would be unintelligible, at least to the uninitiated. . . .

My dear Sir/—I called & left S's opinion tonight[1]—& was truly glad to hear you can answer all his queries.—If my presence is indispensable a letter from you to N[ewstea]d will recall me—but I think if *you* can *answer* the *queries*—I can *answer you*—which will do just as well if not better.—In course you will leave word for Mr. C[laughto]n of your intended return on Tuesday—

ever dr. Sir yrs.

BN

To be delivered *before* [you] go do[wn] in ye. morning.—

My dear Ly. M[elbourn]e.—As I shall not leave town till Monday I have time to hear once by return of post—if convenient to yourself.— That you may judge exactly how *Ph* [Frances Webster] & I are at present with regards to each other I send you her last epistle—the first part is girlish & romantic—& the whole not much to the purpose—as to the "telling" I believe no one but yourself has any foundation but their own suspicions—and after all there is nothing to be told.———I had an odd dialogue lately with her sister—we were talking of passing time in the country—and I said that my usual & favourite method was to pass several hours of the day *quietly* and *alone*.—"Alone—but not *quietly*" she answered——"what do you mean?["] "what I have said— I have seen you when you did not *see me*.—["] I asked as you may be sure for an explanation—which she gave me as follows—"the morning before we all left N[ewstead] I had been walking with *Ph* [Frances] in the cloisters where I left her to go to my room—when I got to the hall door which was half open I stopped as I am short-sighted to look through my glass at a person leaning alone near the fire—& whom I could not at first distinguish—it was *you*—but I really did not know you immediately—you were perfectly *convulsed*—["] "why did not you walk on & speak to me?["] ["]because I was frightened & did not know what to do—but I turned back to *Ph.*["] "did you mention this to her?["] ["]No—I had reasons for keeping it to myself.["]——I perfectly recollect being where she describes—and some of my sensations—but I was not aware of betraying them to any one—the hall at N[ewstead] is in the *Abbey* part of that enormous mansion—& quite remote from any but my own rooms—and this was the last day but one we passed together.—You may perhaps judge from this that I *do feel* sometimes—& that for her at that time I *did* feel enough.———You will think this *scene* a little in C[aroline]'s style—but recollect first—it is not *my* description—and 2dly. it was not before 500 people—nor was I aware that anyone had seen it at all—and that I laid no great stress on it you may suppose by my never having told it even to you before.———So—you have his R[oyal] H[ighness] on Tuesday—well—I envy him his visit—and [word crossed out] many years of his life—much more than I do his *Regency.*—It is cruel to mention Middleton—when I daily regret not going.—How does C[aroline] go on? I do think between her *theory* & my system of Ethics you will begin to think that our first parents had better have paused before they plucked the tree of knowledge.———

ever yrs. most truly

B<small>N</small>

[TO JOHN MURRAY]   [*January 15, 1814*]

Dear Sir/—Before any proof goes to Mr. G[ifford] it may be as well to revise this—where there are *words omitted*—faults committed— and the Devil knows what.—As to the ded[icatio]n I cut out the parenthesis of *Mr.*[1]—but not another word shall move unless for a better—Mr. M[oor]e has seen & decidedly preferred the part your tory bile sickens at—if every syllable were a rattle-snake or every letter a pestilence—they should not be expunged—let those who cannot swallow chew the expressions on Ireland—⟨though⟩ or Mr. Croker should array himself in all his terrors against them—I care for none of you except Gifford and he won't abuse me unless I deserve it—which will at least reconcile me to his justice. As to the poems in H[obhouse]'s volume the translation from ye. Romaic is well enough— but the best of the other vol—(of *mine* I mean) have been already

---

[1] In the dedication to Moore in *The Corsair* Byron had written after the words "Scott alone", in parenthesis, "He will excuse the *Mr.*—we do not say Mr. Cæsar."

printed.[2]——But do as you please—only as I shall be absent when you come out—*do pray* let Mr. *Dallas* & *you* have a care of ye. press.—

yrs. ever
Bℕ

[TO JOHN MURRAY]   *[January 16, 1814]*

Dear Sir/—I do believe that the Devil never created or perverted such a fiend as the fool of a printer.—I am obliged to inclose you *luckily* for me this *second* proof—*corrected*—because there is an ingenuity in his blunders peculiar to himself.—Let the press be guided by the present sheet.

yrs.
B

Burn the other[.] Correct *this also* by the other in some things which I may have forgotten—there is one mistake he made—which if it had stood—I would most certainly have broken his neck.——

[TO LADY MELBOURNE]   *January 16th. 1814*

My dear Lady M[elbourn]e.—Lewis is just returned from Oatlands[1] where he has been quarrelling with Stael about every thing and every body.—She has not even let poor quiet *me* alone—but has discovered first that I am affected—& 2dly. that I *"shut* my *eyes* during dinner!"*—what this last can mean I don't know unless *she* is opposite— if I *then* do—she is very much obliged to me—and if at the same time I could continue to shut my ears—she would be still more so.——If I really have so ludicrous a habit—will *you* tell me so—& I will try and break myself of it—In the mean time I think the charge will amuse you—I have more faults to find with *her* than *"shutting* her eyes"— one of which is opening her mouth too frequently.———Do not you think people are very naught[y]—what do you think I have this very day heard said of poor M [Mary Chaworth-Musters]? it provoked me beyond any thing—as *he* was named as authority—why—the abomin-

[2] Hobhouse had published in his *Journey through Albania* . . . (2nd edition, 1813), pp. 1149–1150, Byron's translation of a "Romaic love-song". The "other volume" was Hobhouse's *Imitations and Translations* (1809), in which nine of Byron's poems had appeared. From that volume he reprinted in *The Corsair* the "Inscription on the Monument of a Newfoundland Dog."

[1] Estate of the Duke of York near Weybridge, Surrey.

able stories they circulate about Lady *Wd.*[2] of which I can say no more—all this is owing to "dear friend" and yet as far as it regards "dear friend" I must say I have very sufficing suspicions for believing them totally false—at least she must have altered strangely within these nine years—but this is the age of revolution.——The ascendancy always appeared to me that of a cunning mind over a weak one.—but—but—why the woman is a fright—which after all is the best reaon for not believing it.————————I still mean to set off tomorrow—unless this snow adds so much to the impracticability of the roads as to render it useless—I don't mind anything but delay—and I might as well be in London as at a sordid inn waiting for a thaw—or the subsiding of a flood & the clearing of snow.—I wonder what *your* answer will be on *Ph's letter*—I am growing rather partial to the younger sister who is very pretty—but fearfully young—and I think a *fool*—a wife you say would be my salvation—now—I could have but one motive for marrying into that family—and even *that* might possibly only produce a scene & spoil every thing—but at all events it would in some degree be a *revenge*—and in the very face of your compliment (*ironical* I believe) on the want of *selfishness*—I must say that I never can quite get over the *"not"* of last summer—no —though it were to become *"yea"* tomorrow.———I do believe that to marry would be my wisest step—but whom?—I might manage *this* easily with "Le Pere"—but I don't admire the connection—and I have not committed myself by any attentions hitherto.—But all wives would be much the same—I have no *heart* to spare—& expect none in return—but as Moore says "a pretty wife is something for the fastidious vanity of a roué to *retire* upon."—and mine might do as she pleased so that she had a fair temper—and a *quiet* way of conducting herself—leaving me the same liberty of conscience.—What I want is a companion—a friend—rather than a sentimentalist—I have seen enough of love matches—& of all matches —to make up my mind to the common lot of happy couples.—The only misery would be if I fell in love afterwards which is not unlikely —for habit has a strange power over my affections—in that case I should be jealous—and then—you do not know—what a devil any bad passion makes me—I should very likely *do* all that C[aroline] *threatens* in her paroxysms—and I have more reasons than you are aware of for mistrusting myself on this point.—Heigh ho! Good night.

ever yrs. most truly

BN

[2] Lady Westmorland?

P.S.—The enclosed was written last night—and I am just setting off—you shall hear from Newstead—if one ever gets there in a coach really as large as the cabin of a 74 and I believe meant for the Atlantic instead of the Continent.———1000 thanks for yours of this Morn.— "never loved so before"—well then—I hope never to be loved *so* again—for what is it to the *purpose?*—You wonder how I answered it?—to tell you the *truth* (which I could not tell *her*) I have not answered it at all—nor *shall*—I feel so much inclined to believe her sincere—that I cannot sit down and coolly repay her truth with fifty falsehoods—I do not believe her for the same *reason you believe*—but because by writing she *commits* herself & that is seldom done unless in earnest.———I shall be delighted to hear your *defence* against my insinuations—but you will make nothing of it—and he *is* very much to be envied—but you mistake me—for I do do not mean in *general*—on the contrary I coincide with him in taste but upon *one* instance.——— C[aroline] was right about the poem—I have scribbled a longer one than either of the last—& it is in the press—but you know I never hold forth to you on such topics—why should I?—now you will think this a piece of conceit—but really it is a relief to the fever of my mind to write—& as at present I am what they call popular as an author—it enables me to serve one or two people without embarrassing anything but my brains—for I never have nor shall avail myself of the *lucre*—& yet it would be folly merely to make presents to a bookseller—whose accounts *to* me last year are just 1500 guineas *without* including C[hild]e H[arol]d—now the odd part is that if I were a regular stipendiary & *wanted* it probably I should not be offered *one* half—but such are mankind—always offering or denying in the wrong place.— But I have written more than enough already—& this is my last experiment on *public* patience—and just at present I won't try *yours* any further.—

ever yrs. my dear Ly. Me.
B

[TO JAMES WEDDERBURN WEBSTER]   *January 18th. 1814*

My dear W.—Address your *"plan"* to town where I shall return in a week—I like "plans" of all things particularly where they are likely never to be realized.———I am on my way to the country on rather a melancholy expedition—a very old & early connection or rather friend of mine has desired to see me—and as now we never can be more than friends I have no objection—she is certainly unhappy & I fear ill—& the length & circumstances attending our acquaintance render her request & my visit neither singular nor improper—I mean to return to London in a few days unless prevented by the weather which is very impracticable even at present.—Your Papa & family are still in town— I see them occasionally and of the youngest (Juliana) I should be glad to see more—but she is not yet *out*— & is generally—I don't exactly see why—kept out of sight—she will be very beautiful—as to *more*— I have never seen nor heard enough to judge.—It is said that you are coming to town in Spring—I shall be happy to see you—if I can be of any use to you in the mean time—the distance between us can make little difference—as business can be arranged without the parties meeting—I don't mean to press any offers of service upon you—but I hope you know already that I will at least treat you in a *Christian* like manner.—I wrote to you shortly before you left Aston on the subject you wished to hear upon—it is the last you shall hear upon it—till convenient to yourself.—If you are disposed to write—write—and if not I shall forgive your silence—and you will not quarrel with mine.

Believe me yrs. very affectly
B<small>N</small>

P.S.—I presume your illness is merely the cold compliment of the New year—at all events I hope this will find you better.——

[TO JOHN MURRAY]   *January 22d. 1814*

Dear Sir/—You will be glad to hear of my safe arrival here [Newstead]—the time of my return will depend upon the weather— which is so impracticable that this letter has to advance through more Snows than ever opposed the Emperor's retreat.——The roads are impassable—and return impossible—for ye. present—which I do not regret as I am much at my ease and *six* and *twenty* complete this day— a very pretty age if it would always last.——Our coals are excellent— our fire places large—my cellar full—and my head empty—and I have not yet recovered my joy at leaving London—if any unexpected turn occurred with my purchaser—I believe I should hardly quit the place at all—but shut my doors & let my beard grow.——————I forgot to mention—(& I hope it is unnecessary) that the lines beginning *"Remember him"* &c. must *not* appear with the *Corsair*—you may slip them in with the smaller pieces newly annexed to C[*hild*]e H[*arol*]d— but on *no* account permit them to be appended to the Corsair—have the goodness to recollect this particularly.—The books I have brought with me are a great consolation for the confinement—& I bought more as we came along—in short—I never consult the thermometer—and shall not put up prayers for a *thaw* unless I thought it would sweep away the rascally invaders of France—was ever such a thing as Blucher's proclamation?[1]—Just before I left town Kemble paid me the compliment of desiring me to write a *tragedy*—I wish I could—but I find my scribbling mood subsiding—not before it was time—but it is lucky to check it at all.—If I lengthen my letter you will think it is coming on again—so Good bye—

yrs. alway
B_N

P.S.—If you hear any news of Battle or retreat on ye. part of the Allies (as they call them) pray send it—he has my best wishes to manure the fields of France with an *invading* army—I hate invaders of all countries—& have no patience with the cowardly cry of exultation over him at whose name you all turned whiter than the Snow to which (under Providence and that special favourite of Heaven Prince Regency) you are indebted for your triumphs.————I open my letter to thank [you] for yours just received.—The lines "to a Lady weeping" must go with the Corsair—I care nothing for consequences on this point[2]—my politics are to me like a young mistress to an old man the worse they grow the fonder I become of them.—As Mr. G[ifford] likes the "Portuguese translation"[3] pray insert it as an Ad[ditio]n to the Corsair—Lady West[morlan]d thought it so bad—that after making me translate it she gave me her *own version*—which is for aught I know the best of the two.—But—I cannot give up my *weeping* lines—and I *do* think them good & don't mind what *"it looks*

---

[1] *The Times* of Feb. 5, 1814 (page 2, column 5) contained this comment: ". . . present papers contain an address from Marshall Blucher to the inhabitants of the left bank of the Rhine, which we own we are not much pleased to see . . . it seems obscurely to hint that the countries in question may, after all, be handed over again to the foreign Tyrant who has done the greatest violence to their national feelings by cutting them up into departments of his pretended empire, confiscating their lands . . . trampling on their rights and laws and customs and extinguishing their language. If it be, and we trust it is, the irrevocable determination of the Allies to treat on no other terms than the independence of *all and every* state politically existing at the commencement of the fatal Revolution then they ought to declare it in stronger, manlier and less equivocal language than that employed in the Proclamation of which we are speaking." Byron must have seen some earlier report of this Proclamation.

[2] The "Lines to a Lady Weeping", published first anonymously in the *Morning Chronicle*, March 7, 1812. When Byron added the poem to *The Corsair*, the author-ship was revealed, and he was attacked venomously by the Tory press.

[3] Byron's translation of the Portuguese poem "Tu mi chamas" was first pub-lished at the end of the 7th edition of *Childe Harold*, which appeared about the same time as *The Corsair*.

like." —————In all points of difference between Mr. G[ifford] & Mr. D[allas]—let the first keep his place—& in all points of difference between Mr. G[ifford] & Mr. anybody else I shall abide by the former—if I am wrong—I can't help it—but I would rather not be right with any other person—so there is an end of that matter.— After the trouble he has taken about me & mine—I should be very ungrateful to feel or act otherwise—besides in point of judgement he is not to be lowered by a comparison.—————In *politics* he may be right too—but that with me is a *feeling* and I can't *torify* my nature.

[TO JOHN HANSON] *January 24th. 1814*

Dear Sir/—The roads are quite impracticable at present—and promise no better for some time to come—it would be useless to set out with the prospect of detention before a single stage was passed—& even the Mails when they are forwarded—come on horseback—I don't think my carriage though a stout one could make way to Nottingham.—————The moment it is possible I shall set out—but the weather or rather roads must fix the time.—————I am willing to deal in course *fairly* and at the same time *not* harshly with Mr. Claughton and to come into any arrangement most adapted to be tolerable to both parties—I suppose the question of *title* is pretty nearly decided.——The only thing is that I wish to meet my *debts* & *Rochdale*—it is a pity to have the last lying fallow—& if I have not funds to arrange with Deardon & work the collieries—I must sell the Manor—the regular payment of the *past*—*present* & future *interest* is in course indispensable—if a Mortgage for the ninety or hundred thousand on this property is safe to ourselves—we can have no objection—and I feel no irritation against Mr. C[laughton] for any part of the past—though he must be aware that *if* I have made good my *title*—the Contract places him in an awkward situation.—But let that pass—I will do as I would be done by—only whatever arrangement is made—let it be one—on which no further suits & cavils may arise—if possible.——I have (as I have always had) unreserved confidence in your integrity & judgment—and I now submit to your own consideration to decide upon our plan of proceeding—you can in the mean time go on *clearing up*—& he may be making his arrangements to complete—on the lesser points of wine &c. on which Mr. C[laughton] & I held some correspondence I shall be very glad to do any thing to conciliate & keep up good humour between us.——I wish as much as you can wish me to meet you in town—& I am sorry that the weather is so uncertain—or rather so *certain* against my immediate return—Buonaparte's Moscow retreat was much easier—you have no idea of the state of the roads.—In the mean time—*use your discretion*—I shall of course as I have hitherto abide by your advice—and arrangements—*Rochdale* is the principal point—& my debts—with the last we can perhaps arrange—for Rochdale is surely the principal object.—

ever yrs. most truly
Bn

P.S.—The first payment should doubtless be *thirty thousand*—*twenty* will not be sufficient for the objects I have stated.—

[TO LADY MELBOURNE]   *January 29th. 1814*

My dear Lady M[elbourn]e.—I wrote a long letter to you yesterday—and in case it should not reach you I may as well do the like today—never was such weather—one would imagine Heaven wanted to raise a Powder-tax & had sent the Snow to lay it on.—However being in no want of combustibles (you know that Notts is famous for coals & the fa[ir se]x) and my books & cellar being both in tolerable order I can laugh even though looking through a window—though I almost suspect myself of the rheumatism in one of my joints—and a chilblain besides—two very unsentimental maladies. My yesterday's was an epistle almost of business—and what this will be I can't tell—no matter—if you don't quarrel with it or the writer.—I have at last *heard* (the weather wont let me *see* her) M's [Mary Chaworth-Musters] intentions—she says (*since* yesterday) she believes *return impossible*—and that she will "soon act for herself" and then talks of being in town in Spring.—What she proposes to herself in coming there—or why she cannot kiss & be friends with *him*—I do not know & shall not enquire—but she appears to me to be acting injudiciously in both instances.—As a woman of an old family & large fortune—(of which from the circumstances she may probably retain a considerable income) and of unimpeached character—it will not perhaps be difficult for her to enter into good society—but she is shy & singular & will be terribly out of her element—but though pretty (at least she was so) I should not think her liable to get into any scrape—but a great deal of discomfort.—In one of her epistles—she tells me that I have always been represented as "totally without principle with regard to her sex"—against which charge she invariably thought it right to defend me—

in *my* opinion very justly doubtless—but I think it very imprudent in her to select at this time a man of that supposed description for her "to consider as a friend or a beloved *brother*" (I believe I quote correctly) and the more so—because I am quite convinced she herself has no idea of ever regarding me as any thing more—and would be exceedingly surprised & vexed if she found the world saying otherwise.—The next absurd thing is making a mystery of our correspondence—which she does in every possible way—and at ye. same time writing almost every day—in short—thus her proceedings stand at present——I have *hinted* as delicately as I could—pretty nearly what you have read in this letter—I told her not to "consider me for a moment but to act entirely according to her own wishes & ideas of propriety &c."—& the answer is "that there will be *no* impediment to our correspondence which at all events may continue" and that in ten days her fate will probably be decided (meaning I suppose the separation) and then she adds her regrets at my selling N[ewstea]d—and wishes me to delay my journey to town for a short time.—I do not believe that *he* as yet has any notion that she won't return—and if she does not—there are probably some who will believe that I have been tampering with her in the way of dissuasion—which will arise entirely from her *timing* things ill—it is however not the fact if I have said anything on ye. subject it has rather been in favour of her return—at least when she thought of it I told her she was quite right.————I should not have said so much on this subject but you expressed a wish to hear of it—& if it bores you it shan't be repeated—you see there is no love in the case—& that I do not write of it "con Amore" as I did from Aston.——All places are I presume nearly alike in this Lapland but N[ewstea]d has always suited me better than any other—& I do not dislike it more now than heretofore.—————I mentioned yesterday that Augusta was here—which renders it much more pleasant—as we never yawn nor disagree—and laugh much more than is suitable to so solid a mansion—and the family shyness makes us more amusing companions to each other—than we could be to any one else.———

ever yrs.

B

P.S.—Will you address your answer to *London*.

[TO JOHN HANSON]   *January 31st. 1814*

Dear Sir/—I have not yet "started" nor as long as this weather lasts—am I likely to be able to start.—It is said that Mr. Claughton will be here on Wednesday—*how* I don't know if the Snow continues to fall—& *why*—unless he means to return to town to complete—I cannot very well comprehend.———His difficulties in *letting* &c. are of his own making as you very well know—and all the delays are none of ours—I have seen Rushton[1] & have talked him into tractability as far as regards Mr. C[laughto]n—though I believe it will cost me something in ye. way of compensation for the stock &c.—but this is a matter of hereafter discussion—in the mean time he promises not to oppose further.—Bowman[2] I have not seen & have no notion of seeing. Mr. C[laughton] must deal with him himself.———Do you know when & where we are to meet & complete? you may as well address to me *here* as my departure depends entirely on ye. weather. Go on— doing what you think best for ye. interests of all parties—& let us have *good security* at all events.—

yrs. ever
B_N

[TO JOHN MURRAY]   [*February, 1814*]

Dear Sir/—In your letter to N[ewstea]d which I have just received you say that you have saved two other of the *Strictures* in the C[ourie]r—were they sent? or have you them still in town—if so will you send them by the bearer

ever yrs.
B_N

[AN ANSWER TO THE *Courier*]   [*February, 1814?*]

In the reign of Richard 3d. the following couplet is said to have been written

"The Cat, the Rat, & Lovel the Dog
Rule all England under the Hog.["]

Catesby and Ratcliffe were the Cat and the Rat—history records that the narrator of this simple fact paid the price of his untoward allegory with his life.—In the present day though the "Rats" may be in as high request as ever and the ⟨dogs very staunch⟩ curs louder in their yelping yet as the Hog has ceased to be an animal emblematic of Sovereignty— the courtly Cats do not kill their mice but merely play with them in the

---

[1] Rushton was the father of Byron's "little page", Robert Rushton, and one of the Newstead tenants.

[2] Bowman was a Newstead tenant. See June 28, 1810, to his mother (Vol. 1, pp. 251–52).

agreeable feline & most approved method.——If the present were not the best of all possible sovereigns—and his favourites the most indulgent & respectable of their respective species it would not probably be in my power to recall the above anecdote to the Reader's recollection—or to thank them[1] as I ought for being permitted to survive the two stanzas of what the *Courier* calls "impudent doggerel," first published in the *Morning Chronicle* early in 1812, now reprinted and annexed, with some other pieces, to a production entitled *The Corsair*.[2]

The lines are doubtless very bad, since the *Courier* says so. The most convincing proof of this lies in the indignation which they have excited, and the still foaming torrent of abuse against their author. Had they been good, so impartial a Critic would never have condescended to stain his hitherto unsullied columns with invective. The lines must have some peculiar demerit in themselves, as the subject is simply "a Lady's weeping;" she is said to be of "royal line" and to lament a "Sire's disgrace, a realm's decay;" but what realm, or what Sire, or who the weeper might be, was not stated till the *Courier* thought proper to instruct all whom it may concern, that this happy, unindebted, and untaxed country,—and that most honoured of Princes were assailed in this "insolent doggerel." a discovery for which the publisher is much indebted to the said *Courier*, inasmuch as the occasional propensity of mankind to be curious when their attention is awakened has led to a more extensive circulation of the obnoxious verses than they might otherwise have obtained.

They are said to be founded on an almost forgotten fact. It was asserted, in the beginning of the year 1812, that the Prince discarded his friends and his opinions, and that on one occasion his daughter, whom he had educated in his former public principles and private friendships, finding it difficult at that early period of life when the heart is warm and the soul open, to revoke at once the best feelings of our nature, was so astonished at a convivial display of the new doctrines, that she shed tears—an unamiable weakness and a formidable precedent for Heirs Apparent. Such was the cause of the lines in question; the effect—is it not written in the *Courier*?

This "doggerel" is said further to be calculated[3] or intended to raise dissention between & separate mother and—I beg pardon—I mean *father* and daughter—a writer's intentions are but known to

[1] There is a double page missing from the manuscript, here supplied from this word from *L.J.*, III, 29–30n.

[2] The "impudent doggerel" was Byron's "Lines to a Lady Weeping". See Jan. 22, 1814, to Murray, note 2.

[3] The manuscript text resumes after this word.

himself—& the author of the lines knew that no such effect could be produced or he would never have written them,—a child may lament a parent's error without disobediance—and the decay of a realm without rebellion.———It is a maxim of English law—that the Sovereign can do no wrong—& perhaps it may soon be extended by some ex post facto kind of expurgation to the principle that he never can have done wrong even before his attainment of the Sovereignty—but as it now stands—though a Sovereign may be & must be perfectly right in abjuring the friends & principles & promises of the heir apparent— yet an Heir apparent may not be quite so justifiable in adopting & cherishing friends & principles & promises for the purpose of denying them on his becoming Sovereign. Louis 12th. said that it was beneath him to retain the enmities of the Duke of Orleans—it seems to have been above George (not yet) the 4th. to recollect the friendships of the Prince of Wales.————A Realm overwhelmed with debt— may be fairly said to be a little out of repair—and if the tax paper & the obnoxious expression of a "realm's decay" should happen to meet the reader's eye at the same time—he will probably be more disposed to quarrel with the Collector—than the author.————The tears are said to be "Virtue's tears" and the wish that they may be repaid by a people's smiles—is not the best foundation for a charge of disloyalty.— So much for these notorious verses—I have yet a few words to say not as their author—but as the victim of a suppressed production now revived for the purpose of proving that I once was hostile to those with whom I am now reconciled—it is for higher stations to convert their friends into enemies.——
⟨In 1808⟩

[TO JOHN HANSON]   *January—February 1st. 1814*

My dear Sir/—By all I hear—& some of it very tolerable authority —*Leigh* & not Claughton is the *real* purchaser[1]——if so—he is well

---

[1] Chandos Leigh, born in 1791, a landed gentleman of considerable wealth, had just come of age when Claughton entered into contract for the purchase of Newstead Abbey in 1812. His second thoughts or indecisions, or difficulty in raising the money, may have accounted for the delays and procrastinations of Claughton. Byron first mentioned Leigh as the possible purchaser in a letter of July 18, 1813, to Lady Melbourne. Since Claughton (or Leigh?) finally forfeited his down payment and gave up the purchase, we learn no more of Leigh, who is not mentioned again in Byron's letters. Of course, Byron may have been wrong in his conjecture that Leigh was the real purchaser and Claughton only his agent. It is an interesting coincidence that Leigh, who was raised to the peerage in 1839, was not only rich but was also a poet, and an apparent admirer of Byron, for he owned a Phillips portrait of the author of *Childe Harold*.

able to adhere to the contract and the only question is have we made good our title?—Leigh has certainly *been here* with Mr. C[laughton]—& his *own* people talk openly of it being for him the purchase was made—& from Mr. C[laughton]'s asking him frequently "would he like this—that or the other done" I think there can be little doubt of it.—I submit this however to your own consideration—but before we complete it will be as well to *know* that we cannot enforce the old conditions—I have acted openly & fairly by Mr. Claughton—*his* whole conduct to me has been a system of cavilling—& at any rate justifies some suspicion on my part——but more of this when we meet.—I suppose & hope you have hit upon some expedient for adjusting this business finally—if we take a mortgage—see that it be ye. firmest of all possible mortgages—& the interest enforceable.—What shall we do about Rochdale—must I sell or work it—I do believe this famous sale which was to set all right will perplex me more than ever.—From this place there is no stirring till the weather is better—Mrs. L[eigh] is with me & being in ye. family way—renders it doubly necessary to remain till the roads are quite safe.—Pray write—we desire our best remembrances to all.—

ever yrs.
BN

P.S.—I am told *Leigh* likes the place particularly & by no means repents his purchase—so that all this shuffling is simply to make a better bargain—If I was certain this was the case by G[od] I would make it personal with one of them—for I do abhor that low system of tricking.———He is of age & has ample funds to make good a much larger purchase.———

[TO JOHN MURRAY] *February 4th. 1814*

My dear Sir/—I need not say that your obliging letter was very welcome & not ye. less so for being unexpected[1]—at ye. same time I received a very kind one from Mr. D'Israeli[2] which I shall acknowledge & thank him for tomorrow.—It doubtless gratifies me much that our *Finale* has pleased—& that the Curtain drops gracefully—*you* deserve

[1] This was Murray's letter of Feb. 3, announcing the phenomenal success of *The Corsair*: "I sold on the day of publication, a thing perfectly unprecedented, 10,000 copies—and I suppose Thirty People who were purchasers (strangers) called to tell the people in the Shop how much they had been delighted and satisfied." (LJ, III, 21n.)

[2] Isaac D'Israeli, a friend of Murray, whose *Curiosities of Literature* Byron much admired.

it should for your promptitude & good nature in arranging immediately with Mr. D[alla]s—& I can assure you that I esteem your
entering so warmly into ye. subject—& writing to me so soon upon it
as a personal obligation.—We shall now part I hope satisfied with
each other—I *was* & *am* quite in earnest in my prefatory promise not
to intrude any more—& this not from any affectation—but a thorough
conviction that it is ye. best policy—& is at least respectful to my
readers—as it shews that I would not willingly run ye. risk of forfeiting their favour in future.—Besides I have other views & objects—&
think that I shall keep *this* resolution—for since I left London—
though shut up—*snow*bound—*thaw*bound—& tempted with all kinds
of paper—the dirtiest of ink—and the bluntest of pens—I have not
even been haunted by a wish to put them to their combined uses—
except in letters of business—my rhyming propensity is quite gone—
& I feel much as I did at Patras on recovering from my fever—weak
but in health and only afraid of a relapse—I do most fervently hope I
never shall.—I see by the Mo[rning] C[hronicl]e there hath been discussion in ye. *Courier* & I read in ye. M[orning] Post—a wrathful
letter about Mr. *Moore*—in which some Protestant Reader has made a
sad confusion about *India* & Ireland.——You are to do as you please
about ye. smaller poems—but I think removing them *now* from ye.
Corsair—looks like *fear*—& if so you must allow me not to be pleased
—I should also suppose that after the *fuss* of these Newspaper
Esquires—they would materially assist the circulation of the Corsair—
an object I should imagine at *present* of more importance to *yourself*—
than C[hild]e H[arol]d's 7th. appearance. Do as you like—but don't
allow the withdrawing that *poem*—to draw any imputations of *dismay*—
upon me—I care about as much for the Courier as I do for the Prince—
or all Princes whatsoever—except Koslovsky.[3]—Pray make my respects to Mr. Ward—whose praise I value most highly as *you* well
know—it is in the approbation of such men that fame becomes worth
having.—To Mr. G[ifford] I am always grateful & surely not less so
now than ever—& so Good Night to my Authorship.————I
have been sauntering & dozing here very quietly & not unhappily—
you will be glad to hear that I have completely established my title
[deeds] as *marketable* & that the Purchaser has succumbed to the terms
& fulfils them—or is to fulfill them forthwith—he is now here—& we
go on very amicably together—one in each *wing* of ye. Abbey.—We
set off on Sunday—I for town—he for Cheshire.———Mrs. Leigh

[3] Prince Kozlovsky, a Russian diplomat whom Byron had met through Lady
Melbourne and others.

is with me—much pleased with the place—& less so with me for parting with it—to which not even the price can reconcile her.————
Your parcel has not yet arrived—at least the *Mags* &c. but I have received C[hild]e H[arol]d & ye. Corsair I believe both are very correctly printed—which [is] a great satisfaction.————I thank you for wishing me in town—but I think one's success is most felt at a distance—& I enjoy my solitary self importance—in an agreeable sulky way of my own—upon the strength of your letter for which I once more thank you & am very truly

yrs.

B

P.S.—Don't you think *Bonaparte's* next *publication* will be rather expensive to the Allies? Perry's Paris letter of yesterday looks very reviving—what a Hydra & Briareus it is—I wish they would pacify— there is no end to this campaigning.——

[TO JOHN MURRAY] *February 5th. 1814*

My dear Sir/—I quite forgot in my answer of yesterday to mention that I have no means of ascertaining whether the Newark *Pirate*[1] has been doing what you say—if so—he is a rascal & a *shabby* rascal too— & if his offence is punishable by law or pugilism he shall be fined or buffeted—do you try & discover—& I will make some enquiry here— perhaps some *other* in town *may* have gone on printing & used the same deception.————The *fac simile* is omitted in C[hild]e H[arol]d which is very awkward—as there is a *note* expressly on the subject[2]— pray *replace* it as *usual*—On second & third thoughts the withdrawing the small poems from the *Corsair* (even to add to C[hil]de H[arol]d) looks like shrinking & shuffling—after the fuss made upon one of them by the tories[3]—pray replace them in the Corsair's appendix.—I am sorry that C[hil]de H[arol]d requires some & such allotments to make him move off—but if you remember I told you his popularity would not be permanent—it is very lucky for the author—that he had made up his mind to a temporary reputation in time—the truth is—I do not

---

[1] John Ridge had published *Hours of Idleness* in 1807. See Feb. 6. 1814, to Murray.

[2] The facsimile was probably that of the letter in Greek from the Bey of Corinth, which was appended with a note to the first (quarto) edition of *Childe Harold*.

[3] Byron refers of course to the "Lines to a Lady Weeping", appended to *The Corsair*, and which Murray wanted to shift to a less conspicuous place at the end of the new edition of *Childe Harold*.

think that any of the present day—(and least of all one who has not consulted the flattering side of human Nature) have much to hope from Posterity—& you may think it affectation very probably—but to me my present & past success has appeared very singular—since it was in the teeth of so many prejudices—I almost think people like to be *contradicted*.—If C[hil]d[e] H[arol]d flags—it will hardly be worth while to go on with the engravings—but do as you please I have done with the whole *concern*—& the enclosed lines written years ago & copied from my Skull cup are among the last with which you will be troubled.—If you like—add them to C[hild]e H[arol]d if only for the sake of another outcry.—You received so long an answer yesterday that I will not intrude on you further than to repeat myself

yrs. very truly
B

P.S.—Of course in reprinting (if you have occasion) you will take great care to be *correct*—the present E[ditio]ns seem very much so— except in the last note of C[hilde] H[arol]d where the word *"responsible"* occurs twice nearly together convert the second into *"answerable"*—

[TO JOHN MURRAY]   *Newark Fy. 6th. 1814*

My dear Sir/—I am thus far on my way to town.——Master Ridge I have seen—& he owns to having *reprinted* some *sheets* to make up a few complete remaining copies!—I have now given him fair warning— & if he plays such tricks again—I must either get an injunction—or call for an acct. of profits—(as I never have parted with the Copyright) or—in short—any thing vexatious to repay him in his own way.—If the weather does not relapse I hope to be in town in a day or two.—

yrs. ever
Bn

[TO LADY MELBOURNE]   *Newark—February 6th. 1814*

My dear Ly. M[elbourn]e.—I am thus far on my return to town & having passed the Trent—(which threatens a flood on ye. first opportunity)—I hope to reach town in tolerable plight.—Mr. Claughton has been with us during the last two days at N[ewstea]d & this day set off for Cheshire—& I for the South to prepare for a final

& amicable arrangement.———M[ary Chaworth-Musters] I have not seen—business and the weather and badness of roads and partly a late slight illness of her own have interfered to prevent our meeting for the present—but I have heard a good deal from & of her—him I have not heard from nor of—nor have I seen him—nor do I know exactly where he is—but somewhere in the county I believe—You will very probably say that I ought to have gone over at all events—& Augusta has also been trying her rhetoric to the same purpose—& urging me repeatedly to call before I left the County—but I have been one day too busy—& another too lazy—and altogether so sluggish upon the subject—that I am thus far on my return without making this important visit in my way.—She seems in her letters very undecided whether to return to——[Musters] or no—& I have always avoided both sides of the topic—or if I touched on it at all it was on the *rational* bearing of the question. I have written to you two long letters from the Abbey and as I hope to see you soon I will not try your eyeglass and patience further at present.—

Ever yrs.
B

[Fragment preserved with above letter] . . . prospect) I never shall.—One of my great inducements to that brilliant negociation with the Princess of Parallellograms [Annabella Milbanke] was the vision of our *family party*—& the quantity of domestic lectures I should faithfully detail with our mutual comments thereupon.———You seem to think I am in some scrape at present by my unequal spirits—perhaps I am—but you shan't be shocked—so you shan't—I wont draw further upon you for sympathy.—You will be in town so soon—& I have scribbled so much—that you will be glad to see a letter shorter than usual.— I wish you would *lengthen* yours.—

ever my dear Ly. Me.
B

[TO JOHN MURRAY] *Fy. 7th. 1814*

Dear Sir/—As you will not want to *reprint* for some time—I wish you would make an *errata page* from this *corrected copy*—& annex it to your own—& to all copies in the hands of the trade.—Let me find a note on my arrival to say merely that you have received this copy.—

yrs. ever
B_N

I see all the papers in a sad commotion with those 8 lines—& the M[orning] Post in particular has found out that I am a sort of R[ichar]d 3d.——deformed in mind & *body*—the *last* piece of information is not very new to a man who passed five years at a public school— I am very sorry you cut out those lines for C[hilde] H[arol]d pray re-insert them in their old place in "the Corsair.—"[1]

[TO JOHN MURRAY]   [*Wandsford February 8th, 1814*]

Dear Sir/—I have just sent by this night-Coach a parcel from Wandsford which if you do not receive I will trouble you to enquire for—I have not received the Magazines you mentioned—but it is of no consequence. This parcel I wish you to attend to—there are directions with it

                                                      Yrs. ever
                                                         B<small>N</small>

The Coach which conveys this parcel goes to ye. Saracen's Head— Town Hall[1]

[TO LEIGH HUNT]   *Fy. 9th. 1814*

My dear Sir/—I have been snow-bound and thaw-swamped (2 compound epithets for you) in the "valley of the Shadow" of Newstead Abbey for nearly a month—& have not been four hours returned to London.—Nearly the first use I make of my benumbed fingers is to thank you for yr. very handsome note in the volume you have just put forth[1]—only—I trust—to be followed by others on subjects more worthy your notice than the works of contemporaries.—Of myself you speak only too highly—& you must think me strangely spoiled—or perversely peevish—even to suspect that any remarks of yours in the

---

[1] See Feb. 5, 1814, to Murray, note 2.
[1] This letter is in the handwriting of Mrs. Leigh.
[1] In his *Feast of the Poets*, published first in the *Reflector* and later in book form (1814), Hunt referred in a note to Byron as "a young nobleman who has been lately rising into celebrity, and who, as far as the world is concerned, is now moving in the very thick of the lustre." In Byron's poetry he found "a general vein of melancholy,—a fondness for pithy, suggesting, and passionate modes of speech, —and an intensity of feeling, which appears to seek relief in its own violence." (pages 130, 131.)

spirit of candid criticism could possibly prove unpalatable.—Had they been harsh—instead of being written as they are in the most indelible ink of good Sense & friendly admonition—had they been the harshest—as I knew & know that you are above any personal bias at least *against* your fellow bards—believe me—they would not have caused a word of remonstrance nor a moment of rankling on my part.—Your poem I redde long ago in "the Reflector" & it is not much to say it is the best *"Session"* we have—& with a more difficult subject—for we are neither so good nor so bad (taking the best & worst) as the wits of the olden time.—To your smaller pieces I have not yet had time to do justice by perusal—and I have a quantity of unanswered & I hope unanswerable letters to wade through before I sleep—but tomorrow will see me through your volume.—I am glad to see you have tracked *Gray* among the Italians—you will perhaps find a *friend* or *two* of yours there also though not to the same extent—but I have always thought the Italians the *only* poetical *moderns*:—our Milton & Spenser & Shakespeare (the last through translations of their tales) are very Tuscan and surely it is far superior to the French School.———You are hardly fair enough to *Rogers*—why *"tea?"*[2] you might surely have given him supper—if only a Sandwich.—Murray has I hope sent you my last bantling "the Corsair"—I have been regaled at every Inn on the road by lampoons and other merry conceits on myself in the ministerial gazettes—occasioned by ye. republication of two stanzas inserted in 1812 in Perry's paper. The hysterics of the Morning Post are quite interesting—and I hear (but have not seen) of something terrific in a last week's Courier, all which I take with *"the calm indifference"* of Sir Fretful Plagiary.[3]—The M[orning] P[ost] has one copy of devices upon my deformity—which certainly will admit of no "historic doubts"[4] like "Dicken my Master's"[5]—another upon my Atheism—which is not quite so clear—and another very down-rightly says I am the *Devil* (*boiteux* they might have added) and a rebel and what not—possibly my accuser of Diabolism may be Rosa Matilda—& if so it would not be difficult to convince her that I am a

[2] In the *Feast of the Poets* Hunt had written that "Spencer—Rogers—Montgom'ry" had presented their cards and Apollo "begged the landlord to give his respects to all three. And say he'd be happy to see them to tea."

[3] In Sheridan's *The Critic* (Act I, scene 1) Sir Fretful Plagiary says: "your disrespect will affect me no more than the newspaper criticisms—and I shall treat it—with exactly the same calm indifference and philosophic contempt—and so, your servant."

[4] H. Walpole's *Historic Doubts on the Life and Reign of King Richard the Third* (1768).

[5] *King Richard III.* Act V, scene 3.

mere Man.—I shall break in upon you in a day or two—distance has hitherto detained me—& I hope to find you well & myself welcome.—

ever yr. obliged & sincere

Bn

P.S.—Since this letter was written I have been at your text which has much *good* humour in every sense of the word—and your notes are of a very high order indeed—particularly on Wordsworth.—

[TO THOMAS MOORE]

[TO THOMAS MOORE] *February 10th, 1814*

I arrived in town late yesterday evening, having been absent three weeks, which I passed in Notts, quietly and pleasantly. You can have no conception of the uproar the eight lines on the little Royalty's weeping in 1812 (now republished) have occasioned. The R * * [Regent], who had always thought them *yours*, chose—God knows why—on discovering them to be mine, to be *affected* "in sorrow rather than anger."[1] The Morning Post, Sun, Herald, Courier, have all been in hysterics ever since. M[urray] is in a fright, and wanted to shuffle— and the abuse against me in all directions is vehement, unceasing, loud—some of it good, and all of it hearty. I feel a little compunctious as to the R * *'s [Regent's] *regret*;—"would he had been only angry! but I fear him not."[2]

Some of these same assailments you have probably seen. My person (which is excellent for "the nonce") has been denounced in verses, the more like the subject, inasmuch as they halt exceedingly. Then, in another, I am an *atheist*—a *rebel*—and, at last, the *Devil* (*boiteux*, I presume). My demonism seems to be a female's conjecture: if so, perhaps, I could convince her that I am but a mere mortal,—if a queen of the Amazons may be believed, who says αριϛον χολος οιφει.[3] I quote from memory, so my Greek is probably deficient; but the passage is *meant* to mean * * * * * * * *

Seriously, I am in, what the learned call, a dilemma, and the vulgar, a scrape; and my friends desire me not to be in a passion, and like Sir Fretful, I assure them that I am "quite calm,"—but I am nevertheless in a fury.

Since I wrote thus far, a friend has come in, and we have been

---

[1] *Hamlet*, Act I, scene 2.
[2] Unidentified.
[3] ἄριστα χολος οιφει? = "The lame mount (cover) best" (generally referring to animals). Mimnermus, fragment No. 23, *Loeb Classical Library*, I, 102–103.

talking and buffooning, till I have quite lost the thread of my thoughts; and, as I won't send them unstrung to you, good morning, and

Believe me ever, &c.

P.S.—Murray, during my absence, *omitted* the Tears in several of the copies. I have made him replace them, and am very wroth with his qualms;—"as the wine is poured out, let it be drunk to the dregs."[4]

[TO JOHN MURRAY (*a*)]   [*February 10, 1814*]

Dear Sir/—I am much better this [sic] & indeed quite well this morning—I have received *two*—but I presume there are more of the *Ana*—subsequently—and also something previous to which the M[orning] C[hronicl]e replied[1]—you also mentioned a parody on the *Skull*[2]—I wish to see them all because there may be things that require notice either by pen or person.

yrs. truly
BN

P.S.—You need not trouble yourself to answer this but send me the things when you get them.—

[TO JOHN MURRAY (*b*)]   [*February 10, 1814*]

Dear Sir/—Pray send a copy of "the Corsair" to Mr Hunt—(with the smaller poems in) & one of the last E[ditio]n of C[hil]d[e] Harold as soon as possible.—Make with a *pen* the corrections I sent for "the Corsair."

yrs ever
BN

The address is L[eig]h Hunt Esqre. Surrey Jail—

---

[4] Unidentified. Perhaps adapted from *Macbeth*, Act II, scene 3, ll. 102–03.
[1] A poem defending Byron's "Lines to a Lady Weeping" appeared in the *Morning Chronicle* on Feb. 8, 1814.
[2] In the *Courier* of Feb. 1, 1814, was printed some verses "On reading the lines written by Lord Byron, and engraven on the Silver Mounting of a Human Skull, formerly used as a Goblet, at his residence, Newstead Abbey." The substance of it was that he profaned this "palace of the soul": "Is this, thou feverish Man, thy festal bowl?"

My dear Lady M[elbourn]e.—On my arrival in town on Wednesday I found myself in what the learned call—a dilemma—and the vulgar a scrape—such a clash of paragraphs and a conflict of Newspapers—lampoons of all descriptions—some good and all hearty—the Regent (as reported) wroth—Ld. Carlisle in a fury—the Morning Post in hysterics and the Courier in convulsions of criticism and contention.— To complete the farce the Morning Papers this day announce the intention of some zealous Rosencrantz or Guildenstern to "play upon this pipe" in our house of hereditaries.—This last seems a little too ludicrous to be true—but even if so—and nothing is too ridiculous for some of them to attempt—all the motions—censures—sayings—doings & ordinances of that august body shall never make me even endeavour to explain or soften a syllable of the twenty words which have excited —*what*—I really do not yet exactly know—as the accounts are contradictory—but be it what it may—"as the wine is tapped it shall be drunk to the lees."[1]—You tell me not to be "violent" & not to "answer"—I *have not* & shall *not* answer—and although the consequences may be for aught I know to the contrary exclusion from society—and all sorts of disagreeables—"the Demon whom I still have served—has not yet cowed my better part of Man—["]² and whatever I may & have or shall feel—I have that within me that bounds against opposition.—I have *quick feelings*—& not very *good nerves*—but somehow they have more than once served me pretty well when I most wanted them—and may again—at any rate I shall try.— Did you ever know any thing like this?—at a time when peace & war— & Emperors & Napoleons—and the destinies of the things they have made of mankind are trembling in the balance—the Government Gazettes can devote half their attention & columns day after day to *8 lines* written two years ago—& now *republished only*—(by an Individual) & suggest them for the consideration of Parliament probably about the same period with the treaty of Peace.—I really begin to think myself a most important personage—what would poor Pope

---

[1] Unidentified.

[2] This is compounded from two passages in *Macbeth* (Act V, scene 8), brought together and distorted for Byron's purpose:
  "Macduff: Despair thy charm,
     And let the angel whom thou still hast served
     Tell thee Macduff was from his mother's womb
     Untimely ripped.
  Macbeth: Accursed be that tongue that tells me so;
     For it hath cowed my better part of man. . . . ."

have given to have brought down this upon his "epistle to Augustus"?
—I think you must allow considering all things public & private—that
mine has been an odd destiny.—But I prate—& will spare you.—Pray
when are you most visible? or will any of your "predilections"[3] interfere between you & me?——How is C[aroline]?—it is a considerable
compensation for all other disturbances—that she has left us in peace—
& I do not think you will ever be further troubled with her Anniversary
scenes.—I am glad you like the Corsair—& was afraid he might be too
larmoyant a gentleman for your favour—but all these externals are
nothing to *that within* on a subject to which I have not alluded[4]—

ever yrs. most affectly.

Bn

P.S.—Murray took fright & shuffled in my absence—as you say—
but I made him instantly replace the lines as before—it was no time to
shrink now—and if it were otherwise—they should never be expunged
& never shall—all the edicts on earth could not suppress their circulation—after the foolish fuss of these journalists who merely extend the
demands of curiosity by the importance they attach to two "doggerel
[stanzas]" as they repeatedly call them.—

[TO ANNABELLA MILBANKE] *Fy 12th 1814*

I am just returned to London after a month's absence and am indeed
sorry to hear that your own will be so much longer—and the cause is
not of a description to reconcile your friends to it entirely although the
benefit you will derive to your health will prevent us from regretting
anything but the time—if the effect is accomplished.—All expressions
of my good wishes to you and for you would be superfluous.———
Mr. Ward postponed our Dutch expedition—but as I have now nearly
arranged my domestic concerns—or at least put them in train—and
the Newstead business is set at rest in my favour—"the world is all
before me" and all parts of it as much a country to me as it was to
Adam—perhaps more so—for Eve as an atonement for tempting him
out of one habitation might probably assist him in selecting another &

---

[3] The word "predilections" was used in the Prince Regent's famous letter to the
Duke of York, Feb. 13, 1812, in which he repudiated his Whig friends, a letter
that precipitated the scene at Carlton House which inspired Byron's "Lines to a
Lady Weeping". The Prince had written: "I have no predilections to indulge, no
resentments to gratify."

[4] Probably his emotional involvement with his half-sister Augusta Leigh.

persuade him into some "valley of sweet Waters" on the banks of the Euphrates.———In thanking you for your letter will you allow me to say that there is one sentence I do not understand—as you may have forgotten I will copy it—it follows one which is in itself a maxim & which I need not repeat—"How I may have forsaken *that*—and under the influence of an ardent zeal for Sincerity—is an explanation that cannot benefit either of us—should any disadvantage arise from the original fault it must be only where it is deserved—Let this then suffice for I cannot by total silence acquiese in that which if supported when it's delusion is known to myself would become deception."———This I believe is word for word from your letter now before me.—I do not see in what you have deceived yourself—& you have certainly never been otherwise than candid with me—and I have endeavoured to act accordingly—in regard to your kind observations on my adoption [sic] of my conduct to your wishes—I trust I should have been able to do so even without your suggestion—the moment I sunk into your friend—I tried to regard you in no other light—our affections are not in our own power—but it would seem strange indeed—because you could not like me that I should repine at the better fortune of another— if I had ever possessed a preference—the case would have been altered—and I might not have been so patient in resigning my pre- tensions—but you never did—never for an instant—trifle with me nor amuse me with what is called encouragement—a thing by the bye— which men are continually supposing they receive without sufficient grounds—but of which I am no great judge—as except in this instance I never had an opportunity.—When I say "this instance" I mean of course any advances on my part towards that connection which re- quires duty as well as attachment—and I begin to entertain an opinion that though they do not always go together—their separate existence is very precarious.———I have lately seen a singular instance of ill fortune.—You have perhaps heard that in my childhood I was ex- tremely intimate with the family of my nearest neighbours—an inheri- tor of the estate of a very old house & her mother—she is two years older than me—and consequently at so early a period any proposal on my part was out of the question—although from the contiguity of our lands—& other circumstances of no great importance—it was sup- posed that our union was within the probabilities of human life.—I never did propose to her—and if I had it would have answered very little purpose—for she married another.—From that period we met rarely—and I do not very well know why—but when we did meet—it was with coldness on both sides.—To cut short a tale which is growing tedious—eight years have now elapsed—and she is separated from her husband at last after frequent dissentions arising entirely from *his* neglect and I fear—injuries still more serious.——At eight & twenty —still in the prime of life—beautiful (at least she was so) with a large fortune—of an ancient family—unimpeached & unimpeachable in her own conduct—this woman's destiny is bitter.—For the first time in many years I heard from her—desiring to see me—there could be nothing improper in this request—I was the friend of her youth—and I have every reason to believe—to be certain—that a being of better principles never breathed—but she was once deep in my heart—and though she had long ceased to be so—and I had no doubts of her—yet I had many of myself—at least of my own feelings if revived rather than of any consequences that might arise from them—and as we had not met since I was 21—to be brief—I did not see her.—There is the whole history of circumstances to which you may have possibly heard some allusion from those who knew me in the earlier part of my life— I *confide* them to you—& shall dwell upon them no further—except to state—that they bear no relation whatever to what I hinted at in a former letter as having occurred to prevent my reviving the topic discussed between us—at least with a view to renewal.———I have to ask for an answer—when you have leisure—and to thank you for your description which brings the scene fully before me—are you aware of an *amplified* coincidence of thought with Burns—?

"Or like the snowflake on the river
A moment shine—then melts forever.["]¹

The verses are very graceful & pleasing—my opinion of your powers in that way I long ago mentioned to another person—who perhaps transmitted it to you.²— I am glad you like "the Corsair" which they tell me is popular.—God bless you—ever yrs

B

P.S.—I am not perhaps an impartial judge of Lady M. as amongst other obligations I am indebted to her for my acquaintance with yourself—but she is doubtless in talent a superior—a *supreme* woman—& her heart I know to be of the kindest—in the best sense of the word.— Her defects I never could perceive—as her society makes me forget them & every thing else for the time.—I do love that woman (*filially*

---

¹ Burns, "Tam o Shanter", stanza 7. The lines in Burns are: "Or like the snow falls in the river/A moment white—then melts forever."
² Byron refers to his comments on Annabella's poetry to Caroline Lamb. See May 1, 1812, to Caroline (Vol. 2, pp. 175–76).

or *fraternally*) better than any being on earth—& you see—that I am therefore unqualified to give an opinion.————

[TO JOHN MURRAY (*a*)]   [*February 12, 1814*]

Dear Sir/—I will trouble you for the Courier of tonight.—

                                                   yrs. truly
                                                   Bn

[TO JOHN MURRAY (*b*)]   [*February 12, 1814*]

If you have copies of the "intercepted letters"[1] Ly. H[ollan]d would be glad of a volume—and when you have served others have the goodness to think of yr. humble Sert.——You have played the Devil— by that injudicious *suppression*—which you did totally without my consent——some of the papers have exactly said what might be expected—now I *do not* & *will* not be supposed to shrink—although myself & every thing belonging to me were to perish with my memory.———

                                                   yrs. &c.
                                                   Bn

P.S.—Pray attend to what I stated yesterday on *technical* topics.———

[TO LADY HOLLAND?]   [*February 12, 1814?*]

I can I think venture to prophecy that the more you allow my friend Hobhouse to become acquainted with you the more you will like him—He possesses all the qualities you mention and I can add from experience that he is sincere active & unalterable in his friendships— God knows—I have but too often tried his patience very severely.— Nothing can give me greater pleasure than your partiality in his favour and I really think you would find him an addition to that society which—if *I* had not the honour sometimes of being admitted into it—I should say was the best.——Do you mean by asking me if I intend to see Kean—that I may go to your box?—I do wish to see him (particularly in Richard) very much.——You ask me after my

---

[1] Murray published in 1814 *Letters and Despatches of the Generals, Ministers, etc., at Paris, to the Emperer Napoleon, at Dresden: intercepted by the advanced Troops of the Allies in the North of Germany.*

probable scribblings in the country?——nothing whatever—and I sincerely hope that I shall be able to say so through the rest of my life—if it were to begin again I would be anything rather than what I am.———My head is at present in a chaotic state of all possible jarrings—not from the clash of paragraphs—& the conflict of journalists—to whose good pleasure I resign my person—politics and poesy—but from a variety of other circumstances which in the words of the wary—are "best known to oneself" and best kept there.—However—"I breathe and I can bear"—excuse the only home-made quotation I ever ventured upon.—I shall send to enquire after the "intercepted letters."—Did I formally say "Ladyship?"—why then in return you must call me by my *own* name as a punishment—and as one of my nearest relatives said to me more than once when I was a child—you could not give me a worse.—Bad as it is for want of a better I must sign myself by it

> ever yrs. very truly
> Bn

[TO ————————]   *Fy. 14th. 1814*

Sir/—The very pleasing volume which accompanied your letter I had redde before but I am not the less obliged by the gift from the Author.—To have obtained for any work of mine your approbation and to have afforded a moment's gratification to a mind like yours requires—& I beg you—you will receive—my very sincere thanks.—My absence from London for some time past prevented me from receiving and acknowledging your kind present for which I remain

> most truly yr. obliged Sert.
> Byron

[TO JOHN MURRAY (*a*)]   *Monday—[February 14, 1814]*

Dear Sir/—Before I left town yesterday I wrote you a note which I presume you received.——I have heard so many different accounts of *your* proceedings or rather of those of others towards *you*—in consequence of the publication of these everlasting lines—that I am anxious to hear from yourself the real truth of the case.—Whatever responsibility obloquy or effect is to arise from the publication should surely *not* fall upon you in any degree—and I can have no objection to your stating as distinctly & publicly as you please—*your* unwillingness to publish them—& my own obstinacy upon the subject.—Take any course you please to vindicate *yourself*—but leave me to fight my own way—and as I before said do not *compromise* me—by anything which may look like *shrinking* on *my* part—as for your own—make the best of it—

yrs.

B<small>N</small>

[TO JOHN MURRAY (*b*)]   *Monday Night [February 14, 1814]*

I humbly conceive that the Admiralty in laying an embargo upon some of your publications (if it be so) did not extend it to an answer to a note—I have sent you two—one containing a question to which I have received no reply.—However—as you please—I shall not trouble you with another.—

yrs.

B<small>YRON</small>

[TO LORD HOLLAND]   *February 15th. —1814*

My dear Lord—I called today for the purpose of answering your letter in person—but others being present & more agreeable topics occurring I would not touch on a subject on which I am still rather at a loss how to express myself.—It is now nearly two years since I suppressed the publication in question[1] in consequence of a conversation with Mr. Rogers, & I may add, my perfect concurrence in his opinion, and I have since declined a large offer from the publisher to reprint it—I mention this last merely because it more completely establishes the *fact* of the *suppression*—on any other account it neither merits nor met with a moment's notice.—I have also—as far as in me lay—regretted not only in conversation—but as lately as publicly in my letter to Mr. Moore prefixed to the Corsair—the composition and circulation of that satire.—To yourself this has appeared sufficient—for those who are less *liberal*—or more injured—I have no further redress to offer—but such as they may win & wear—they must take it.—Of all times this happens to be the period when I cannot concede even if *my* judgement & feelings incline me to regret the bitterness of many expressions in that production—but I can not blame nor accuse anyone—I have made myself enemies—some powerful—and all

---

[1] *English Bards and Scotch Reviewers.*

zealous & I must meet them as I best can—when I know them I shall be better able to determine *how*.—To Lady Holland & yourself I can only repeat that I have been & ever am

most truly your obliged sert.

BYRON

[TO ANNABELLA MILBANKE] *Feby. 15th 1814*

In my letter of ye 12th in answer to your last I omitted to say that I have not for several years looked into the tract of Locke's which you mention—but I have redde it formerly though I fear to little purpose since it is forgotten—& have always understood *that* and Butler's Analogy to be the best treatises of the kind. Upon the subject of which it treats—I think I have already said—that I have formed no decided opinion—but I should regret any *sceptical bigotry* as equally pernicious with the most credulous intolerance. Of the Scriptures themselves I have ever been a reader & admirer as compositions particularly the *Arab—Job*—and parts of Isaiah—and the song of Deborah.——Your kind congratulations on the subject of certain prejudices against me having subsided is a little premature—for in discussing more agreeable topics—I quite forgot to mention what you perhaps have seen in some of the journals—viz—a series of attacks—some good and all hearty which have been called forth by the republication & avowal of some lines on the P[rinces]s C[harlott]e weeping in 1812—at the time when the Prince assailed Ld. Lauderdale at a public dinner—soon after his own abandonment of Grey & Grenville.——These still continue and rather more violently than ever—except that I think the destruction of the Custom House has a little interfered with mine—and Buonaparte's recent advantage has usurped the column generally devoted to the abuse of a personage who however unimportant appears to be very obnoxious.—I have hitherto been silent—& may probably remain so—unless something should occur to render it impossible. ————You will have received so long a letter from me before this arrives—that I will not at present intrude upon you further.—Pray take care of yourself—consider how many are interested in your health and welfare—and reconcile us to your absence by telling us that you are the better for it.—

ever yrs
BYRON

P.S.—My best respects to Lady M[ilbank]e. & Sir Ralph.

My dear Rogers—I wrote to Lord Holland briefly but I hope distinctly on the subject which has lately occupied much of my conversation with him & you.—As things now stand—upon that topic my determination must be unalterable.——I declare to you most sincerely that there is no human being on whose regard & esteem I set a higher value than on Lord Holland's—and as far as concerns himself & Lady H[ollan]d I would concede even to humiliation—without any view to the future—& solely from my sense of his conduct as to the past.— For the rest I conceive that I have already done all in my power—by the suppression—if that is not enough—they must act as they please— but I will not "teach my tongue a most inherent baseness" come what may.[1]——I am sorry that I shall not be able to call upon you today— & what disappoints me still more—to dine with you tomorrow—I forwarded a letter from Moore to you—he writes to me in good spirits—which I hope will not be impaired by any attack brought upon him by his friendship for me.——You will probably be at the Marquess Lansdowne's tonight—I am asked—but am not sure that I shall be able to go—Hobhouse will be there—I think if you knew him well—you would like him.——

Believe me always yours very affectly
B

My dear Rogers,—If Lord Holland is satisfied, as far as regards himself and Lady Holland, and as this letter expresses him to be, it is enough.

As for any impression the public may receive from the revival of the lines on Lord Carlisle,[1] let them keep it,—the more favourable for him, and the worse for me,—the better for all.

All the sayings and doings in the world shall not make me utter another word of conciliation to any thing that breathes. I shall bear what I can, and what I cannot I shall resist. The worst they could do would be to exclude me from society. I have never courted it, nor, I may add, in the general sense of the word, enjoyed it—and "there is a world elsewhere!"[2]

---

[1] *Coriolanus*, Act III, scene 2, line 123: "teach my mind a most inherent baseness."

[1] *English Bards and Scotch Reviewers*, lines 719–726.

[2] *Coriolanus*, Act III, scene 3, line 133.

Any thing remarkably injurious, I have the same means of repaying as other men, with such interest as circumstances may annex to it.

Nothing but the necessity of adhering to regimen prevents me from dining with you to-morrow.

I am, yours most truly,
Bn

[TO THOMAS MOORE]   *February 16th, 1814*

You may be assured that the only prickles that sting from the Royal hedgehog are those which possess a torpedo property, and may benumb some of my friends. *I* am quite silent, and "hush'd in grim repose."[1] The frequency of the assaults has weakened their effects,— if ever they had any;—and, if they had had much, I should hardly have held my tongue, or withheld my fingers. It is something quite new to attack a man for abandoning his resentments. I have heard that previous praise and subsequent vituperation were rather ungrateful, but I did not know that it was wrong to endeavour to do justice to those who did not wait till I had made some amends for former and boyish prejudices, but received me into their friendship, when I might still have been their enemy.

You perceive justly that I must *intentionally* have made my fortune, like Sir Francis Wronghead.[2] It were better if there were more merit in my independence, but it really is something nowadays to be independent at all, and the *less* temptation to be otherwise, the more uncommon the case, in these times of paradoxical servility. I believe that most of our hates and likings have been hitherto nearly the same; but from henceforth, they must, of necessity, be one and indivisible,—and now for it! I am for any weapon,—the pen, till one can find something sharper, will do for a beginning.

You can have no conception of the ludicrous solemnity with which these two stanzas have been treated. The Morning Post gave notice of an intended motion in the House of my brethren on the subject, and God he knows what proceedings besides;—and all this, as Bedreddin in the "Nights" says, "for making a cream tart without pepper."[3] This last piece of intelligence is, I presume, too laughable to be true;

[1] Gray, *The Bard*, II, stanza 2.
[2] In *The Provoked Husband*, by Vanbrugh and Cibber.
[3] From the *Arabian Nights* "Tale of Núr al-Din Ali and his Son". See Richard Burton's *Arabian Nights*, Vol. I, p. 79ff. Byron's edition of the *Arabian Nights* was Scott's, 6 vols., 1811.

and the destruction of the Custom-house[4] appears to have, in some degree, interfered with mine;—added to which, the last battle of Buonaparte has usurped the column hitherto devoted to my bulletin.

I send you from this day's Morning Post the best which have hitherto appeared on this "impudent doggerel," as the Courier calls it. There was another about my *diet*, when a boy—not at all bad—some time ago; but the rest are but indifferent.

I shall think about your *oratorical* hint;[5] but I have never set much upon "that cast,"[6] and am grown as tired as Solomon of every thing, and of myself more than any thing. This is being what the learned call philosophical, and the vulgar, lack-a-daisical. I am, however, always glad of a blessing; pray, repeat yours soon,—at least your letter, and I shall think the benediction included.

Ever, &c.

[TO ROBERT CHARLES DALLAS]   *Fy. 17th. 1814*

My dear Sir/—The Courier of this Evening accuses me of having "received & pocketed" large sums for my works.—I have never yet received nor wished to receive a farthing for any—Mr. M[urra]y offered a thousand for the G[aiou]r & B[rid]e which I said was too much—& that if he could afford it at the end of 6 months I would then direct him [how] it might be disposed of—but neither then nor at any other period have I ever availed myself or shall avail myself of the profits on my own account.—For the republication of the Satire I refused 400 gs. & for the previous editions I never asked nor received a sou—nor for any writing whatever.—I do not wish you to do anything disagreeable to yourself—there never was nor shall be any conditions nor stipulations with regard to any accommodation that I could afford you—& on your part I can see nothing derogatory in receiving the copyrights—it was only assistance afforded to a worthy man by one not quite so worthy.—Mr. M[urra]y is going to contradict this—but your *name* will not be mentioned, for your own part you are a free agent & are to do as you please—I only hope that now as always you will think that I wish to take no unfair advantage of the

---

[4] Fire totally destroyed the Custom House on February 12, 1814.

[5] Moore had urged Byron to take part in parliamentary affairs, but by this time he had resolved to "strut no more upon that stage", not being able to play the politician's compromising game.

[6] *King Richard III*, Act V, scene 4: "Slave, I have set my life upon a cast,/And I will stand the hazard of the die."

accidental opportunity which circumstances permitted me of being of use to you.—

ever yrs. most truly
BIRON

P.S.—It is a cruel & bitter thing on all parties to be obliged to notice this—but the statement is made in such a manner as requires it to be done away with—founded as it is on utter falsehood.—

[TO JOHN MURRAY]   [*February 17, 1814*]

You must take care in stating D[allas]'s acknowledgement of the receipt of C[hilde] H[arol]d not to make a mistake as if I had *purchased* this dedication—he mentioned it quite *uncalled for* & indeed unknown to me previous to publication—in his preface to his Novels[1] —nearly a year afterwards.—

Dr. Sir—
yrs.
BN

[TO ROBERT CHARLES DALLAS]   *Fy. 18th. 1814*

My dear Sir/—Since I wrote to you last night—it is determined that M[urray] shall say nothing (& certainly *I* shall not) but allow them to sail on & lie to the uttermost.—Do *not* you therefore think of involving yourself in the squabble by any statement but let it rest.[1]—

ever yrs.
BN

[TO LADY MELBOURNE]   *Fy. 18th. 1814*

My dear Lady M[elbourn]e.—R[ogers] I should conceive not [to] be a very exact thermometer as to "spirits" but if his statement be true—it may not be necessary for me to tell *you* that there are better reasons for my so being—than all the paragraphs that ever were [ground?]. But to talk of common things—the Hollands &c. have been

---

[1] Byron had been somewhat embarrassed by the pompous and fulsome tone of Dallas's dedication to *The Miscellaneous Works and Novels of R. C. Dallas*, 7 Vols., 1813.

[1] Dallas had nevertheless written a long letter on Feb. 18, saying that Byron had never received a shilling from any of his works, and acknowledging Byron's gifts of the copyrights of *Childe Harold* and *The Corsair*. This letter was published on February 21 in the *Morning Post* and other newspapers.

worrying me to say & do I know not what about Lord Carlisle and I will neither do that nor anything else but be silent which has put them in no very good humour.———The Courier has lastly been most savage to Rogers—who appears to me to feel it angrily—but I may be mistaken.———I do not know to what you allude—nor does it matter—whatever they *can*—they will say—but if stepping across the room would stop them I would not cross it.—If they once get to a certain pitch—I shall do something or other probably—and effectual if possible—but I will go to the fountain-head—& not to the muddy little stream that flows from it.—I was near meeting you at Lady Lansdowne's & Miss Berrys' but did not go—Rogers says I should— as it looks as if I was disturbed—but you know I did not go out much last year—& have still less inclination this—but if I felt all *this* so deeply—what should prevent my leaving town—or the country?— The fact is I believe that I am much as usual—& they tell me in high health which is more than usual.—I don't think that I shall be able to call upon you before C[aroline]'s arrival—& that will stop my visits for a still longer period—she has been quite silent—and all I most sincerely desire is that she may continue so—& I dare say she will.— At least I hope it—for I do believe if one thing more than another would drive me out of my senses at this moment—it would be any renewal or intercourse with her even by letters.—

Pray believe me ever yrs. most truly & affectly.

B

[TO JOHN MURRAY]   [*February 18, 1814*]

The copy of the Corsair entitled 5th. Ed[itio]n just sent—contains every *single error* which more than a fortnight ago—I so particularly requested might be cancelled & altered—this is really too *bad*—& I will not permit it—after so much as I have said upon the subject. I once more request that the alterations be made & that an *Errata* be made for these copies which are out[;] have you lost the alterations?— if so I will do it over again—but don't go on—with these eternal errors.—

yrs.
B

[TO ANNABELLA MILBANKE]   *Feby 19th 1814*

Many thanks for your answer which has cut the knot—but I had no right to interrogate you on such a subject—& had I been at all aware

65

that my question would have led to any explanation of feelings to which you do not like to recur—of course I should have remained in silence & in darkness.————Still it is not [to] be regretted in one point of view even on your own account—as it sets all apprehension of the revival of a subject already discussed long ago between us—at rest:—it is true that it was not in any great peril of revival before—but it is now more completely "numbered with the things that were"[1] and never can be again.—Ignorant as I am of the person & the circumstances to whom & which you allude—I can form no opinion—except —that if he has put it out of his power to avail himself of such a disposition in his favour—he is fortunate in not knowing that it ever existed.————I was rather sorry (though probably *they* would not believe me) for Bankes & Douglas—who are both very clever & excellent men—& attached to you—and as I had contrived to make my own fortune like Sir Francis Wronghead[2]—I confess that (that terrible pronoun *I* being put out of the question) I should have been glad to have seen one of them in a fair way for happiness—but I shall grow impertinent which will do them no good—& me some harm—& so Adieu to the subject.————Since my last letter I believe I have sent another of *omitted* replies to part of your own—and I must shorten this—or you will think me more tedious than usual.—I am at present a little feverish.—I mean mentally—and as usual—on the brink of something or other—which will probably crush me at last— & cut our correspondence short with every thing else[3]—till then—I take as much of it as I can get—& as to my own epistolary offerings— you will only find them too profuse. Besides these domestic stimulants—I have the further satisfaction of still finding the P[rinc]e Regent's friends & Newspapers in gallant array against me—the latter very loud—the former I don't see—if I did our dialogue would probably be very short—but more to the purpose.—I am told also that I am "out of Spirits" which is attributed to the said paragraphs—he must however be a happy man who has nothing deeper to disturb him. —Ly. M[elbourn]e. I have not yet seen—but I believe she is well— and I hope to find her so shortly.—Pray how old are you?—it is a question one may ask safely for some years to come—I begin to

---

[1] Unidentified.

[2] In *The Provoked Husband* by Vanbrugh and Cibber. Sir Francis did everything wrong and almost ruined himself and his family.

[3] This is the kind of hint Byron frequently gave Lady Melbourne that he might in desperation elope with Augusta.

count my own—a few weeks ago I became six & twenty in summers—six hundred in heart—and in head & pursuits about six.—

ever yrs very truly

Bɴ

Pray make my best respects acceptable to Sir R[alph] & Ly. Milbanke.—

[ᴛᴏ ᴊᴀᴍᴇs ᴡᴇᴅᴅᴇʀʙᴜʀɴ ᴡᴇʙsᴛᴇʀ]   *February 20th. 1814*

My dear W—Your arrival at A[ston] was unknown to me till my own in London—& had it been otherwise—I could not have availed myself of your invitation from the state of ye. roads &c. but I am equally indebted to your intended hospitality as if it had taken effect.—If you are serious in your intention of visiting London—Fletcher shall look out for ye. abode you require or I will do it myself if you think me more likely to obtain what will suit you—but you neither mention terms—time—nor place—& I shall wait your answer.———I have been again in ye. country but for a shorter time & distance—which has occasioned partly my delay in answering your first letter—you know that I am a very irregular correspondent & I have lately been a good deal occupied with business of one kind or another.—There is a new Actor named Kean come out—he is a wonder—& we are yet wise enough to admire him—he is superior to Cooke certainly in many points—& will run Kemble hard—his style is quite new—or rather *renewed*—being that of Nature.———Nobody knows as yet what is to become of Bonaparte—the reports are various—but the war party have it hollow at home—a few days will probably see him all or nothing.———

Hobhouse is returned to England[1]—full of health good humour & anecdote—I was most agreeably surprized by his arrival.———I have been living very quietly—& declined such invitations as have offered themselves—Ld. [Mountnorris][2] or his family I have not lately seen—[Ly. Julia] seems to promise a splendid debût—& will perhaps be the finest pearl of the string—they are all very handsome but there is *more* of ye. youngest—& her head is very *Greek*—I speak merely as a "formarum spectator" for I have long passed the happy time when

---

[1] Hobhouse had returned from his Continental tour on Feb. 8. He had been gone for eight months, visiting most of the central European capitals not in the hands of the French.

[2] Webster's father-in-law, 1st Earl of Mountnorris and 8th Viscount Valentia.

one's heart is turned by a pretty face, & can give my opinions as impartially as I would of a Statue.———

Believe me

yrs. very truly
BIRON

[TO JOHN HAMILTON REYNOLDS[1]] *February 20th, 1814*

Sir,—My absence from London till within these last few days, and business since, have hitherto prevented my acknowledgment of the volume I have lately received, and the inscription which it contains, for both of which I beg leave to return you my thanks, and best wishes for the success of the book and its author. The poem itself, as the work of a young man, is highly creditable to your talents, and promises better for future efforts than any which I can now recollect. Whether you intend to pursue your poetical career, I do not know, and can have no right to inquire—but, in whatever channel your abilities are directed, I think it will be your own fault if they do not eventually lead to distinction. Happiness must in course depend upon conduct—and even fame itself would be but a poor compensation for self-reproach. You will excuse me for talking to a man perhaps not many years my junior, with these grave airs of seniority;—but though I cannot claim much advantage in that respect, it was my lot to be thrown very early upon the world—to mix a good deal in it in more climates than one— and to purchase experience which would probably have been of greater service to any one than myself. But my business with you is in your capacity of author—and to that I will confine myself.

The first thing a young writer must expect, and yet can least of all suffer, is *criticism*—I did not bear it—a few years, and many changes, have since passed over my head, and my reflections on that subject are attended with regret. I find, on dispassionate comparison, my own revenge more than the provocation warranted—it is true, I was very young—that might be an excuse to those I attacked—but to *me* it is none: the best reply to all objections is to write better—and if your enemies will not then do you justice, the world will. On the other hand,

---

[1] John Hamilton Reynolds had sent Byron a copy of his *Safie, an Eastern Tale* (1814). It bore the dedication: "This Tale is inscribed with every sentiment of gratitude and respect, to the Right Honourable Lord Byron". Reynolds was later to be the close friend of Keats, and his sister friend Jane married Thomas Hood. He had great ambition and talent. He wrote a very clever parody-satire of Wordsworth called "Peter Bell: A Lyrical Ballad" (1819). But his talent was dissipated in other activities in later years.

you should not be discouraged—to be opposed, is not to be vanquished, though a timid mind is apt to mistake every scratch for a mortal wound. There is a saying of Dr. Johnson's, which it is as well to remember, that "No man was ever written down except by himself." I sincerely hope that you will meet with as few obstacles as your self can desire—but if you should, you will find that they are to be *stepped* over; to *kick* them down, is the first resolve of a young and fiery spirit—a pleasant thing enough at the time—but not so afterwards: on this point I speak of a man's *own* reflections—what others think or say, is a *secondary* consideration,—at least, it has been so with me, but will not answer as a general maxim: he who would make his way in the world, must let the world believe that it made it for him, and accommodate himself to the minutest observance of its regulations. I beg once more to thank you for your pleasing present, and have the honour to be,

Your obliged, And very obedient servant,
Byron

[TO LADY MELBOURNE]   *Fy. 21st. 1814*

My dear Lady M[elbourn]e.—I am not "forbidden" by —— [Augusta] though it is very odd that like *every one*—she seemed more assured (and not very well pleased) of your influence than of any other—but—I suppose being pretty certain of her own power—always said "do as you please—& go where you like" and I really know no reason for my not having been where I ought—unless it was to punish myself—or—I really do not know why exactly.——You will easily suppose—that—twined as she is round my heart in every possible manner—dearest & deepest in my hope & my memory—still I am not easy—it is *this*—if any thing—my own—in short I cannot write about it.—Still I have not lost all self-command—for instance—I *could* at this moment be where I have been—where I would rather be than anywhere else—and yet from some motive or other—but certainly not indifference—I am here—& here I will remain [London]—but it costs me some struggles.—It is the misery of my situation—to see it as *you* see it—& to *feel* it as *I* feel it—on *her* account—& that of others—as for myself—it is of much less—& may soon be of no consequence.—But—I will drop ye. subject.———I am glad that you think poor Dallas acted rightly[1]—I told him that I saw no reason why he should interpose—& Hobhouse said it was better not—but it was

---

[1] See Feb. 18, 1814, to Dallas, note 1.

his own doing—& the facts are exactly as he stated—I neither forbade nor encouraged him—but left him as I hitherto always had—a free agent—if he was ever under any obligation to me—it is amply cancelled by the acknowledgement.———As for the Courier gentleman—he has gone upon the wrong plan—a little *fun* would have done me more harm than all this exceeding gravity and rage—who he is—I know not—they tell me many different names—and I observe that Rogers & all of them fix upon *that* person *they each* most dislike—is not this human Nature? & worth all the paragraphs to catch the trait?—I am perhaps not so angry as I ought to be—but that won't alter me a jot—the instant I can find a clue—I shall not be at all less summary—because I have hitherto been silent—as to law—that would be no revenge at all—& besides it is so slow—the person will either betray himself—or be betrayed—if a hireling he must be left to his wages—if in a higher circle as is suspected—he will answer it.—To apply to the Editor—or involve myself in a squabble personally with a man who sells advertisements would I am told be ridiculous—or else I have no particular objection—anything to amuse anybody is much the same to me at present.———As for the *world*—I neither know nor enquire into it's notions—you can bear me witness that few ever courted it—or flattered it's opinions less—if it turns or has turned against me I cannot blame it—my heart is not in it—& my head better without it.—I don't know why I have scribbled this sheet full—for I mean to call upon you tomorrow—if I don't find you I shall be more lucky some other day

ever yrs. most affectly.

B

[TO JOHN MURRAY]   *Fy. 25th.—1814*

Pray what the Devil may all this be?—you never heard from me of any "letter" nor did I ever hear a word on the subject from D[allas] nor do I know that he is about to say any more on ye. subject.—With regard to the truth & the "whole truth" which you speak of to him—to what do you allude?—did anyone ever require of you on my part anything but the truth?—& is there anything in his former statement that you *can* contradict?—I am quite in the dark & really confounded between you & him

yrs.

B<small>N</small>

Do you mean to tell *me* as you told Me. de Stael that you actually *paid* the sum you *offered* or that *I* received it—or that any one else did—if so—Bravo![1]

I have not availed myself of your kind introduction to Mrs. Baillie[1] —because I hope time or chance will one day bring us into the same society—& then you will do it in person—& although I wish much to be acquainted with her & have the sincerest admiration of all I see & hear of her—yet—in short I have a strange awkwardness & repugnance in making new acquaintances—& have had ever since I was a child—& you will easily believe this is not at all diminished by the respect I may entertain for the person to whom I am to undergo presentation.—This is constitutional—& not all I have seen—or all I may see—can or could ever cure it entirely—I conceal it as much as possible—so well indeed—that many would believe it affectation in me to say this—with *you* I have no such apprehensions in stating the simple truth.————I am *very* glad that she likes ye Corsair— because she is one of the very few—who can understand the passions & feelings I have endeavoured to describe—but not even my Vanity can get the better of me in ye respect I have mentioned above.———I have troubled you lately with so much scribbling—that I feel some remorse in intruding on you again so soon—

ever yrs. most sincerely
BYRON

Sir/—The purpose for which the produce of the Bride & Giaour is to be appropriated—is for a friend as you will perceive when the time

[1] In his letter to the *Morning Post* and other papers Dallas, after acknowledging Byron's gift of the copyrights of *Childe Harold* and *The Corsair* to him, added: "with respect to his two other poems, *The Giaour* and *The Bride of Abydos*, Mr. Murray, the publisher of them, can truly attest that no part of the sale of these has ever touched his hands or been disposed of for his use." This irritated Murray, for Dallas did not say that Murray had offered Byron 1000 guineas for the copyrights, but that Byron had not accepted it, postponing the decision until such time as the volumes had shown themselves profitable, and then he did not intend to take the money for himself. Dallas, on the other hand, was piqued that Byron had left the copyrights with Murray instead of giving them to him.
[1] Joanna Baillie, poet and dramatist, was a friend of the Milbankes.

comes.—Our discussions upon that point took place as you will perceive by *dates*—before the publication of the *Bride*—which was never left in abeyance—as the Giaour had been until that period.————
With regard to the disposal of copyrights it is enough that I do not avail *myself* of any personal profit from them—if the works succeed there is the fair advantage to the publisher from the residue—& if they do not—they would be of no service to you nor any one else.————I have always I believe kept clear accounts with you—& settled all my bills regularly—these cannot be much now—but if there is I should wish to discharge them immediately.—Your distinctions between "paid" & "given" seem to me without a difference—but as you had done neither one nor the other in the usual sense of those words—you will permit me to think that your statement to Me. de Stael was a little premature.————Upon the subject of these last I shall merely say that if I had been anxious on the subject I might have received the sum you offered at the time—& had it been on my own acct. I probably should—I declined it at that time—because I wished to accommodate you till the expiration of a period sufficient to ascertain your probable profit or loss.—What you mean by "the Gift" of the G[iaou]r I do not know—unless you mean that by not coming hastily to any arrangement—I never intended to arrange it at all—had it been given—the copyright would have been made over as in the other cases.—I have now done with the subject—& I think you may as well follow the example

yrs.

B<small>N</small>

[TO THOMAS MOORE]   *Feb. 26th, 1814*

Dallas had, perhaps, have better kept silence;—but that was *his* concern, and, as his facts are correct, and his motive not dishonourable to himself, I wished him well through it.[1] As for his interpretations of the lines, he and any one else may interpret them as they please. I have and shall adhere to my taciturnity, unless something very particular occurs to render this impossible. Do *not you* say a word. If any one is to speak, it is the person principally concerned. The most amusing thing is, that every one (to me) attributes the abuse to the *man they personally most dislike*!—some say C * * r [Croker], some C * * e [Coleridge], others F * * d [Fitzgerald], &c, &c. &c. I do not know,

[1] See Feb. 25, 1814, to Murray, note 1.

and have no clue but conjecture. If discovered, and he turns out a hireling, he must be left to his wages; if a cavalier, he must "wink, and hold out his iron."[2]

I had some thoughts of putting the question to C * * r [Croker], but H[obhouse], who, I am sure, would not dissuade me, if it were right, advised me by all means *not*;—"that I had no right to take it upon suspicion," &c. &c. Whether H. is correct, I am not aware, but he believes himself so, and says there can be but one opinion on that subject. This I am, at least, sure of, that he would never prevent me from doing what he deemed the duty of a *preux* chevalier. In such cases—at least, in this country—we must act according to usages. In considering this instance, I dismiss my own personal feelings. Any man will and must fight, when necessary,—even without a motive. *Here*, I should take it up really without much resentment; for, unless a woman one likes is in the way, it is some years since I felt a *long* anger. But, undoubtedly, could I, or may I, trace it to a man of station, I should and shall do what is proper.

* * was angerly, but tried to conceal it. *You* are not called upon to avow the "Twopenny," and would only gratify them by so doing. Do you not see the great object of all these fooleries is to set him, and you, and me, and all persons whatsoever, by the ears?—more especially those who are on good terms,—and nearly succeeded. Lord H[olland] wished me to *concede* to Lord Carlisle—concede to the devil! —to a man who used me ill? I told him, in answer, that I would neither concede, nor recede on the subject, but be silent altogether; unless any thing more could be said about Lady H[olland] and himself, who had been since my very good friends;—and there it ended. This was no time for concessions to Lord C[arlisle].

I have been interrupted, but shall write again soon. Believe me ever, my dear Moore, &c.

[TO SAMUEL ROGERS] *Fy. 26th. 1814*

My dear R.—I shall call on you—but regret that I cannot dine— who is Sir Proteus? I have neither seen nor heard of him—pray send him to me & I will return him immediately.—

ever yrs.

B

[2] *Henry V*, Act II, scene 1.

Your non-attendance at Corinne's[1] is very *à propos*, as I was on the eve of sending you an excuse. I do not feel well enough to go there this evening, and have been obliged to despatch an apology. I believe that I need not add one for not accepting Mr. Sheridan's invitation on Wednesday, which I fancy both you and I understood in the same sense:—with him the saying of Mirabeau, that *"words* are *things,"*[2] is not to be taken literally. I leave town for a day or two. Tomorrow or Tuesday—probably Tuesday.—

Ever, yrs.

I will call for you at a quarter before *seven*, if that will suit you. I return you *Sir Proteus*,[3] and shall merely add in return, as Johnson said of, and to, somebody or other, "Are we alive after all this censure?"[4]

Believe me, etc.[5]

[TO FRANCIS HODGSON] *February 28th, 1814*

There is a youngster—and a clever one, named Reynolds, who has just published a poem called "Safie," published by Cawthorne. He is in the most natural and fearful apprehension of the Reviewers—and as you and I both know by experience the effect of such things upon a *young* mind, I wish *you* would take his production into dissection and do it *gently*.[1] I cannot, because it is inscribed to me; but I assure you this is not my motive for wishing him to be tenderly entreated, but because I know the misery, at his time of life, of untoward remarks upon first appearance.

Now for *self.* Pray thank your *cousin*—it is just as it should be, to my liking, and probably *more* than will suit any one else's. I hope and trust

---

[1] *i.e.*, at Madame de Staël's.
[2] Byron used this phrase of Mirabeau in *Don Juan*, Canto III, stanza 88.
[3] *Sir Proteus*; *A Satirical Ballad*, by P. M. O'Donovan, Printed for T. Hookham and E. T. Hookham, 1814, had a satirical inscription to Byron, expressing admiration for "versification undecorated with the meretricious fascinations of harmony, for sentiments unsophisticated by the delusive ardour of philanthropy, for narrative enveloped in all the Cimmerian sublimity of the impenetrable obscure."
[4] After reading a newspaper satire abusing Reynolds and himself, Johnson called out: "Are we alive after all this satire?" Boswell's *Life of Johnson*, 1780.
[5] This postscript is added in *LJ*, III, 89–90. It is not in the manuscript, and is possibly a separate letter since Byron did not usually add a closing to his postscripts.
[1] Hodgson reviewed *Safie* by John Hamilton Reynolds in the *Monthly Review* for Sept., 1814 (N. S., Vol. LXXV, page 60). See [Feb. 20, 1814] to Reynolds.

that you are well and well doing. Peace be with you. Ever yours, my dear friend.

My dear W.—I have but a few minutes to write to you.—*Silence* is the only answer to the things you mention—nor should I regard that man as my friend—who said a word more on the subject.—I care little for attacks—but I will not submit to *defences* & I do hope & trust that *you* have never entertained a serious thought of engaging in so foolish a controversy.—Dallas's letter was to his credit—merely as to facts which he had a right to state.—*I* neither have nor shall take the least *public* notice—nor permit anyone else to do so.—If I discover the writer—then I may act in a different manner—but it will not be in writing.——An expression in your letter has induced me to write this to you—to entreat you not to interfere in any way in such a business—it is now nearly over—& depend upon it—*they* are much more chagrined by my silence than they could be by the best defence in ye. world.—I do not know anything that would vex me more—than any further reply to these things.

ever yrs. in haste

B

[TO LADY MELBOURNE]   [*March, 1814?*]

My dear Ly. M[elbourn]e.—I return A[nnabella]'s letter with many thanks—I have had *one too.*—Next week—I hope to see you—I am going down to Harrow for a day.——"*Prosecute*"—Oh No—I am a great friend to the liberty of the press—even at the expence of myself—besides—do I not deserve all this? and am I not in reality much worse than they make me?—they shall not break my heart or my spirit—*personally* or *paragraphically*—but if the man whoever he is were delivered bound hand & foot into my hands—I would cut the cords—though if he turned out a gentleman—I must cut his throat instead—but that is to oblige the world & it's regulation—& not myself.—I can be as savage & revengeful as anybody—but then it must be on someone in one's way—or at least my equal—I could have no great pastime in torturing earwigs—though I dislike them as much as wolves.—But I was the *beginner*—and as long as I can be patient I

will—& when I cannot—depend upon it—I will break out effectually
or not at all.—————

ever yrs.

Bɴ

[ᴛᴏ ᴊᴏʜɴ ᴍᴜʀʀᴀʏ]   *March 1st. 1814*

Dear Sir/—I have just heard I trust falsely—of a letter purporting
to be from *me* in some *paper* of yesterday—to Sir W. [Garrow?]![1]—
I wish you would enquire if such a forgery has appeared—as it must
be some "invention of the enemy" of which I neither dreamed nor can
guess at it's writer.———

yrs. ever truly

Bɴ

[ᴛᴏ ᴊᴏʜɴ ᴍᴜʀʀᴀʏ]   *March 2d. 1814*

My dear Sir/—I am afraid that what you call *"trash"* is plaguily to
the purpose & very good sense into the bargain—& to tell the truth
for some little time past I have been much of the same opinion—which
serves to confirm me in my present resolution.———Are you fond of
Cyder & Perry?—I have a hogshead of each in Worcestershire which
I don't know what to do with & if you like it it shall be sent Carriage
free—& presented to you for your "bye drinkings"[1] without expence
and as little trouble as I can give you with it.———I want all my
boxes of papers & trunks that may contain others—as some I have at
present or wish to refer to—let them be sent down when convenient.

ever yrs.

B

[ᴛᴏ ᴛʜᴏᴍᴀs ᴍᴏᴏʀᴇ]   *March 3, 1814*

My dear Friend.—I have a great mind to tell you that I *am* "uncomfortable," if only to make you come to town; where no one ever
more delighted in seeing you, nor is there any one to whom I would
sooner turn for consolation in my most vapourish moments. The truth
is, I have "no lack of argument" to ponder upon of the most gloomy

[1] Sir William Garrow (1760–1840) was made Solicitor-General in 1812, and
Attorney-General in 1813.
[1] *Henry IV*, Part I, Act III, scene 3.

description, but this arises from *other* causes. Some day or other, when we are *veterans*, I may tell you a tale of present and past times; and it is not from want of confidence that I do not now,—but—but—always a *but* to the end of the chapter.

There is nothing, however, upon the *spot* either to love or hate;—but I certainly have subjects for both at no very great distance, and am besides embarrassed between *three* whom I know, and one (whose name, at least) I do not know.[1] All this would be very well, if I had no heart; but, unluckily, I have found that there is such a thing still about me, though in no very good repair, and, also, that it has a habit of attaching itself to *one*, whether I will or no. "Divide et impera," I begin to think, will only do for politics.

If I discover the "toad," as you call him, I shall "tread,"—and put spikes in my shoes to do it more effectually. The effect of all these fine things, I do not inquire much nor perceive. I believe * * felt them more than either of us. People are civil enough, and I have had no dearth of invitations,—none of which, however, I have accepted. I went out very little last year, and mean to go about still less. I have no passion for circles, and have long regretted that I ever gave way to what is called a town life;—which, of all the lives I ever saw (and they are nearly as many as Plutarch's), seems to me to leave the least for the past and future.

How proceeds the Poem? Do not neglect it, and I have no fears. I need not say to you that your fame is dear to me,—I really might say *dearer* than my own; for I have lately begun to think my things have been strangely overrated; and, at any rate, whether or not, I have done with them for ever. I may say to you, what I would not say to every body, that the last two were written, the Bride in four, and the Corsair in ten days,—which I take to be a most humiliating confession, as it proves my own want of judgment in publishing, and the public's in reading things, which cannot have stamina for permanent attention. "So much for Buckingham."[2]

I have no dread of your being too hasty, and I have still less of your failing. But I think a *year* a very fair allotment of time to a composition which is not to be Epic; and even Horace's "Nonum prematur"[3] must

[1] The three women most in Byron's thoughts at this time were Lady Frances Webster, Augusta, and Annabella Milbanke; the one whose name he did not know must have been one of the many women who wrote him anonymously or came to see him during his years of fame.

[2] *Richard III* (as altered by Cibber), Act IV, scene 3.

[3] Horace, *Ars Poetica*, line 388. Byron was fond of citing Horace's advice to keep one's manuscript for nine years before publishing.

have been intended for the Millenium, or some longer-lived generation than ours. I wonder how much we should have had of *him,* had he observed his own doctrines to the letter. Peace be with you! Remember that I am always and most truly yours, &c.

P.S.—I never heard the "report" you mention, nor, I dare say, many others. But, in course, you, as well as others, have "damned good-natured friends,"[4] who do their duty in the usual way. One thing will make you laugh * * * * * *

[TO ANNABELLA MILBANKE]   *March 3d. 1814*

My dear Friend—In your last you stated that you were about to quit Seaham for a short time—I trust that you have derived benefit— that is better health—from your excursion.—I have to regret having perhaps alarmed you by something I said—writing hastily in one of my late letters[1]—I did not very well—at least I do not recollect— exactly what I said—it was the "hectic of a moment" probably— occasioned by a variety of unpleasant circumstances pressing upon me at the time—and arising from follies (or worse) into which I betray myself—& escape I cannot tell how—unless there be such a thing as Fate in this best of all possible worlds.————You allude in your last to the very indignant newspapers—whose assaults I would most willingly encounter every morning for the residue of my life—provided I could exchange for them some of my own reflections & recollections on very different subjects which assail me much more formidably.—I thank you very much for your suggestion on Religion—but I must tell you at the hazard of losing whatever good opinion your gentleness may have bestowed upon me—that it is a source from which I never did—& I believe never can derive comfort—if I ever feel what is called devout—it is when I have met with some good of which I did not conceive myself deserving—and then I am apt to thank anything but mankind—on the other hand when I am ill or unlucky—I philosophize as well as I can—& wish it over one way or the other without many glimpses at the future—why I came here—I know not—where I shall go it is useless to enquire—in the midst of myriads of the living & the dead worlds—stars—systems—infinity—why should I be anxious about an atom?————I am writing to you with "the night almost at

---

4 Sir Fretful Plagiary in Sheridan's *The Critic,* says: "if there is anything to one's praise, it is a foolish vanity to be gratified at it, and if it is abuse—why one is always sure to hear of it from one damned good-natured friend or another!"

1 See Feb. 19, 1814, to Annabella Milbanke, note 3.

odds with morning" and you are asleep—perhaps I were better so too—& for fear my letter should prove a commentary on Pope's line "sleepless himself to give his readers sleep"[2] I will conclude by wishing that you may awake to the most agreeable day-dreams which the "pure in heart" desire & deserve

ever yrs most truly

B

P.S.—I was told today that you had refused me "a *second* time" so that you see I am supposed to be the most permanent of your plagues— & persevering of Suitors—a kind of successor to Wellesley Long Pole[3]—if this multiplication table of negatives don't embarrass you— I can assure you it don't disturb me—if it vexed me I could not—& if I thought it would do otherwise than amuse *you*, I certainly *should* not have mentioned it.—

[TO THOMAS PHILLIPS?］ *March 6th. 1814*

Dear Sir/—I regret troubling you—but my friend H[obhouse] who saw the pictures today suggests to me that the *nose* of the smaller portrait is too much turned *up*—if you recollect I thought so too—but as one never can tell the truth of one's own features—I should have said no more on the subject but for this remark of a friend whom I have known so long that he must at least be aware of the length of that *nose* by which I am so easily led.———Perhaps you will have the goodness to retouch it—as it is a feature of some importance—the Albanian wants nothing—if you can—excuse my plaguing you with this request.—

yrs. very truly
BIRON

[TO THOMAS MOORE] *March 12th, 1814*

Guess darkly, and you will seldom err. At present, I shall say no more, and, perhaps—but no matter. I hope we shall some day meet, and whatever years may precede or succeed it, I shall mark it with the "white stone" in my calendar. I am not sure that I shall not soon be in

---

[2] Pope, *Dunciad*, Book I, lines 92–93: "While pensive poets painful vigils keep,/Sleepless themselves to give their readers sleep."

[3] William Wellesley Pole, wastrel nephew of the Duke of Wellington, married in 1812 Catherine, daughter of Sir James Tylney Long. He added his wife's double name to his own and became William Wellesley Pole Tylney Long Wellesley. He proceeded to spend his wife's fortune and finally left her.

your neighbourhood again. If so, and I am alone (as will probably be the case), I shall invade and carry you off, and endeavour to atone for sorry fare by a sincere welcome. I don't know the person absent (barring "the sect") I should be so glad to see again.

I have nothing of the sort you mention but *the lines* (the Weepers),[1] if you like to have them in the Bag. I wish to give them all possible circulation. The *Vault*[2] reflection is downright actionable, and to print it would be peril to the publisher; but I think the Tears have a natural right to be bagged, and the editor (whoever he may be) might supply a facetious note or not, as he pleased.

I cannot conceive how the *Vault* has got about,—but so it is. It is too *farouche*; but, truth to say, my satires are not very playful. I have the plan of an epistle in my head, *at* him and *to* him; and, if they are not a little quieter, I shall imbody it. I should say little or nothing of *myself*. As to mirth and ridicule, that is out of my way; but I have a tolerable fund of sternness and contempt, and, with Juvenal before me, I shall perhaps read him a lecture he has not lately heard in the C————t [Cabinet]. From particular circumstances, which came to my knowledge almost by accident, I could "tell him what he is—I know him well."

I meant, my dear M.. to write to you a long letter, but I am hurried, and time clips my inclination down to yours, &c.

P.S.—*Think again* before you *shelf* your Poem. There is a youngster (older than me, by the by, but a younger poet), Mr. G. Knight, with a vol. of Eastern Tales,[3] written since his return,—for he has been in the countries. He sent to me last summer, and I advised him to write one in *each measure*, without any intention, at that time, of doing the same thing. Since that, from a habit of writing in a fever, I have anticipated him in the variety of measures, but quite unintentionally. Of the stories, I know nothing, not having seen them; but *he* has some lady in a sack, too, like the Giaour:—he told me at the time.

The best way to make the public "forget" me is to remind them of yourself. You cannot suppose that *I* would ask or advise you to publish, if I thought you would *fail*. I really have *no* literary envy; and I do not believe a friend's success ever sat nearer another than yours do

---

[1] "Lines to a Lady Weeping".

[2] The savage lines on the Prince Regent, who was present at the opening of the tomb at Windsor which held the remains of Henry VIII and Charles I, had been circulated in manuscript but not published during Byron's lifetime.

[3] Henry Gally Knight (1786–1846) wrote several Eastern tales: *Ildirim, a Syrian Tale* (1816), *Phrosyne, a Grecian Tale* (1817), and *Alashtar, an Arabian Tale* (1817).

to my best wishes. It is for *elderly gentlemen* to "bear no brother near," and cannot become our disease for more years than we may perhaps number. I wish yoú to be out before Eastern subjects are again before the public.

My dear Sir/—I have not time to read the whole M.S. but what I have seen seems very well written (both *prose* & *verse*) & though I am & can be no judge (at least a *fair* one on this subject) containing nothing which you *ought* to hesitate publishing upon *my* account.[1]— If the author is not Dr. *Busby* himself[2]—I think it a pity on his *own* account that he should dedicate it to his subscribers—nor can I perceive what Dr. B. has to do with the matter except as a translator of Lucretius—for whose doctrines he is surely not responsible.—I tell you openly & really most sincerely—that if published at all there is no earthly reason why you should *not*—on the contrary I should receive it as the fairest compliment *you* could pay to your good opinion of my candour—to print & circulate that or any other work attacking me in a manly manner—& without any malicious intention from which as far as I have seen I must exonerate this writer.—He is wrong in one thing— *I am no Atheist*—but if he thinks I have published principles tending to such opinions—he has a perfect right to controvert them.—Pray— publish it—I shall never forgive myself—if I think that I have prevented you.———Make my compts. to the Author—& tell him I wish him success—his verse is very deserving of it—& I shall be the last person to suspect his motives.—

yrs. very truly.—
BYRON

P.S.—If *you* do not publish it—some one else will—you cannot suppose me so *narrow* minded—as to shrink from discussion—I repeat once for all—that I think it a good poem (as far as I have redde) and that is the only point—*you* should consider. How odd that *8 lines* should have given birth I really think to *8000* including *all* that has been said & will be on the subject!

[1] This was a long solemn satire called *Anti-Byron*, which had been sent to Murray.
[2] See [Oct. 17?], 1812, to Murray (*a*), note 1 (Vol. 2, p. 228, note 1).

To rob you of my conversion some pious person has written & is about to publish a long poem—an "Anti-Byron" which he sent to *Murray*—who (not very fairly) sent it to me—and I advised him to print it—but some strange sort of book-selling delicacy won't let him—however some one else will.—I thought some parts of the verse very good—the author's object is to prove that I am the *systematic* reviver of the dogmata of Epicurus—& that I have formed a promising plan for the overthrow of these realms their laws & religion by dint of certain rhymes (Runci (?) I suppose) of such marvellous effect that he says they have already had the "most pernicious influence on civil society".—Howbeit—with all this persuasion of mine evil intents— what I saw was very decent invective & very grave—no humour nor much personality—a great deal about Gassendi Locke &c.[1] and a learned refutation of my supposed doctrines. The preface is all about the 8 lines (ye. tears)—which have I believe given birth to as many volumes of remarks answers epigrams &c. &c. so you see like the fly on the wheel in the fable "what a dust we create."—In addition to these—I do not think that there be 50 lines of mine in all touching upon religion—but I have an ill memory—& there may be more— however I had no notion of my being so formidable an Encyclopedist— or a Conspirator of such consequence.—Now—can anything be more ludicrous than all this?—yet it is very true—I mean the Anti-person of whom I am speaking—he assumes at first setting out my *Atheism* as an incontrovertible basis & reasons very wisely upon it—the real fact is I am none—but it would be cruel to deprive one who has taken so much pains of so agreeable a supposition—at least unless he believed that he had convinced me of that which I never doubted.——I will send it to you ye. moment it is out to shew you what an escape you have had—for there is a long prose passage against *my marrying*—or rather anyone's marrying me—on account of ye. presumed philosophy wherewithal I am incessantly to lecture ye. future Ly. B. and the young Spinozas tutored in the comfortable creed with which I have already inoculated "civil society" & which they are to take instead of the Vaccine.—You do not know how much I wish to see you—for there are so many things *said* in a moment—but tedious upon the tablets— not that I should ever intrude upon your confidence any thing (at least

[1] Pierre Gassendi, French philosopher and savant (1592–1655), noted for his empirical views, and John Locke, whose rational system and his preaching of "Toleration" were both more congenial to Byron than to the author of *Anti-Byron*.

I hope not) you should *not* hear—yet there are several opinions of yours I want to request—& though I have two or three able & I believe very sincere *male* friends there is something preferable to me in ye. delicacy of a woman's perceptions.—Of this at least I am sure— that I am more liable to be convinced by their arguments.—As for ye *report* I mentioned—*I* care not how often it is repeated—it would plague me much more to hear that I was *accepted* by anybody else than rejected by you.————I have passed the bourne of my paper—& must leave Me. de Stael—Miss B[yro]n and somewhat more of Egotism for another opportunity.—You are better—and God knows I am glad of it.—I am interrupted by a visitor—and you won't regret it—and I must not.—

ever yrs.

B

[TO JOHN MURRAY] *March 19th. 1814*

Dear Sir/—The only resource left me against the conspiracy of yourself & printer not to attend to one word I say—is to require the proofs—pray send them—& for the present *copies* make me an errata page—with the addition & corrections—marked in this & the *other* copies I sent you.—

ever yrs.

B

I have *marked* the pages on the cover of the book.—

[TO JAMES WEDDERBURN WEBSTER] *March 21st. 1814*

Dear Webster/—I am sorry to say that in consequence of a disappointment for the present in the *amount* of the remittance I expected I am obliged to decline advancing the sum which I would readily have done had it been within my power.—With regard to joining you as a security—I should have no objection—but on the terms & with the persons to whom you have applied—I should only become instrumental in involving *both* without any permanent benefit to yourself.— I speak from experience—as my own difficulties have arisen from similar sources.—Your own agent could surely direct you to more reputable lenders—and better terms—and as you must have security to give on your own property—I should think the business might be arranged without your having recourse to the Advertisers in papers.

———I regret very much that it is not now in my power to advance this *myself*—& I think you know that I would have done so had it been practicable

very truly yrs.

B

Dear Sir,—I have been out of town, otherwise your letter should have been answered sooner. When a letter contains a request, the said request generally figures towards the *finale,* and so does yours, my good friend. In answering perhaps the other way is the better: so not to make many words about a trifle, (which any thing of mine must be,) you shall have a touch of my quality for your first Number—and if you print that, you shall have more of the same stuff for the successors. Send me a few of your proofs, and I will set forthwith about something, that I at least hope may suit your purposes. So much for the Poetic Mirror,[2] which may easily be, God knows, entitled to hang higher than the prose one.

You seem to be a plain spoken man, Mr. Hogg, and I really do not like you the worse for it. I can't write verses, and yet you want a bit of my poetry for your book. It is for you to reconcile yourself with yourself.—You shall have the *verses.*

You are mistaken, my good fellow, in thinking that I (or, indeed, that any living verse-writer—for we shall sink *poets*) can write as well as Milton. Milton's Paradise Lost is, as a whole, a heavy concern; but the two first books of it are the very finest poetry that has ever been produced in this world—at least since the flood—for I make little doubt Abel was a fine pastoral poet, and Cain a fine bloody poet, and so forth; but we, now-a-days, even we, (you and *I, i.e.*) know no more of their poetry than the *brutum vulgus*—I beg pardon, the swinish multitude, do of Wordsworth and Pye. Poetry must always exist, like drink, where there is a demand for it. And Cain's may have been the brandy of the Antedeluvians, and Abel's the small [?] still.

Shakespeare's name, you may depend on it, stands absurdly too high and will go down. He had no invention as to stories, none whatever.

---

[1] James Hogg, the Ettrick Shepherd.

[2] Hogg had planned a volume consisting of contributions from contemporary poets but finally wrote clever parodies of Wordsworth, Byron, Southey, Coleridge, Wilson, Scott, and himself, and published them with an ingenious preface in 1816 as "The Poetic Mirror, or the Living Bards of Great Britain."

He took all his plots from old novels, and threw their stories into a dramatic shape, at as little expense of thought as you or I could turn his plays back again into prose tales. That he threw over whatever he did write some flashes of genius, nobody can deny: but this was all. Suppose any one to have the *dramatic* handling for the first time of such ready-made stories as Lear, Macbeth, &c. and he would be a sad fellow, indeed, if he did not make something very grand of them. [As] for his historical plays, properly historical, I mean, they were mere re-dressings of former plays on the same subjects, and in twenty cases out of twenty-one, the finest, the very finest things, are taken all but *verbatim* out of the old affairs. You think, no doubt, that *A horse, a horse, my kingdom for a horse*! is Shakespeare's. Not a syllable of it. You will find it all in the old nameless dramatist. Could not one take up Tom Jones and improve it, without being a greater genius than Fielding? I, for my part, think Shakespeare's plays might be improved, and the public seem, and have seemed for to think so too, for not one of his is or ever has been acted as he wrote it; and what the pit applauded three hundred years past, is five times out of ten not Shakespeare's, but Cibber's.

Stick you to Walter Scott, my good friend, and do not talk any more stuff about his not being willing to give you real advice, if you really will ask for real advice. You love Southey, forsooth—I am sure Southey loves nobody but himself, however. I hate these talkers one and all, body and soul. They are a set of the most despicable impostors —that is my opinion of them. They know nothing of the world; and what is poetry, but the reflection of the world? What sympathy have this people with the spirit of this stirring age? They are no more able to understand the least of it, than your *lass*—nay, I beg her pardon, *she* may very probably have intense sympathy with both its spirit, (I mean the whisky,) and its body (I mean the bard.) They are mere old wives. Look at their beastly vulgarity, when they wish to be homely; and their exquisite stuff, when they clap on sail, and aim at fancy. Coleridge is the best of the trio—but bad is the best. Southey should have been a parish-clerk, and Wordsworth a man-midwife—both in darkness. I doubt if either of them ever got drunk, and I am of the old creed of Homer the wine-bibber. Indeed I think you and Burns have derived a great advantage from this, that being poets, and drinkers of wine, you have had a new potation to rely upon. Your whisky has made you original. I have always thought it a fine liquor. I back you against beer at all events, gill to gallon.

By the bye, you are a fine hand to cut up the minor matters of verse-writing; you indeed think harmony the all-in-all. My dear sir, you may depend upon it, you never had *name* yet, without making it rhyme to *theme*. I overlook all that sort of thing, however, and so must you, in your turn, pass over my real or supposed ruggedness. The fact is, that I have a theory on the subject, but that I have not time at present for explaining it. The first time all the poets of the age meet— it must be in London, glorious London is the place, after all—we shall, if you please, have a small trial of skill. You shall write seventeen odes for me, anything from Miltonian blank down to Phillupian [sic] namby, and I a similar number for you, and let a jury of good men and true be the judges between us. I name Scott for foreman—Tom Campbell may be admitted, and Mrs. Baillie, (though it be not exactly a matron case.) You may name the other nine worthies yourself. We shall, at all events, have a dinner upon the occasion, and I stipulate for a small importation of the peat reek.

> Dear sir, believe me sincerely yours,
> BYRON

[TO SCROPE BERDMORE DAVIES]   *March 26th 1814*

My dear Scrope—The bills are discounted & I have sent a draft on Hoares for the whole sum to your bankers[1]—I trust tonight—or tomorrow will apprize you of the receipt of the same.—I shall merely add that I by no means consider the obligation cancelled with the bond—though I much regret [first page of MS. cut off here] Tomorrow at 6—the *Cocoa*[2]—shall you order? or shall *I*—if you do—remember *fish*—and what meats you please.—

> ever yrs. most truly—
> BYRON

[TO LADY MELBOURNE]   *March 30th. 1814*

My dear Ly. M[elbourn]e.—I have turned over ye. book at least ye. part of it.—& think the *coincidence* unlucky for many reasons—in the 1st. place every body will read Me. D'Arblay[1]—& though in a

[1] This was the final payment of Byron's debt to Scrope Davies, for the money he had borrowed before he went abroad in 1809. He had paid £1500 of the debt in November, 1812, after receiving his first payment from Claughton.

[2] The Cocoa Tree Club, of which Byron and Scrope Davies were members.

[1] In Madame D'Arblay's novel *The Wanderer, or Female Difficulties* there was an episode that might have reminded readers of Caroline Lamb's cutting herself with some broken glass at Lady Heathcote's party in 1813. In Volume I, Elinor, rejected by Harleigh, takes out a poniard as if to stab herself.

thousand points there is no resemblance nor design to make one—yet the *main* fact at least as represented & believed by several—will be recalled afresh to people's recollection—& what is worse to *her own*—and then Lady B[essborough] will have her flutters—& C[aroline] be in one of her tempers—of which I can hardly tell whether the bad or the good are most to be dreaded by what I have seen & heard of her disposition.—I have very little doubt—that though this was written long ago—she might not erase it with her many corrections—as something like it having really occurred (and of which she must have heard) would at least prevent her from being charged with *over* colouring her portraits—as the *scene* and the *assembly* and the *public display* would otherwise have certainly been thrown upon her as *French*—& not English *manner*.—I am in *my* & *your* Albany rooms[2]—I think you should have been included in the lease.—I am sadly bewildered with hammering—and teaching people the left hand from the right—and very much out of humour with a friend—who tells me of a serious report that I am turning Methodist!—I suppose you will say so I am "in good works" (I don't mean scribblings) which with them are as nought—

ever yrs.

B

P.S.—I have seen the E[dinburgh] R[eview][3] and the compliment—which *Rogers* says—"*Scott* & *Campbell* won't like" kind Soul!—It is very handsome of Jeffrey nevertheless—& what a little mind would not dare in favour of a former enemy—& it is further valuable as coming from the monarch of existing criticism.—

[TO CHARLES HANSON]   *March 30th. 1814*

My dear Charles/—All words are useless—but I think your own manliness of mind will support you—the more so—as others will require that consolation from you which the helplessness of their sex more especially demands at such a moment.[1]—Whenever your father &

2 Byron had just moved into his bachelor quarters in Albany House in Piccadilly just a few steps from Murray's office in Albemarle Street. This was the house in which the Melbournes had lived until 1789, when, to oblige the Duke of York and Albany, who had taken a fancy to it, they traded it for the residence in Whitehall, where Byron first met them and Lady Caroline Lamb.

3 In the April number of the *Edinburgh Review* Francis Jeffrey reviewed *The Corsair* and *The Bride of Abydos*, giving high praise to Byron's poetic qualities and to his "tenderness and humanity".

1 John Hanson's wife (Charles's mother) died in March 1814. She had been something of a substitute mother to Byron during his early years in London.

yourself feel it proper and desire to see me I shall wait upon you—till then believe me your

afflicted & affectionate friend
BYRON

Wednesday Noon
[*March 30–April 6 1814?*]

[TO JAMES WEDDERBURN WEBSTER]

Dear W.—I hear that you are in town & *unwell*—the last report I shall be very glad to have contradicted by yourself.—When you have nothing better to do I shall be happy to see you—if you are not disposed to stir in this weather I can call upon you when you like.

yrs. very truly
B

[TO HARRIETTE WILSON[1]]   *Albany* [*April?*] *1814*

If my silence has hurt "your pride or your feelings", to use your own expressions, I am very sorry for it; be assured that such effect was far from my intention. Business, and some little bustle attendant on changing my residence, prevented me from thanking you for your letter as soon as I ought to have done. If my thanks do not displease you, now, pray accept them. I could not feel otherwise than obliged by the desire of a stranger to make my acquaintance.

I am not unacquainted with your name or your beauty, and I have heard much of your talents; but I am not the person whom you would like, either as a lover or a friend. I did not, and do not suspect you, to use your own words once more, of any design of making love to me. I know myself well enough to acquit anyone who does not know me, and still more those who do, from any such intention. I am not of a nature to be loved, and so far, luckily for myself, I have no wish to be so. In saying this, I do not mean to affect any particular stoicism, and may possibly, at one time or other, have been liable to those follies, for

1 Harriette Wilson, the famous courtesan and demi-mondaine, who had at one time by her own account kept the Duke of Wellington waiting in the rain while she entertained another lover, claimed in her *Memoirs* that she had met Byron at a masquerade in 1814. It is more likely that she just saw him, for she wrote to him asking for his acquaintance, and when he did not reply, she wrote again reprimanding him for his discourtesy. This was his answer to her second letter. She continued to write to him while he was in Italy, and he once sent her £50 when she was in dire need in Paris. The manuscript of this letter is not preserved, but it is very Byronic and probably authentic. He preserved a number of her letters which are sophisticated and clever.

which you sarcastically tell me, I have now no time: but these, and everything else, are to me, at present, objects of indifference; and this is a good deal to say, at six-and-twenty. You tell me that you wished to know me better, because you liked my writing. I think you must be aware that a writer is in general very different from his productions, and always disappoints those who expect to find in him qualities more agreeable than those of others; I shall certainly not be lessened in my vanity, as a scribbler, by the reflection that a work of mine has given you pleasure; and, to preserve the impression in its favour, I will not risk your good opinion, by inflicting my acquaintance upon you.

Very truly your obliged servant,

B

[TO JOHN MURRAY]   *April 2d 1814*

Dear Sir/—Mr. Dallas disclaims all connection with the last Ed[ition] of C[hilde] H[arold]—some proofs were sent in an irregular manner—but no attention paid to his wish for the whole.—All I can say is—that the carelessness with which the last E[ditio]ns of that work have been allowed to be published—is very unpleasant to me—& not very creditable to you.

yrs.

B

[TO ———————France[1]]   *April 3d. 1814*

Dear Sir/—In the present distress of Mr. Hanson & his family I would not venture to intrude on him with business of whatever consequence to myself, this must be my excuse for troubling *you* with this letter. Mr. Claughton was expected in town daily will *you* have the goodness to enquire after & see him.—& urge the *indispensable* necessity of his fulfilling as far as in his power & immediately the terms—of which the satisfactory adjustment has been again delayed— solely by himself.———His address will be I believe the Grecian Coffee House.—

ever yr. obliged & obedt. Sert.

BYRON

---

[1] France was Hanson's clerk or assistant in his law office. Byron did not want to disturb Hanson because of the recent death of his wife.

I have been out of town since Saturday & only returned last Night from my visit to Augusta.——I swallowed the D———l in ye. shape of a collar of brawn one evening for supper (after an enormous dinner too) and it required all kinds of brandies & I don't know what besides to put me again in health & good humour—but I am now quite restored—& it is to avoid your congratulations upon *fatness* (which I abhor & *you* always inflict upon me after a return from the country) that I don't pay my respects to you today—besides which I dislike to see Ld. M[elbourn]e standing by the chimney piece all horror & astonishment at my appearance while C[aroline] is within reach of the two-penny postman.—Today I have been very sulky—but an hour's exercise with Mr. Jackson of pugilistic memory—has given me spirits & fatigued me into that state of languid laziness which I prefer to all other.—I left all my relations—at least my niece & her mamma very well—L[eigh] was in Yorkshire—& I regret not having seen him of course very much.—My intention was to have joined a party at Cambridge—but somehow I overstaid my time—& the inclination to visit the University went off—& here I am alone—& not over pleased with being so.—*You* don't think the "Q[uarterl]y so very complimentary"[1] most people do—I have no great opinion on the subject—& (except in the E[dinburg]h) am not much interested in any criticisms favourable or otherwise.—I have had my day—& have done with all that stuff—& must try something new—politics— or rebellion—or methodism—or gaming—of the 2 last I have serious thoughts as one can't travel till we see how long Paris is to be the quarter of the Allies.[2]—I can't help suspecting that my little Pagod will play them some trick still—if Wellington or one hero had beaten another—it would be nothing—but to be worried by brutes—& conquered by recruiting sergeants—why there is not a *character* amongst them.—

ever yrs. most affectly.

B

---

[1] *The Giaour* and *The Bride of Abydos* were reviewed in the January number of the *Quarterly Review*, which under Gifford's editorship was usually two or three months late in appearing.

[2] At the end of March Paris capitulated and the allies entered the city. Napoleon was forced to abdicate and was sent to Elba. Byron was right in his prediction that he would "play them some trick still."

April 9th. 1814

Dear Sir/—All these news are very fine—but nevertheless I want my books if you can find or cause them to be found for me—if only to lend them to N[apoleo]n in the "island of Elba" during his retirement. —I also—(if convenient & you have no party with you)—shd. be glad to speak with you for a few minutes this Even. as I have had a letter from Mr. Moore and wish to ask you as the best judge of the best time for him to publish the work he has composed—I need not say that I have his success much at heart—not only because he is my friend—but something much better—a man of great talent of which he is less sensible than I believe any even of his enemies.————If you can so far oblige me as to step down do so—& if you are otherwise occupied—say nothing about it—I shall find you at home in ye course of next week.——

yrs. truly
B

P.S.—I see Sotheby's tragedies advertised—the D[eath] of Darnley is a famous subject[1]—one of the best I should think for the Drama— pray let me have a copy when ready.———Mrs. L[eigh] was much pleased with her books—& desired me to thank you—she means I believe to write to you her acknowledgements.

[TO THOMAS MOORE] *2, Albany, April 9th, 1814*

Viscount Althorpe is about to be married,[1] and I have gotten his spacious bachelor apartments in Albany, to which you will, I hope, address a speedy answer to this mine epistle.

I am but just returned to town, from which you may infer that I have been out of it; and I have been boxing, for exercise, with Jackson for this last month daily. I have also been drinking,—and, on one occasion, with three other friends at the Cocoa Tree, from six till four, yea, unto five in the matin. We clareted and champagned till two— then supped, and finished with a kind of regency punch composed of

---

[1] Sotheby published *Five Tragedies* in 1814: *The Confession, Orestes, Ivan, The Death of Darnley, Zamorin and Zama.* Byron preferred *Orestes*: "And Sotheby, with his damned 'Orestes,' (Which, by the way, the old Bore's best is)",—"Epistle to Dr. Polidori from Mr. Murray".

[1] John Charles Spencer, Viscount Althorp (afterward the 3rd Earl Spencer) (1782–1845) married in 1814, Esther, only daughter and heiress of Richard Acklom, of Wiseton Hall, Notts. When he gave up his bachelor apartment in Albany, Byron sublet it from him.

madeira, brandy, and *green* tea, no *real* water being admitted therein. There was a night for you!—without once quitting the table, except to ambulate home, which I did alone, and in utter contempt of a hackney-coach and my own *vis*, both of which were deemed necessary for our conveyance. And so,—I am very well, and they say it will hurt my constitution.

I have also, more or less, been breaking a few of the favourite commandments; but I mean to pull up and marry,—if any one will have me. In the mean time, the other day I nearly killed myself with a collar of brawn, which I swallowed for supper, and *in*digested for I don't know how long;—but that is by the by. All this gourmandize was in honour of Lent; for I am forbidden meat all the rest of the year, —but it is strictly enjoined me during your solemn fast. I have been, and am, in very tolerable love;—but of that hereafter, as it may be.

My dear Moore, say what you will in your Preface; and quiz any thing, or any body,—me, if you like it. Oons! dost thou think me of the *old*, or rather *elderly*, school? If one can't jest with one's friends, with whom can we be facetious? You have nothing to fear from * *, whom I have not seen, being out of town when he called. He will be very correct, smooth, and all that, but I doubt whether there will be any "grace beyond the reach of art;"[2]—and, whether there is or not, how long will you be so d————d modest? As for Jeffrey, it is a very handsome thing of him to speak well of an old antagonist,[3]—and what a mean mind dared not do. Any one will revoke praise; but—were it not partly my own case—I should say that very few have strength of mind to unsay their censure, or follow it up with praise of other things.

What think you of the review of *Levis?*[4] It beats the Bag and my hand-grenade hollow, as an invective, and hath thrown the Court into hysterics, as I hear from very good authority. Have you heard from * * * * * * * *

No more rhyme for—or rather, *from*—me. I have taken my leave of that stage, and henceforth will mountebank it no longer. I have had my day, and there's an end. The utmost I expect, or even wish, is to have it said in the Biographia Britannica, that I might perhaps have been a poet, had I gone on and amended. My great comfort is, that the temporary celebrity I have wrung from the world has been in the very

[2] Pope, *Essay on Criticism*, Part I, line 153.

[3] Jeffrey's review of *The Corsair* and *The Bride of Abydos* in the *Edinburgh Review* of April, 1814, Vol. XXII, pp. 198–229.

[4] *Souvenirs et Portraits*, par M. de Levis (*Edinburgh Review*, April, 1814, Vol. XXII, page 281).

teeth of all opinions and prejudices. I have flattered no ruling powers; I have never concealed a single thought that tempted me. They can't say I have truckled to the times, nor to popular topics (as Johnson, or somebody, said of Cleveland), and whatever I have gained has been at the expenditure of as much *personal* favour as possible; for I do believe never was a bard more unpopular, *quoad homo*, than myself. And now I have done;—"ludite nunc alios."[5] Every body may be d————d, as they seem fond of it, and resolved to stickle lustily for endless brimstone.

Oh—by the by, I had nearly forgot. There is a long Poem, an "Anti-Byron," coming out, to prove that I have formed a conspiracy to overthrow, by *rhyme*, all religion and government, and have already made great progress! It is not very scurrilous, but serious and ethereal. I never felt myself important, till I saw and heard of my being such a little Voltaire as to induce such a production. Murray would not publish it, for which he was a fool, and so I told him; but some one else will, doubtless. "Something too much of this."[6]

Your French scheme is good, but let it be *Italian*; all the Angles will be at Paris. Let it be Rome, Milan, Naples, Florence, Turin, Venice, or Switzerland, and "egad!" (as Bayes saith), I will connubiate and join you; and we will write a new "Inferno" in our Paradise. Pray, think of this—and I will really buy a wife and a ring, and say the ceremony, and settle near you in a summer-house upon the Arno, or the Po, or the Adriatic.

Ah! my poor little pagod, Napoleon, has walked off his pedestal. He has abdicated, they say. This would draw molten brass from the eyes of Zatanai.[7] What! "kiss the ground before young Malcolm's feet, and then be baited by the rabble's curse!"[8] I cannot bear such a crouching catastrophe. I must stick to Sylla, for my modern favourites don't do,—their resignations are of a different kind. All health and prosperity, my dear Moore. Excuse this lengthy letter. Ever, &c.

P.S.—The Quarterly quotes you frequently in an article on America;[9] and every body I know asks perpetually after you and yours. When will you answer them in person?

[5] Byron quoted slightly inaccurately the inscription on the sarcophagus of L. Annias Octavius in the Lateran Museum in Rome: Evasi, Effugi, Spes et Fortuna valete;/Nil mihi Vobiscum; ludificate alios." "I have escaped, I have fled. Hope and Fortune farewell; You will get no more from me; make game of others."

[6] *Hamlet*, Act III, scene 2.

[7] Satan.

[8] *Macbeth*, Act V, scene 7.

[9] *Inchiquen the Jesuit's Letters, during a late Residence in the United States . . .* (By Charles Jared Ingersoll). *Quarterly Review*, Vol. 10, pp. 494–539 (Jan., 1814).

Dear Sir/—I have written an ode on the fall of Nap[oleo]n which if you like I will copy out & make you a present of—Mr. Merivale has seen part of it & likes it—you may shew it to Mr. G[iffor]d & print it or not as you please—it is of no consequence.—It contains nothing in *his* favour—& no allusion whatever to our own Government or the Bourbons.

yrs. ever
B

P.S.—It is in the measure of my stanzas at the end of C[hilde] H[arol]d—which are much liked—beginning "and thou art dead" &c. &c.—There are ten stanzas of 90 lines in all.—

Dear Sir/—If the enclosed is deemed worth printing by itself—let it be *without* a name—though I have no objection to it's being *said* to be mine—if you could also get it *stopped*[1] you will oblige

yrs. truly
Bn

Dear Sir—I enclose you a letter*et* from Mrs. L[eig]h.———It will be best *not* to put my name to our *Ode*[1] but you may *say* openly as you like that it is mine—& I can inscribe it to Mr. Hobhouse from ye. *Author* which will mark it sufficiently.—After the resolution of not publishing—though it is a thing of little length & less consequence it will be better altogether that is is anonymous—but we will incorporate it in the first *tome* of ours that you find time or the wish to publish.—

yrs alway
B

P.S.—I hope you got a note of alterations sent this Matin.

P.S.—Oh my books! my books! will you never find my books?— Alter "*potent* spell" to "*quickening* spell" the first (as Polonius says)

---

[1] *i.e.*, punctuated.
[1] The "Ode to Napoleon Buonaparte".

"is a vile phrase" & means nothing besides being common place &
Rosa Matildish.—

[TO JOHN MURRAY (*a*)]   *April 12th. 1814*

Dear Sir/—I send you a few notes and trifling alterations and an
additional motto from Gibbon,[1]—which you will find *singularly
appropriate.* A "Goodnatured friend" tells me there is a most scurrilous
attack on *us* in the Anti-jac[obin] R[revie]w[2]—which you have *not*
sent—send it—as I am in that state of languor which will derive
benefit from getting into a passion.—

                                                        ever yrs.
                                                              B

[TO JOHN MURRAY (*b*)]   *A[pri]l 12th. 1814*

Dear Sir/—I am very glad you like it—as I am anxious that the
whole should be ready tomorrow—perhaps I can have a proof early in
the morning—or if you can thoroughly read my detestable scrawl—
& could correct *very carefully* the whole yourself—it may save time &
do well without my superintendence.

                                                        yrs. truly
                                                              B

[TO JOHN MURRAY (*c*)]   *April 12th. 1814*

Dear Sir/—I send you some replicatory notes for *"the Corsair"*
which you must insert there the very first opportunity.—In the mean
time strike me off a proof of them to be ready for occasion—& I think
your Reviewer (whoever he may be) should see what I quote for "the
Corsair" in behalf of his being in Nature—yrs. ever

                                                              B

---

[1] The motto from Gibbon did not appear with the published poem.

[2] *The Antijacobin Review and True Churchman's Magazine* for March, 1814,
reviewed *The Bride of Abydos* and *The Corsair* with high moral indignation, comparing the dedications to Lord Holland and Moore with what he had said of them in
English Bards and Scotch Reviewers, and ended with a moral judgment: "Let him
examine, impartially, whether he has written a single sentence worthy to be
impressed on the mind of youth; whether he has composed a single line serviceable
to the cause of religion, morality, or virtue."

[to john murray (*d*)]   *April 12th. 1814*

Dear Sir/—Will you consult some of your literati on the pointing &
the propriety of the notes—& attend to the corrections & alterations.—
Perhaps we had better have one more revise.—

yrs. ever—

B

P.S.—I have read the Anti-jac[obin] it is a bagatelle & reprint of
Courier.—

[to john murray (*e*)]   *April 12, 1814*

Dear Sir—I send you *2* new Stanzas to the 2d and third[1]—if they
are tolerable insert them—and let me have a proof of the whole.—

Ever yrs.

B

[to john cam hobhouse]   *April 12th. 1814*

My dear H[obhous]e—I take the earliest opportunity of telling you
that to my regret *my* Parisian scheme is knocked up[1]—by some
intelligence received in letters this morning on business & other con-
cerns/—pray excuse this & yrs. ever

B

[to martin archer shee]   *2 Albany—April 15th. 1814*

Dear Sir/—I have received your letter with great—and the accom-
panying volume with greater pleasure.—In the latter—(with the
exception of the memorial you are kind enough to bestow on me)[1] I
am furnished with an additional proof that he who duly & publicly

---

[1] Byron was preparing a new edition of *The Corsair*.

[1] Hobhouse had determined to go to Paris "whilst yet any part of the Napoleon
vestiges yet remain", and Byron had consented to accompany him, but the fact that
Claughton had failed to make good his promise to pay another £5000 on account,
and his loyalty to Augusta who was approaching childbirth, caused him to cancel
his plans.

[1] Martin Archer Shee, portrait painter and later president of the Royal
Academy, sent Byron *The Commemoration of Reynolds; and Other Poems*. It was
published by Murray, who had presented a copy of *The Corsair* to Shee.

appreciates the merit of your productions is merely paying a compliment to his own taste.—Believe me with great regard & sincerity

yr. obliged & very obedt. Sert.

BYRON

[TO LADY SITWELL[1]]   *Albany A[pri]l 15th. 1814*

I shall have ye. honour of joining your party on Thursday evening. The song you have been good enough to send had escaped my observation or my memory when in Greece—I will endeavour to comply with your request.—The copy has a few errors which I will try to expunge— though I have nearly forgotten my Romaic—I believe the words should be thus arranged—

Pagoe is ten (the next word I cannot make out but pagē is I think "a fountain") dia nera Pago honta na eido [;] montana I scarcely recollect as a Romaic word—but na eido is "to see" or literally "that I may see" honta is "near" Ola tais Romaikais edo Ma te Agape mou den (or then is pronounced) einai edo.[2]—Where I am wrong Mr. Gell[3] will easily set it right—and knows much more of the subject than I can pretend to.—

I have the honour to be very

respectfully yr. obliged Sert.

BYRON

[TO BERNARD BARTON[1]]   *Albany April 16th. 1814*

Sir/—All offence is out of the question—my principal regret is that it is not in my power to be of service.—My own plans are very un-

---

[1] Sarah Caroline, daughter of James Stovin of Whitgift Hall, Yorkshire, married Sir Sitwell Sitwell. It was at Lady Sitwell's party in June, 1814, that Byron saw his cousin Mrs. Wilmot in a spangled dress, and was inspired to write his lyric: "She walks in Beauty like the Night".

[2] The Greek song which Lady Sitwell sent to Byron he translated, but it was not published in any of his collected works during the nineteenth century. His translation began: "I wander near that fount of waters/Where throng my country's daughters—" The manuscript, dated April 15th, 1814, is with the holograph letter to Lady Sitwell in the Yale Library.

[3] Sir William Gell (1777–1836), archaeologist and traveller, had published *Topography of Troy* (1804), *Geography and Antiquities of Ithaca* (1807), and *Itinerary of Greece* (1810), Byron had ridiculed him in *English Bards and Scotch Reviewers*, calling him "rapid Gell" because he spent only three days at Troy, and yet he had respect for Gell's knowledge of Greece and the Greek language.

[1] Bernard Barton (1784–1849), the Quaker poet, a friend of Lamb and Southey.

settled—& at present from a variety of circumstances embarrassed—
and even were it otherwise—I should be loth to offer anything like
dependence to one who from education and acquirements must
doubly feel sensible of such a situation—however I might be disposed to
render it tolerable.—As an adviser I am rather qualified to point out
what should be avoided than what may be pursued—for my own life
has been but a series of imprudences & conflicts of all descriptions—
from these I have only acquired experience—if repentance were added
perhaps it might be all the better, since I do not find the former of
much avail without it.—

[TO JOHN MURRAY]   [*April 16, 1814*]

Perhaps you may have leisure & inclination to step up here for a
few minutes—I have something to say about an *Irish piracy* of the
E[nglish] B[ards] which must be stopped.—

yrs. ever
B

[TO JOHN MURRAY]   [*April 17–18? 1814*]

Dear Sir/—Thanks—if you can get the stanza enclosed in—do.—I
send you Hunt with his ode[1]—the thoughts are good—but the
expressions *buckram* except here & there.—

ever yrs.
B

[TO ————————]   *2 Albany April 18th. 1814*

Sir/—I have to thank you for your present—& request that in
future the numbers be sent to my bookseller *Mr. Ridgway* at the time
of publication—who will receive my orders to account for them
regularly to the Publisher.————If you think the Ode worth sending
for[1]—Mr. Murray will deliver a copy to anyone sent in my name for
that purpose.—A friend of mine left town for Paris this morning[2]—

---

[1] Hunt's "Ode for the Spring of 1814" appeared in the *Examiner* on April 17,
1814. It was concerned with Napoleon's downfall.
[1] Byron's "Ode to Napoleon Buonaparte".
[2] Hobhouse left for Paris on April 18, 1814.

otherwise I should avail myself of your obliging offer.—The latter part of your letter I will consider & am

very truly yr. obliged Sert.
BYRON

P.S.—If you wish to have the Ode—it will be better to delay till Wednesday—as there is a slight addition which will then be published.————

[TO LADY MELBOURNE]   *April 18th. 1814*

My dear Ly. M[elbourn]e.—As I had no chance of seeing you except under that living padlock fixed upon you yesterday—I did not venture to your palace of Silence this afternoon.—I have as yet no intention of serving my sovereign "in the *North*"[1] and I wish to know whether (if I did incline that way) you would not put Richard's question to me?[2]—Though I think *that chance* off the cards—& have no paramount inclination to try a fresh deal—yet as what I may resolve today—may be unresolved tomorrow—I should be not only unwilling but unable to make the experiment without your acquiescence.—Circumstances which I need not recapitulate may have changed *Aunt's* mind—I do not say that *Niece's* is changed—but I *should* laugh if their judgments had changed places & exactly reversed upon that point.—In putting this question to you—my motive is all due selfishness—as a word from you—could & would put an end to that or any similar possibility—without my being able to say anything but "thank you".—Comprenez vous?—all this mystery?[3] it is what no one else will—I think I need hardly be more intelligible.—To conclude with a quotation "all this may be mere speculation if so think no more of it."—

ever yrs.
B

[TO DR. WILLIAM CLARK]   *2, Albany—April 19th. 1814*

Dear Sir/—Certainly—& I only regret that circumstances will not

[1] *i.e.*, Annabella Milbanke.

[2] *King Richard III*, Act I, scene 2. Richard's question was: "Was ever woman in this humour woo'd?/Was ever woman in this humour won?".

[3] Byron is hinting that Lady Melbourne may have changed her mind about fostering a match with her niece, Annabella Milbanke, because of Byron's involvement with his half-sister.

permit me to join you there immediately.[1]—I have only [to] add that if we meet either at home or abroad within a reasonable time I hope you will allow me to renew our acquaintance & joint expedition if the last should not interfere with more agreeable pursuits on your part.— You will find Hobhouse at Paris, & your sword & trunk here in your way.—

ever yrs.

B

[TO THOMAS MOORE]   *Albany, April 20th, 1814*

I *am* very glad to hear that you are to be transient from Mayfield so very soon, and was taken in by the first part of your letter.[1] Indeed, for aught I know, you may be treating me, as Slipslop says, with "ironing"[2] even now. I shall say nothing of the *shock*, which had nothing of *humeur* in it; as I am apt to take even a critic, and still more a friend, at his word, and never to doubt that I have been writing cursed nonsense, if they say so. There was a mental reservation in my pact with the public, in behalf of *anonymes*; and, even had there not, the provocation was such as to make it physically impossible to pass over this damnable epoch of triumphant tameness. 'Tis a cursed business; and, after all, I shall think higher of rhyme and reason, and very humbly of your heroic people, till—Elba becomes a volcano, and sends him out again. I can't think it all over yet.

My departure for the continent depends, in some measure, on the *in*continent. I have two country invitations at home, and don't know what to say or do. In the mean time, I have bought a macaw and a parrot, and have got up my books; and I box and fence daily, and go out very little.

At this present writing, Louis the Gouty is wheeling in triumph into Piccadilly, in all the pomp and rabblement of Royalty.[3] I had an offer of seats to see them pass; but, as I have seen a Sultan going to mosque, and been at *his* reception of an ambassador, the most Christian King "hath no attractions for me:"—though in some coming year of the

---

[1] Dr. Clark, anatomist, Fellow of Trinity College, Cambridge, whom Byron had planned to accompany abroad in the summer of 1813, had finally decided to leave for the Continent by himself.

[1] Moore had begun his letter with the pretence that he thought Byron's anonymous "Ode to Napoleon Buonaparte" was written by Fitzgerald or Rosa Matilda.

[2] Fielding, *Joseph Andrews*, Book I, Chapter 6.

[3] Louis XVIII made a triumphal entry into London on April 20, 1814, escorted by the Prince Regent and a long procession of French and English nobility.

Hegira, I should not dislike to see the place where he *had* reigned, shortly after the second revolution, and a happy sovereignty of two months, the last six weeks being civil war.

Pray write, and deem me ever, &c.

If I could flatter myself that my visit would not be disagreeable to you nor yours I should very willingly avail myself of Sir Ralph's possible invitation.—Distance is no object with me—and time can hardly be misspent in your society—besides a good deal of mine is generally passed in my own company—so that I could almost hope that I should not be found an intruder upon your studies or amusements.—you will do as you please—only let it be *as you* please—& not to gratify any supposed or real wish of mine that you make this sacrifice at the shrine of Hospitality.———I quite coincide with you upon religious discussion—it should at all events be treated with some degree of respect—if for no other reason than that it is so easy—so common and so unfit a subject for would be witticisms.—Upon that score I may have as a scribbler something to answer for—(I allude to some notes on some of the things of the last 2 years) but they have been as it were wrung from me—by the outcry on the subject—the common effect of contradiction upon human Nature.———It gave me much pleasure to hear from you again—I thought you unwell or indisposed to correspond with me farther—in either case I had no claim to trespass upon your health or patience.———All ye world are for Paris—Italy is my Magnet—but I have no particular wish to be of the vanguard or forlorn hope of foolish travellers—& shall take my time without much regretting a *summer* month or two in this country more or less—besides I have some previous business to arrange—for if I do once cross the channel I know my own loitering disposition well enough to fix no precise period for my return.—Buonaparte has fallen—I regret it—& the restoration of the despicable Bourbons— the triumph of tameness over talent—and the utter wreck of a mind which I thought superior even to Fortune—it has utterly confounded and baffled me—and unfolded more than "was dreamt of in my philosophy."—It is said the Empress has refused to follow him—this is not well—men will always fall away from men—but it may generally be observed that no change of Fortune—no degradation of rank or even character will detach a woman who has truly loved—unless there has been some provocation or misconduct towards herself on the part of the man—or she has preferred another for whom her affection will endure the same.—I have brought my politics & paper to a close—and have only room to sign my abdication of both.—

ever yrs.

B

[TO JOHN MURRAY]   *April 21st. 1814*

Dear Sir/—Many thanks with ye. letters which I return.—You know I am a jacobin & could not wear white nor see the installation of Louis the gouty.—This is sad news—& very hard upon the sufferers at any but more at *such* a time—I mean the Bayonne Sortie.[1]———You should *urge* Moore to come *out.*——

ever yrs.

B

P.S.—Perry hath a piece of compliment today[2]—but I think the *name* might have been as well omitted—no matter they can but throw the old story of inconsistency in my teeth—let them—I mean as to *not* publishing—however *now* I will keep my word—nothing but the occasion which was *physically* irresistible made me swerve—and I thought an *anonyme* within my *pact* with ye public—it is the only thing I have or shall set about.——

P.S.—I want *Moreri*[3] to purchase for good & all—I have a Bayle[4] but I want M. too.

[TO JOHN MURRAY]   *April 22d. 1814*

I think you told me that you wanted some smaller poems for the small Edition you intended some time or other to print—For this purpose I transmit you ye. enclosed and if I can find—or create any more you shall have them.

yrs. ever

B

[1] On April 14, 1814, after the fall of Toulouse, the French in a sortie from Bayonne, engaged the English and their allies, and about a thousand men on both sides were lost before news of the peace reached them.

[2] The *Morning Chronicle* for April 21, 1814, reported: "Lord Byron has written a very beautiful *Ode to Napoleon Buonaparte.* The noble poet speaks with becoming indignation of the manner in which the tyrant has borne himself in his fall."

[3] Louis Moreri's *Grand Dictionnaire Historique,* first published in 1674. Byron acquired the edition of 1759 published in Paris in ten volumes.

[4] Byron's copy of Pierre Bayle's *Dictionnaire Historique et Critique* was the edition of 1734.

Dear Sir/—I send you a poem as sent to me in M.S. for criticism with the Author's letter—& will feel obliged if you will send it back to the man tomorrow (see his address in ye. letter) with any or no answer.——The title & subject would be thought original—but in Rochester's poems mention is made of a *play* with the like delicate appellation.—Who the man is I know not—by his letter he seems silly—& by his poem—insane.—

ever yrs.

B

[TO LADY MELBOURNE]   *April 24th. 1814*

My dear Lady M[elbourn]e.—I wish to know whether *I* may go to Ly. Hard[wick]e's¹ on Thursday or not—because you may be sure I will do what *you* like on that point—as on *all* others—saving one—though methinks I am vastly obedient there too. +—What became of you last night? I don't know but I got into a roundabout conversation with Miss M—& was obliged to call carriages a service in which I got wet through & consequently took refuge in my own & came away. ——Today I am going with your Chevalier of Troy² to the Prin[ce]ss of W[ale]s to dine & dawdle away the Evening.—I suppose at least that C[aroline] is quiet—and I really think you pay me too great a Compliment—& her none—to imagine any doubts of our mutual decorum & discretion & all that—

ever yrs. most inveterately

B

[TO JOHN MURRAY]   *April 25th* [1814]

Dear Sir/—Let Mr. G[ifford] have ye. letter & return it at his leisure—I would have offered it had I thought that he liked things of the kind.—Do you want the last page filled up *immediately?*—I have doubts about the lines being worth printing—at any rate I must see them again & alter some passages before they go forth in any shape into the *Ocean* of circulation—a very conceited phrase by the bye—

¹ Elizabeth, third daughter of James Lindsay, 5th Earl of Balcarres and sister of Lady Anne Barnard, the authoress of *Auld Robin Gray*, married Philip Yorke, 3rd Earl of Hardwicke.
² Sir William Gell.

well then—*channel* of publication will do.———"I am not i' the vein"[1] or I could knock off a stanza or 3 for the Ode that might answer the purpose better[2]—at all events—I *must* see the lines again *first*—as there be two I have altered in my mind's manuscript already—has any one seen & judged of them? that is the criticism by which I will abide— only give me a *fair* report—& "nothing extenuate"[3] as I will in that case do something else.—

ever yrs.
B

I want *Moreri*—& an *Athenaeus*[4]

[TO LADY MELBOURNE]   *A[pri]l 25th. 1814*

My dear Ly. M[elbourn]e.—Thanks as to C[aroline]—though the task will be difficult—if she is to determine as to kindness & unkindness—the best way will be to avoid each other *without appearing* to do so—or if we jostle—at any rate *not to bite.*———Oh! but it is "worth while"—I can't tell you why—and it is *not* an *"Ape"* and if it is—that must be my fault[1]—however I will positively reform—you must however allow—that it is utterly impossible I can ever be half as well liked elsewhere—and I have been all my life trying to make some one love me—& never got the sort that I preferred before.—But positively she & I will grow good—& all that—& so we are *now* and shall be these three weeks & more too.———Yesterday I dined at the Princess's—where I deported myself like a White stick till as the Devil would have it—a man with a flute played a solemn & somewhat tedious piece of Music—well—I got through that—but down sate Lady Anne H.[2] to give evidence at the Pianoforte with a Miss Somebody (the "privy purse") in a pair of spectacles—dark green— and these & the fluteman—& the "damnable faces" (as Hamlet says)

---

[1] *King Richard III*, Act IV, scene 2.

[2] Murray had asked Byron for some more stanzas for his Ode, to make it more than a single sheet and thus avoid the stamp duty. In subsequent printings he added stanzas, increasing the original eleven to nineteen. The last stanza paid tribute to Washington, "the first—the last—the best—/The Cincinnatus of the West."

[3] *Othello*, Act V, scene 2.

[4] In the sale catalogue of Byron's books, April 5, 1816 is this: "Athenaeus: G. et Lat., Casauboni, Lugd., 1657".

[1] This passage has been offered as evidence that Medora Leigh was Byron's incestuous daughter, but see a rational discussion of this in Doris Langley Moore's *The Late Lord Byron*, pp. 301–302.

[2] Lady Anne Hamilton.

of the whole party threw me into a convulsion of uncourtly laughter—
which Gell & Lady Crewe[3] encouraged—at least the *last* joined in it so
heartily—that the hooping-cough would have been an Æolian harp in
comparison to us both—at last I half strangled it & myself with my
handkerchief—and here I am grave & sedate again.——You will be
sorry to hear that I have got a physician—just in time for an old
complaint—"troublesome but not dangerous" like Lord *Stair* & Ld.
Stair's [?][4] of which I am promised an eventual removal.—It is very
odd—he is a staid grave man—and puts so many questions to me
about *my mind* and the state of it—that I begin to think he half suspects my senses—he asked me—how I felt "when anything weighed
upon my mind—" and I answered him by a question why he should
suppose that anything did?——I was laughing & sitting quietly in my
chair the whole time of his visit—& yet he thinks me horribly rest-
less—and irritable—and talks about my having lived *excessively* "out
of all compass" some time or other—which has no more to do with the
malady he has to deal with—than I have with the Wisdom of Solomon.
———Tomorrow—I go to the Berry's on Wednesday to the
Jerseys—on Thursday I dine at Ld. Grey's and there is Ly. Hard
[wick]e's in the Evening—& on Friday I am asked to a Lady Charleville's[5] whom I don't know—& where I shan't go—we shall meet I
hope at one or two of these places.——I don't often bore you with
rhyme—but as a wrapper to this note—I send you some upon a
brunette[6]—which I have shewn to no one else—if you think them not
much beneath the common places—you may give them to any of your
"Album" acquaintances.—

ever yrs. most truly.—
B

[TO SIR W. GELL?[1]]   *A[pri]l 26th.* [*1814*]

My dear Sir/—Many thanks for ye. epistles which I will duly

---

[3] Frances Anne, Lady Crewe (died 1818), daughter of Fulke Greville, and
wife of the 1st Baron Crewe, was a fashionable beauty and friend of Fox, Burke, and
Sheridan.
[4] For Lord Stair see Aug. 5, 1813, to Lady Melbourne, note 2 (Vol. 3, p. 85)
[5] Lady Charleville was the wife of the 2nd Earl of Charleville. She was educated
in a convent and was the widow of James Tindall when she married the Earl, then
1st Baron Tullamore of Charleville Forest, in 1798.
[6] It is not known what these verses were, unless they were those entitled
"Magdalen", of which there is a facsimile in *Astarte* (privately printed, 1905).
These are dated April 18, 1814.
[1] See April 15, 1814, to Lady Sitwell, note 3.

restore this evening.—At ten I will call at your Hostel with great pleasure—The Parrot (I grieve to speak it) is in excellent noise & very troublesome spirits.—

> very truly yr. obliged Sert.
> BIRON

[TO CHARLES HANSON]   *April 26th* [*1814*]

Dear Charles/—How is your father?—& have you any news of C[laughton]? I need not say how very important it is that he should be brought to *immediate* peace or war—payment—or law—as it is—it is sad shuffling—& utter ruin by delays.—

> ever yrs.
> B

[TO JOHN MURRAY (*a*)]   *April 26th. 1814*

Dear Sir/—I have been thinking that it might be as well to publish no more of the Ode separately—but incorporate it with any of the other things—and include the smaller poems too (in that case)— which I must previously correct nevertheless.—I can't for the head of me add a line worth scribbling—my "vein" is quite gone—and my present occupations are of the gymnastic order—boxing and fencing— & my principal conversation is with my Maccaw & Bayle—I want my Moreri—& I want Athenæus.[1]————

> yrs. always
> B

P.S.—I hope you sent back that poetical packet to the address which I forwarded to you on Sunday—if not—pray do—or I shall have the author screaming after his Epic.————

[TO JOHN MURRAY (*b*)]   *April 26th 1814*

Dr. Sir/—I have no guess at your Author but it is a noble poem[1]— & worth a thousand odes of anybody's.——I suppose I may keep this copy—after reading it I really regret having written my own—I say

---

[1] See April 21, 1814, to Murray, notes 3 and 4: April 25, 1814, to Murray, note 4.

[1] The poem entitled *Bonaparte* was written, as Byron later discovered, by Stratford Canning.

this very sincerely albeit unused to think humbly of self.—I don't like the additional stanzas *at all*—and they had better be left out—the fact [is] I can't do anything I am asked to do—however gladly I *would*— and at the end of a week—my interest in a composition goes off— this will account to you for my doing no better for your "stamp duty" Postscript.[2]——The S. R. is very civil[3]—but what do they mean by C[hil]d[e] H[arol]d resembling Marmion?—& the next *two* G[aiou]r & B[rid]e *not* resembling Scott?—I certainly never *intended* to copy him—but if there is any copyism—it must be in the 2 poems—where the same versification is adopted—however they exempt the Corsair from all resemblance to any thing—though I rather wonder at his escape.———If ever I did anything original it was in C[hil]d[e] H[arol]d—which *I* prefer to the other things always after the 1st. week—yesterday I *reread* E[nglish] B[ar]ds—(bating the *malice*) it is the *best*.—

ever yrs.

B

[TO LADY CHARLEVILLE]   *Friday Morning [April 29, 1814][1]*

Ld. Byron presents his Compliments to Lady Charleville & regrets very much that by a mistake on the part of *his* servants he did not receive the honour of Ly. C's invitation till this morning—when he is truly sorry that it is not in his power to accept it without breaking another though less agreeable engagement.—

[TO JOHN MURRAY]   *2 Albany—April 29th. 1814*

Dear Sir/—I enclose a draft for the money—when paid send the copyrights—I release you from the thousand pounds agreed on for the Giaour & Bride—and there's an end.——If any accident occurs to me—you may do then as you please—but with the exception of two copies of each for *yourself* only—I expect and request—that the advertisements be withdrawn—and the remaining copies of *all* destroyed—and any expence so incurred I will be glad to defray.——

---

2 See April 25, 1814, to Murray, note 2.

3 The "S. R.' 'is a reference to the *Scottish Review*, the name of a section of the *Scot's Magazine*. It reviewed *The Bride of Abydes* in the number of January, 1814 (Vol. LXXVI, pp. 48–51).

1 See April 25, 1814, to Lady Melbourne, note 5. The date of this letter is established by Byron's remarks in his letter to Lady Melbourne.

For all this it might be as well to assign some reason—I have none to give except my own caprice, and I do not consider the circumstances of consequence enough to require explanation.[1]——In course I need hardly assure you that they never shall be published with my consent—directly or indirectly by any other person whatsoever, and that I am perfectly satisfied & have every reason so to be with your conduct in all transactions between us as publisher & author.———It will give me great pleasure to preserve your acquaintance—and to consider you as my friend—Believe me very truly and for much attention

yr. obliged & very obedt. St.
BYRON

P.S.—I do not think that I have overdrawn at Hammersley's—but if *that* be the case I can draw for the superflux on Hoare's—the draft is 5 £ short—but that I will make up—on payment—*not* before—return [of?] the copyright papers.—

[TO CHARLES HANSON]   *April 29th. 1814*

Dear Charles/—They are charging & surcharging for the taxes (assessed) at Newstead of last year—which *were paid* to Mr. Reeves of St. James's in London—whose certificate has been sent to Mansfield—& I have also written—to no purpose.—Let the proper *legal* steps be taken immediately to resist *this*—& pray do not lose a moment in writing to Mealey with instructions how to proceed—I shall certainly not submit to it.—

ever yrs.
BYRON

P.S.—Pray write tonight.—

[TO LADY MELBOURNE]   *April 29th. 1814*

I delivered "Mamma's message" with anatomical precision—the *knee* was the refractory limb—was it not? injured I presume at prayers —for I cannot conjecture by what other possible attitude a female knee could become so perverse.—Having given an account of my embassy— I enclose you a note which will only repeat what you already know—— but to obviate a possible *Pharisaical* charge—I must observe that the

---

1 Byron rescinded this order a few days later but he never gave an explanation of his sudden whim to cease publication of his poems.

first part of her epistle[1] alludes to an answer of mine—in which talking about that eternal Liturgy—I said that I had no great opinion one way or the other—assuredly no decided unbelief—and that the *clamour* had wrung from me many of the objectionable passages—in the pure quintessence of the spirit of contradiction &c &c.—She talks of "talking" on these same metaphysics—to shorten the conversation I shall propose the Litany—"from the crafts & *assau*—" ay—that will do very well—what comes next—"Deliver us"—an't it?—Seriously—if she imagines that I particularly delight in canvassing the creed of St. Athanasius—or prattling of rhyme—I think she will be mistaken—but *you know* best—I don't suspect myself of often talking about poets or clergymen—of rhyme or the rubrick—but very likely I am wrong—for assuredly no one knows *it*self—and for aught I know—I may for these last 2 years have inflicted upon you a world of theology—and the greater part of Walker's rhyming dictionary.————I don't know what to say or do about going—sometimes I wish it—at other times I think it foolish—as assuredly my design will be imputed to a motive—which by the bye—if once fairly there is very likely to come into my head—and *failing* to put me into no very good humour with myself—I am not now in love with her—but I can't at all foresee that I should not be so if it came "a warm June" (as Falstaff observes) and seriously—I do admire her as a very superior woman a little encumbered with Virtue—though perhaps your opinion & mine from the laughing turn of "our philosophy" may be less exalted upon her merits than that of the more zealous—though in fact less benevolent advocates of charity schools & Lying in Hospitals.——By the close of her note you will perceive that she has been "frowning" occasionally and has written some pretty lines upon it to a friend (he or she is not said) as for rhyme I am naturally no fair judge & can like it no better than a Grocer does figs.[2]————I am quite irresolute—and undecided—if I were sure of *myself* (not of her) I would go—but I am not—& never can be—and what is still worse I have no judgement—& less common sense than an infant—this is *not affected humility*—with *you* I have no affectation—with the world I have a part to play—to be diffident there is to wear a drag-chain—and luckily I do so thoroughly despise half the people in it—that my insolence is almost natural.—I enclose you also a letter written some time ago and of which I do not remember the precise contents—most likely they contradict every

[1] Annabella Milbanke's letter.
[2] Fielding says of Parson Barnabas (*Joseph Andrews*, Book I, chapter 17) that he "loved sermons no better than a grocer doth figs."

syllable of this—no matter.—Don't plague yourself to write—we shall meet at Mrs. Hope's[3] I trust—

ever yrs.

B

My dear Lady M[elbourn]e.—*You*—or rather *I* have done *my A*—[Augusta] much injustice—the expression which you recollect as objectionable meant only "loving" in the *senseless* sense of that wide word—and—it must be some selfish stupidity of mine in telling my own story—but really & truly—as I hope mercy & happiness for her—by that God who made me for my own misery—& not much for the good of others—*she* was not to blame—one thousandth part in comparison—she was not aware of her own peril—till it was too late—and I can only account for her subsequent "*abandon*" by an observation which I think is not unjust—that women are much more *attached* than men—if they are treated with any thing like fairness or tenderness. ————————As for *your* A—[Annabella] I don't know what to make of her—I enclose her last but one——and *my* A's last but one—from which you may form your own conclusions on *both*—I think you must allow *mine*—to be a very extraordinary person in point of *talent*—but I won't say more—only do not allow your good nature to lean to my side of *this* question—on all others I shall be glad to avail myself of your partiality.—Now for *common* life.—There *is* a party at Lady J[ersey]'s on Monday and on Wednesday—I am asked to both—and excused myself out of Tuesday's dinner because I want to see Kean in Richard again—pray *why* did you say—I am getting into a *scrape* with R's moiety?[1]—one must talk to somebody—I always give you the preference when you are disposed to listen—and when you seem fidgetted as you do now & then—(and no wonder—for latterly I do but repeat—) I turn to anyone and she was the first that I stumbled upon—as for anything more—I have not even advanced to the tip of her little finger—and never shall—unless she gives it.—You won't believe me—& won't care if you do—but I really believe that I have more true regard and affection for yourself than for any other existence—as for my A— my feelings towards her—are a mixture of good

---

[3] The wife of Thomas Hope, the author of *Anastasia* (1819), and collector and patron of sculpture. Mrs. Hope was a well known hostess in Whig society during the Regency.
[1] Lady Rancliffe?

& diabolical—I hardly know one passion which has not some share in them—but I won't run into the subject.—Your Niece has committed herself perhaps—but it can be of no consequence—if I pursued & succeeded in that quarter—of course I must give up all other pursuits— and the fact is that my wife if she had common sense would have more power over me—than any other whatsoever—for my heart always alights upon the nearest *perch*—if it is withdrawn—it goes God knows where—but one must like something.—

ever yrs.

B

[TO LADY MELBOURNE]   *April—May 1st. 1814*

My dear Lady M[elbourn]e.—She says "*if* la tante" neither did she imagine nor I assert that you did have an opinion of what Philosopher Square calls "the fitness of things."[1]—You are very kind in allowing *us* the few merits we can claim—*she* surely is very clever—and not only so—but in some things of good judgement—her expressions about A[nnabell]a are exactly your *own*—and these most certainly without being aware of the coincidence—and excepting our one *tremendous* fault—I know her to be in point of temper—& goodness of heart almost unequalled——now grant me this—that she is in truth a very *loveable* woman—and I will try and *not* love any longer—if you don't believe me—ask those who know her *better*—I say *better*—for a man in love is blind as that Deity.——You yourself soften a little in the P. S. and say the letters "make you melancholy—" it is indeed a very triste and extraordinary business—& what is to become of us I know not—and I wont think just now.—Did you observe that she says "*if* la tante approved she should" she is little aware how much "la tante" has to *dis*approve—but you perceive that without intending it she pays me a compliment by supposing you to be my friend and a sincere one—where *approval* could alter even *her* opinions.——— Tomorrow I am asked to Ly. Jersey's in the evening—and on Wednesday again—tuesday—I go to Kean & dine after the play with Ld. Rancliffe—and on Friday there is Mrs. Hope's[2] we shall clash at some of them.—*What* on *earth* can plague you?—I won't ask—but am very very sorry for it—it is very hard that one who feels so much for others—should suffer pain herself—God bless you—Good night—

ever yrs. most truly

B

---

[1] Fielding, *Tom Jones*, Book III, Chapter 3.
[2] See April 29, 1814, to Lady Melbourne, note 3.

P.S.—A thousand loves and excuses to Mrs. Damer[3] with whom— I weep—*not* to dine.

P.S. 2d.—It indeed puzzles me to account for————[Augusta's marriage?] it is true she married a fool—but she *would* have him— they agreed—& agree very well—& I never heard a complaint but many vindications of him—as for me brought up as I was & sent into the world as I was both physically & morally—nothing better could be expected—and it is odd that I always had a foreboding—and remember when quite a child reading the Roman History—about a *marriage* I will tell you of when we me[et]—asking ma mere—why I should not marry +

Since writing this—I have received yr. enclosed—I will not trouble you with another—but *this* will I think enable you to appreciate *her* better.—she seems very triste—and I need hardly add that the reflection does not enliven me.————

[TO JOHN MURRAY]　　　　　　　　　　　　　　　*May 1st. 1814*

Dear ⟨Murray⟩ Sir/—If your present note is serious—and it really would be inconvenient—there is an end of the matter—tear my draft— & go on as usual[1]—in that case we will recur to our former basis.— That *I* was perfectly *serious* in wishing to suppress all future publication is true—but certainly not to interfere with the convenience of others—& more particularly your own.—Some day I will tell you the reason of this apparently strange resolution—at present it may be enough to say that I recall it at your suggestion—and as it appears to have annoyed you I lose no time in saying so

yrs. truly

B

[TO MISS MERCER ELPHINSTONE]　　　　　*2 Albany May 3d. 1814*

I send you the Arnaout garments[1]—which will make an admirable

---

[3] Anne, only daughter of Lady Ailesbury, married in 1767 Joseph Damer. She was a widow after 1776. She obtained a high reputation as a sculptress. Among those of whom she left portraits were Fox, George IV, Mrs. Siddons, the Princess of Wales and Miss Berry, who was a close friend and mentions her frequently in her Diary.

[1] See April 29, 1814, to Murray.

[1] This was the Albanian costume which Byron had bought in Jannina, and which he wore for a portrait by Thomas Phillips. It is now in the Museum of Costume in Bath.

costume for a Dutch Dragoon.—The Camesa or *Kilt* (to speak Scottishly) you will find very long—it is the custom with the Beys and a sign of rank to wear it to the ancle—I know not why—but so it is— the million shorten it to the knee which is more antique—and becoming—at least to those who have legs and a propensity to show them.— I have sent but one camesa—the other I will dispatch when it has undergone the Mussulman process of ablution.———There are greaves for the legs—2 waistcoats are beneath—one *over* the Jacket—the cloak—a sash—a short shawl and cap—and a pair of garters (something of the Highland order—) with an ataghan wherewithal to cut your fingers if you don't take care—over the sash—there is a small leathern girdle with a buckle in the centre.———It is put off & on in a few minutes—if you like the dress—keep it—I shall be very glad to get rid of it—as it reminds me of one or two things I don't wish to remember.———To make it more acceptable—I have worn this very little—& never in England except for half an hour to Phillips—I had more of the same description but parted with them when my Arnaouts went back to Tepalen and I returned to England, it will do for a masquerade. One word about *"caprice"* I know you were merely in jest—and that my *caprices*—supposing such to exist—must be a subject of laughter or indifference—but I am not unconscious of something not unlike them in the course of our acquaintance.—Yet you must recollect that from your situation you can never be *sure* you have a friend—(as somebody has said of Sovereigns I believe) and that any apparent anxiety on my part to cultivate your acquaintance might have appeared to yourself like importunity—and—as I happen to know— would have been attributed by others to a motive *not* very creditable to me—and agreeable to neither.—This is quite enough—& more than I have a right to trouble you with on this or any other subject.—

ever yrs. very sincerely
B

[TO THOMAS MOORE (*a*)]   *May 4th, 1814*

"Last night we supped at R[anclif]fe's board, &c."[1]

* * * * * * * * *[2]

I wish people would not shirk their *dinners*—ought it not to have been a dinner?—and that d————d anchovy sandwich!

[1] George Augustus Henry Anne Parkyns, 2nd Baron Rancliffe, M.P. for Nottingham, married in 1807 Lady Elizabeth Forbes, daughter of the 6th Earl of Granard.

[2] Moore's note on the asterisks: "An epigram here followed, which, as founded on a scriptural allusion, I thought it better to omit."

That plaguy voice of yours made me sentimental, and almost fall in love with a girl who was recommending herself, during your song, by *hating* music. But the song is past, and my passion can wait, till the *pucelle* is more harmonious.

Do you go to Lady Jersey's to-night? It is a large party, and you won't be bored into "softening rocks,"[3] and all that. Othello is to-morrow and Saturday too. Which day shall we go? when shall I see you? If you call, let it be after three and as near four as you please. Ever, &c.

[TO THOMAS MOORE (*b*)]   *May 4th, 1814*

Dear Tom,—Thou hast asked me for a song, and I enclose you an experiment, which has cost me something more than trouble,[1] and is, therefore, less likely to be worth your taking any in your proposed setting. Now, if it be so, throw it into the fire without *phrase*.

Ever yours,
BYRON

[TO THOMAS MOORE]   *May 5th, 1814*

Do you go the the Lady Cahir's[1] this even? If you do—and when-ever we are bound to the same follies—let us embark in the same "Shippe of Fooles." I have been up till five, and up at nine; and feel heavy with only winking for the last three or four nights.

I lost my party and place at supper trying to keep out of the way of * * * *. I would have gone away altogether, but that would have appeared a worse affectation than t'other. You are of course engaged to dinner, or we may go quietly together to my box at Covent-garden, and afterwards to this assemblage. Why did you go away so soon?

Ever, &c.

P.S.—*Ought not* R * * * fe's [Rancliffe's] supper to have been a dinner? Jackson is here, and I must fatigue myself into spirits.

---

[3] *Two Gentlemen of Verona*, Act III, scene 2: "For Orpheus' lute was strung with poet's sinews,/Whose golden touch could soften steel and stones." Moore was often asked to sing his Irish melodies at social gatherings.
  [1] This was the poem, evidently addressed to Augusta, beginning: "I speak not, I trace not, I breathe not thy name".
  [1] Emily, daughter of James St. John Jeffries, of Blarney Castle, married in 1793 Richard Butler, Baron Caher of Ireland.

Will you and Rogers come to my box at Covent, then? I shall be there, and none else—or I won't be there, if you *twain* would like to go without me. You will not get so good a place hustling among the publican *boxers*, with damnable apprentices (six feet high) on a back row. Will you both oblige me and come,—or one—or neither—or, what you will?

P.S.—An you will, I will call for you at half-past six, or any time of your own dial.

[TO THOMAS MOORE]   *Sunday matin* [*May 8?, 1814*]

Was not Iago perfection?[1] particularly the last look. I was *close* to him (in the orchestra), and never saw an English countenance half so expressive. I am acquainted with no *im*material sensuality so delightful as good acting; and, as it is fitting there should be good plays, now and then, besides Shakespeare's, I wish you or Campbell would write one:—the rest of "us youth" have not heart enough.

You were cut up in the Champion—is it not so? this day, so am I[2]— even to *shocking* the editor. The critic writes well; and as, at present, poesy is not my passion predominant, and my snake of Aaron has swallowed up all other serpents, I don't feel fractious. I send you the paper, which I mean to take in for the future. We go to M's together. Perhaps I shall see you before, but don't let me *bore* you, now nor ever.

Ever, as now, truly and affectionately, &c.

[TO AUGUSTA LEIGH]   *May 9th. 1814*

Dearest A—I enclose you Hammersley's answer—I have money at Hoare's & more coming in soon—so don't mind me—you can't be off

---

1 Kean acted Iago in *Othello* at Drury Lane, May 7, 14, and 21, 1814. Michael Kelly wrote in his *Reminiscences* (Vol. II, p. 317): "The first night he acted it at Drury Lane, I sat in my seat in the orchestra, which was appropriated to me, as Director of the Music, and next to me was Lord Byron, who said, 'Mr. Kelly, depend upon it, this is a man of genius.'"

2 The *Champion* published a series of literary portraits. That on Moore appeared Feb. 27, 1814, and that on Byron on May 7, a blistering diatribe against "the selfish misanthrope", etc.

of this sum now[1]—& I heartily hope it may be useful—and adequate to ye. occasion.—Now—don't "affront" me by any more scruples—

ever yrs.

B

[TO LADY MELBOURNE] *May 16th. 1814*

My dear Ly. M[elbourn]e.—Your letter is not without effect— when I tell you that I have *not written* to-day—& shall weigh my words when I write to——[Augusta] to-morrow.—I *do* thank you— and as somebody says—I hope *not* Iago—"I think you know I love you well."[1]—As for C[aroline] we both know her for a foolish wicked woman—I am sorry to hear that she is still fermenting her weak head and cold heart to an *ice-cream* which will only sicken every one about her—as I heard a girl say the other night at Othello—when I asked her how she liked it—"I shall like it much better when that woman (a bad actress in Desdemona) is fairly smothered" so—if C[aroline] were fairly shut up—& bread & watered into common sense & some regard to truth—no one would be the worse & she herself much better for the process.—By the bye—(*entre nous* remember) she has sent for Moore—on some mysterious concern—which he will tell me probably —at least if it regards the old—eternal—& never sufficiently to be bored with—story.—I dine at Ld. Jersey's tomorrow—that is I am asked—and (to please you) I am trying to fall *in* love—which I sup- pose will end in falling *out* with somebody—for I am perplexed about 2—& would rather have both—I don't see any use in one without a chance at least of the other.—But all this is nonsense—I won't say a word more about your grievance—though I cannot at all conceive what there can be more *now* than ever to plague you anywhere— particularly as C[aroline] has nothing to do with it.———Horace Twiss has sent me melodies—which I perceive are inscribed to you— don't you think yourself lucky to have escaped one of *my* dedications?— I am going to dine at Wm. Spencer's[2] today—I believe I told you the *Claret* story at Mrs. Hope's—last ball but one.—

ever yrs. most affectly.

B

---

[1] Byron sent Augusta £3,000 to help clear her husband's debts. It was ostensibly a loan but really a gift. The gift was made possible by his receiving some additional money as part of Claughton's down payment for Newstead.

[1] Iago said to Cassio: "I think you think I love you." *Othello*, Act II, scene 3.

[2] William Robert Spencer, son of Lord Charles Spencer, was a wit and poet, a friend of Sheridan and others.

P.S.—I am just elected into Watier's[3]—shall I resume *play?* that will be a change—& for the better.—

May 18th, 1814

Thanks—and punctuality. *What* has passed at ＊ ＊ ＊ ＊ House? I suppose that *I* am to know, and "pars fui" of the conference. I regret that your ＊ ＊ ＊ ＊s will detain you so late, but I suppose you will be at Lady Jersey's. I am going earlier with Hobhouse. You recollect that to-morrow we sup and see Kean.

P.S.—*Two* to-morrow is the hour of pugilism.

[TO THOMAS MOORE]   *May 23d, 1814*

I must send you the Java government gazette of July 3d, 1813,[1] just sent to me by Murray. Only think of *our* (for it is you and I) setting paper warriors in array in the Indian seas. Does not this sound like fame—something almost like *posterity?* It is something to have scribblers squabbling about us 5000 miles off, while we are agreeing so well at home. Bring it with you in your pocket;—it will make you laugh, as it hath me.

Ever yours,
B

P.S.—Oh the anecdote! ＊ ＊ ＊ ＊ ＊ ＊ ＊ ＊ ＊ ＊ ＊ ＊ ＊ ＊

[TO JOHN MURRAY]   *May 24—1814*

Dear Sir—The note at 2 months paid to my account at Mess[rs]. Hoare's (Fleet Street) will do very well.—I do not think less highly of "Bonaparte" for knowing this author[1]—I was aware that he was a man of talent—but did not suspect him of possessing *all* the *family* talents in such perfection.

ever yrs.
B

---

[3] Watier's was a famous gambling Club, patronized by Brummell and other Dandies.
[1] Byron recalled this incident in his Ravenna Diary (Jan. 15, 1821) and again in his "Detached Thoughts" (No. 52) as an evidence of fame. He said he and Moore discussed it on their way to dine with Earl Grey.
[1] The author of the poem "Bonaparte" was Stratford Canning. See April 26, 1814, to Murray (*b*), note 1; and Sept. 2, 1814, to Murray.

I have gotten a box for Othello to-night, and send the ticket for your friends the R[anclif]fes. I seriously recommend to you to recommend to them to go for half an hour, if only to see the third act—they will not easily have another opportunity. We—at least, I—cannot be there, so there will be no one in their way. Will you give or send it to them? it will come with a better grace from you than me.

I am in no good plight, but will dine at * *'s with you if I can. There is music and Covent-g—Will you go, at all events, to my box there afterwards, to see a *début* of a young 16 in the "Child of Nature?"[1]

[TO JOHN HANSON]   *May 27th. 1814*

My dear Sir/—I have received the enclosed letter from Mr. Randall[1] to which I add *my* answer—if not *actionable* send it—*his* letter is without exception the most insolent I ever heard of.—It will give me great pleasure to see you in better spirits—I have been *silent*— for words are useless—& time and business are the only comforters[2]— but I have not been insensible & ever am

very truly yrs.
BYRON

[TO WILLIAM SOTHEBY[1]]   *May 27th. 1814*

My dear Sir/—I have received ye "Song of Triumph"[2] and if my praise were worth having it would be yours—it is a very noble poem.————It is with much regret that I plead a prior engagement— but I did not receive the card or rather *per*ceive it (owing to the

---

[1] Maria Foote, after acting at Plymouth, made her first appearance in London on May 26, 1814, at Covent Garden as Amanthis in Mrs. Inchbald's *Child of Nature*. She was pretty but was not much of a success as an actress. She later (1831) retired from the stage and married Charles Stanhope, 4th Earl of Harrington.

[1] Perhaps one of Byron's creditors.

[2] Hanson's wife had died in March.

[1] William Sotheby gained fame first as a translator, of Wieland's *Oberon* (1798), and then of Virgil's *Georgics*. His original poetry and dramatic efforts were less successful. Byron was friendly with him in England, and recommended his *Ivan* for Drury Lane. But after he went abroad, Byron took offence at an imagined underhand criticism by Sotheby and ridiculed him as "bustling Botherby" (*Beppo*, stanza 72).

[2] Sotheby's "Song of Triumph on the Peace" was published in 1814.

negligence of a servant of my own) till yesterday & in the meantime I had accepted an invitation from Mr. Nugent[3] for the very day,—or rather renewed one—for the engagement was of long standing but the day unfixed till last week.—Pray make my best respects acceptable to Mrs. Sotheby & believe me ever & very truly yrs.

Byron

[TO LADY MELBOURNE] *May 28th. 1814*

Dear Lady M[elbourn]e.—I have just received a wrathful epistle from C[aroline] demanding letters—pictures—and all kinds of gifts which I never requested & am ready to resign as soon as they can be gathered together—at the same signal it might be as well for her to restore *my* letters—as every body has read them by this time—and they can no longer be of use to herself and her five hundred sympathizing friends.—She also complains of some barbarous usage—of which I know nothing except that I was told of an *inroad* which occurred when I was fortunately out—and am not at all disposed to regret the circumstance of my absence either for her sake or my own.— I am also menaced in her letter with immediate *marriage*—of which I am equally unconscious—at least *I* have not proposed to anybody— and if anyone has to me—I have quite forgotten it—if she alludes to Ly. A[delaide] F[orbes][1] she has made a sad mistake—for not a syllable of love ever passed between us—but a good deal of heraldry & mutual hatred of Music[2]—the merits of Mr. Kean—and the excellence of white soup and plovers eggs for a light supper—besides—Lady R[ancliffe] who is good authority—says that I do not care about Ly. A—nor Lady A. about me—and that if such an impossibility did occur—she could not possibly approve of it—nor anyone else—in all which I quite acquiesce with ye. said Lady R. with whom however I never had a moment's conversation on the subject—but hear this from a friend—who is in very bad humour with her—& not much better with me—why—I can't divine—being as innocent & ill used as C[aroline] herself in her very best story.—If you can *pare* her down to good humour—do—I am really at this moment—thinking as little of

---

[3] Byron mentions Nugent as a friend of Henry Luttrell, the Irish wit and society poet. See Sept. 11, 1822, to Murray.

[1] Lady Adelaide Forbes was the daughter of the 6th Earl of Granard, and hence a sister of Lady Rancliffe. Her mother was Lady Selina Rawdon, daughter of the 1st Earl of Moira.

[2] See May 4, 1814, to Moore.

the person with whom She commits me to Matrimony—as of herself
—and I mean to leave London next week if I can—in the meantime I
hope we shall meet at Lady Grey's or Clare's this evening—

ever yrs most affectly.

B

[TO THE COUNTESS OF JERSEY[1]]   *May 29th. 1814*

Dear Lady Jersey/—Don't be very angry with me—I send you
something of which—if ill done—the shame can only be mine.—No
one has seen them, and they were begun & finished since ten o clock
tonight[2]—so that whether good or bad they were done in good
earnest—do with them what you please—whether they amuse your
friends or light your fire I shall be quite content, so they don't offend
you.

ever yrs.

BYRON

[TO THOMAS MOORE]   *May 31st, 1814*

As I shall probably not see you here to-day, I write to request that,
if not convenient to yourself, you will stay in town till *Sunday*; if not
to gratify me, yet to please a great many others, who will be very
sorry to lose you. As for myself, I can only repeat that I wish you
would either remain a long time with us, or not come at all; for these
snatches of society make the subsequent separations bitterer than ever.

I believe you think that I have not been quite fair with that Alpha
and Omega of beauty, &c. with whom you would willingly have united
me.[1] But if you consider what her sister[2] said on the subject, you will

[1] Lady Sarah Sophia Fane, daughter of the 10th Earl of Westmorland, married,
1804, George Villiers, who succeeded his father as the 5th Earl of Jersey in
1805. Lady Jersey was a favourite of the Prince Regent until he quarrelled with
her. She was a reigning beauty and held a commanding position in Whig society.
[2] The verses were entitled "Condolatory Address to Sarah Countess of Jersey,
on the Prince Regent's Returning Her Picture to Mrs. Mee," when they were
printed. Mrs. Mee was a miniaturist who had painted a gallery of beauties for the
Prince Regent. Byron was later embarrassed by the verses, which contained lines of
impudent lèse majesté, being printed without his knowledge or leave in the
Champion on July 31, 1814. See Aug. 3, 1814, to Moore.
[1] Moore had tried to promote a match between Byron and Lady Adelaide
Forbes.
[2] Lady Rancliffe.

less wonder that my pride should have taken the alarm; particularly as nothing but the every-day flirtation of every-day people ever occurred between your heroine and myself. Had Lady * * [Rancliffe] appeared to wish it—or even *not* to oppose it—I would have gone on, and very possibly married (that is, *if* the other had been equally accordant) with the same indifference which has frozen over the "Black Sea" of almost all my passions. It is that very indifference which makes me so uncertain and apparently capricious. It is not eagerness of new pursuits, but that nothing impresses me sufficiently to *fix*; neither do I feel disgusted, but simply indifferent to almost all excitements. The proof of this is, that obstacles, the slightest even, *stop* me. This can hardly be *timidity*, for I have done some impudent [imprudent?] things too, in my time; and in almost all cases, opposition is a stimulus. In mine, it is not; if a straw were in my way, I could not stoop to pick it up.

I have sent this long tirade, because I would not have you suppose that I have been *trifling* designedly with you or others. If you think so, in the name of St. Hubert (the patron of antlers and hunters) let me be married out of hand—I don't care to whom, so that it amuses anybody else, and don't interfere with me much in the daytime.

Ever &c.

[TO JOHN HANSON]   *June 6th. 1814*

Dear Sir/—I have been unable to call as I proposed—& was in the meantime in hopes of some further intelligence from Mr. Claughton.— Enclosed is a letter from Joseph Murray—from which you will perceive that Mr. C[laughton] has been at Newstead.—My affairs appear in every manner worse than ever—I wish to know what I could get for Rochdale—I am willing to sell it for what it will bring—so that it could be sold immediately—for such is the pressure of my debts that I am unable to describe the perplexity in which they involve me.—

yrs ever
B

[TO SAMUEL ROGERS]   *Tuesday [June 7, 1814?]*

My dear Rogers—Sheridan was yesterday at first too sober to remember your invitation but in the dregs of the third bottle he fished up his memory—& found that he had a party at home. I left & leave any other day to him & you—save Monday & some yet undefined dinner at Burdett's.[1]—Do you go to-night to Lord Eardley's?[2] & if you do—shall I call for you—(anywhere) it will give me great pleasure.

ever yrs. entire

ß

P.S.—The Stael out-talked Whitbread—overwhelmed his spouse—was *ironed* by Sheridan—confounded Sir Humphry—& utterly perplexed your slave.—The rest (great names in the red book nevertheless) were mere segments of the circle—Ma'mselle daunced a Russ saraband with great vigour—grace—& expression—though not very pretty—I think her eyes & figure promise a lively part in bed.——

[TO HENRIETTA D'USSIÈRES[1]]   *June 8th. 1814*

Excepting your compliments (which are only excusable because you don't know me) you write like a clever woman for which reason I hope you *look* as *un*like one as possible—I never knew but one of your country—Me. de Stael—and she is frightful as a precipice.—As it seems impracticable my visiting you—cannot you contrive to visit me? telling me the time previously that I may be in ye. way—and if this same interview leads to the "leap into the Serpentine" you mention—we can take the jump together—and shall be very good company—for I swim like a Duck—(one of the few things I can do well) and you say that your Sire taught you the same useful acquirement.— I like your education of all things—it in some degree resembles my own—for the first ten years of my life were passed much amongst mountains—and I had also a tender and peremptory parent who indulged me sometimes with holidays and now and then with a box on the ear.—If you will become acquainted with me—I will promise not to make love to you unless you like it—and even if I did there is no occasion for you to receive more of it than you please:—you must however do me two favours—the first is not to mistake me for *S*[2]—

---

[1] Sir Francis Burdett.

[2] See June 29, 1813, to Lady Melbourne, note 1 (Vol. 3, p. 69).

[1] Henrietta D'Ussières was one of the many women who wrote to Byron after he achieved fame. She apparently wrote him several letters before he replied. A number of her epistles are published in *To Lord Byron* by George Paston and Peter Quennell (1939), pp. 121–141.

[2] Unidentified. Southey? Sotheby?

who is an excellent man—but to whom I have not the honour to bear the smallest (I won't say *slightest* for he has the circumference of an Alderman) resemblance—and the next is to recollect that as "no man is a hero to his Valet" so I am a hero to no person whatsoever—and not treat me with such outrageous respect and awe—which makes me feel as if I was in a strait waistcoat.—you shall be a *heroine* however if you prefer it and I will be and am

yr. very humble Sert.

B

P.S.—"Surprized" oh! no!—I am surprized at nothing—except at your taking so much trouble about one who is not worth it.——You say—what would "my servants think?" 1stly. they seldom think at all—2dly. they are generally out of the way—particularly when most wanted—3dly. *I* do not know you—and I humbly imagine that they are no wiser than their Master.—

[TO LADY MELBOURNE]   *June 10th. 1814*

Dear Lady M[elbourn]e.—I don't remember one syllable of such a request—but the truth is that I do not always read ye. letters through —she[1] has no more variety than my Maccaw—& her note is not much more musical—judge then—whether (being also in ye. delectable situation which winds up the moral of your note) I can attend the ye. [*sic*] same tones—if there is a Nightingale or a Canary bird to be got by love or money.——All you say is exceeding true—but who ever said or supposed that you were not shocked and all that?—you *have* done every thing in your power—& more than any other person breathing would have done for *me*—to make me act rationally—but there is an old saying (excuse the Latin—which I wont quote but translate) "whom the Gods wish to destroy—they first madden" I am as mad as C[aroline] on a different topic and in a different way—for I never break out into scenes—but am not a whit more in my senses——I will however not persuade *her* into any *fugitive* piece of absurdity—but more I can't promise—I love no one else (in a proper manner) and whatever you may imagine—I can not or at least do not put myself in the way of——let me see—Annabella is the most prudish & correct person I know—so I refer you to the last emphatic substantive in her last letter to you.——There is that little Lady R.[2]—tells me that C[aroline] has taken a sudden fancy to *her*—what can that be for?—

1 Lady Caroline Lamb.
2 Rancliffe?

C[aroline] has also taken some offence at Lady G. Sloane's[3] frigid appearance—& supposes that Augusta who never troubles her head about her—has said something or other on my authority—*this* I remember is in C[aroline]'s last letter—one of her twaddling questions I presume——she seems puzzled about me—& not at all near the truth—the Devil who ought to be civil on such occasions will probably keep her from it still—& if he should not—I must invent some flirtation to lead her from approaching it.—I am sorry to hear of your tristesse—& conceive that I have at last guessed or perceived the real cause—it won't trouble you long—besides what is it or anything else compared with our melodrame? *Take* comfort—you very often give it

ever yrs.

B

[TO JAMES WEDDERBURN WEBSTER] *June 11th. 1814*

Dear W—My arrangements with Mr. Claughton are still so undefined—that I am not sure whether I can comply with your request or not—however—I will enquire—and if I have the power you may depend upon the permission.—I did but receive *one note* from you during your last visit to town and I had been up all night for a week together—& being at ye. same time in expectation of seeing you here or meeting you somewhere I delayed answering till you were gone—our avocations seem to have led in different ways—& yet at that time I was a good deal *out*—as it is called.———I thank you for your invitation—which you may repeat with great safety—and ever am

very truly yours.

B

P.S.—I hope you settled every thing to your wish with your *M. P.*——and that if you go over to N[ewstea]d you will pass your time pleasantly.—I shall always be happy to hear that you are doing well.——Your Lady Sitwell[1] has sent me a card for to night, but I shan't go. I have had enough of parties—for this summer at least.

[3] Unidentified.
[1] See April 15, 1814, to Lady Sitwell, note 1. Webster wrote a manuscript note on this letter: "I *did* take him to Lady Sitwell's party in Seymour Road. He there for the first time saw his cousin, the beautiful Mrs. Wilmot. When we returned to his rooms in Albany, he said little, but desired Fletcher to give him a *tumbler* of *Brandy*, which he drank at once to Mrs. Wilmot's health, then retired to rest, and was, I heard afterwards, in a sad state all night. The next day he wrote those charming lines upon her—She walks in Beauty like the Night. . . ."

My dear Charles/—I will be at home—but don't let him out of town again without some definitive arrangement.—He need not think I shall meet (if we meet) him with ill-temper—I trust that under any circumstances however vexatious—that where offence is not intended—none will be taken by me.————I have no intention of blaming anyone—but merely wished to suggest that *every day* is now a serious loss to me—and that something conclusive must be determined upon.——

yrs. ever
B

[TO THOMAS MOORE] *June 14th, 1814*

I *could* be very sentimental now, but I won't. The truth is, that I have been all my life trying to harden my heart, and have not yet quite succeeded—though there are great hopes—and you do not know how it sunk with your departure. What adds to my regret is having seen so little of you during your stay in this crowded desert, where one ought to be able to bear thirst like a camel,—the springs are so few, and most of them so muddy.

The newspapers will tell you all that is to be told of emperors, &c.[1] They have dined, and supped, and shown their flat faces in all thoroughfares, and several saloons. Their uniforms are very becoming, but rather short in the skirts; and their conversation is a catechism, for which and the answers I refer you to those who have heard it.

I think of leaving town for Newstead soon. If so, I shall not be remote from your recess, and (unless Mrs. M detains you at home over the caudle-cup and a new cradle) we will meet. You shall come to me, or I to you, as you like it;—but *meet* we will. An invitation from Aston has reached me, but I do not think I shall go. I have also heard of * * * [Mary Chaworth-Musters?]—I should like to see her again, for I have not met her for years; and though "the light that ne'er can shine again" is set, I do not know that "one dear smile like those of old"[2] might not make me for a moment forget the "dulness" of "life's stream."

I am going to R * *'s [Rancliffe's] to-night—to one of those suppers

---

[1] This was what Byron called "the summer of the sovereigns", when the Emperor of Russia, the King of Prussia, and various famous diplomats and generals came to England to celebrate the victory over Napoleon.

[2] The refrain of Moore's ballad, "One dear smile".

which *"ought* to be dinners." I have hardly seen her, and never *him*, since you set out. I told you, you were the last link of that chain. As for * *,³ we have not syllabled one another's names since. The post will not permit me to continue my scrawl. More anon.

Ever, dear Moore, &c.

P.S.—Keep the Journal,⁴ I care not what becomes of it, and if it has amused you, I am glad that I kept it. "Lara"⁵ is finished, and I am copying him for my third vol., now collecting;—but *no separate* publication.

[TO JOHN MURRAY]   *June 14th. 1814*

Dear Sir/—I return your packet of this morning.—Have you heard that Bertrand¹ has returned to Paris with the account of Napoleon's having lost his senses?—it is a *report*—but if true—I must like Mr. Fitzgerald and Jeremiah (of lamentable memory) lay claim to prophecy—that is to say of saying that he *ought* to go out of [his] senses—in the penultimate stanza of a certain ode²—the which having been pronounced *nonsense* by several profound critics has a still further pretension by it's unintelligibility to inspiration.———

ever yrs.

B

[TO AUGUSTA LEIGH]   *June 18th. 1814*

Dearest A.—Well—I *can* "judge for myself" and a pretty piece of judgment it is—you shall hear.—Last night at Earl Grey's¹—or rather this *morning* (about 2 by the account of the said Aurora) in one

³ Lady Adelaide Forbes?
⁴ Byron had given to Moore the journal which he began on November 14, 1813, and continued until April 19, 1814 (with considerable intermissions in 1814). See Vol. 3, pp. 204–258.
⁵ *Lara*, a sort of sequel to *The Corsair*, was published in August, 1814, in a volume with Rogers' poem *Jacqueline*.
¹ Henri Gratien Bertrand (1773–1844), distinguished general of Napoleon's army, followed the Emperor to Elba.
² In the 15th stanza of Byron's "Ode to Napoleon Buonaparte" there is the "prophecy" that unless "All sense is with thy sceptre gone,/Life will not long confine/That spirit pour'd so widely forth."
¹ The 2nd Earl Grey (1764–1845), Whig statesman and staunch opponent of repressive legislation. His house was a centre of Whig social life.

of the cooler rooms sitting on the corner of a great chair wherein was deposited Lady R[ancliffe] *she* talking Platonics and listening to a different doctrine—I observed Mr. Rogers not far off colloquizing with your friend.[2]—Presently he came up and interrupted our duet— and after different remarks—began upon her & hers—what seized me I know not but I desired him to introduce me—at which he expressed much good humour.—I stopped him—and said he had better ask her first—and in the mean time to give her entire option—I walked away to another part of the room separated by a great Screen—so that she had the best opportunity of getting off without the awkwardness of being overheard—or seen &c. &c. all which I duly considered.—My Goddess of the Armchair in the mean time was left to a soliloquy—as she afterwards told me—wondering what Rogers and I were about.— To my astonishment in a minute up comes R[ogers] with *your* Ch[arlott]e at the pas de charge of introduction—the bow was made— the curtsey returned and so far "excellent well" all except the dis- appearance of the said Rogers, who immediately marched off leaving us in the middle of a huge apartment with about 20 scattered pairs all employed in their own concerns.—While I was thinking of a *nothing* to say—the Lady began—"a friend of mine—a great friend of yours" and stopped—wondering what the Devil was coming next I said "per- haps you mean a relation"—"Oh yes—a relation—" and stopped *again*—finding this would never do—and being myself beginning to break down into shyness—she too confused—I uttered your respect- able name and prattled I know not what syllables—and so on for about 3 minutes—and then how we parted I know not—but never did two people seem to know less what they said or did.—Well—we met again 2 or 3 times in passages &c. where I endeavoured to improve this dialogue into something like sense—still taking you and people she knew—(and the dead Marquis of Granby[3] I believe) for the topics— in this interval she lost her party and seemed in an agony—"shall I get your shawl"—I have got it—(they were going—by the bye—La Mere was not there) "is it your brother that you want—he is not gone"— no—but have you seen Lady (or Mrs. Somebody) oh—there she is— and away she went.———She is shy as an Antelope and unluckily as

[2] Lady Charlotte Leveson-Gower, whom Augusta wanted Byron to marry, was the daughter of Lord Gower, half-brother of Lord Granville. Charlotte met Augusta at Castle Howard, the home of the Carlisles. Lady Charlotte, Lady Gertrude Howard, and Augusta were inseparable.

[3] John Manners, Marquis of Granby (1721–1770). From the Manners family also came the Duke of Rutland, a son-in-law of Lord Carlisle. Lady Charlotte Leveson-Gower was related to the Carlisles.

pretty or we should not remark it.—By the bye—I must say—that it looked more like *dislike* than shyness—and I do not much wonder— for her first confusion in calling you a *friend*—forgetting the relationship set me off—not laughing—but in one of our *glows*—and stammers—and then all I had heard from you and others of *her* diffidence— brought our own similar malady upon me in a double degree.————
The only thing is that she might have not been introduced unless she had liked—as I did not stand near as people usually do so that the introduc*ee* can't get off—but was out of sight and hearing—then I must say that *till* the first sentence there was a deal of valour on both sides—but after that—Oh—Dear—this is all your fault.—The Duchess of Somerset[4] also to mend matters insisted on presenting me to a Princess *Biron* Duchess of Hohen[5]—God knows—what—and another person to her two sisters—Birons too—but I flew off—& *would* not—saying I had enough of introductions for that night at least.—Devonshire asked me *twice* (last night) to come to Chiswick on Sunday!—is not *that* a little odd?[6]—I have seen Blucher &c. &c. and was surprized into an introduction after all to a Prince Radzivil a Pole[7] and a Potentate—a good and great man but very like a Butler.

————

God bless you, my dear.

Ever yours most affectionately,
BYRON

[TO SAMUEL ROGERS]   *June 19th. 1814*

Dear Rogers/—I am always obliged to trouble you with my awkwardnesses—and now I have a fresh one.—Mr. Wrangham[1] called on me several times—and I have missed the honour of making

---

[4] The Duchess of Somerset was the wife of the 11th Duke. She was the second daughter of the 9th Duke of Hamilton.

[5] Perhaps an emigrée daughter of the Princess Biron, Duchess of Hohen, who was killed in the Terror in 1793.

[6] A little odd, Byron felt, because the Devonshires were connected with the family of Lord Carlisle, the 6th Duke of Devonshire's sister Georgiana having married Carlisle's eldest son. Never having made up with or forgiven Lord Carlisle for having failed to introduce him in the House of Lords, he felt uncomfortable in the presence of any of the Carlisles. The Duke's party (June 19, 1814) was for the Emperor of Russia, the King of Prussia, and other celebrities.

[7] The Prince was of a family of famous Polish aristocrats which still exists.

[1] Francis Wrangham (1769–1843) was an editor of Plutarch, and a translator and imitator of Petrarch. He later took orders and became Archdeacon of Cleveland, Archdeacon of the East Riding of Yorkshire, and Prebend of York and of Chester.

his acquaintance, which I regret—but which *you* who know my desultory and uncertain habits will not wonder at—& will I am sure attribute to any thing but a wish to offend a person who has shown me much kindness—and possesses character and talents entitled to general respect.—My mornings are late and passed in fencing and boxing and a variety of most unpoetical exercises—very wholesome, &c. but would be very disagreeable to my friends—whom I am obliged to exclude during their operation—I never go out till the evening and I have not been fortunate enough to meet Mr. W[rangham] at Lord Lansdowne's or Lord Jersey's, where I had hoped to pay him my respects.——I would have written to him—but a few words from you will go further than all the apologetical *sesquipedalities* I could muster on the occasion—it is only to say that without intending it I contrive to behave very ill to every body—and am very sorry for it.—

Ever dear R. yrs.
BYRON

[TO LADY MELBOURNE]   *June 21st 1814*

Since I wrote last night I have received the 2 enclosed—what shall I do about Ph [Lady Frances Webster] and her epistles? since by her own account they run great hazard in their way to her. I am willing to give them up—but she says not a syllable about mine—no matter.— The other is from A[nnabella] and prim & pretty as usual—somebody or other has been seized with a fit of amazement at her correspondence with so naught[y] a personage—and this has naturally given a fillup [sic] of contradiction in my favour which was much wanted.—

ever yrs.
B

[TO JOHN MURRAY]   *June 21st. 1814*

Dear Sir/—I suppose "Lara" is gone to the Devil—which is no great matter—only let me know that I may be saved the trouble of copying the rest—and put the first into the fire—I really have no anxiety about it—& shall not be sorry to be saved the copying—which goes on very slowly and may prove to you that you may *speak out*— or I should be less sluggish.—

yrs. truly
B

I have delayed writing from day to day first because you were absent from Seaham—and 2dly. I wished to fix a time when I might have the pleasure of availing myself of Sir Ralph's very welcome invitation. ——You may be assured that "my kindness" as you are pleased to call it—*is* "undiminished" you have much more cause to apprehend it's troublesome progress—than conjecture its decay.—You make me laugh about "forms & expressions" I will not say that I wish you to be less formal because I had rather you pleased yourself—but Me. Scudery herself could not have imagined a more correct correspondent —as to "meanings" I hope you do not think that I have presumed to mistake them—and if I do not—I know not who else has any business with them except Sir. R. & Lady Milbanke—who have permitted our correspondence.—————I shall wait your answer and your convenience before I pretend to name any period when I can hope to see you—believe me—it will give me great satisfaction—I do not find my comparisons very favourable to those in the crowd where I have lately mingled—and this may in some measure augment a regret which is now useless.——You have been "charged with this correspondence" might I ask by whom?—it is no great matter—unless with these very discerning persons who think that between people of our time of Life and in our situation there can be but one topic of discussion.—If all this has not alarmed you—let me hear from you again and at all events believe me

very affectly. & truly yrs
BYRON

My dearest Augusta—"Certainty" is a strong word—particularly as applied to the most capricious of beings—but the probabilities are surely strong against any right feeling or action from a black heart and a foolish head.—More I need not say—except that I have had *no* conversation with Lady M[elbourn]e on the subject.—There is no occasion for so much scrupu*losi*ty about the transfer[1]—I did it on your account—& that I would do for any one I know in a similar situation— he need not consider himself under the least obligation—nor in fact is

---

[1] Augusta apparently was embarrassed to receive the £3,000 Byron was transferring to her from Hammersley's.

there any—I must—and will at all events get *you* out of debt—and in the mean time while this is proceeding—let him think well of some plan of regulating his expenditure[2]—*I* will have no interest—nor bond—nor repayment—unless his father left him so rich as to make it easy & pleasant to himself—what is the whole amount of his debts now?—I mean after the sum at Hammersley's has liquidated a part—do conceal nothing from me—& for Godsake let me have the satisfaction of at least relieving you from the most worrying & pressing of petty vexations—if this Prince should *come* forward at last or the General *go*[3]—he can then repay it or not as he likes—I am sure I don't care———if any accident happened to G[eorge]—you know my dearest A—that as your *father's* son—I am more deeply interested than your *Mamma['s]* brothers can be—I am also unconnected & less incumbered—& am merely doing now—what I must do then—trying to make you less uncomfortable—and then consider the *children*—& my Georgiana in particular—in short I need say no more.—Well—now for *nothings*.—Last night at Lady Jersey's—after as many movements as ever were upon a Chess-board—your friend[4] & I got fairly checkmated in a corner—& talked a very good half-hour—& by persuading her that I was in a greater fright than herself she got over much of her shyness—and we prated something like you & me at our second or third interview—I only heard her say one disagreeable thing—& that is that Lady S.[5] & the whole family leave town very soon for Scotland—I think her so very pretty—& pleasing—I ⟨think you⟩ perhaps might do something to improve our acquaintance.—God bless you—my dear—

ever yrs, most affectionately
BYRON

P.S.—You know that some years ago—my only reason for not doing what was then required—was that it was not in my power—now—that it is—you hesitate—were there ever such people? We are all mad.———

P.S.—Last night a presentation to Princes Metternich Radzivil &

---

[2] Augusta's husband George Leigh was heavily in debt from betting on the horses and from other extravagant habits.
[3] George Leigh had quarrelled with the Prince Regent. As an Equerry, he was dependent on the Prince's bounty and favours for his livelihood. It was uncertain whether he would inherit much from his father General Leigh.
[4] Lady Charlotte Leveson-Gower.
[5] Lady Stafford, mother of Lady Charlotte.

Czartoriski[6]—you may suppose my horror—as I have no French—luckily they speak Italian which I once spoke fluently & have not quite forgotten. Radzivil said his Spouse (not in England) was a great *Englist*--& would admire poesy &c. &c.

[TO JOHN MURRAY (*a*)]   *June 24th. 1814*

Dear Sir/—I hope the next proof will be better—this was one which would have consoled Job had it been of his "enemy's book."—Let Mr. Dallas—have the next for the *pointing's* sake—& let me have a more correct revise for my own.—

yrs. truly
B

[TO JOHN MURRAY (*b*)]   [*June 24th, 1814*]

Dear Sir/—Let me have a correct revise of the whole[1]—I have corrected some of the most *horrible* blunders that ever crept into a proof

yrs. ever
B

[TO LADY MELBOURNE]   *June 26th. 1814*

My dear Ly. M[elbourn]e.—(⟨I have⟩ to continue the conversation which Ld. C[owpe]r has broken off by falling asleep—& his wife by keeping awake—) I know nothing of C[aroline]'s last night adventures; to prove it there is her letter—which I have not read through—nor answered—nor written these two months—& then only by *desire* to keep her quiet.———You talked to me—about keeping her out—it is impossible—she comes at all times—at any time—& the moment the door is open in she walks—I can't throw her out of the window—as to getting rid of her—that is rational—& probable—but *I* will not receive her.—The Bessboroughs may take her if they please—or any steps they please—I have no hesitation in saying—that I have made up my mind as to the alternative—and would sooner—much sooner be

---

[6] Adam Jerzy Czartoryski, a Polish Prince, once minister of foreign affairs under Czar Alexander of Russia, was dismissed in 1806 because of his Polish nationalism, but came out of his retreat after the check of Napoleon in 1813, and tried vainly to get recognition for the independence of Poland at the Congress of Vienna.

[1] The proofs of *Lara*.

with the dead in purgatory—than with her—*Caroline* (I put the name at length as I am not jesting) upon earth.——She may hunt me down— it is in the power of any mad or bad woman to do so by any man—but *snare* me she shall not—torment me she may—how am I to bar myself from her!—I am already almost a prisoner—she has no shame—no feeling—no one estimable or redeemable quality.—These are strong words—but I know what I am writing—they avail nothing but to convince you of my own determination—my first object in such a dilemma would be to take ⟨Augusta?⟩ with me—that might fail—so much the better—but even if it did—I would lose an hundred souls rather than be bound to C[aroline]—if there is one human being whom I do utterly *detest* & *abhor*—it is she—& all things considered—I feel to myself justified in so doing—she has been an adder in my path ever since my return to this country—she has often belied—& sometimes betrayed me—she has crossed me every where—she has watched—& worried & *guessed*—& been a curse to me & mine.——You may shew *her* this if you please—or to anyone you please—if these were the last words I were to write upon earth—I would not revoke one letter— except to make it more legible.—

ever yours most sincerely
BYRON

[TO SAMUEL ROGERS]   *June 27th, 1814*

My dear Rogers,—You could not have made me a more acceptable present than *Jacqueline*.[1] She is all grace and softness and poetry; there is so much of the last, that we do not feel the want of *story*, which is simple, yet enough. I wonder that you do not oftener unbend to more of the same kind. I have some sympathy with the *softer* affections, though very little in *my* way, and no one can depict them so truly and successfully as yourself. I have half a mind to pay you in kind, or rather *un*kind, for I have just "supped full of horror"[2] in two cantos of darkness and dismay.

Do you go to Lord Essex's[3] to-night? if so, will you let me call for you at your own hour? I dined with Holland-house yesterday at Lord Cowper's; my Lady very gracious, which she can be more than any

[1] Rogers sent Byron the manuscript of his poem *Jacqueline*, which was later published in a volume with Byron's *Lara*.
[2] *Macbeth*, Act V, scene 5.
[3] George, 5th Earl of Essex was afterward associated with Byron on the Drury Lane Sub-Committee of Management.

one when she likes. I was not sorry to see them again, for I can't forget that they have been very kind to me.

Ever yours most truly,
Bn

P.S.—Is there any chance or possibility of making it up with Lord Carlisle,[4] as I feel disposed to do any thing reasonable or unreasonable to effect it? I would before, but for the *Courier*,[5] and the possible misconstructions at such a time. Perpend, pronounce.

[TO JOHN MURRAY (*a*)]   *June 27th. 1814*

Dear Sir/—You demanded more *battle*—there it is—[1]

yrs. truly
B

[TO JOHN MURRAY (*b*)]   *June 27th. 1814*

Dear Sir/—I have not looked over the proofs—but send you *more additions* &c. & request a correct revise of the whole—when convenient.—

yrs. truly
B

[TO LADY MELBOURNE]   *June 28th. 1814*

My dear Ly. M[elbourn]e.—I must assure you that I did not see nor hear of C[aroline] on Saturday and—that all bolts bars & silence can do to keep her away are done daily & hourly.—I had written a long savage letter about her last night—which I will send another time.—You must send me back the inclosed *both A's*[1] & the other immediately—as *one* must be returned by the post.—I need not say be

---

[4] It was probably through Augusta's urging, and because of his interest in Lady Charlotte Leveson-Gower, who had family connections with Lord Carlisle, that Byron was at this time willing to make up the quarrel, but nothing ever came of the resolution.

[5] The *Courier*, at the time that Byron was being attacked for his poem "Lines on a Lady Weeping", brought up again Byron's attack on Carlisle in *English Bards and Scotch Reviewers*.

[1] Byron probably refers to stanza 15, which was added to the description of the battle in the second canto of *Lara* after the first draft was completed.

[1] Augusta and Annabella.

secret—though after all neither are of any importance—but will amuse you as they do me with the *fusses* into which our friendships quarrels & relationships appear to involve people to the 3d. & 4th. generation.—You will see how *demure* I must have been—and the passage about *Ma* (and the separate answer) is something in A's style—and like all very correct people when they set about secrecy. ————Pray forgive—& laugh—& be silent—& believe me

most affectly. yrs.

B

P.S.—You need not write—but enclose these back by the bearer— if you can.————I must send *this* back by the Post.——

[TO ————]   *June 29th. 1814*

Sir/—I have to thank you for the perusal of your work—and assure You that I perfectly coincide with your judges in their opinion of it's merits.—Excuse my having detained it so long.—I have the honour to be

yr. very obedt. Sert.

BYRON

[TO LADY MELBOURNE (*a*)]   *July 2d. 1814*

Dear Lady M[elbourn]e.—I leave town tomorrow for 2 or 3 days and as I shall probably be occupied at Cambridge I may as well "say my say" with regard to C[aroline].—"Conquer" oh no—*crush*—if you please & not unlikely whether she goes or stays.——She perplexed me very much with questions & guesses—and as I verily believe her growing actually & seriously disordered in her intellects—there is no conjecturing what she may assert or do——as far as I can judge from observation—not less towards myself than others (though in a different way to the last) she can not be in her senses—I was obliged to talk to her—for she laid hold of Hobhouse & passed before where another person & myself were discussing points of Platonism—so frequently—& remarkably—as to make us anticipate a scene and as she was masked & dominoed[1] & it was daylight there could be little

---

[1] This was at a masked ball at Burlington House in honour of the Duke of Wellington on July 1, 1814. All the *haut ton* of society was there and also, hiding behind the masks, some demi-mondaines such as Harriette Wilson, who claimed she met Byron there.

harm & there was at least a probability of more quiet.—Not all I
could say could prevent her from displaying her green *pantaloons*
every now & then—though I scolded like her grandfather upon these
very uncalled for and unnecessary gesticulations.—Why do you say
that I was mistaken about another mask with you?—I never even pretended to guess at so pious a person nor supposed they were in so profane an assembly—& now I am convinced they were not there at all—
since you tell me of the illness of the little boy—who so happily recovered by the timely devotion of *her* staying away to take care of
him.————To be sure I thought I saw somebody very like—but
there is no trusting to likenesses and it is not easy to unmask anybody
even without their pasteboard.————I don't wonder at your dislike
to C[aroline] &c.—and whatever absurdity or enormity her madness
may plunge me into—I do think you have already done at least tenfold
more than anyone on earth would have done—& if you were to do
more—I should conceive you no less mad than herself—I thank you
for the past for the thousandth time—and as to the present & future I
shall parry her off as well as I can—and if foiled I must abide by the
consequence—so there's an end—after all it is not much your concern
(except as far as Good Nature went) and rests between me & the
Blarneys [Bessboroughs]—whom I regard not—to *yourself* I own that
I am anxious to appear as having done all that could be done to second
your wishes in breaking off the connection—which would have been
effectual with any or every other person.——I am glad you were
amused with ——'s correspondent————is very much astonished
but in very good humour—and I too—on account of my *theory*, of
which by the bye I despaired very much at first in the present instance.
I think I should make a good Tartuffe—it was by paring down my
demeanour to a very quiet & hesitating deportment—which however
my natural shyness (though that goes off at times) helped to forward
—that I ensured the 3 days recollection of ——'s amiable ally.
——— Good bye—for the present—I am still sadly sleepy with the
wear & tear of the last 2 nights & have had nothing for my trouble—I
wanted very much to tell [it?] to you but you preferred Robinson[2]—
the next time he breaks a leg I shall be less sorry—& send you to
nurse him.——I am in amity (the purest & of course most insipid)
with a person[3]—and one condition is that I am to tell her her faults

---

[2] Robinson seems to have been a servant of Lady Melbourne who had injured a
leg and was the object of the Lady's solicitation, and apparently she went home
early from the ball on his account.
[3] Unidentified.

without reserve—how long do you think such a treaty fully observed would endure?—I will tell you—five minutes.—I was assailed by a Mask for some time—teazing enough but with a sweet voice—& some one of whom all I could learn was that I had said of her she *had been* very beautiful—this quite cured my desire of discovery—as such a speech could never be forgiven—so I told her—& got away.— — Good bye—again—

ever most affectionately yr. servitor
B

[TO LADY MELBOURNE (*b*)]   *July 2d. 1814*

My dear Ly. M[elbourn]e.—As the last 2 letters amused you perhaps *these* may (they seem to arrive *both* always by the same post) only have the goodness to think of the return of the said *post* & to let me have it for the impatient—who will be in such a fidget if not possessed of it again immediately.—I was up till 7 this morning—& the last person who left the room (I believe) I had a long conversation with C[aroline] (closely masked that is *she* but always trying to *indicate* who she was not to me so much as to every body) but nothing more or very particular.—I am so sleepy that I hope you will say something to enliven or at least awaken me—as you went to bed earlier—but don't trouble yourself to write *now* as I know your fusses in a morning—believe me

ever yrs. most truly
B

[TO FRANCIS HODGSON]   *Albany. July 8th. 1814*

My dear Hodgson/—I send this in the chance of your being still at Hastings—if so—pray answer by return of Post.—Will you take a house for me at Hastings—by the *week* will be best as my stay will be short—it must be good and tolerably large—as Mrs. Leigh—her *4* children—& three maids will be there also—besides my own Valet & footman—my Coachman (& his horses) may be boarded out—I shall also want a housemaid and *extempore* & pro tempore cook of the place—and wish all this to be settled as soon as you are disposed to take the trouble.— —It is very tiresome to bore you in this manner—but I have no other acquaintance at H[astings] & prefer the place for that reason & *quiet*—for this last—let my bedroom be some way from

137

the *Nursery* or children's apartments—and let the women be near together—and as far from me as possible.—I don't much care about the price—so that they are comfortable—but I wish this soon—& I hope you will excuse the trouble—as I have no other way of arranging without coming down myself.—If I don't hear from you directly I shall conclude that you are not at H[astings] & bend my steps & my enquiries elsewhere.——[end of letter cut away—balance of letter from copy of the original given to Mrs. Goodall] There will be room wanted for *two* carriages—but only one pair of horses—& those can be anywhere—I suppose & hope there is good *bathing*—as that is one of my principal objects—will you favour me with an early response to this? & believe me

> Ever yrs truly & affectly.
> BYRON

[TO THOMAS MOORE] *July 8th, 1814*

I returned to town last night, and had some hopes of seeing you to-day, and would have called,—but I have been (though in exceeding distempered good health) a little head-achy with free living, as it is called, and am now at the freezing point of returning soberness. Of course, I should be sorry that our parallel lines did not deviate into intersection before you return to the country,—after that same non-suit,[1] whereof the papers have told us,—but, as you must be much occupied, I won't be affronted, should your time and business militate against our meeting.

Rogers and I have almost coalesced into a joint invasion of the public.[2] Whether it will take place or not, I do not yet know, and I am afraid Jacqueline (which is very beautiful) will be in bad company. But, in this case, the lady will not be the sufferer.

I am going to the sea, and then to Scotland; and I have been doing nothing,—that is, no good,—and am very truly, &c.

[TO THOMAS MOORE] [*July, 1814*]

I suppose, by your non-appearance, that the phil*a*sophy of my note, and the previous silence of the writer, have put or kept you in *humeur*. Never mind—it is hardly worth while.

---

[1] Moore had been summoned to London to appear as a witness in a suit of his musical publisher James Power against a literary pirate.
[2] Byron refers to the joint publication of *Lara* and Rogers's *Jacqueline*.

This day have I received information from my man of law of the *non*—and never likely to be—performance of purchase by Mr. Claughton, of *im*pecuniary memory. He don't know what to do, or when to pay; and so all my hopes and worldly projects and prospects are gone to the devil. He (the purchaser, and the devil too, for aught I care) and I, and my legal advisers, are to meet to-morrow,—the said purchaser having first taken special care to inquire "whether I would meet him with temper?"—Certainly. The question is this—I shall either have the estate back, which is as good as ruin, or I shall go on with him dawdling, which is rather worse. I have brought my pigs to a Mussulman market. If I had but a wife now, and children, of whose paternity I entertained doubts, I should be happy, or rather fortunate, as Candide or Scarmentado.[1] In the mean time, if you don't come and see me, I shall think that Sam's bank is broke too; and that you, having assets there, are despairing of more than a piastre in the pound for your dividend.

Ever, &c.

[TO FRANCIS HODGSON] *July 11th, 1814*

My dear Hn./—The retired house by all means—that is Hastings House—I believe—the month will do very well only *if* I stay longer—they must reckon only *weekly* after it—let the H[astings] servitors sleep out—I have told you our numbers & have the goodness to arrange for me as well as you can—with a thousand thanks to you for taking so much trouble.—I should hope next week (but am not sure what day) to be there—and to make and receive all the presentations of our mutual acquaintance.—Cowell is & always was a fine fellow[1]—I don't like anybody much—but him as well as most—of course I except all my old friends from this sweeping [sway?] of Cynicism.———Do whatever is expedient—and make me responsible for any expence—I am so glad to hear of quiet—for I would not be at a *regular* fashashashionable watering place—for all the gems of Ocean and it's Cod-fisheries into the bargain.—

[signature cut out]

---

[1] In Voltaire's tale, *Histoire des Voyages de Scarmentado Écrite par lui-même* (1756), the hero like Candide decides after his travels to stay at home, not to cultivate his garden, but "Je me mariai chez moi: je fus cocu, et je vis que c'était l'état le plus doux de la vie."

[1] Byron had met John Cowell at Brighton in 1808 and had patronized him as he had the younger boys at Harrow.

P.S.—You will like Augusta much—she is as shy as an Antelope—but the best hearted gentle inoffensive being in the *world*.—And one of the children is a Beauty—and the rest fine—but damnable Squallers.————

[TO CHARLES HANSON]   *July 11th. 1814*

Dear Charles/—I called just now with some expectation of hearing further of Mr. Claughton & your conference with him.——Whatever is done must be done *now*. I cannot wait till your father's return—& have lost too much by delay already—pray have the goodness to tell me if you have seen him—and what will be the conditions supposing me to be disposed to relieve him & take back the property.—I must once more represent to you the necessity of some actual *conclusion*—for years & years I have been sinking gradually deeper & deeper—I do not mean to exonerate myself—my own extravagance has doubtless been the principal cause—but at the same time I must add that *delay* never ending—still beginning—delay has materially contributed to assist my own imprudence in adding to my involvements.—It is now 2 months since I spoke of Rochdale—nothing has been done—nor even said—I am & was willing to sell it for what it will bring—why cannot this be attempted at least?—and immediately—let me hear something of Mr. Claughton whom I am willing to meet anywhere or anyhow—& come to something decisive one way or the other.—

                                                    yrs. ever truly
                                                        BYRON

[TO JOHN MURRAY]   [*July 11, 1814*]

Dear Sir/—You shall have one of the pictures.—I wish you to send the proof of "Lara" to Mr. Moore 33—Bury Street *tonight*—as he leaves town tomorrow—& wishes to see it before he goes—and I am also willing to derive the benefit of his remarks.—

                                                        yrs. truly
                                                            B

[TO JOHN MURRAY]   *July 12th. 1814*

Dear Sir,—Mr. Moore has gone to the country & carried off Lara with him—I suppose it is of no consequence & that another can be sent to me exactly the same.—At your leisure (not now when at dinner) you can answer this.—

yrs truly
B

July 13th. 1814

Dear Charles/—I called again today—your father is *not* come— all I have to request is—that if Mr. C[laughton] cannot wait till he comes—something may & must be done immediately—I leave town myself on *Monday*—and shall call on Mr. C[laughton] & settle with him in person in case your father does not arrive directly.———I would sooner lose anything or everything—than bear the suspense a day longer.—

yrs truly
B

July 15th. 1814

Dear Charles/—I presume that by this time Mr. Hanson is re- turned—at least I hope so—& should regard it as a little extra- ordinary—that at a time of such peculiar importance to one of his clients—and being already acquainted with Mr. C[laughton]'s arrival in London—he should allow him to return to the country—& myself to leave London (as I must on Monday) without meeting either—or even answering the letter I suppose you have addressed to him on the subject.——In case he should not be arrived I must (however un- willingly) take it upon myself to meet Mr. Claughton *tomorrow*—& request *you* to be present & to fix an hour for that purpose in Chancery Lane.—

ever yrs. truly—
BYRON

July 17th. 1814

Dear Sir/—Whatever arrangements Mr. C[laughton] may mean to make—I trust that they will be *speedy*—when *he* talks of *sacrifices*— he forgets the confusion into which the *non*-performance of his engagements plunges my affairs—and if he has involved his own—he should have recollected both *his* & *mine* before he began to purchase *Welsh* or other reversions—If he can complete his purchase in proper time & method—very well—if not—I humbly conceive in law & equity—that the loss ought not to fall upon the person who is ready to fulfil *his* engagements—or him who has given Mr. C[laughton] *time* & every accommodation in his power and to whom when Mr. C[laughton] has refused a security upon his own property—for the safety of the seller—you will have the goodness to use your own discretion as to making him acquainted or not with my sentiments.—surely *you* cannot be so sanguine *now* as to place much reliance on any *promises* after what has already passed.—I shall not leave town till Tuesday—I think you should see or *write* to him once more before Mr. Claughton leaves London.—Pray—remember *Rochdale*—& let something be done directly about it—I have nothing else to trust to——believe me

yrs ever truly
BYRON

P.S.—My respects to the Earl & Coun[te]ss. I am glad to hear from Charles that he is better.—Do pray give a serious glance at my concerns—& don't let me be *fooled*.

[TO JOHN MURRAY] *J[ul]y 18th. 1814*

Dear Sir,—I think *you* will be satisfied even to *repletion* with our Northern friends[1]—& I wont deprive you longer of what I think will give you pleasure—for my own part my modesty or my vanity must be silent.—

ever yrs. truly
BN

P.S.—If you could spare it for an hour in the Evening—I wish you to send it up to Mrs. L[eig]h your neighbour at the London Hotel A[lbemarl]e Street.

[TO FRANCIS HODGSON] *July 18th. 1815 [1814][1]*

My dear Hodgson—Tomorrow (Tuesday) or Wednesday at

---

[1] The *Edinburgh Review*, in the April number which appeared in July, gave high praise to Byron's "unequalled force and fidelity" in depicting "the workings of those deep and powerful emotions which alternately enchant and agonize the minds that are exposed to their inroads", in *The Corsair* and *The Bride of Abydos*. The review was by Francis Jeffrey.

[1] Misdated in Sotheby catalogue. The context shows that this was written in July, 1814, before Byron left for Hastings. July 19, 1814 was a Tuesday.

furthest expect us *all*—Capt. Byron (whom you know or will know) accompanies us—if there is not convenient room we can dispose of him at the Hotel—excuse haste—in the hope of seeing you &c. &c.

ever yrs.
BYRON

P.S.—Many thanks for today's epistle—I shall be happy to m[eet] *you so.*

[TO JOHN HANSON] *July 19th. 1814*

Dear Sir/—I called in the hope of seeing you before I left town tomorrow—& to say that if Mr. C[laughto]n will give 25–000—or even 20–000—I will close with him—& take back the estate—so much am I convinced that he is a man of neither property nor credit.—He has never *once* kept his word since the sale was concluded—and at all events I will do any thing to be rid of him—so tell him in what words you please—for such I appeal to you if he has not proved himself— without faith—& as far as I can perceive without funds.—*You* will cling & cling to the fallacious hope of the fulfilment—already shown to be so—till I am ruined entirely—in short it was a pity to let him go out of town again—without a conclusion—it was only to gain time— *close* with him on any terms—and let us have done with the equivoca- tor.——Pray think of Rochdale—it is the delay which drives me mad —I declare to God—I would rather have but ten thousand pounds clear & out of debt—than drag on the cursed existence of expectation & disappointment which I have endured for these last 6 years—for 6 months longer—though a million came at the end of them.—Address me at *Hastings House*—Hastings—& believe me

very truly yours
B

P.S.—I hope Charles is better—tell Lord & Lady P[ortsmouth] that Mrs. Chaworth is in town—I believe the Countess knows her is it not so?————

[TO JOHN CAM HOBHOUSE] *July 23d. 1814*

My dear H[obhous]e—The name of *Lara* only is *Spanish*—I have no country whatever in my view—and the name was *liquid* which put it into my head for it's smooth & antique sound—if it be right to say

143

this—put a *note tantamount*—and I shall be your debtor.———The motion of Tuesday is tempting inasmuch as it promises a *dinner* with you—the rest is "all but leather & Prunella"—Ly. J[erse]y has written to me to speak & write and the Devil knows what[1]—I *can* do neither—which is a good excuse for refusing though self-love won't allow it to be an *alledgeable* one—I shall say politely I *wont*—in very truth I wonder that the heiress apparent's intimate friend should condescend to such a solicitation.[2]———H[odgso]n is here happy in expectation—a second son of Ld. E[rskine]'s Harry Erskine[3]—happy in *possession* as he *says*—so that here in a county of downs—and a town of fishery—I have met with a pair of actual & reversionary *Optimists*—I suppose they will end like Pangloss & Scarmentado[4]—no matter—you & I will be Cacambo and Martin[5]—and our "El Dorado" shall be God knows where.———My scrawl will be illegible—but I have drank two bottles of Claret—and I have hobbled two miles *up* hill— and stumbled as many down hill—and here I am again upon even ground and ever my dear H[obhous]e most truly yours

B

[TO JOHN MURRAY] *July 23d. 1814*

Dear Sir/—I am very sorry to say that the print[1] is by no means approved by those who have seen it—who are pretty conversant with the original as well as the picture—from whence it is taken—I rather suspect that it is from the *copy* & not the *exhibited* portrait—and in this dilemma would recommend a suspension—if not abandonment of the *prefixion* to the vols—which you purpose inflicting on the public.—— With regard to *Lara* don't be in any hurry—I have not yet made up my mind on the subject—nor know what to think or do—till I hear from you—and Mr. R[ogers] appeared to me in a similar state of in-

---

[1] Byron was being urged to come to town to vote against the Government Bill providing for the stricter execution of the laws in Ireland. The bill was read a second time in the House of Lords on July 27. It was opposed by Lord Holland, but it passed and became law.

[2] Lady Jersey was an intimate friend of Princess Charlotte.

[3] Henry David Erskine, son of the first Baron Erskine, entered Harrow at the same time as Byron and later went to Trinity College, Cambridge. He afterwards became a clergyman and was Dean of Ripon.

[4] See [July, 1814], to Moore, note 1.

[5] Byron's memory of *Candide* was somewhat faulty. Candide and Cacambo were in El Dorado together. Martin joined Candide later.

[1] An engraving by Agar from the Phillips portrait of Byron, which Murray proposed to use as a frontispiece to a collected edition of Byron's poems.

determination.—I do not know that it may not be better to *reserve* for the *entire* publication you proposed and not adventure in hardy singleness—or even backed by the fairy Jacqueline—I have been seized with all kinds of doubts &c. &c. since I left London.——Pray let me hear from you & believe me

yrs. ever

B

[TO JOHN MURRAY] *[July 23–24? 1814]*

I have read the article & concur in opinion with Mr. Rogers & my friends that I have every reason to be satisfied.—You best know as Publisher how far the book may be injured or benefited by the critique in question.[1]—I can only say that I do not see how more could have been said, though perhaps it might have been done more good-humouredly.—

yrs. very truly

B

[TO JOHN HANSON] *July 24th. 1814*

Dear Sir/—I wrote to you before I left town on a subject of some importance to which I shall be glad to receive an answer.—I hope all the family are well & remain yours very truly

BYRON

[TO JOHN MURRAY] *July 24th. 1814*

Dear Sir/—The minority must in this case carry it—so pray let it be so—for I don't care a sixpence for any of the opinions you mention on such a subject—and Phillips must be a dunce to agree with them[1]— for my own part I have no opinion at all—but Mrs. L[eigh] & my cousin must be better judges of the likeness than others—and they

---

1 Since the manuscript is undated, it is difficult to determine what "the critique in question" was. Prothero has placed it between letters of July 23 and 24, but if it refers to a review of *Lara*, which seems likely, most of the reviews in important periodicals appeared in September and October. A likely one is a review by George Ellis of *The Corsair* and *Lara* in the *Quarterly Review* of July, which did not appear, however, until after October 20th.

1 See July 23, 1814, to Murray, note 1.

hate it—& so I wont have it at all.———Mr. Hobhouse is right as for his conclusion—but I deny the premises—the name only is Spanish—the country is not Spain but the Moon.—Waverley is the best & most interesting novel I have redde since—I don't know when—I like it as much as I hate Patronage & Wanderer—& O'donnel[2] and all the feminine trash of the last four months—besides—it is all easy to me—because I have been in Scotland so much—(though then young enough too) and feel at home with the people lowland & Gael.———A *note* will correct what Hob[hous]e thinks an error—(about the feudal system in Spain) it is *not* Spain—if he puts a few words of prose any where it will set all right.—I have been ordered to town to vote—I shall disobey—there is no good in so much prating—since "certain issues strokes should arbitrate."[3]—If you have nothing to say let me hear from you—

yrs. ever
B

[TO JOHN MURRAY]   *July 28th. 1814*

Dear Sir/—I am very glad indeed that Mr. G[iffor]d thinks so—& it shall be as he recommends.—You had better not publish till the E[dinburgh] R[eview] has been out at least a week—& it is not yet arrived.—In fact—wait till you hear from me again before you publish it at all.—Remember—*we positively will not have that same print* by Phillips' engraver,—your parcel of Clarke & letters has not arrived yet—but I suppose it will.—

ever yrs.
B

[TO JOHN MURRAY (*a*)]   *July 29th. 1814*

Dear Sir/—I am sorry to say that all enquiry after this parcel which should have arrived 24 hours ago have been in vain—and I am in a fuss about my letters which had they been sent as desired by the *Post* would have been now in my possession.———Pray allow some enquiry to be made after them—and never in future trust to a *parcel* with my address for mine always miscarry.—

yrs. truly
B

---

[2] *Patronage*, by Maria Edgeworth; *The Wanderer*, by Fanny Burney (Madame D'Arblay); and *O'Donnel*, by Sydney Owenson (Lady Morgan).
[3] *Macbeth*, Act V, scene 4.

July 29th. 1814

Dear Sir/—There is neither arrival nor hope of the parcel—I am sorry for the books—but a good deal more so for the letters—some of which may be on business—and at all events it is a vexation to lose them &c. &c.—I trust that you will let some enquiry be made at the accursed Coach Office—it is strange enough—since my servants tell me that every thing else has found it's way here without delay or puzzlement.—

ever yrs. truly
B

P.S.—Don't do anything about "Lara" till I return to town—& do not *print* in *any* number—at present.———Capt. Byron[1] will deliver this—which will reach you before the post.—

[TO JOHN HANSON] *July 29th. 1814*

Dear Sir/—I have twice written to you & received no answer—from which I infer that ill health on your part or that of Charles has prevented you from replying as the business was of some consequence to me—& I think required some notice from you.—Pray let me hear from you—or I must be reduced to the necessity of conducting my treaty with Mr. C[laughto]n myself.—

yrs. truly
BYRON

[TO JOHN MURRAY] *July 31st. 1814*

Dear Sir/—The parcel is come at last—it had made all sorts of circumvolution on ye. way—but no matter.—So the E[dinburgh] R[eview] is out—I thought I had requested you to send me a copy for Mrs. L[eigh] which I beg you will immediately and a little more carefully than the last.—I shall expect it with the answer to this on Tuesday—and by the same *post* any letters at Albany—*not* in the parcel with the E[dinburgh] Re[vie]w—which can be sent separately.—Many thanks for Sir J. Malcolm[1]—I wish to the skies—he had been of

1 His cousin, Captain George Anson Byron.
1 Sir John Malcolm (1769–1833), who had served in India as soldier, administrator, and diplomat, was in England from 1812 to 1816. He wrote a *History of Persia* (published in 1815), and also apparently a poem, which he sent to Byron through Murray (see Aug. 2, 1814, to Murray).

the party with R[ogers] & me—I can as yet give no positive answer about *Lara*. I will return *Persia*[2] in a day or two—but I must read it at my leisure.———I send back the *Butlers*[3]—you forget that I can only *frank* from Hastings.—

ever yrs.
B

P.S.—Don't forget the E[dinburgh] R[eview] for I have given my copy to Mr. H[odgson?]———

[TO CHARLES HANSON]   [*August, 1814*]

Dear Charles—I wish to know when your father will be in town and whether Mr. C[laughton] is actually in *possession* of N[ewstead] or not—my reason for the last question you will perceive by the enclosed *note* of a friend of mine to another[1]—pray favour me with an answer— I don't want to stay till Saturday—but will if actually expedient—

ever yrs.
B

[TO ANNABELLA MILBANKE]   *Hastings, August 1st. 1814*

Your letter has only reached me this day from London (where I shall return in a short time)—otherwise it had been answered immediately.———Allow me to avail myself of your permission to request "an explanation" which—as I do not recollect the "*ambiguous* expression" to which you allude in my last letter is necessary for me to understand yours.—I am the more anxious to receive it as *this* is my second answer to your letter—the first I have destroyed—because on considering yours more attentively—it appeared to me that I had misunderstood you and that my reply would in that case only produce perplexity.—Pray then—write to me openly and *harshly* if you please —if there is anything you wish to know or to say—I am ready to

---

[2] Murray must have sent Byron the manuscript of Sir John Malcolm's *History of Persia*, for it was not published until the following year.

[3] Unidentified.

[1] The enclosed note, signed B.H. [possibly Hobhouse's father Benjamin Hobhouse], says that there is a danger, if Byron takes possession of Newstead before everything is arranged, that the purchaser, if "hostilely disposed" may threaten him with an action for disturbing his property.

answer or to listen—but whether present or absent—in enmity or in charity you are the last person I would wish to misunderstand.———
My best thanks are due to Sir R. for the invitation which accompanied your letter—it is however as well that I have delayed accepting it—as I have not interfered with your Durham gaieties of the 6th.—I hope on my return to London to receive your reply—I shall be there next week.—————

ever most affectionately yours

BYRON

[P.S.]—I have read your letter once more—and it appears to me that I must have said something which makes you apprehend a misunderstanding on my part of your sentiments—and an intention of renewing a subject already discussed between us.—Of this I am not conscious—and whatever my regrets or my regards might have been—or may be—I have not so far lost all self-command as to betray either to an extent that would render them troublesome to you; and my memory is still retentive enough not to require the repetition that you are attached to another.———

[TO JOHN MURRAY]   *August 2d. 1814*

Dear Sir—Enclosed is a letter from Mr. Moore.——Thanks for the letters—but you have neither sent nor said a word of sending the Edin[burg]h Rev[ie]w though I particularly requested it—pray send it—as I have not my copy—Ridgway generally saves one for me—and if you have none by you, you can obtain mine from him.——I am sorry to see that the papers have by some means obtained & published a copy (an imperfect one by the bye) of some lines[1]—I cannot divine how—as none were ever given except to the person to whom they were addressed—but there they are with some errors and my name to them—it cannot be helped now—but it is very unfair in the E[dito]rs to do this without at least asking a writer's consent—besides—putting a name without permission is not much better—but no matter—it seems fated that I am never to be left quiet even when disposed to remain so.—Do not forget the E[dinburgh] R[eview] again—and

---

[1] The *Condolatory Address* to Lady Jersey. See May 29, 1814, to Lady Jersey, note 2.

present my best thanks to Sir Jno. Malcolm for a very beautiful poem.[2]—

ever yrs truly

B

P.S.—[two lines crossed out]

[TO JOHN HANSON]   *August 3d. 1814*

Dear Sir/—Very well—twenty five thousand is the forfeit[1]—but there are little subordinate things of furniture expences on the estate—&c.—how have you discussed them?—Whatever our agreement is to be—let it be such as may bring *no more law*—and with regard to the business altogether—Mr. C[laughton] may be a loser—but I am certainly no great gainer—by the concern—altogether—when delay—confusion—and expence consequent on his demurs are considered.—The next thing *we* have to consider is something immediate in arrangement as to letting the property &c.—somebody must go down and settle the rents—neither the *keeper* nor Mealey—nor any of the old set must remain—the *first* (the keeper) is the greatest rascal and sells the game—in short—we must turn over a new leaf—and since the property is still to be mine—at all events it shall not be as it has been.———Then Rochdale—I suppose you will look about for a purchaser there—no matter what—or who—I would sell it for half it's value—so that I could extricate myself once *clear* with the creditors.—I shall be in London early next week—in the mean time let me hear from you.—

ever yrs. truly

B

[TO JOHN MURRAY]   *August 3d. 1814*

Dear Sir/—It is certainly a little extraordinary that you have not sent the E[dinburgh] R[eview] as I requested—and hoped it would not require a note a day to remind you.—I see *advertisements* of Lara & Lara & Jacqueline—pray *why?* when I requested you to postpone publication till my return to town.—[two lines crossed out] I have a

2 See July 31, 1814, to Murray, note 1
1 Claughton finally forfeited £25,000 of his down payment of £28,000, and Newstead reverted to Byron. But Hanson made no serious effort to sell the estate and continued to lend a sympathetic ear to Claughton's professed wish to renew the contract, which he never did.

most amusing epistle from the Ettrick Bard Hogg[1]—in which speaking
of his bookseller—whom he denominates the "shabbiest" of the
trade—for not "lifting his bills" he adds in so many words "G–d d—n
him and them both" this is a pretty prelude to asking *you* to adopt him
(the said Hogg) but this he wishes—and if you please you & I will
talk it over—he has a poem ready for the press (and your *bills* too if
"*lift*able") and bestows some benedictions on Mr. R[ogers] for his
abduction of Lara from the forthcoming Mis[cellany].—

yrs. ever
B

P.S.—Seriously—I think Mr. Hogg would suit you very well—and
surely he is a man of great powers and deserving of encouragement
——I must knock out a tale for him—and *you* should at all events
consider before you reject his suit.—Scott is gone to the Orkneys in a
Gale of wind[2]—and Hogg says that during the said Gale "he is sure
that S[cott] is not quite at his ease to say the best of it"—Ah! I wish
these home keeping bards could taste a Mediterranean White Squall
or the Gut[3] in a Gale of wind—or even the bay of Biscay with no wind
at all.—

[TO THOMAS MOORE]   *Hastings, August 3d, 1814*

By the time this reaches your dwelling, I shall (God wot) be in
town again probably. I have been here renewing my acquaintance with
my old friend Ocean; and I find his bosom as pleasant a pillow for an
hour in the morning as his daughter's of Paphos could be in the twi-
light. I have been swimming and eating turbot, and smuggling neat
brandies and silk handkerchiefs,—and listening to my friend Hodgson's
raptures about a pretty wife-elect of his,—and walking on cliffs, and
tumbling down hills, and making the most of the "dolce far-niente" for
the last fortnight. I met a son of Lord Erskine's, who says he has been
married a year, and is the "happiest of men;" and I have met the
aforesaid H[odgson], who is also the "happiest of men;" so, it is
worth while being here, if only to witness the superlative felicity of

---

[1] James Hogg, the Ettrick Shepherd, was planning at this time a volume of
poetry of the most distinguished writers of the day. Byron had promised him something, but the project fell through, and Hogg published instead *The Poetic Mirror*,
a series of parodies of the leading poets, including Byron.

[2] Scott had gone on a cruise of the Orkney and Shetland Islands and the
Hebrides. Hogg had helped Scott prepare his *Border Minstrelsy*.

[3] An epithet that Byron used for the Strait of Gibraltar.

these foxes, who have cut off their tails, and would persuade the rest to part with their brushes to keep them in countenance.

It rejoiceth me that you like "Lara." Jeffrey is out with his 45th Number, which I suppose you have got. He is only too kind to me, in my share of it, and I begin to fancy myself a golden pheasant, upon the strength of the plumage wherewith he hath bedecked me. But then, "surgit amari," &c.—the gentlemen of the Champion, and Perry, have got hold (I know not how) of the condolatory address to Lady J[ersey] on the picture-abduction by our R * * *[Regent]. and have published them[1]—with my name, too, smack—without even asking leave, or inquiring whether or no! D--n their impudence, and d--n every thing. It has put me out of patience, and so, I shall say no more about it.

You shall have Lara and Jacque (both with some additions) when out; but I am still demurring and delaying, and in a fuss, and so is R[ogers] in his way.

Newstead is to be mine again. Claughton forfeits twenty-five thousand pounds; but that don't prevent me from being very prettily ruined. I mean to bury myself there—and let my beard grow—and hate you all.

Oh! I have had the most amusing letter from Hogg, the Ettrick minstrel and shepherd. He wants me to recommend him to Murray, and, speaking of his present bookseller, whose "bills" are never "lifted," he adds, *totidem verbis,* "God d--n him and them both." I laughed, and so would you too, at the way in which this execration is introduced. The said Hogg is a strange being, but of great, though uncouth, powers. I think very highly of him, as a poet; but he, and half of these Scotch and Lake troubadours, are spoilt by living in little circles and petty societies. London and the world is the only place to take the conceit out of a man—in the milling phrase. Scott, he says, is gone to the Orkneys in a gale of wind;—during which wind, he affirms, the said Scott, "he is sure, is not at his ease,—to say the best of it." Lord, Lord, if these home-keeping minstrels had crossed your Atlantic or my Mediterranean, and tasted a little open boating in a white squall—or a gale in "the Gut"—or the "Bay of Biscay," with no gale at all—how it would enliven and introduce them to a few of the sensations!—to say nothing of an illicit amour or two upon shore, in the way of essay upon the Passions, beginning with simple adultery, and compounding it as they went along.

[1] *The Champion* of July 31, 1814, published Byron's verses on the episode of the Prince Regent's returning Lady Jersey's picture, naming Byron as the author, and Perry's *Morning Chronicle* quoted the lines on August 1, 1814.

I have forwarded your letter to Murray,—by the way, you had addressed it to *Miller*. Pray write to me, and say what art thou doing? "Not finished!"—Oons! how is this?—these "flaws and starts" must be "authorised by your grandam,"[2] and are unbecoming of any other author. I was sorry to hear of your discrepancy with the * * s, or rather your abjuration of agreement. I don't want to be impertinent, or buffoon on a serious subject, and am therefore at a loss what to say.

I hope nothing will induce you to abate from the proper price of your poem, as long as there is a prospect of getting it. For my own part, I have, *seriously*, and *not whiningly* (for that is not my way—at least, it used not to be) neither hopes, nor prospects, and scarcely even wishes. I am, in some respects, happy, but not in a manner that can or ought to last,—but enough of that. The worst of it is, I feel quite enervated and indifferent. I really do not know, if Jupiter were to offer me my choice of the contents of his benevolent cask,[3] what I would pick out of it. If I was born, as the nurses say, with a "silver spoon in my mouth," it has stuck in my throat, and spoiled my palate, so that nothing put into it is swallowed with much relish,—unless it be cayenne. However, I have grievances enough to occupy me that way too;—but for fear of adding to yours by this pestilent long diatribe, I postpone the reading them, *sine die*. Ever, dear M., yours, &c.

P.S.—Don't forget my godson.[4] You could not have fixed on a fitter porter for his sins than me, being used to carry double without inconvenience. * * * * * * *

[TO JOHN JACKSON]   *August 3d. 1814*

Dear Jack—Grimaldi has sent me some tickets for his benefit at the Wells[1] which I only received the other day and not in time to go there.—Will you pay him five guineas for them & I will settle with you when I come to town—his address is—Prospect Cottage Spa fields—

ever yrs. truly
BYRON

[TO JOHN MURRAY]   *August 4th. 1814*

Not having received the slightest answer to my last 3 letters—nor

[2] *Macbeth*, Act III, scene 4.
[3] *Iliad*, Book XXIV, lines 527–533. According to Homer, Zeus bestowed gifts from two urns, one of evils and one of blessings.
[4] Moore's child was not a son but a daughter, born August 14, 1814, and christened Olivia Byron Moore. She died soon after she was born.
[1] Joseph Grimaldi (1779–1837), actor and pantomimist, began his career at Sadler's Wells, but he also played for many years at Drury Lane.

the book (the last Number of the E[dinburgh] R[eview]) which they requested—I presume that you were the unfortunate person who perished in the Pagoda[1] on Monday last—and address this rather to your executors than yourself—regretting that you should have had the ill luck to be the sole victim on that joyous occasion.——I beg leave then to inform these gentlemen (whoever they may be) that I am a little surprised at the previous neglect of the deceased—and also at observing an advertisement of an approaching publication on Saturday next—against the which I protested & do protest—for the present.[2]———

yrs. (or theirs) &c.

B

[TO JOHN MURRAY]   *August 5th. 1814*

Dear Sir/—E[dinburgh] R[eview] is arrived—thanks—I enclose Mr. Hob[hous]e's letter from which you will perceive the work you have made—however—I have done—you must send my rhymes to the Devil your own way.—It seems also that the "faithful & spirited likeness" is another of your publications—I wish you joy of it—but it is no likeness—that is the print—seriously—if I *have* delayed your journey to S[cotland] I am sorry that you carried your complaisance so far—particularly as upon trifles you have a more summary method—witness the grammar of H[obhouse]'s "bit of prose" which has put him & me into a fever.[1]—You don't condole with me about the Champion's seizure & publication of the lines on the picture[2]—of which I knew nothing and am in a very bad humour at the proceeding—I gave no copy whatever (except to Ly. J[ersey]) and had not even one of my own.—Hogg must translate his own words—"*lifting*" is a quotation from his letter—together with "God d—n &c." which I suppose requires no translation.—I was unaware of the contents of Mr. M[oore]'s letter—I think your offer very handsome—but of that you & he must judge—If he can get more—you won't wonder that he should accept it—Out with Lara—since it must be—the tome looks pretty enough—

---

[1] The reference is to a grand national jubilee on August 1, 1814, celebrating the anniversary of the Battle of the Nile and the centenary of the accession of the family of Brunswick, during which a Chinese pagoda in St. James's Park caught fire and at least one person was lost in the fire.

[2] Byron had not given his permission for the publication of *Lara*, but Murray went ahead and published it.

[1] Byron had asked Hobhouse to write a note to *Lara* explaining that the name only was Spanish and that the setting was in no particular country.

[2] See Aug. 3, 1814, to Moore, note 1.

on the outside.————I shall be in town next week—& in the mean-time wish you a pleasant journey.—[nine lines crossed out]

yrs. truly
B

[TO JOHN HANSON] *August 10th. 1814*

Dear Sir/—I returned to town last night—what news?—I would call but my horses do not return till tomorrow—some person called here to make some enquiries about Newstead (selling or letting) during my absence—the servant directed him to you—has such a person appeared?——*when—how—& where*—is our finale with Mr. C[laughto]n to take place?—soon I trust—as I wish to leave town again in a few days.—

yrs. ever truly
B

[TO ANNABELLA MILBANKE] *August 10th 1814*

I will answer your question as openly as I can.—I did—do—and always shall love you—and as this feeling is not exactly an act of will—I know no remedy and at all events should never find one in the sacrifice of your comfort.—When an acquaintance commenced—it appeared to me from all that I saw and heard—that you were the woman most adapted to render any man (who was neither inveterately foolish nor wicked) happy—but I was informed that you were attached if not engaged—and very luckily—to a person for whose success—all the females of the family—where I received my intelligence—were much interested.——Before such powerful interest—and your supposed inclinations—I had too much humility or pride to hazard importunity or even attention—till I at last learned—almost by accident—that I was misinformed—as to the engagement[1]—the rest you know—and I will not trouble you with "a twice told tale" "signifying nothing."————————What your own feelings and objections were and are I have not the right and scarcely the wish to enquire—it is enough for me that they exist—they excite neither astonishment nor dis-pleasure—it would be a very hard case—if a woman were obliged to account for her repugnance—you would probably like me if you could —and as you cannot—I am not quite coxcomb enough to be surprized at a very natural occurrence.——You ask me how far my peace is— or may be affected by those feelings towards you?——I do not know— not quite enough to invade yours—or request from your pity what I cannot owe to your affection.————I am interrupted—perhaps it is as well upon such a subject.—

ever most truly yrs.
B

[1] Annabella's supposed engagement to George Eden.

155

I was *not* alone, nor will be while I can help it. Newstead is not yet decided. Claughton is to make a grand effort by Saturday week to complete,—if not, he must give up twenty-five thousand pounds, and the estate, with expenses, &c. &c. If I resume the Abbacy, you shall have due notice, and a cell set apart for your reception, with a pious welcome. Rogers, I have not seen, but Larry and Jacky[1] came out a few days ago. Of their effect, I know nothing.

* * * * * * * * * * * * * * *

There is something very amusing in *your* being an Edinburgh Reviewer.[2] You know, I suppose, that T[hurlow] is none of the placidest, and may possibly enact some tragedy on being told that he is only a fool. If, now, Jeffrey were to be slain on account of an article of yours, there would be a fine conclusion. For my part, as Mrs. Winifred Jenkins says, "he has done the handsome thing by me,"[3] particularly in his last number; so, he is the best of men and the ablest of critics, and I won't have him killed,—though I dare say many wish he were, for being so good-humoured.

Before I left Hastings, I got in a passion with an ink-bottle, which I flung out of the window one night with a vengeance;—and what then? why, next morning I was horrified by seeing that it had struck, and split upon, the petticoat of Euterpe's graven image in the garden, and grimed her as if it were on purpose. Only think of my distress,—and the epigrams that might be engendered on the Muse and her misadventure.[4]

I had an adventure, almost as ridiculous, at some private theatricals near Cambridge—though of a different description—since I saw you last. I quarrelled with a man in the dark for asking me who I was (insolently enough, to be sure), and followed him into the green-room (a *stable*) in a rage, amongst a set of people I never saw before. He turned out to be a low comedian, engaged to act with the amateurs, and to be a civil-spoken man enough, when he found out that nothing very pleasant was to be got by rudeness. But you would have been amused with the row, and the dialogue, and the dress—or rather the undress—of the party, where I had introduced myself in a devil of a hurry, and the astonishment that ensued. I had gone out of the theatre,

---

[1] *Lara* and *Jacqueline*.
[2] Moore reviewed four volumes of Lord Thurlow's poems (*Edinburgh Review*, Vol. XXIII, page 411 ff. Sept., 1814).
[3] The last letter in *Humphry Clinker*.
[4] For an account of this misadventure see Moore, I, 575n.

for coolness, into the garden;—there I had tumbled over some dogs, and, coming away from them in very ill-humour, encountered the man in a worse, which produced all this confusion.

Well—and why don't you "launch?"[5]—Now is your time. The people are tolerably tired with me, and not very much enamoured of * * [Wordsworth], who has just spawned a quarto of metaphysical blank verse, which is nevertheless only a part of a poem.[6]

Murray talks of divorcing Larry and Jacky—a bad sign for the authors, who, I suppose, will be divorced too, and throw the blame upon one another. Seriously, I don't care a cigar about it, and I don't see why Sam should.

Let me hear from and of you and my godson. If a daughter, the name will do quite as well.[7] * * * * *

Ever, &c.

August 13th, 1814

I wrote yesterday to Mayfield,[1] and have just now enfranked your letter to mamma. My stay in town is so uncertain (not later than next week) that your packets for the north may not reach me; and as I know not exactly where I am going—however, *Newstead* is my most probable destination, and if you send your despatches before Tuesday, I can forward them to our new ally. But, after that day, you had better not trust to their arrival in time.

* * [Lord Kinnaird] has been exiled from Paris, *on dit*, for saying the Bourbons were old women.[2] The Bourbons might have been content, I think, with returning the compliment. * * * *

I told you all about Jacky and Larry yesterday;—they are to be separated,—at least, so says the grand M[urray], and I know no more of the matter. Jeffrey has done me more than "justice;" but as to tragedy—um!—I have no time for fiction at present. A man cannot paint a storm with the vessel under bare poles, on a lee-shore. When I

[5] Moore's *Lalla Rookh* was finished but was not published until 1817.

[6] Wordsworth's *The Excursion* was published in 1814, with a preface saying that it was part of a longer poem to be called *The Recluse*.

[7] See Aug. 3, 1814, note 4.

[1] Moore had moved into Mayfield Cottage, near Ashbourne, Derbyshire, in June, 1813.

[2] Charles, 8th Lord Kinnaird (1780–1826), M.P. for Leominster, was a collector of pictures and lived abroad a great deal. He later, with his brother Douglas Kinnaird, visited Byron in Venice. He was twice expelled from France because of his disrespect for the Bourbons, in 1814, and again in 1816.

get to land, I will try what is to be done, and, if I founder, there be plenty of mine elders and betters to console Melpomene.[3]

When at Newstead, you must come over, if only for a day—should Mrs. M[oore] be *exigeante* of your presence. The place is worth seeing, as a ruin, and I can assure you there *was* some fun there, even in my time; but that is past. The ghosts, however, and the gothics, and the waters, and the desolation, make it very lively still.

Ever, dear Tom, yours, &c.

[TO LADY MELBOURNE]   *August 15th. 1814*

Dear Lady M[elbourn]e.—Perceiving by the papers that you are in town—(where I have only been within these last few days) I have sent you some grouse (4 brace) and hope that they are fresh & in eatable order.——I shall leave London before ye. end of the week—or about it—and if you are not inscrutable and unvisitable by mortals will take my chance of finding you some morning at home.—I have been at the Sea and in it—and am going to Newstead I believe for a week or so—& thence I know not whither.—You will not be sorry to hear that of C[aroline] I have heard nothing for some time—and that there is every reason to believe that we are come to a conclusive and happy separation.——[two lines crossed out] I see that the Continent is happy in the presence of Lady Blarney[1]—the Princess of Wales and various other persons of honour—and I hear that our friend of indifferent memory Me. de Stael has been bowed out of Paris for some of those bright remarks which will doubtless appear in her next preface.—

ever yrs.

B

[TO ANNABELLA MILBANKE]   *August 16th. 1814*

Very well—now we can talk of something else.[1]——Though I do not think an intimacy which does not extend beyond a few letters and still fewer interviews in the course of a year could be particularly injurious to either party—yet—as—if I recollect rightly—you told me

---

[3] Jeffrey had written to Moore expressing a wish that Byron would write a tragedy.

[1] Byron's nickname for Lady Bessborough.

[1] In reply to Byron's letter of Aug. 10, 1814, Annabella had written so convoluted a response to his frank confession of love for her, that he concluded that his suit there was hopeless.

that some remarks had been made upon the subject—it is perhaps as well that even that should end—this is a point upon which yourself can best determine—and in which I have nothing to do but to acquiesce.——I shall leave London in a few days—but any letter addressed to me here will be forwarded—should you deem it proper to answer this.———You have not said anything of your health lately from which I infer that it is improved—you have had a good escape from the last town winter which was bustling beyond precedent and has I dare say provided invalids for the next ten years.——Pray make my best respects to Sir R. and Lady M. and accept them for yourself.—

ever yrs. very sincerely
B

[TO ————¹] *Albany—August 17th. 1814*

Madam—I have only been favoured with your letter this evening or it had been acknowledged before—a mistake in the address has occasioned some delay in it's delivery.—With your son's talents I am acquainted—I need hardly add that I sincerely admire them—nor have I ever encountered a difference of opinion upon the subject amongst the many I have heard express their sentiments on his abilities natural and acquired—he is indeed a wonderful young man & will I trust continue to be a comfort to you—an honour to himself—and—one day—to his country.—But to the point—the Review you mention would undoubtedly be of considerable service in forwarding your object—but with it's conductors I have a very slight acquaintance and no influence whatsoever—the Editor I have never even seen —but I believe that the principal persons connected with the critical journals are very jealous of any interference—and that mine would have no good effect upon their decision—be assured—if I thought I had the power—it's exertion should not be wanting.—The poem from which you have done me the honour to enclose some extracts—I saw in M.S. last year in the hands of Mr. Murray and expressed my wonder that he did not publish it—his answer was neither one thing nor the other—and since that time I heard no more of it—you must be well aware that amongst "the *trade*" as they are called—there is a caprice and a quackery and a fashion and a disregard of unsupported Merit which is astonishing when their interest would be so much

---

¹ A note at the end of the Hobhouse proof of this letter suggests that it was written to Mrs. Dallas, whose son's poems were published by Murray.

advanced by a contrary conduct—and even Mr. M[urray] though a worthy and an able man is not at times wholly free from this leaven of his profession.—In ninety nine instances out of a hundred I should advise a young man who had his way to make in the world—by all means to discontinue the unprofitable and "profane art of poem making" but I could not conscientiously do so by your son—whose poems have been so very generally felt and acknowledged.— —I had last year some conversation with a young friend of mine and schoolfellow of Mr. Walker's at Salthill[2] on the subject of this letter—to whom I expressed myself as sincerely & more particularly than I can to you within the limits of a letter.—

[TO JOHN HANSON]   *August 18th. 1814*

Dear Sir/—Mr. C[laughto]n called on me today but of course we came to nothing decisive—I wish you could see him tomorrow—and on Saturday we shall come to something definitive one way or the other.

ever yrs. truly

B

[TO JOHN MURRAY]   *August 18th. 1814*

Dear Sir/—There is no occasion to put yourself out of humour in your answer to Mr. St. G.[1] nor would it answer my purpose so to do— I dare say his opinion is very sincere and that you will find many more of the same; it only proves that it had been better for me (& you too) if I had adhered to my intention and is a good lesson for the future.— I shall probably hear something of N[ewstea]d today.— —Penrose[2] is most amusing—I never read so much of a book at one sitting in my life—he kept me up half the night and made me dream of him the other half:—it has all the air of truth—and is most entertaining & interesting in every point of view.— —

yrs. truly

B

2 Unidentified.
1 Unidentified.
2 See Nov. 28, 1813, to Murray (*a*), note 1 (Vol. 3, p. 176).

You can hardly have a better modern work than Sismondi's[1]—but he has since published another on the Literature of Italy—Spain &c. which I would willingly recommend though it is not completed and contains only the South as yet—if you have not got it—on my return to London I would gladly forward it.—In his Italian Commonwealths there are two characters which interested me much—Eccelin,—and Giovanni Galeazzo[2] to say nothing of many others—I am a very bad French scholar—but can read when I like the subject—though I prefer Italian.—Davila—Guicc[i]ardini[3]—Robertson—& Hume—you know without my telling you are the best "modern Historians"—and Gibbon is well worth a hundred perusals—Watson's Philips' [sic] of Spain—& Coxe's Spain & Austria are dry enough[4]—but there is some advantage to be extracted even from them—Vertot's Revolutions[5]—(but *he* writes not history but romance)—the best thing of that kind I met with by accident at Athens in a Convent Library in old & not "very choice Italian" I forget the title—but it was a history in some 30 tomes of all Conjurazioni whatsoever from Cataline's down to Fiesco of Lavagna's in Genoa—and Braganza's in Lisbon—I read it through (having nothing else to read) & having nothing to compare it withal thought it perfection.—I have a Tacitus with Latin on one page & Italian on the other among my books in town—I should think the original by itself a little severe on a feminine reader & will send you that if you would like it—it is a foreign edition.————The only books I brought with me here are a few Novels—Essayists—and plays—with one classic—and a volume of Machiavel containing his

[1] Byron owned the 1813 Paris edition of Sismondi's *De la Littérature du Midi de l'Europe* (4 Vols.), and later he drew on Sismondi's *Histoire des Républiques Italiennes du Moyen Age* for the background of his historical drama *Marino Faliero*.

[2] In his journal of March 20, 1814, Byron mentioned that he was much taken, in reading Sismondi, with the characters of Giovanni Galeazzo and Eccelino, and he referred to a fine picture by Fuseli of "Ezzelin" over the body of Meduna. (But see *LJ*, II, 405n.)

[3] Enrico Caterino Davila (1576–1631) wrote *Istoria delle Guerra Civile di Francia*, which went into 200 editions; Francesco Guicciardini (1483–1540), Italian historian and statesman, wrote *Storia d'Italia* (1561–1564), a scientific history full of details observed objectively, dealing with the period from 1494 to 1532.

[4] Robert Watson, *The History of the Reign of Philip the Second*; William Coxe, *Memoirs of the Kings of Spain of the House of Bourbon, from the Accession of Philip the Fifth to the Death of Charles the Third: 1700 to 1788*. (3 vols. 1812.)

[5] René Aubert de Vertot (1655–1735), *Histoire des Révolutions Arrivées dans le Gouvernement de la République Romaine*. He also wrote histories of revolutions in Portugal and Sweden.

Principe and life of Castruccio.—You should read Denina's Greece[6] also—and Roscoe's Lorenzo—& Leo[7]—but I shall only bore you with my *shoulds* and suggestions—so there's an end.———You ask me what my "occupations" are?—the "dolce far niente"—nothing—— what my "projects" are?—I have none—how my "health" is?—very well.—I quite agree with you on the score of "fashionable" life— though I don't perceive that any other is either better or worse—all contemplative existence is bad—one should *do* something—since

"All partial evil's universal Good"[8]

even mischief is remotely productive of advantage to some one or something in this best of all possible worlds—now the worst of civilization & refinement is that we are reduced to a most insipid medium between good and harm and must get very much out of the beaten path to do either.——It will give me much gratification some day or other to see the "early essays" you mention and in the mean time I shall not like my own the worse for resemblance.—

very sincerely yrs.
B

P.S.—I wrote my last so hurriedly being on ye eve of leaving London—that I omitted to mention (with my best thanks & respects to Sir R.) that I regret it will not be in my power to proceed to Seaham during the present year.—My Northern expedition (with a son of Sir Jno. Sinclair's to his father's) during the commencement of which I could have had the pleasure of joining you for a few days has been put off—and I shall not see Scotland with which I wished to have renewed my acquaintance for some time to come.—

[TO JOHN MURRAY]   *August 27th. 1814*

Dear Sir,—I have nothing particular to trouble you with but a letter which I yesterday franked to you from Mr. Hogg & which I hope will lead to a lucrative alliance between you.—If any thing occurs I shall avail myself of your good-natured offer to undertake any slight commission in my behalf—

ever yrs.
B

[6] Carlo Giovanni Maria Denina, *Istoria Politica e Letteraria della Grecia*. 4 tom. Torino, 1781.

[7] William Roscoe, *The Life of Lorenzo de Medici called The Magnificent*, and *The Life and Pontificate of Leo the Tenth*.

[8] Pope, *Essay on Man*, I, 292.

Newstead. August 31st. 1814

Dear Sir/—I enclose a letter on the subject of a small purchase of land which was to have been bought by Mr. Claughton—the owner wants £1500 for about 80 acres.—I want your advice about the matter—and a speedy answer—I send you both plan & letter.—From Mr. Claughton I have heard—stating "that he is ready now & at all times to renew & fulfil" his quondam "contract"—I have kept the letter which I wish you to see—& I told him in reply to write to you if he continued in the same mind—perhaps you have heard from him & will let me know—at all events—I suppose you have made the *papers* elucidatory of our title be *restored*.—These last are particularly important & I hope have been attended to.———I wish much to hear from you—& what has been done about Rochdale?—& I propose to sell this property if we can find an adequate purchaser—it is with a view to this that I think of purchasing the parcels of Blidworth land (if Mr. C[laughton] meant to do so) but I think the man wants too much for them.—With my best rem[embrance]s to you & yours believe me very truly

yr. friend & Sert.
B

P.S.—I ordered Mealey to write to you about the *taxes*—they persist in surcharging although *paid* in *St. James's* last year to *Mr. Reeves* who has written again & again & certified to no purpose—what is to be *done*? I will not submit to this—if law or justice can be had pray direct me as I am determined [not] to submit to the imposition—we must go to law with them—let me know the proper steps—as I can't answer for my temper if they attempt to seize—and am at the same time unwilling to do any thing violent if it can be helped.

———

Newstead Abbey—Septr. 2d. 1814

Dear Sir,—I am obliged by what you have sent[1]—but would rather not see anything of the kind—we have had enough already of these things good & bad—& next month you need not trouble yourself to collect even the *"higher"* generation—on my account.—It gives me much pleasure to hear of Mr. Hob[hous]e's & Mr. Meriv[a]le's good

---

[1] Periodicals with reviews of Byron's poetry.

entreatment by the Journals you mention.—I still think Mr. Hogg & yourself might make out an alliance—*Dodsley's*[2] was I believe the last decent thing of the kind & *his* had great success in it's day & lasted several years—but then he had the double advantage of editing & publishing;—the Spleen—& several of *Gray's* odes—much of *Shenstone* & many others of good repute made their first appearance in his collection—now with the support of Scott—Wordsworth—Southey—&c.—I see little reason why you should not do as well—and if once fairly established you would have assistance from the youngsters I dare say—Stratford Canning (whose Bonaparte is excellent)[3] & many others—and Moore & Hobhouse & I would try a fall now & then (if permitted) and you might coax Campbell too into it—by the bye—*he* has an unpublished (though printed) poem on a Scene in Germany (Bavaria I think)[4] which I saw last year—that is perfectly magnificent & equal to himself—I wonder he don't publish it.————Oh—do you recollect Sharpe (the engraver's) mad letter about not engraving Phillips' picture of Lord *Foley?*[5] (as he blundered it)—well—I have traced it I think—it seems by the papers a preacher of Johanna Southcote's[6] is named *Foley*—& I can no way account for the said Sharpe's confusion of words & ideas—but by that of his head's running on Johanna & her apostles—it was a mercy he did not say Lord *"Tozer"*:[7] you know of course that Sharpe is a believer in this new (old) Virgin of spiritual impregnation.————I long to know what she will produce—her being with child at 65 is indeed a miracle—but her getting any one to beget it—a greater.————If you were not going to Paris

---

[2] Robert Dodsley (1703–1764) published a *Collection of Poems, by Several Hands* in three volumes in 1748. It was enlarged and grew to six volumes by 1758, and became the source through which most readers discovered contemporary poetry. Dodsley's fame rests, however, chiefly upon his collection of Old English Plays. James Hogg was preparing a collection of contemporary poets, which Byron was encouraging Murray to publish.

[3] See April 26, 1814, to Murray (*b*), note 1.

[4] Thomas Campbell's poem was called "Lines on Leaving a Scene in Bavaria."

[5] Thomas Foley, 3rd Baron Foley of Kidderminster (1780–1833). William Sharp (1729–1824) was the engraver, who later attached himself to Joanna Southcott.

[6] Joanna Southcott (Byron regularly misspelled her name Southcote) (1750–1814) became a Methodist in 1791. She began prophesying in 1792, and in 1813 she announced that she was to become the mother of Shiloh, a new Messiah. In March, 1814, she became ill. She had a great following of believers, including Sharp the engraver. She died on December 27, 1814. The autopsy revealed dropsy as the cause of the symptoms and of her death.

[7] The Rev. Mr. Tozer had announced to a crowded audience in his chapel that the birth of Shiloh would take place in November.

—or Scotland I could send you some game—if you remain—let me
know.———

yrs. very truly
BYRON

P.S.—A word or two of "Lara" which your enclosure brings before
me.—It is of no great promise separately but as connected with the
other tales—it will do very well for the *vols* you mean to publish—I
would recommend this arrangement—Childe H[arold]—the smaller
poems—Giaour—Bride—Corsair—Lara—the last completes the
series—and it's very likeness renders it necessary to the others.—
Cawthorne writes that they are publishing *E[nglish]* *B[ards]* in
Ireland—pray enquire into this—because *it must* be stopped—

[TO THOMAS CLAUGHTON]   *Newstead Abbey.—Septr. 4th. 1814*

Dear Sir—Whenever your business or leisure prompts you to visit
this place you can take your choice of it's apartments[.] I will take care
that they are ready for your reception.—The key of the cellar will be
left with Murray so that I hope you will not find it more uncomfortable than heretofore.———I cannot yet fix any day for my departure—
but probably it will take place within the ensuing ten days—but if you
are disposed to come here before that period I trust you will not doubt
that you will be very welcome. I have to thank you for your answer on
the subject of Mr. Kirkby's lands—and shall come to some agreement
with him on the subject.—Upon the subject of Newstead I will be
explicit with you—it *is* my intention to sell the estate—and I would
certainly rather renew the sale with yourself on the same terms—than
part with it to any other—even should chance or circumstances offer a
more advantageous purchase—upon this point you can determine for
yourself—you have the preference.—In the mean time I have not
interfered with the new tenants—nor disturbed or removed any of the
furniture—perhaps it may be as well even to leave the things which
you directed to be sent to Haydock (spoons &c.) till you arrive and
may choose to order their removal in person—as the plate may hardly
be safe in a parcel—but if required they shall be forwarded now.———
I hope you are now satisfied that "the channel of Negotiation is left
open" nor would it ever have been closed on my part—but for the
necessity that existed of some decision one way or the other for the
time being; but I am by no means insensible to the handsome part you
have acted in not seeking fresh litigation for the purpose of delay, nor

to the whole of your recent conduct, and have only to regret the untoward circumstances which produced the temporary (or final) relinquishment of your purchase.—

Believe me very truly yrs.

BYRON

P.S.—I believe there is a Gun of yours here—I have long given up sporting—but you will find plenty of game (by all accounts) and if you like to bring any friend with you there will be room & birds enough for both.—The gun (if here) shall be taken care of & not used except by yourself.——

[TO JOHN HANSON] *Newstead Abbey.—Septr. 6th. 1814*

My dear Sir/—I enclose you my letters from Mr. Claughton which you will take care to preserve.—In answer I told him that it *is* my intention to sell the Estate—and that I give him the preference on the old terms.—Surely if he could or can complete—it would be but fair that he should be permitted so to do rather than any other—as he has already made such a sacrifice.—I have referred him to you—with his propositions—if any are intended—of course he must be ready with a large sum & security for all—before we proceed.—He wants the loan of a room &c. on a visit on business—this I could not refuse him nor any civility in my power—for as things now stand—he has paid pretty dearly for his non-completion.—I will write again in a day or two—but let me hear that you have received these letters safely—and your opinion thereupon.——About the taxes I will fight till the last—Mealey can tell all particulars—he has got receipts from Mr. Reeves—it is a *job* of the Clerks in this neighbourhood to get a few pounds—but cost what it may I must & will resist them.—I see no great use in keeping Newstead *now* (after having resolved long ago to part with it) but I will do as you like about it—if C[laughton] can complete—or we can get a tolerable purchaser——but no matter—let us do what can be done about Rochdale.——Pray answer—

ever yrs.

BYRON

P.S.—Many thanks for the *Venison offer*—but *not yet*—I will write when I have an appetite—but thank you once more.—I write in great hurry.——

Newstead Abbey.—Septr. 7th. 1814

Dear Sir/—I should think Mr. Hogg for his own sake as well as yours would be "critical" as Iago himself[1]—in his editorial capacity—and that such a publication would answer his purpose & yours too with tolerable management—you should however have a good number to start with—I mean good in *quality*—in these days there be little fear of not coming up to the mark in quantity.—There must be many "fine things" in Wordsworth—but I should think it difficult to make 6 quartos (the amount of the whole) all fine—particularly the Pedlar's portion of the poem—but there can be no doubt of his powers to do about any thing.———I *am* "very idle" I have read the few books I had with me—& been forced to fish for lack of other argument—I have caught a great many perch and some carp which is a comfort as one would not lose one's labour willingly.—Pray who corrects the press of your vols? I hope "the Corsair" is printed from the copy I corrected with the additional lines in the first Canto.—& some *notes* from Sismondi & Lavater which I gave you to add thereto—the arrangement is very well.—————My cursed people have not sent my papers since Sunday—and I have lost Johanna's divorce from Jupiter—who hath gotten her with prophet?—is it Sharpe?[2]—& how? for I am sure the common materials would not answer so pious a purpose—I should like to buy one of her seals[3]—if salvation can be had at half a guinea a head—the landlord of the Crown & Anchor should be ashamed of himself for charging double for tickets to a mere terrestrial banquet: —I am afraid seriously—that these matters will lend a sad handle to your profane Scoffers and give a loose to much damnable laughter.—I have not seen Hunt's sonnets nor descent of Liberty[4]—he has chosen a pretty place wherein to compose the last.———Let me hear from you before you embark—

ever yrs. very truly
B

P.S.—Mrs. L[eigh] and the children are very well—I have just read to her a sentence from your epistle—and the remark was "how *well* he writes"—so you see—you may set up as Author in person whenever you please.———

[1] "For I am nothing, if not critical." *Othello*, Act II, scene 1.

[2] See Sept. 2, 1814, to Murray, notes 5 and 6.

[3] Joanna Southcott began by sealing up her prophesies, and then she sealed papers containing a text of scripture and a promise of beatitude hereafter. These sealed papers were apparently sold by her followers to the faithful.

[4] *The Descent of Liberty, a Masque,* which Leigh Hunt wrote in prison, was published in 1815.

It is Porson's letter to Travis[1] to which you allude and—if I recollect rightly—one of his remarks (the highest praise to be passed on an Historian) is—that amidst the immensity of reading through which he had tracked Gibbon—not *one* of his *authorities* was misquoted or perverted even unto a syllable—perhaps I am wrong in giving this as from P's preface—for years have elapsed since I saw it—but of the fact as P's opinion—and no one could be a better judge—I am certain.—Porson was slowly extinguishing—while I was a Cantab—I have seen him often—but not in "his happier hour" for to him that of "social pleasure" could not be so termed—he was always—that is daily—intoxicated to brutality ———I hate to think of it—for he was a perfect wonder in powers and attainments.———Newstead is mine again—for the present—Mr. C[laughton] after many delays in completion—relinquished his purchase———I am sorry for it—he has lost a considerable sum in forfeiture by his temporary inability or imprudence—but he has evinced a desire to resume or renew his contract with greater punctuality—& in justice to him—though against the advice of lawyers—and the regrets of relations—I shall not hesitate to give him an opportunity of making good his agreement—but I shall expect—indeed I will not endure such trifling for the future. ——I am much amused with *your* "sovereign good" being placed in *repose*—I need not remind you that this was the very essence of the Epicurean philosophy—and that both the Gods (who concerned themselves with nothing on earth) and the Disciples of the illustrious idler the founder of that once popular sect—defined the *"Τό Καλον"* to consist in literally doing nothing—and that all agitation was incompatible with pleasure.—The truth possibly is that these materialists are so far right—but to enjoy repose we must be weary—and it is to "the heavy laden" that the invitation to "rest" speaks most eloquent music.————You accuse yourself of "apparent inconsistencies"—to me they have not appeared—on the contrary—your consistency has been the most *formidable* Apparition I have encountered—there seem to be no grounds for complaint on one side nor vindication on the other—and as to explanations—*they* are always a puzzle. After one or two letters which lately passed between us—and to which—I must request your pardon for recurring—we—at least *I* (to speak for

---

[1] Richard Porson's most widely read work was his *Letters* to Archdeacon Travis on a disputed passage in the Bible, *I John*, V, 7: "For there are three that bear record in heaven, the Father, the Word, and the Holy Ghost: and these three are one."

myself) could hardly have met without some embarrassment—possibly on both sides—certainly on one—this has been avoided—and so far is a subject of congratulation.——Your letters are generally answered on the day of their arrival so that it can't be very "irksome to me to write soon."——On my return to London which will not take place immediately I shall have great pleasure in forwarding the book offered in my last.—The "Agricola"[2] is beautiful—it is a pity that there are so many objections to a like perusal of Suetonius also; whose portraits are but too faithful even in their coarsest features.———You must be partial to Sallust—but after all there are none like Tacitus & him you have.——

ever yours
B

[TO ANNABELLA MILBANKE] *Newstead Abbey. Septr. 9th 1814*

You were good enough in your last to say that I might write "soon"—but you did not add *often*—I have therefore to apologize for again intruding on your time—to say nothing of patience.—There is something I wish to say—and as I may not see you for some—perhaps for a long time—I will endeavour to say it at once.——A few weeks ago you asked me a question—which I answered—I have now one to propose—to which if improper—I need not add that your declining to reply to it will be sufficient reproof.—It is this.—Are the "objections" —to which you alluded—insuperable?—or is there any line or change of conduct which could possibly remove them?—I am well aware that all such changes are more easy in theory than practice—but at the same time there are few things I would not attempt to obtain your good opinion—at all events I would willingly know the worst—still I neither wish you to promise or pledge yourself to anything—but merely to learn a *possibility* which would not leave you the less a free agent.———When I believed you attached—I had nothing to urge— indeed I have little now—except that having heard from yourself that your affections are not engaged—my importunities may appear not quite so selfish however unsuccessful—It is not without a struggle that I address you once more on this subject—yet I am not very consistent —for it was to avoid troubling you upon it that I finally determined to remain an absent friend rather than become a tiresome guest—if I offend it is better at a distance.———With the rest of my sentiments

---

[2] *De Vita et Moribus Iulii Agricolae* by Tacitus.

you are already acquainted—if I do not repeat them it is to avoid—or at least not increase you displeasure.—

ever yrs. most truly
B

[TO JOHN HANSON] *Septr. 11th. 1814*

My dear Sir,—Since my last I have received the enclosed also from Mr. C[laughto]n.—My meaning is this—if Mr. C[laughton] is disposed to renew & fulfil the contract in such a manner as seems proper to my legal advisers & myself—let him—that is within a reasonable time—if in the interim any other purchaser offers—and Mr. C[laughto]n cannot then complete—why there is an end—I think *November* is the furthest period we can well afford him.————I think it but fair to give him such an opportunity in consideration of the sacrifice he has made.—As to his hints about the delay of furnishing the title &c.—you know a man is loth to blame *himself* in all cases— and as he has paid so round a sum you can't expect him to be in the best of humours—I wonder for my part that he is not in a worse. This place I fully intend to dispose of—unless a wife—a legacy or a lottery ticket—(and I have put in for neither) induced me to retain it:—so if you hear of any monied personage inclined to purchase—we can in the first place let Mr. C[laughto]n have the refusal on the old terms—and in the event of his want of ability or inclination—in the second place— treat with those who are inclined to negociate.———Mealey shall furnish the tax detail forthwith.—I have received a very kind invitation from Lord & Lady P[ortsmouth] for the present month—but I very much doubt if it will be in my power to have the honour of seeing Hurstbourne[1] so soon.—At any rate I must write to thank them—but wait a day or two to be more certain whether I may be able or not to go there.—In the mean time pray present them with my best respects.————I wish very much to have something done about Rochdale or this place—*soon*———

ever yrs. truly
B

[TO JOHN CAM HOBHOUSE] *Newstead Abbey, Septr. 14th. 1814*

My dear Hobhouse—Clau[ghton] has relinquished his purchase and twenty five thousand pounds out of twenty eight do. paid on account—

[1] Hurstbourne was Lord Portsmouth's estate in Hampshire.

and I am Abbot again—it is all signed—sealed and *re*-delivered——
So much for your enquiry—he wishes to *renew*—but I will first see an'
the monies be palpable and tangible—before I recontract with him or
others—though if he could complete I should have no objection, on the
old terms.—But now for other matters:—if a circumstance (which
may happen[1]—but is as unlikely to happen as Johanna's establishing
herself the real Mrs. Trinity)[2] does not occur—I have thoughts of
going direct and directly to Italy—if so—will you come with me?—I
want your opinion first—your advice afterwards—and your company
always:—I am pretty well in funds—having better than £4000 at
Hoares—a note of Murray for £700 (the price of *Larry*) at a *year's*
date last month—and the Newstead Michaelmas will give me from a
thousand to 15– if not 1800—more—I believe it is raised to between
3 & 4000—but then there is land upon *hand* (which of course payeth no
rent for the present & be damned to it) altogether I should have
somewhere about £5000 tangible—which I am not at all disposed to
spend at home—now I would wish to set apart £3000—for the tour—
do you think *that* would enable me to see all *Italy* in a gentlemanly
way?—with as few servants & luggage (except my aperients) as we
can help.—And will you come with me?—you are the only man with
whom I could travel an hour except an *"ιατρος"*[3]—in short you know
my dear H—that with all my bad qualities—(and d————d bad they
are to be sure) I like you better than any body—and we have travelled
together before—and been old friends and all that—and we have a
thorough fellow-feeling & contempt for all things of the sublunary
sort—and so do let us go & call the "Pantheon a cockpit" like the
learned Smelfungus.[4]—The Cash is the principal point—do you think
that will do—viz £3000 clear from embarkation onwards. I have a
world of watches & snuffboxes & telescopes—which would do for the
Mussulmans if we liked to cross from Otranto & see our friends again.
——They are all safe at Hammersleys.——would my *coach* do?—
beds I have & all canteens &c. from *your* Man of Ludgate Hill—with
saddles—pistols—tromboni—& what not.———I shall know tomorrow
or next day—whether I can go—or not—and shall be in town next
week—where I must see you or hear from you—if we set off—it

[1] Byron was waiting for an answer to his tentative proposal (see letter of Sept.
9, 1814) to Annabella Milbanke.
[2] See Sept. 2, 1814, to Murray, note 6.
[3] Physician.
[4] In his *Sentimental Journey through France and Italy* Sterne thus referred to
Smollett whose ill-tempered *Travels in France and Italy* irritated him.

should be in October—and the earlier the better.—Now don't engage yourself—but take up your map—& ponder upon this.—ever dear H.

yrs most affectly.

B

[TO THOMAS MOORE (a)]

Newstead Abbey, September 15, 1814

This is the fourth letter I have begun to you within the month. Whether I shall finish it or not, or burn it like the rest, I know not. When we meet, I will explain *why* I have not written—*why* I have not asked you here, as I wished—with a great many other *whys* and wherefores, which will keep cold. In short, you must excuse all my seeming omissions and commissions, and grant me more *re*mission than St. Athanasius will to yourself, if you lop off a single shred of mystery from his pious puzzle. It is my creed (and it may be St. Athanasius's too) that your article on T * * [Thurlow] will get somebody killed, and *that*, on the *Saints*, get him d——d afterwards, which will be quite enow for one number.[1] Oons, Tom! you must not meddle just now with the incomprehensible; for if Johanna Southcote turns out to be * * * * * * * * * *

Now for a little egotism. My affairs stand thus. To-morrow, I shall know whether a circumstance of importance enough to change many of my plans will occur or not. If it does not, I am off for Italy next month, and London, in the mean time, next week. I have got back Newstead and twenty-five thousand pounds (out of twenty-eight paid already),—as a "sacrifice," the late purchaser calls it, and he may choose his own name. I have paid some of my debts, and contracted others; but I have a few thousand pounds, which I can't spend after my own heart in this climate, and so, I shall go back to the south. Hobhouse, I think and hope, will go with me; but, whether he will or not, I shall. I want to see Venice, and the Alps, and Parmesan cheeses, and look at the coast of Greece, or rather Epirus, from Italy, as I once did—or fancied I did—that of Italy, when off Corfu. All this, however, depends upon an event, which may, or may not, happen. Whether it will, I shall know probably to-morrow, and, if it does, I can't well go abroad at present.

[1] Moore had reviewed four volumes of the poetry of Edward, Lord Thurlow, in the *Edinburgh Review* of September, 1814. The tone of the review was light and condescending and not likely to please Lord Thurlow.

Pray pardon this parenthetical scrawl. You shall hear from me again soon;—I don't call this an answer.

Ever most affectionately, &c.

I have written to you one letter to-night, but must send you this much more, as I have not franked my number, to say that I rejoice in my god-daughter, and will send her a coral and bells, which I hope she will accept, the moment I get back to London.

My head is at this moment in a state of confusion, from various causes, which I can neither describe nor explain—but let that pass. My employments have been very rural—fishing, shooting, bathing, and boating. Books I have but few here, and those I have read ten times over, till sick of them. So, I have taken to breaking soda water bottles with my pistols, and jumping into the water, and rowing over it, and firing at the fowls of the air. But why should I "monster my nothings"[1] to you, who are well employed, and happily too, I should hope. For my part, I am happy too, in my way—but, as usual, have contrived to get into three or four perplexities, which I do not see my way through. But a few days, perhaps a day, will determine one of them.

You do not say a word to me of your Poem. I wish I could see or hear it. I neither could, nor would, do it or its author any harm. I believe I told you of Larry and Jacquy. A friend of mine was reading—at least a friend of his was reading—said Larry and Jacquy in a Brighton coach. A passenger took up the book and queried as to the author. The proprietor said "there were *two*"—to which the answer of the unknown was, "Ay, ay—a joint concern, I suppose, *summot* like Sternhold and Hopkins."[2]

Is not this excellent? I would not have missed the "vile comparison" to have scaped being one of the "Arcades ambo et cantare pares."[3] Good night. Again yours.

[TO ANNABELLA MILBANKE]

Newstead Abbey—Septr. 18th 1814

Your letter has given me a new existence—it was unexpected—I need not say welcome—but *that* is a poor word to express my present

---

[1] "To hear my nothings monster'd" *Coriolanus*, Act II, scene 2.

[2] Thomas Sternhold and John Hopkins published a collection of the *Psalms* in metrical verse in 1547, and added to the number in subsequent editions, which were long popular.

[3] Virgil, *Eclogues*, vii, 4, 5.

feelings—and yet equal to any other—for express them adequately I cannot.—I have ever regarded you as one of the first of human beings —not merely from my own observation but that of others—as one whom it was as difficult *not* to love—as scarcely possible to deserve;— I know your worth—& revere your virtues as I love yourself and if every proof in my power of my full sense of what is due to you will contribute to *your* happiness—I shall have secured my own.——It *is* in your power to render me happy—you have made me so already.—I wish to answer your letter immediately—but am at present scarcely collected enough to do it rationally—I was upon the point of leaving England without hope without fear—almost without feeling—but wished to make one effort to discover—not if I could pretend to your present affections—for to these I had given over all presumption—but whether time—and my most sincere endeavour to adopt any mode of conduct—that might lead you to think well of me—might not eventually in securing your approbation awaken your regard.———These hopes are now dearer to me than ever; dear as they have ever been;— from the moment I became acquainted my attachment has been increasing—& the very follies—give them a harsher name—with which I was beset & bewildered—the conduct to which I had recourse for forgetfulness only made recollection more lively & bitter by the comparisons it forced upon me in spite of Pride—and of Passions which might have destroyed but never deceived me.—————I am going to London on some business which once over—I hope to be permitted to visit Seaham;—your father I will answer immediately & in the mean time beg you will present my best thanks & respects to him & Lady Milbanke.—Will you write to me? & permit me to assure you how faithfully I shall ever be

> yr most attached and obliged Sert.
>
> [BYRON]

[TO JOHN HANSON] *Newstead Abbey. Septr. 18th. 1814*

Dear Sir/—I shall be in London this week where it is highly expedient that I should see you immediately—on business—as I am engaged to a lady with whose name you are not unacquainted—Miss Milbanke—the daughter of Sir R. Milbanke—I have this day received her acceptance—& an invitation from Sir R. to join them in the country. —You will *keep this a secret for the present*—& let me see you soon for obvious reasons—to discuss the state of my affairs—& the expediency

174

of retaining or selling Newstead or Rochdale—also what settlements it will be proper for me to make—with various other details which will arise at our meeting.—Under these circumstances you will see that I shall not be able to have the honour of joining your Son in law the Earl—at Hurstbourne—for the present—(to whom & the Countess I beg my best respects) & I do hope you will do me the favour to meet me in London as soon after the receipt of this as you conveniently can—I have written to Mr. Hodgson about *Newton*[1]—& you shall have his answer on my receiving it—I think him the best man in the world in temper—character—& learning to make your child all you wish him.

very truly yrs.
B

P.S.—I expect to be in town on Thursday next.———[on cover] If absent to be *forwarded immediately*.——

[TO LADY MELBOURNE]   *Newstead Abbey—Septr. 18th. 1814*

My dear Lady M[elbourn]e.—Miss Milbanke has accepted me:—and her answer was accompanied by a very kind letter from your brother—may I hope for your consent too? without it I should be unhappy—even were it not for many reasons important in other points of view—& with it I shall have nothing to require except your good wishes now—and your friendship always.——I lose no time in telling you how things are at present—many circumstances may doubtless occur in this as in other cases to prevent it's completion—but I will hope otherwise.—I shall be in town by thursday—& beg one line to Albany to say you will see me at your own day—hour—& place. ————In course I mean to reform most thoroughly & become "a good man and true" in all the various senses of these respective & respectable appellations—seriously—I will endeavour to make your niece happy not by "my deserts but what I will deserve"[1]—of my deportment you may reasonably doubt—of her merits you can have none.——I need not say that this must be a *secret*—do let me find a few words from you in Albany & believe me ever most affectly yrs.

B

---

1 Hanson's son Newton became, on Byron's recommendation, a pupil of Francis Hodgson.
1 "Plead what I will be not what I have been." *Richard III*, Act IV, scene 4.

Newstead Abbey. Septr. 19th. 1814

I wrote to you yesterday—not very intelligibly I fear—and to your father in a more embarrassed manner than I could have wished—but the fact is that I am even now apprehensive of having misunderstood you and of appearing presumptuous when I am only happy—in the hope that you will not repent having made me more so than I ever thought to have been again.————Perhaps in some points our dispositions are not so contrasted as at times you have supposed—but even if they were—I am not sure that a perfect sameness of character (a kind of impossibility by the bye) would ensure the happiness of two human beings any more than an union of tempers and pursuits of very dissimilar qualities.—Our *pursuits* at least I think are not unlike—you have no great passion for the *world* as it is called—and both have those intellectual resources which are the best—if not the only preventatives of ennui of oneself or others;—*my* habits I trust are not very anti-domestic—I have no pleasure in what is named Conviviality—nor is Gaming nor Hunting my vice or my amusement—and with regard to other and perhaps far more objectionable faults & levities of former conduct—I know that I cannot exculpate myself to my own satisfaction—far less to yours—yet there have been circumstances which would prove that although "sinning" I have also been "sinned against." —I have long stood alone in life—and my disposition though I think not unaffectionate—was yet never calculated to acquire the friendships which are often *born* to others—the few that chance or circumstances have presented I have been fortunate enough to preserve—& some whom I could little have hoped to number amongst them.———I wont go on with this Egotism—will you write to me soon?—I shall be in London on Thursday I think—I do not answer oftener than is least irksome—but permit me to address you occasionally till I can see you —which I wish so much—and yet I feel more tremblingly alive to that meeting than I quite like to own to myself—when your letter arrived my sister was sitting near me and grew frightened at the effect of it's contents—which was even painful for a moment—not a long one—nor am I often so shaken.—I have written—yet hardly a word that I intended to say—except that you must pardon me for repeating so soon how entirely I am

yr. attached & sincere

Byron

P.S.—Do not forget me to your father & mother—whom I hope to call mine.—

There is one point on which—though you have not lately pressed it—I am sure you feel anxious on my behalf—and to this will I speak, I mean—Religion.—When I tell you that I am so convinced of it's importance in fixing the principles—that I could never have had perfect confidence in any woman who was slightly impressed with it's truth—you will hardly believe that I can exact more tolerance than I am willing to grant.—I will not deny that my own impressions are by no means settled—but that they are perverted to the extent which has been imputed to them on the ground of a few passages in works of fiction—I cannot admit to those whose esteem I would secure— although from a secret aversion from explanations & vindications I have hitherto entered into none to those who would never have made the charge but from a wish to condemn rather than convert.—To you —my conduct must be different—as my feelings—I am rather bewildered by the variety of tenets—than inclined to dispute their foundation—in a word—I will read what books you please—hear what arguments you please—and in leaving the choice to your judgment—let it be a proof that my confidence in your understanding & your virtues is equal.—You shall be "my Guide—Philosopher and friend" my whole heart is yours—and if possible let me make it not unworthy of her to whom it is bound—& from whom but one event can divide it.—This is my third letter in three days—I will therefore shorten it—I proceed on my way to London tomorrow.—With every sentiment of respect—and—may I add the word?—Love—

ever yours
BYRON

> Here's to her who long
>   Hath waked the poet's sigh!
> The girl who gave to song
>   What gold could never buy.

My dear Moore, I am going to be married—that is, I am accepted, and one usually hopes the rest will follow. My mother of the Gracchi (that *are* to be) *you* think too strait-laced for me, although the paragon of only children, and invested with "golden opinions of all sorts of

177

men,"[1] and full of "most blest conditions,"[2] as Desdemona herself. Miss Milbanke is the lady, and I have her father's invitation to proceed there in my elect capacity,—which, however, I cannot do till I have settled some business in London, and got a blue coat.

She is said to be an heiress, but of that I really know nothing certainly, and shall not inquire. But I do know, that she has talents and excellent qualities, and you will not deny her judgment, after having refused six suitors and taken me.

Now, if you have any thing to say against this, pray do; my mind's made up, positively fixed, determined, and therefore I will listen to reason, because now it can do no harm. Things may occur to break it off, but I will hope not. In the mean time, I tell you (a *secret*, by the by, —at least, till I know she wishes it to be public) that I have proposed and am accepted. You need not be in a hurry to wish me joy, for one mayn't be married for months. I am going to town to-morrow; but expect to be here, on my way there, within a fortnight.

If this had not happened, I should have gone to Italy. In my way down, perhaps, you will meet me at Nottingham, and come over with me here. I need not say that nothing will give me greater pleasure. I must, of course, reform thoroughly; and, seriously, if I can contribute to her happiness, I shall secure my own. She is so good a person, that—that—in short, I wish I was a better.

Ever, &c.

[TO LADY MELBOURNE] *Albany Septr. 23d. 1814*

My dear Ly. M[elbourn]e.—Many thanks—I am just arrived.—I thought—at least heard that *C[aroline]* was gone to France—see her I will not—if I can help it—and if I did nothing could come of it now—though the consequences might be as unpleasant—but—no matter—much plague—if not misery had probably been saved by her absence.—Perhaps it would be as well to tell her at once—it can hardly be kept a secret long—and the quantity of letters which lately passed between Seaham & Newstead—can hardly have escaped the servants (the letter bags being lost since my last visit) a species of persons from whom I suspect C[aroline] derives most of her information.—If Annabella has any firmness—if she has even any *woman* in her composition—C[aroline] will only lose her labour by trying to mar

[1] "And I have bought/Golden opinions from all sorts of people." *Macbeth*, Act I, scene 7.
[2] *Othello*, Act II, scene 1.

the match—I am glad you liked A[nnabella]'s letter to you—Augusta said *that* to *me* (the decisive one) was the best & prettiest she ever read—it was really perfect—and so much the more welcome—as almost all the former ones were written evidently under embarrassment of feeling & expression.—I have written to my Agent—who is coming to town—to get my property in matrimonial array—whether A[nnabella] is to have any fortune or not—I do not know—and am not very anxious—at least *I* will not be *off* under any circumstances unless she sets me the example—the only thing is this—if she has nothing I had better sell N[ewstea]d again as I can thus give her a better settlement—Mr. C[laughto]n has renewed his offers (on the *old* terms) and begs the refusal—that is to *complete* his former bargain —if I sell——but of these things hereafter—I could also sell R[ochdale] for a round sum—however I can only repeat and very sincerely—that I will settle on her all I can—and that her circumstances will make no difference to me—(if Sir R[alph] is dipped as I have heard is the case) and my property such as it is—shall go as far as it may for her—I would do about any thing rather than lose her now.— Pray let me hear from you—I only wait for my lawyer's arrival—and a day or two's consultation with him—to go down to Seaham—where I am invited "most cordially."—But I must see *you* first—I have so much to say—and am writing to no purpose—but answer me.—

ever yrs. most affectly.

B

P.S.—I heartily hope this will go on—to say nothing of your niece & myself—how much more comfortable we should all be—(if C[aroline] were but rational) meeting occasionally like other people— and not in this half-hostile way—I really shall be all the better for it— one half of my faults & scrapes have arisen from not being settled— and I think that the (Bourbon) Philips of Spain were not more disposed to be docile to their moieties than your nephew (I hope) that is to be.—As to An[nabell]a you cannot think higher of her than I do— I never doubted anything but that she would have me.—After all it is a match of *your* making—and better had it been had *your* proposal been accepted at the time—I am quite horrified in casting up my *moral* accounts of the two intervening years—all which would have been prevented and the heartache into the bargain—had she—but I can't blame her—and there is time yet to do very well.————My Pride (which my Schoolmaster said was my ruling passion) has in all events been spared—she is the only woman to whom I ever proposed in that way—and it is something to have got into the affirmative at last—I wish one or two of one's idols had said No instead—however all that is over—I suppose a married man never gets anybody else—does he?— I only ask for information.————

[TO JOHN HANSON]   *Albany. Septr. 24th. 1814*

My dear Sir/—I only got your letter (& to town) last night—I fear I cannot well come down to F[arleig]h or H[urstbourn]e at present— but I wish so much to see you that I hope it will not be inconvenient for you to come to London—as till we meet—I know not what to settle or how—or even what proposition to make—*we are engaged*— so that there is nothing but our worldly concerns to discuss—& I thought it better to see you first—than to go down to Sir R[alph]'s to come away again so far on business without at least trying to make some previous arrangement.—I have Mr. H[odgso]n's answer about Newton which I will shew you—when we meet.—With my best respects to the Earl and Countess—believe me

yrs. ever truly
BYRON

[TO LADY MELBOURNE]   *Septr. 26th. 1814*

My Dear Ly. M[elbourn]e.—I sent you a long letter on *Saturday* which I hope you received safely.—Annabella has written to me—and says that "a continuance of secrecy appears unnecessary" and that she has already told her own friends.—I only wait to see my Agent—and arrange my worldly affairs—to go down to S[eaham]—but do let me see you first—or at any rate write to me in answer to my last—you had better tell C[aroline] at once—it cannot be helped—she must do her worst—if so disposed—I am very sorry for it if such is her dis- position—& must bear it as well as I can.—Excuse this scrawl—it is the 100th of today—& believe me ever my dear *Zia*

yrs. most dutifully
B

[TO ANNABELLA MILBANKE (*a*)]   *Septr. 26th. 1814*

Your letter has relieved me from the remaining doubts which still lingered round me—it is difficult at first to believe our dearest hopes

180

realized.—I had struggled on in the full conviction that your heart was another's—and at times in the delusion of having recovered mine—but the sight of your handwriting—the casual mention of your name by any third person—all and every thing which recalled you to my memory— and there were few things that did not by connection or *contrast*— conspired to tell me in the sensations they produced that I still coveted "a pearl—worth all my tribe."[1]—I did not require nor expect the explanation you have afforded—but it has removed a weight from my heart—and a restlessness from my brain that would have made me—I know not what—now I am yours—and being dear to you will I hope make me better as it has left me nothing to desire beyond deserving your affection and retaining it.———I came to town on business—which I thought it as well to arrange before I proceed to Seaham—my Agent is in the country whence I expect him in a few days—if not—I shall join him there for a day—I thought the delay would sit easier at present—for if I had been with you it had been painful to me to quit you so soon—and yet expedient—since "the heart that little *world* of ours"[2] is not the only world we must live in—and I have some points to discuss with him upon the subject of Newstead (which is mine again) and a property I have in Lancashire— with a view to your comfort as well as mine—all I can do shall be done—and in all my future views you must be my principal object— and my tenderest care.——I am glad that you have heard from Lady Melbourne—her conduct has been uniformly kind—considerate—and even indulgent to me—and I have only to regret the unhappy circumstances which prevent my being on the same terms of friendship with all her family.——It is some satisfaction to me to have retained hers—and had my conduct been altogether inexcusable all things considered I could hardly have retained it—she has much regard for you— but that is not extraordinary—*I* have also heard from her—and perhaps I may see her before we meet.—I am anxious—and shall be uneasy till I see you—yet I cannot fix a day till I have seen my lawyer—and you know the "the law's delay"—extends to the personal movements of it's professors—I try to keep myself in patience but I begin to think the famous exclamation of "Ye Gods—*annihilate* both *time* & *space*— and make two &c."[3]—not half so absurd as I used to do.—Dearest

---

[1] ". . . threw a pearl away/Richer than all his tribe." *Othello*, Act V, scene 2.

[2] Perhaps an adaptation of Rogers's "Ode to Superstition": "That little world, the human mind"; or *Richard II*, Act II, scene 1: "This Little World".

[3] Pope's "Martinus Scriblerus—Peri Bathous: or The Art of Sinking in Poetry" (1728), chapter 11: "Ye Gods—annihilate but space and time,/And make two lovers happy."

Annabella—allow me for the first time to use that expression—do write to me—and do not grow tired of hearing me repeat seemingly by rote but really by *heart* how faithfully I am your most attached and unalterable

B

P.S.—I have just been going through a curious scene [.] Sir W. Knighton brought Spurtzheim[4] (I believe is the name) the *craniologist* to see me—a discoverer of faculties & dispositions from heads.—He passes his hand over the head & then tells you—curious things enough—for I own he has a little astonished me.—He says all mine are strongly marked—but very antithetical for every thing developed in & on this same skull of mine has its *opposite* in great force so that to believe him my good & evil are at perpetual war—pray heaven the last don't come off victorious.———

[TO ANNABELLA MILBANKE (*b*)]   *Septr. 26th. 1814*

I wrote in the morning but I cannot go to rest without once more conversing with you as well as I can at this distance.—My letters always leave me dissatisfied—something—so much is unsaid:—since I have given way to those feelings—which almost since our first acquaintance I have repressed but never could conquer even when I thought them most hopeless—you have never left me for a moment— you never shall—you never can.—*You* do not perhaps recollect the first time we ever met—at M[elbourn]e House—an abode with which—except in the instance of our Aunt that is to be—I cannot always associate the most pleasing ideas—but to me it is a yesterday—although I have lived nearly a life of events since that day.—You struck me (as it is called) particularly—I did not know your name and the room was full of morning-visitors—I was myself almost a stranger & felt awkward & shy—for which I have a *natural* talent at that time increased by my recent return from a country where society comprised of men & women is unknown—I set you down as the most puzzling person there—for there was a quiet contempt of all around you & the nothings they were saying & doing in your manner that was so much after my own heart—I could hardly refrain from telling you so—still & calm as you appeared—you went away at last—with Miss Mercer I

---

[4] Johann Christoph Spurzheim (1776–1832), the German phrenologist, had studied medicine at Vienna. He lectured extensively in England at a time when phrenology was taken seriously as a science.

think—and the moment you were gone I enquired all the *who's* & *whats* of mine hostess—your name was answer sufficient for I had heard of you long before—even while I was abroad through particular circumstances—little dreaming then how much I should in future dream of you.—There was a simplicity—an innocence—a beauty in your deportment & appearance which although you hardly spoke— told me I was in company with no common being.—Not very long after this I confided to one whom I then thought only a friend how much I admired—for I dared not do more—how superior you seemed to me to all I perceived in the crowds where I was wandering;—at first my confidante was all acquiescence and approbation—but I was soon informed that you were—but why should I retrace misrepresentations & their consequences for which I shall never forgive myself? I thought you attached & engaged—regret was useless—but how much would have been spared to me had I been aware that your heart was your own—that it could even be exchanged for mine—in very truth— from my heart of hearts—dearest Annabella—I can now tell you— that then—at the very time when I became unworthy of being yours— it was to you my attachment had turned—it was you from whom it was wrenched—those feelings cannot be quelled—only removed—and my sole resource was to suppose that I felt for another the love which you would not accept.———In the autumn I was undeceived with regard to your prepossession for another—but confirmed by the ill success of my kind friend Ly. M[elbourn]e in my opinion that we never should be what I still tremulously hope—for till you are mine I shall tremble—well—"Rebellion lay in my way" and like Hotspur— "I found it"—I became the fool of a similar delusion—loving *you* still.——Since that time I have proceeded "seeking for rest & finding none" at moments retiring within myself and gathering my thoughts and the recollection of my passions & observations into rhimes—with which as the world are pleased to take them well—at least in quantity —I have only to be pleased too—and think myself a very clever gentleman—you will think this affectation—but it is not—I have never thought very highly of poetry nor poets *merely as poets*—and my becoming one—if indeed I am so—is the result of temporary solitude & accident—it is not "my vocation" and I once thought I was meant for something better—but that is past.—I yet wish to be good—with you I cannot but be happy—but I never shall be what I would have been— luckily I do not wish to be so now—reflection & experience have taught me that all pursuits which are not founded on self-esteem & the good of others—lead but to the same result—and far astray as it has led me—I am thankful that the wildness of my imaginations has not altogether prevented me from recovering the path of peace.—What an unmerciful prose have I sent you—or rather am sending—but pardon me—I will compress in future my language—as I have already my feelings—my plans—my hopes—my affection into love—I could almost say—devotion to you—forgive my weaknesses—love what you can of me & mine—and I will be—I am whatever you please to make me.—I am at least above the paltry reluctance of not submitting to an understanding which I am sure is superior to mine—I do not flatter you—I am certain that you are wiser than me—more reflective —more dispassionate—surely more good—you say that "you will look up to me" were you my inferior I should perceive it—I should require it—but it is not so—and yet I do not think humbly of myself when I estimate you more highly.—I do not mean that *I* should rely on you for that protection which it is *my* part to give—and my pride to prove—but that you should be not only my Love—but my first friend—my adviser—my reprover—when necessary—that my head should at times be as much indebted to your counsels—as my heart is to your regard.—In difficulty or danger I would not call upon you to share it or extricate me—I would not throw upon you the weight of my griefs or my perils—but I would ask you if I had done well or ill— and upon your answer would materially depend my estimation of my conduct.——I write to you as if you were already my wife—"the wife of my bosom" you assuredly are—for it does not contain a thought which I can separate from you—it is "almost at odds with morning" so—if not a Hibernicism—Good *Night*— I must try to sleep.—Heaven bless and protect you.—Ever your most attached

and sincere
BYRON

Tuesday—[Sept. 27]

P.S.—I have just heard a distressing piece of intelligence to our family—my first cousin Sir Peter Parker[1] is killed in the late action with the Americans—he was a very gallant & popular officer—young & not long married——and his death will be very generally regretted.—I have not seen him since we were boys—but my sister knew him very well—and I do not [know] whether—or *how* to tell

[1] Sir Peter Parker was Byron's first cousin, son of Charlotte Augusta Byron, daughter of Admiral John Byron, who had married Christopher Parker. She was a widow living in Nottingham when Byron first came to Newstead. Sir Peter Parker's sister Margaret was one of Byron's early cousinly loves. Her early death inspired his "first dash into poetry".

her or not—Lady P[arke]r was particularly attached to him—in short—
it is very bitter to us all.————

[TO LADY MELBOURNE]   *Septr. 28th. 1814*

My dear Ly. M[elbourn]e.—I am truly grieved to hear of Lady
Cowper's illness—as she must ever be one of the most honoured of
my new relatives (that are to be) do tell me when she is better—as I
shall feel anxious not only for her but you till I know.—All *my* connections are in great grief on the loss of my first cousin Sir Peter
Parker—a very gallant and popular character—whom even his wife
could not help loving—poor fellow—you will have seen his death in
the Gazette of our late American victory.—I have not seen him since
we were boys together—but all our family even to the selfishness of
the Howards must be sorry for him; Lady P[arke]r was much attached
to him.—The secret is a secret no longer—for A[nnabella] has written
to her Uncle Ld. W[entworth] who is pleased to be pleased with it—
and it has besides been imparted to the whole *city* of Seaham which it
seems is very glad too—and as (to use her words) "her happiness"
has thus far been "made known" it may probably reach the ears of
C[aroline] & in that case interfere confoundedly with mine.—I don't
much admire this kind of publicity on account of the fuss & fooling it
produces—it has always seemed to me very odd that so much ceremony should be made of a thing so very simple in itself—& it is so
much worse in the country—that I would rather be married—no
matter where—but I should think any place better than the house of
one's papa.—I quite agree with you that it were best over—but I have
several previous arrangements that must take place before I can even
go down there.—I shall make no hesitation about settlements as far
as my property will go—nor did I pay my addresses to her with the
notion of her being a very considerable parti—so that I am much
more afraid of her & hers being disappointed in that respect than
myself——Don't let me bore you but when Ly. C[owpe]r is better—
& you have leisure allow me to hear from you & believe me

                                        ever & affectly yrs.

                                                      B

P.S.—I have heard & seen nothing of C[aroline] and of course hope
I shall not.——

Dear Sir—I had hoped to be able to come down yesterday or today—but I find that it will not be in my power & must wait your leisure.—With regard to Mr. Fellowes[1] I should conceive for his own sake he would preserve some terms—& if he does not—you are well able to cope with & curb him—what *can* he do that can seriously molest you or your son in law?—Upon the subject of my own affairs it will be proper that you should submit their state with the necessary documents to Sir R[alph] Milbanke's solicitor—but I wish to know as I must resell Newstead whether it had not be as well to write to Mr. C[laughto]n on his own proposal of renewal—which if he declines— we must take the best bidder—perhaps Mr. Walker[2]—and then what is to be done about Rochdale?—Miss M[ilbanke] will actually be Baroness Noel and inherit certain property with that title from her uncle Lord Wentworth—there is also something settled from her father's estates and she will have Seaham & all that he can give her— but *entre nous* I believe Sir R[alph] is much involved by electioneering &c. & that her present portion will not be considerable.—Her connections have announced her engagement to all her relations—(& even to the tenantry I believe) so that it is no longer nor need be a secret.— In these circumstances you will easily see how expedient it is for us to meet—and get my property in matrimonial array as speedily as need be—they wish me to go down there—& it will seem singular if I delay it much longer.———

yrs. ever truly
BYRON

[1] Lord Portsmouth had married on March 7, 1814, Mary Anne, eldest daughter of John Hanson. Byron was present at the ceremony and at Hanson's request gave away the bride. The brother of Lord Portsmouth, and next heir, the Hon. Newton Fellowes, not being pleased that his brother should marry a young wife who might provide him with heirs, took out a commission of lunacy to try to annul Lord Portsmouth's marriage. It was because Hanson was much occupied with his son-in-law's affairs that he was dilatory in handling Byron's marriage settlement and other business.

[2] Unidentified.

[TO ISAAC NATHAN[1]]   *Albany, Saturday Morn[in]g [October, 1814?]*

My dear Nathan,—You must dine with me to-day at Seven o'clock.
I take no refusal.

> Yours truly,
> BYRON

[TO LADY MELBOURNE]   *Octr. 1st. 1814*

My dear Ly. M[elbourn]e.—Your description of my uncle is
infinitely inviting—by your account he is an Elzevir Edition of Mr.
Penn of facetious memory[1]—and to crown all the most important
personage of "both your houses"—if so—the longer I stay away the
better—for I never could recommend myself to an old person in my
life—and the circumstance of these expectations of A[nnabella]'s
would do no good—I am sure without intending it I should offend in
some way or other—I never tried to keep anyone in good humour
without blundering.———I cannot go to Seaham—for I know not
how long—my Agent can't leave his son in law Ld. P[ortsmouth] at
present—and wants me to go there—which is not in my power—at
least it is very much out of my way & my inclination—so I must wait
his time—which will not be very long:—the moment I can go to
S[eaham] I will—& yet I feel very odd about *it*—*not her*—it is nothing
but shyness and a hatred of Strangers which I never could conquer.—
I wish so much to see you I have a thousand things to say about—
not C[aroline]—nor any *person* you may imagine—not a *married*
person either—nor a *mistress* either—and yet a woman of course[2]———
in short it is something that was going on very well—not exactly
with *me* but with or through the medium of +[3] (you may guess by

[1] Nathan was a Jewish musical composer, who abandoned theology for music
and studied under Domenico Corri. Nathan had specialized in the music of the
tabernacles, and attempted to adapt some of the ancient Hebrew melodies, for
which he applied to Byron as the most popular poet of the day to write lyrics.
Byron at first was not interested, but through the intervention of his friend Douglas
Kinnaird, he finally undertook the task in October, 1814, and became enthusiastic
about it. The result was *The Hebrew Melodies,* published with the music by Nathan
in April, 1815. Nathan was also a singer and composed light operas. He retained
fond memories of Byron to the end of his life. See his *Fugitive Pieces and Reminiscences of Lord Byron,* 1829. He died in Australia in 1864.

[1] Unidentified.

[2] Lady Charlotte Leveson-Gower. See Byron's more detailed account in the
letter of Oct. 4, 1814, to Lady Melbourne.

[3] The + is Byron's symbol for Augusta. A series of pluses was a secret love
message between them and is found frequently in their correspondence.

those with whom I have lately been—) when lo—upon a scheme—or rather the prospect of a scheme with *another* of the family's speculation—a perplexity ensued—which of course put an end to that—in short it is such an intricate & involved piece of arrangement altogether that I cannot explain it now—but if you guess to whom it refers—do not *breathe* it—for A (*neither* of the A's) would ever forgive me—to say nothing of the other letters of the Alphabet.——My proposal to A[nnabella] followed this—and now—from some fresh circumstances my confidante feels a difficulty in breaking the acceptance which ensued upon it—to her friend—*why*—I cannot exactly see—since it never came to any thing like either with her—and what really was always rather *implied* than expressed by either party.————— Then C[aroline]?—I cannot help any mischief she may do—it will be a pity—because Annabella appears to like me—and I am sincerely disposed to do her justice and love her with all my heart.——I have not seen C[aroline]—nor shall I if I can help it.————————It gives me much pleasure to hear that Ly. C[owpe]r is better—and your *Sprain?* deuce take it—*you* shall leave your friendship for me as an inheritance to Ly. Cow[pe]r and as I hope it will not devolve for these 40 years—by that time I may be "rational" enough to receive my legacy with propriety—

yrs. ever

B

[TO JOHN HANSON] *Octr. 1st. 1814*

My Dear Sir/—By Mr. C[laughto]n's letters to me in your possession you will perceive that he requested the refusal of N[ewstead] & that it was granted.—Things being so circumstanced I wish you to write to him and state that I am about to be married &c. & consequently his determination must be immediate one way or the other— and clear and the *funds* in part and security for the rest—equally palpable & tangible.—If he cannot make this out—I have performed my promise in allowing him the first offer—and we can treat with any other—perhaps Mr. Walker[1] may be the best.—Pray do this—it is better you should write than *I*—but in justice to Mr. C[laughton] as well as myself—this compliment must be paid him—though his letters—or one of them—admits my "free agency."—Do not lose any time in this—& request an immediate answer—the intended marriage

[1] Unidentified.

188

is no secret—& must shew him the necessity of determining forth-with.————Then as to Rochdale I really think without waiting for Deardon[2]—I must sell the other part—though at a loss from that accursed lawsuit which is still undecided.—It would give me great pleasure to visit you & Ld. & Ly. P[ortsmout]h at Hurstbourne but at present I cannot quit London—I am not very well—though apparently robust enough—but still under Sir W. Knighton's[3] care for a tendency to the complaint I brought on 3 years ago by the use or abuse of Acids.—This he gives me great hopes of removing.—The object of Mr. F[ellowes][4] & its motive are equally vain & ridiculous—surely there cannot be a chance of its proving successful—and when it is con-sidered that it was unthought of till Ld. P[ortsmouth] married a woman capable of bringing him an *heir*——in short it seems to me that Mr. F[ellowes] is in more danger than Ld. P[ortsmouth]—particularly *if* there is anything that looks *like Conspiracy* in the attempt—if Ld. P[ortsmouth] is apprehensive—if any outrage is menaced—cannot he have the law to protect him?—is there not the *peace?*—of course I say all this to you in *strict confidence*—and out of regard to your family—and after all *you* must know best.—

ever truly yrs.
B

P.S.—When you write to Mr. C[laughto]n say that the *reply* must be prompt—& clear—& decisive.

P.S.—I think I sent you Mr. C[laughto]n's last letter—it was to the same purport with the others—the moment you can I hope I shall see you here.——If I could come I would—my best compts. & thanks to Ld. & Lady P[ortsmout]h.

[TO ANNABELLA MILBANKE]   *Octr. 3d. 1814*

I am happy to hear that Lady Milbanke is better—but wish to hear that she is well—pray tell me so—you probably know that Lady Cowper has met with an accident—but is not dangerously ill.—I am still detained here waiting for my agent's arrival: it is my intention to

---

[2] James Dearden, who had leased the coal mines at Rochdale from the 5th Lord Byron, finally bought the free part of the estate just before Byron died in Misso-longhi.

[3] Sir William Knighton, 1st baronet (1776–1836), was assistant surgeon at the Royal Naval Hospital and physician to the Prince of Wales, and became private secretary and keeper of the Privy Purse when the Prince became George IV.

[4] See Sept. 28, 1814, to Hanson, note 1.

part with N[ewstead] once more—the late purchaser being unable to fulfil his engagements at the proper time—was under the necessity of forfeiting £25000—and resigning the purchase which was hard upon him but indispensable—he may still have the option of completing his purchase if disposed & competent to renew it.—When I had once determined to sell that estate—I conquered or stifled those feelings which attach one to an old patrimony in the conviction that it was better for many reasons it should be so.—my Lancashire inheritance consists merely of a very extensive & uninclosed manor with the mineral & all other rights—I wished to have sold it instead—but was dissuaded and am still—and told that it will ultimately be very valuable—perhaps more so than the other—on account of the collieries which have never yet been worked to the proper extent because I could not spare the requisite sum and at the same time discharge my debts till N[ewstead] was sold—a part of Rochdale but not the most considerable by any means has been subject to a lawsuit which I have *gained three times* but it is not yet *decided!*—you *know* the *law*—this also would have been arranged by the completion of the N[ewstead] purchase.—My R[ochdale] rights extend over better than eleven thousand acres—and these have been ours since the Conquest I believe—they wish to enclose but cannot without my consent—it is also further valuable on this account—as of course besides the reservation of the minerals to me from the extent of the royalty a considerable portion of land would in that case be added.—Of the actual or exact value of R[ochdale] or of Newstead I cannot speak with any certainty—it is to ascertain this—and to take the proper steps for making every settlement in my power upon you that I wish to see my Agent and determine these points before I join you at Seaham.—My debts are reduced very much within the last three years—and a few thousand pounds will cover the rest—considerably above half have been already paid.— The last price of N. was £140-000—since that time land has fallen— but I can afford to sell for £25000 less at all events—and if the late purchaser renews & completes there will be no loss at all.—The rents have been more than tripled—almost quadrupled—but the income is still far short of what I should derive from the produce of the sale— besides the expence of keeping up the place in any kind of order.—— This is more like a *factor's* letter than anything else—but as you said something on the subject—I thought it as well to get over it at once, your father's agents & mine will of course canvas the business more fully.—With regard to your expectations I have neither conjecture nor curiosity—my motives in addressing you were not founded upon these—and in such respects there will be *no disappointment* to me—and I will make it my endeavour that there shall be as little to you & yours as I can help.————I have said so much—at least so many words on the above topic that I have not left myself time for others:—indeed what I could say would be merely repetition of that which you already know & which years (if spared to me) will only confirm.—You do not yet know how dear you must ever be to

yr. most attached & sincere

B

[TO LADY MELBOURNE]   *Octr. 4th. 1814*

My dear Ly. M[elbourn]e.—+[1] never threw any obstacles in the way—on the contrary she has been more urgent than even you that I should go to S[eaham] and wished me to set out from N[ewstead] instead of London; she wished me much to marry—because it was the only chance of redemption for *two* persons—and was sure if *I* did not that I should only step from one scrape into another—particularly if I went abroad—& I had settled every thing to go to Italy with Mr. Hobhouse if A[nnabella] had not accepted me.————The other was undoubtedly her *favourite*—but no one could acquiesce in this with a better grace as I could convince you by her letters and conduct at that time.——Her friend after a certain time—was seized with a panic[2]—on some family scheme which I will tell you when we meet—of a *compact elsewhere*—the fact is the little girl had no will of her own—and might not be aware of what she had been doing—but her frequent epistles & excessive attachment to + *both* so much more numerous & friendly than ever before—with sentences which were *not* to be answered—or if answered—replied to in a *particular* manner—&c. &c. with a hundred little things which I don't understand but which convinced + of her disposition—all produced this episode in our Drama.—+ always thought her the *only* person perhaps who would suit——it is my suspicion (but I am probably wrong) that la Mere was not ignorant either—but that circumstances—a better prospect in another quarter—and the never to be adjusted family quarrel[3] made her alter—and the young one was perhaps her dupe—of course the demoiselle & + were the only persons who made their appearance on

---

[1] Byron's symbol for Augusta.
[2] Lady Charlotte Leveson-Gower.
[3] Byron's quarrel with Lord Carlisle, who had married in 1770 Lady Caroline, second daughter of Lord Granville Leveson-Gower.

the stage—and *I* was supposed or rather presumed to know nothing of it—and *la Mere* also—but this I can hardly conceive you will recollect that it never came to *yes* or *no* or anything direct. It went off thus —after one very long letter—which + answered—came another full of alarms—"she had been so foolish" & was in such a dilemma—such & such persons were coming—& such & such a scheme was to be brought forward—what was she to do?—I made + write a kind but satisfactory answer taking it *all* on herself—& getting the other out of it completely—and there it ended—& they are all good friends still. ——I then said to + —after consoling her on the subject that *I* would try the next myself—as she did not seem to be in luck—the prospect— (for A[nnabella] had been bewildering herself sadly & did not appear to be much better disposed towards me than formerly) was not very promising—however—the stars I presume did it—the rest you know. ———+ has written to A[nnabella] to express how much all my relatives are pleased by the event &c. &c.—It *is* in the Morning Post of this day—from the Durham paper—so that C[aroline] *will* hear it soon—with regard to any *"hitch"* how *can* either party be off?—it shall not be *my* doing in any case—but surely you cannot wonder that I should wish to arrange my property first—& not proceed hurriedly in a business which is to decide her fate & mine forever.—

ever yrs. most truly

B

P.S.—I enclose a letter which will explain what I have been saying —but *answer* me by return as I shall feel *odd* till I get it again.

[TO JAMES PERRY]   *Albany Octr. 5th. 1814*

Sir—I perceive in your paper of this day the *contradiction* of a paragraph copied from the Durham paper announcing the intended marriage of Ld. B. with Miss M[ilbank]e.—How the paragraph came into the Durham or other papers *I* know not—but as *it is founded on fact*—I will be much obliged if you will inform me—*who* instructed you to contradict this?—I am no great admirer of paragraphs upon such subjects at all—but I cannot help feeling what an awkwardness the positive contradiction of this must occasion—as the paragraph originated in the county where Sir R[alph] M[ilbanke] resides. I leave to yourself to do away by as *few* words as may be proper—(and *without* mentioning that you have heard from *me* of course) the unpleasant impression your contradiction may occasion amongst my present & future connections.—I need not add that I write this in *confidence* & *privately* to *Mr. Perry*—rather than *the Editor*. Do not forget to tell me *why* and *how* you came to deny so positively a truth which has for the last fortnight been no secret,—as I suspect mischief (and consequently a woman) to be your authority.—

yrs. truly & obliged
BYRON

You will be as much surprized as I have been displeased—Dearest Annabella—to perceive in the M[ornin]g Chronicle a *contradiction* of a paragraph in the D[urham] & other papers announcing our intended marriage.—I have written to Perry—but can easily *guess* the personage who has thought proper to perform this piece of petty malignity— which has hurt me—but no matter—I shall probably know in a few hours whence it originated.—My reasons for suspecting the personage to whom I allude—are—that it is not the first nor the fiftieth of these *monkey-tiger* tricks that she has played me—one in particular of *forging* a letter in my name so exactly that the person to whom it was addressed was completely deceived: the *cause* was a picture—and Murray (in whose care it was—& who ought to know my hand writing perfectly, was the dupe[1]—after this (which was above a year ago) you can hardly wonder at my want of Charity on this occasion in fixing upon the same object for my present conjectures.—The *fact* you may depend upon—you cannot conceive what persecution I have undergone from the same quarter—nor the pains I have taken to save that person from herself—I do not mean *very* recently—but since my first acquaintance —she has crossed my every path—she has blighted or at least darkened my every prospect—it is bitter to speak harshly of that which we once thought loved us—& yet in this instance to speak truly & kindly at the same time is difficult—I will therefore close the subject.———Mr. Hanson is still at Ld. Portsmouth's detained by business—but I expect him daily—& have written to him peremptorily—in the mean time I trust he is doing what I have desired him—& will tell me so when we meet—nothing but this—& it is a necessary though irksome delay detains me from you. All *my* connections & friends are delighted —they could not but be proud of you—my feelings are dashed with

---

[1] For Caroline Lamb's forgery of Byron's handwriting in order to get a picture of Byron from Murray, see Jan. 10, 1813, to Murray, note 1; see also Jan. 9, 1813, to Lady Melbourne, note 1 (Vol. 3, p. 11).

doubt—if I valued you less—I should be more confident—but you seem to me so much more than I deserve—that I can scarcely persuade myself that you are to be mine: *yours* I must be ever from my heart of hearts.—

B

P.S.—I enclose you Perry's answer & the note which I retain "pour des raisons"[.] I have seen—& do not think it *is* the person I believed but cannot guess the writer pray have I done right or wrong in this? it could not merely be passed by silently—particularly as it first appeared in the D[urham] paper—the contradiction was like an insult.— As I wish to let you into the character of a man with whom I have passed much of my youth—I send you also *3* epistles of my friend Hobhouse—the son of Sir B[enjamin] H[obhouse]—and my fellow traveller during the first part of my stay in the East—I think the dry & cynical turn of his style will amuse you—but I can assure you he is *all heart* notwithstanding & a great admirer of you—as one of his letters will prove to you.—ever my Love—thine

B

Keep them till we meet.—

[TO JOHN HANSON] *Octr. 5th. 1814*

My dear Sir/—I do not wish to hurry or to plague you but I cannot help saying that *delay* in this business may do me great harm—& that it has even done *some* already.—I hope as I [have] ever shewn not only my confidence in you professionally—but I trust my regard for you & yours personally—that you will not lose much time in seeing me—and that in the mean time you are considering & arranging what may best be done on my approaching marriage.—My relatives that are to be are expecting me—& wondering that I do not come—I can only say that nothing detains me but not seeing you first & making the arrangements.—If I could have come to H[urstbourne] I would willingly but it is not in my power.—

ever yrs. truly
BYRON

[TO LADY MELBOURNE] *Octr. 5th. 1814*

My dear Ly. M[elbourn]e.—C[aroline] I suspect has been at her

194

cursed tricks again—the D[urham] paragraph is *contradicted* in the M[orning] Chronicle—I have written to Perry—but it could only be *her*—no one else has the motive or the malignity to be so *petty.* If she proceeds—I can only appeal to you whether I have not done all in my power to break off—indeed—I have neither heard from nor seen her since July (I think)—well—I must bear it I presume.——+'s friend has written to her just the letter she ought full of congratulations—so that all is right—& + was mistaken.———I did not I assure you *know* the contents of K[innaird]'s letter—but he is an old friend of mine—and if he likes me—you must at least allow him to be a good-natured soul.—The moment I have seen Hanson—to whom I have written most peremptorily—I shall set out for S[eaham]—In the mean time do all for me you can—I assure you these delays are not of my desiring.—

ever yrs. most truly
B

It is *not* C[aroline]—I beg her pardon—I think I know the hand which *Perry* has sent me—& if I can bring it home—woe to the writer.

————

[TO JOHN HANSON]   [*October 5, 1814*]

Dear Sir/—I enclose you the *cover* of a *letter* & a *paragraph* to the *Morning Chronicle* what think *you?*—*Keep both*—if your suspicions agree with mine—at any rate *keep* the *note* and do let me hear from or see you immediately—you *know* the hand—

yrs. truly
B

Compare this with more of Mr. C[laughton]'s writing & then tell me what you think?—

[TO THE COUNTESS OF JERSEY]   *Albany—Oct. 5th. 1814*

Dear Lady Jersey—Your recollection & invitation do me great honour—but I am going to be "married & can't come" my intended is two hundred miles off & the moment my business here is arranged I must set out in a great hurry to be happy.—Miss Milbanke is the good-natured person who has undertaken me—and of course I am very much in love and as silly as all single gentlemen must be in that sentimental situation.—I have been accepted these three weeks—but when the event will take place—I don't exactly know—it depends partly upon lawyers who are never in a hurry—one can be certain of nothing —but at present there appears no other interruption to this intention which seems as mutual as possible—and now no secret though I did not tell first—and all our relatives are congratulating away to right & left in the most fatiguing manner.—You perhaps know the Lady—she is niece to Lady Melbourne—and cousin to Lady Cowper and others of your acquaintance—and has no fault—except being a great deal too good for me—and that *I* must pardon if nobody else should.—It might have been *two* years ago—and if it had would have saved me a world of trouble—she has employed the interval in refusing about half a dozen of my particular friends (as she did me once by the way) and has taken me at last for which I am very much obliged to her.—I wish it was well over—for I do hate bustle—and there is no marrying without some—and then I must not marry in a black coat they tell me & I can't bear a blue one.—Pray forgive me for scribbling all this nonsense—you know I must be serious all the rest of my life—and this is a parting piece of buffoonery which I write with tears in my eyes expecting to be agitated. Believe me most seriously & sincerely

yr. obliged Sert.
BYRON

P.S.—My best rem[embrance]s to Lord J[ersey] on his return.—

[TO ANNABELLA MILBANKE]   *Octr. 7th. 1814*

Mr. Hanson my solicitor is arrived in London—& will be glad to confer with Sir Ralph's—if he will have the goodness to favour me with his address. I believe the etiquette—in short I do not know it— but if I am wrong in addressing this to you to mention to Sir R. instead of writing to him myself will he & you pardon it?—The fact is that I write to you less formally than I could—(with all my sentiments of regard & respect) to your father—& now I shall be quite happy to get these points of discussion out of our heads into those of our lawyers— & may *they* prosper only in proportion to their expedition!————I wrote to you yesterday—Dearest Annabella—exceedingly distempered with conjectures & choler—at the contra*diction* & Contra-*dictor* of the paragraph from the Durham paper announcing our intended marriage—nor can I at this moment fix on the person—there are but—no—there can be but *one*—who could or would play such an idle & yet vexatious trick—after all my only reason for suspecting that personage—is my knowledge of her disposition—of which I must say—nothing.———It gives me much pleasure to hear that Augusta has written to you—she is the least selfish & gentlest creature in being—& more attached to me than any one in existence can be—she was particularly desirous that I should marry and only regretted— what I must regret a little too—that she had not earlier the pleasure of your acquaintance—she was very anxious for the fate and favourable reception of her letter to you.—Your mother "is better—but not yet well—" I must naturally be very desirous to hear her amendment confirmed—this you will tell me doubtless—but *soon?*—answer that question when & how you please I shall still be dissatisfied there is no *soon* for me till we have met—every thing about me seems tedious & tiresome.—When I have the honour of being presented to your Uncle Lord Wentworth I hope I shall not be unmindful of my obligation to him for his favourable opinion taken on *your word*—it is the only point on which he need doubt it—it would delight me to obtain the friendship of all who are dear to you—but I am so unlucky in my approaches to strangers that it is one of the objects on which I am more anxious than sanguine.———I have been writing on skaits—my paper slippery as ice and at full speed—perhaps you will think *with* them by the scrawl—but hastily or tardily believe me ever

yr. most attached & faithful
B

P.S.—I cannot resist sending you the enclosed from Augusta as it will enable you to judge of her disposition—since with me she can be under no constraint—& it will in some parts I think amuse you—"the bets" will I hope be soon decided.—Make my best remembrances to Sir R. & let the first sentence of your answer inform me your mother is quite—*quite* recovered.—

[TO JAMES PERRY]   *Octr. 7th. 1814*

Dear Sir/—I have to thank you for your handsome letter and the *note*—the writer & motive I can only *guess* at.—As far as my own feelings are concerned—misrepresentation can hardly affect one so inured to it—but I cannot willingly allow those of others to be hurt— as had been the case in this instance.———Enclosed I send you some lines which I was desired by our relatives to write on the death of Sir

P. Parker[1] (my first cousin) and one very much beloved & regretted.
——If you think them worth insertion—they are at your service—I
would rather not have my *name* to them at length—but have left an
initial to indicate the writer.——I wish you could persuade our friend
Moore to bring out his work—but I suppose he will now wait till the
first brunt of Scott's newly announced one is over—perhaps he is
right—but there never was a man who had less reason to fear competition or comparison with others than Moore—I wish he could be convinced of this as truly as his friends & readers are.

yr. obliged Sert.
BYRON

P.S.—My handwriting is so horrible that I must entreat your
attention to ye. printing—*if* you print the enclosed.—

[TO LADY MELBOURNE (*a*)]   *Octr. 7th. 1814*

My dear Lady M[elbourn]e.—I cannot fix yet upon the *contradictory*
paragraph-writer—but I think it is *Claughton*—it is very like his hand
but Kinnaird who saw it *doubted*—& so must I.—Let it sleep for the
present.—+ is the least selfish person in the world—you of course
will never believe that either of us can have any right feeling—I won't
deny this as far as regards me—but you don't know what a being she
is—her only error has been my fault entirely—& for this I can plead no
excuse—except passion—which is none.——I forgot to say that +
and her friend had one interview—in the summer—which the friend
came several miles to encounter—and it was that more than any thing
else that made + believe in the practicability of her scheme—when
they parted + said—"may I write whatever I please without getting
you into any dilemma &c.["]—the answer was *yes*—all this made me
believe that the exquisite politician who brought her into the world
could not be altogether ignorant.—The new plan is this—(a secret of
course & do *you* keep it better than *I* have in this instance) young
Howard the Norfolk[1] & a Mr. Bellasyse his uncle or cousin are
invited—& he is to take his choice of the family—so that *both* are in

[1] Sir Peter Parker, Byron's first cousin, was killed in August while leading a
party from his ship the Menelaus in an attack on the American camp near Baltimore.
Byron's "Elegiac Stanzas on the Death of Sir Peter Parker, Bart." was first published by Perry in the *Morning Chronicle*, Oct. 8, 1814, and included in Murray's
edition of the *Hebrew Melodies* in 1815.

[1] Lady Charlotte Leveson-Gower was married before the end of the year to
young Howard, Earl of Surrey, only son of the Duke of Norfolk.

requisition for the present—and as + could not persuade me to wait the reversion—(notwithstanding all the probabilities that the younger would be the winner—) I hope she may secure him—as she is the favourite of the Uncle it is not unlikely—all this the poor little soul wrote clandestinely to + in her eagerness to vindicate herself—and betrayed this pretty piece of policy.—Whether it will do—I don't know—but thus they are at present.—Mr. Hanson comes to town today—so that I hope to get down to S[eaham] soon—I hear nothing but praises & wonders of my wife elect (+ says that she hears her called "very pretty" too by everybody) and it is a most popular match amongst all my relations & acquaintances—you very much mistake me if you think I am lukewarm upon it—quite the reverse— and I have even the conceit to think that I shall suit her better than a better person might—because she is not so cold as I thought her— and if I think she likes me—I shall be exactly what she pleases—it is her fault if she don't govern me properly—for never was anybody more easily managed. *You* ought to like the match—for it is one of your making—& I hope not the worst of your performances in that way.—You can't conceive how I long to call you Aunt—I hope then to see a great deal of you & even of Brocket in the course of time.—

yrs. ever
B

P.S.—I heard from A[nnabella] today—she says Ld. W[entworth] "pleases me by his strong prepossession in your favour—he is proud of his future nephew"—I must insist upon your being equally pre-possessed ma tante. I thought you would be glad to hear this from A[nnabella]—*not* a *word* of or from C[aroline].—

[TO LADY MELBOURNE (*b*)]   *Octr. 7th. 1814*

My dear Ly. M[elbourn]e.—Hanson is come at last & is ready to meet Sir R[alph]'s solicitor the moment we know who he is—£60-000 —that is £3000 a year—is the proposed settlement on our part—if not enough—we can make it more—N[ewstea]d can be charged with it for the present—but subject to Trustees so as *still* to *sell* it & secure that sum to A[nnabella] from the produce. H[anson] still thinks N[ewstea]d must bring about 120-000—as it has been much im-proved—& the rents raised beyond what *I* could have done—because I should not have liked to turn out the old (though stupid) tenants— and all this has been effected.—You know I can *afford* to sell it for

£25000 *less* than before—as that is already received of C[laughto]n's forfeit.—On Rochdale we have not decided but it is certainly valuable —though want of money has prevented me from working it to advantage—many & most of my debts are paid—there are still however several to pay.—H[anson] is decided for the resale of N[ewstead] because although the rents are nearly quadrupled—yet the income is much short of what would arise from the purchase money—and the house requires too much keeping up.—What is to be done about C[*aroline*]—Ought I to write to her?—I am sure no one can be more disposed to pay her every *proper* attention. I hope that she is not the paragraph-mover if she hates me—she cannot hate An[nabella] and should consider her a little——I must do C[aroline] justice in saying that I have neither heard from nor of her—nor have we met.—If you think it right to say anything on the subject—in short I know not what to do or say—any situation is so difficult with her—to preserve a *medium* is what would be desirable—I would willingly follow your judgment—but it seems so hard upon *you*—to make you the arbitress between us.—Whatever new attachments she may have formed should at least induce her to consider the old as entirely cancelled—*if* there be any complaints—methinks I might complain too—but with these things I have nothing to do—though I suspect she means to charge *all* her *wrong* to my account.—If she would but have a little sense & consideration—how much it would conduce to all our comfort—to her own—for there never were persons for whom I felt more kindness than you & all yours—and it will be very hard on me to be proscribed from that intimacy which this connection with your niece will sanction & improve.—

ever yrs. most affectionately

B

Augusta tells me that G[eorge] says they are "betting away at Newmarket—whether I am to be married or not"—she had had a very kind answer from A[nnabella]—is not this amusing or rather provoking?—always a *fuss* whether one wishes it or not.—

[TO THOMAS MOORE]   *October 7th, 1814*

Notwithstanding the contradictory paragraph in the Morning Chronicle, which must have been sent by * * [Caroline Lamb?], or perhaps—I know not why I should suspect Claughton of such a thing, and yet I partly do, because it might interrupt his renewal of purchase, if so disposed; in short, it matters not, but we are all in the road to matrimony—lawyers settling, relations congratulating, my intended as kind as heart could wish, and every one, whose opinion I value, very glad of it. All her relatives, and all mine too, seem equally pleased.

Perry was very sorry, and has *re*-contradicted, as you will perceive by this day's paper. It was, to be sure, a devil of an insertion, since the first paragraph came from Sir Ralph's own County Journal, and this in the teeth of it would appear to him and his as *my* denial. But I have written to do away that, enclosing Perry's letter, which was very polite and kind.

Nobody hates bustle so much as I do; but there seems a fatality over every scene of my drama, always a row of some sort or other. No matter—Fortune is my best friend, and as I acknowledge my obligations to her, I hope she will treat me better than she treated the Athenian, who took some merit to *himself* on some occasion, but (after that) took no more towns. In fact, *she*, that exquisite goddess, has hitherto carried me through every thing, and will, I hope, now; since I own it will be all *her* doing.

Well, now for thee. Your article on * *[1] is perfection itself. You must not leave off reviewing. By Jove, I believe you can do any thing. There is wit, and taste, and learning, and good-humour (though not a whit less severe for that) in every line of that critique.

* * * * * * * * * * * * * * *

Next to *your* being an E[dinburgh] Reviewer, *my* being of the same kidney, and Jeffrey's being such a friend to both, are amongst the events which I conceive were not calculated upon in Mr.—what's his name?'s—"Essay on Probabilities."[2]

But, Tom, I say—Oons! Scott menaces the "Lord of the Isles."[3] Do you mean to compete? or lay by, till this wave has broke upon the *shelves* (of booksellers, not rocks—a *broken* metaphor, by the way). You *ought* to be afraid of nobody; but your modesty is really as provoking and unnecessary as a * *'s. I am very merry, and have just been writing some elegiac stanzas on the death of Sir P[eter] Parker. He was my first cousin, but never met since boyhood. Our relations desired me, and I have scribbled and given it to Perry, who will chronicle it to-morrow. I am as sorry for him as one could be for one I

---

[1] Lord Thurlow. See Sept. 15, 1814, to Moore (*a*).

[2] A review of Laplace's *Essai Philosophique sur les Probabilités* appeared in the *Edinburgh Review* (Vol. XXIII, p. 320).

[3] Scott's *Lord of the Isles* was advertised in the autumn of 1814, but did not appear until January, 1815.

never saw since I was a child; but should not have wept melodiously, except "at the request of friends."

I hope to get out of town and be married, but I shall take Newstead in my way, and you must meet me at Nottingham and accompany me to mine Abbey. I will tell you the day when I know it.

Ever, &c.

P.S.—By the way, my wife elect is perfection, and I hear of nothing but her merits and her wonders, and that she is "very pretty." Her expectations, I am told, are great; but *what*, I have not asked. I have not seen her these ten months.

[TO ANNABELLA MILBANKE] *Octr. 8th. 1814*

I have directed Mr. Hanson to communicate with Mr. Hoar[1] in compliance with your father's kind request which I this day received.— Between them I will for the present leave the discussion.——Were I to follow my own inclination—my *more* than inclination—I should now be with you & yours at Seaham—but my presence here will forward arrangements which must be completed before we can meet free from all anxiety—& then I trust we shall meet never to part till that moment which will be bitterest to the survivor.——I have long accustomed myself to lean as little upon hope—or rather on *certainty*— as I can help—I do not foresee anything that can prevent the accomplishment of our intentions—but if such did occur—I know not how I should bear it now—but were I *with* you—near you—and then to relinquish you—I could not bear it at all.—When I say this—do not imagine—that under any circumstances *I* would now recede—but if malice—or any of the thousand somethings or nothings which so often "give us pause" should interpose between us—it would cost *you* less— & so far be some relief to me—than if we were together only to separate————It is for both our comforts indispensably necessary that a "freedom from embarrassments" should *precede* our marriage— this I am endeavouring—& in this the arrangements I am proposing must ultimately succeed—that delay will arise—I know—but it is expedient & must be borne, & I would much rather owe the extrication to my own endeavours and resources than to those of others— however highly I may regard them.—With this view I told Ly. Mel[bourn]e that your situation—be it what it might—would make no difference to me further than that of parting with N. *now* instead of a

[1] William Hoar was Sir Ralph Milbanke's attorney and business agent.

few months hence—but that I thought it better not to join you till all was settled on *my* worldly concerns.————Lady M[elbourn]e with that uniform friendship she has ever shown me—is very anxious that I should lose no time—I *will lose* none—but I would rather lose every thing—than precipitate you perhaps into repentance.—I do not wish you to "profess"[;] write to me as you feel—or if that seem more than I should request—write to me as you please—I shall find no fault.—So *you* were once called a "savage"—I never was called anything else—but I hope my ferocity resembles yours.—With my best remembrance to Sir R. & your mother (in whose recovery I rejoice) believe me

ever yrs.
B

[TO JOHN HANSON]   *Albany—Octr. 8th. 1814*

My dear Sir/—I have only time (as you set off so soon) to send the enclosed from Sir R[alph] M[ilbanke] as he gives the address of Mr. Hoar you had better write to him—(is it [Stoar?] or Hoar?) a few lines by *this day's* post would save time

yrs. truly
BYRON

[TO ANNABELLA MILBANKE]   *Octr. 9th. 1814*

I have had a letter from a person whose name you will guess without a large expense of conjecture——it is the first I have received from that quarter for some time—and is quiet and rational enough—the passage I have cut out refers to you[1]—and confirms a statement which —I think—I made to you—for that reason I send it.——With regard to the writer—whom I have not seen nor heard from for months—I would fain hope that she may yet retrieve herself[.] I do not speak as far as regards *me*—that has of course been long over but on subsequent circumstances with which I have no concern except to regret—that since there never were so many opportunities of amendment & [remission?] presented to any being as to her—she should not avail herself of them—to me she has been the cause of much wretchedness

[1] Extract from Caroline Lamb's letter to B. enclosed: "Is it not a little strange that almost the first words you ever spoke in confidence to me were concerning Annabella—I was astonished & overpowered—I could not believe it—"

not unattended with self reproach—& yet I did try to preserve her—I would have sacrificed myself at one time to have made her happier but *that* was not called for by her connections nor even herself—her whole disposition is a moral phenomenon (if she be not *mad*) it is not feminine—she has no real affection—or if any it is to the very man she has most injured W[illiam] [Lamb]—but every thing seems perverted in her—she is unlike every body—& not even like herself for a week together. I have not discovered our paragraph-scribe—my mind misgave me it might be Mr. Claughton—on the supposition that he might conceive my marriage would interfere with any intention of repurchase of N. on his part—but Mr. Hanson on comparing the writing says it is unlike—& that he would not be so silly.—It matters not—we shall one day laugh at it—your "assurance"—dearest A—makes mine "double sure"—but I wish our lawyers would be quicker—my Philosophy begins to be a little fractious.———I believe you dislike bustle as much as I do—you shall please yourself & yours as to the where & when the ceremony (which I suppose you would not like to be *very ceremonious*) is to take place—but as it is usual to separate for a time from all but *our*selves I wish to fix on our retreat—Newstead will hardly be in the state I could wish it to be in to receive you—but I will make it my care to provide us a suitable abode.—

ever yr. attached

B

[TO LADY MELBOURNE] *Octr. 9th. 1814*

My dear Ly. M[elbourn]e.—I will answer C[aroline] tomorrow—pray tell her so—& say any thing proper for me.—Your approbation of my intentions gives me great pleasure—Hanson said £50-000 or £2500 a year—but agreed with me that it was best to do things handsomely—and to err on the right side if at all—and acquiesced in making it £3000 instead.——I must run the risk of Sir R[alph]'s "possibility" nevertheless devoutly praying for Ly. M[ilbanke]'s long life—or a young & pretty step-mother in law—in case she should leave us. Enclosed are two letters one from A. and the other from A +—I wish to convince you of the disposition of the one + & to ask your opinion about going—but why—I know it already—& will go to S[eaham] the moment I can.—I shall be delighted to see Ld. M[elbourne]—I do hope C[aroline] will continue in this mood—it becomes her—& it is so provoking to see her throwing away her own happiness by handfuls—when every one is disposed to forgive & treat her kindly if she would but suffer them.—

ever yrs. most affectly.

B

[TO THE EDITOR OF THE *Poetical Register*]   *Octr. 10th. 1814*

Sir—I have just received your obliging present of ye "Poetical Register."[1]—It is a work which deserves & I doubt not will obtain every success and I request that you will accept my sincere thanks for your kindness in deeming me worthy of a copy.—I have the honour to be

yr. obliged & very faithful Sert.

BYRON

[TO LADY MELBOURNE]   *Octr. 11th. 1814*

My dear Ly. M[elbourn]e.—Your Lord has this moment left me— very kind—& I take it kindly—He looked a little suspicious at a *miniature* near the chimney—it was one of Ly. O[xford]—& not of C[aroline] as he probably suspected—but I did not know *how* to make him perceive this as he seems short-sighted & yet I feel uneasy at the idea that he should imagine for a moment that C[aroline]'s was amongst them which upon my honour it is *not*—if you can fall upon any way to assure him of this—I wish you would—perhaps it may be only my fancy as I judge a good deal from looks—but I take his visit as such a compliment that I would not have him think I paid him so bad a one in return.———I enclose you an answer to C[aroline]. It is *short*—& I hope the proper *medium*—I was glad to hear from Ld. M[elbourne] that Lady Cow[pe]r is much better.—

ever yrs. most affectly.

B

[TO LADY MELBOURNE]   *Octr. 12th. 1814*

Dear Lady M[elbourn]e.—Were I in the fortunate situation of Ld. C[1] I don't know whether I should return so "Post-hastily["] but I

---

[1] The *Poetical Register*, published by Rivingtons, the high-church publishers of the *British Critic*, began in 1801 but fell behind in its publication. Its reviews were generally short. It reviewed *Hours of Idleness* in 1811, and *English Bards and Scotch Reviewers* in 1812, both favourably.

[1] Unidentified. Lord Cowper, Lady Melbourne's son-in-law?

am pretty sure I should not have set out without my Penelope—as to being "married 9 years" that to be sure rather enhances the merits of his L[or]dship's conjugal expedition—but don't equal mine—for I would travel twice the distance to see the same person without being married at all.———Well—but I *am* going am I not?—what would mine aunt have? you forget that I shall not be a whit nearer marriage when I get there—& really without being more impatient than other people—you must allow that it is rather a trying situation to be placed near &c. with one's intended & still to be limited to intentions only.—I have bored you with so many letters lately that you will not be sorry to hear that I am interrupted & must conclude this.

ever yrs.

B

[TO JOHN HANSON]   *Octr. 13th. 1814*

Dear Sir/—I have received the enclosed from Lady Mil[bank]e— perhaps you can manage to go with me *next* week—for I have some things to order which must be ready before.—We could take Newstead in our way—but do as you like.—Return the enclosed to me & believe me

truly yrs.

B

[TO ANNABELLA MILBANKE]   *Octr. 13th. 1814*

Mr. Hanson has just left me—he will be in Durham early next week (Wednesday I hope) to meet Mr. Hoar—he is in full possession of my intentions & the proper papers—the legal arrangement I leave to his discretion subject to any observations your father may think proper to make—Mr. Hoar answered his letter & they agree that a personal interview will save time and trouble.———I must be at Newstead for a few days next week after which we shall meet—my Love—I do not know how to thank you for your letter received this morning—I never doubted *you*—I know you to be Truth herself—but I dreaded— I will not say—I dread—lest a happiness which I do not deserve should be dashed from me—but I will not yield to these "thick coming fancies"—forgive me for even hinting at them.———My delays— dearest A—have arisen from various causes & some not very important—though equally provoking—when I addressed you from

N[ewstea]d. it was with so little hope—that I had actually prepared every thing to go abroad with my friend Hobhouse—and now I have to do & undo fifty things connected with my then resolution—I made that as a last effort in the thought that before my return you might perhaps give me some encouragement—or by your answer crush my presumption at once—but I had as little belief that *you* loved me—that you would be mine—as I now have that *I* can ever be another's.———I will not do you nor myself such injustice as to suppose that any misconception could *now* arise on either part—of the state of our affections—our present feelings & our future intentions—it is for common minds to attribute little motives—I have none—nothing but wishes & fears the former I need not repeat—the latter I hardly know how to define—or to account for—except by a Superstition to which I am not generally subject.———But—"something too much of this"—the latter end of next week I intend to be at Newstead & as soon after as some business there will permit—at Seaham.—My best regards to all around you— who will receive them—ever—my beloved Annabella—

yrs.

B

P.S.—Your mother's letter pleased me beyond its kind contents—in confirming your assurance of her recovery.—

[TO ANNABELLA MILBANKE]   *Octr. 14th. 1814*

I have not seen the paragraph you mention—but it cannot *speak* more humbly of me in the comparison than I *think*.—This is one of the lesser evils to which notoriety and a carelessness of fame—in the only good sense of the word—has rendered me liable—a carelessness which I do not now feel since I have obtained something worth caring for.— The truth is that could I have foreseen that your life was to be linked to mine—had I even possessed a distinct hope however distant—I would have been a different and a better being—as it is—I have sometimes doubts—even if I should not disappoint the future nor act hereafter unworthily of you—whether the past ought not to make you still reject me—even that portion of it with which you are not unacquainted. —I did not believe such a woman existed—at least for me—and I sometimes fear I ought to wish that she had not—I must turn from the subject.—Yesterday I answered your letter—will you repeat my thanks to Lady Milbanke for hers—& believe me

yrs. ever

B

P.S.—I am not satisfied with what I have written—but I shall not improve by adding to it—in ten or twelve days the moment I can leave N[ewstea]d we shall meet—till then let me hear from you—I will write tomorrow—my Love—do forgive me—if I have written in a spirit that renders you uncomfortable—I cannot embody my feelings in words—I have nothing to desire—nothing I would see altered in *you* —but so much in myself—I can conceive no misery equal to mine if I failed in making you happy—& yet how can I hope to do justice to those merits—from whose praise there is not a dissentient voice?——

P.S. 2d.—I have since the morning seen the paragraph—it is just to you—& not very unjust to me—merely the old story of "the thorny paths of Satire & the gloomy recesses of Misanthropy" from which the writer hopes you will withdraw me—I'm sure so do I.—He adds laughably enough "we hope so much contradiction will not exist after the ceremony" alluding to the con—& *re*-contradiction.———There are also some epigrams by no means bad & very complimentary to you in which such a "Heraclitus"—as I am—is made to leave off melancholy under your auspices—and a long address in the M[ornin]g P[os]t to me—making me responsible for a sentiment in "the Giaour" though it is in the mouth of a fictitious character—these "paper bullets of the brain" will not penetrate mine—& I could forgive any censure but of *you*.——

[TO THOMAS MOORE]   *October 15th, 1814*

An' there were any thing in marriage that would make a difference between my friends and me, particularly in your case, I would "none on't." My agent sets off for Durham next week, and I shall follow him, taking Newstead and you in my way. I certainly did not address Miss Milbanke with these views, but it is likely she may prove a considerable *parti*. All her father can give, or leave her, he will; and from her childless uncle, Lord Wentworth, whose barony, it is supposed, will devolve on Ly. Milbanke (his sister), she has expectations. But these will depend upon his own disposition, which seems very partial towards her. She is an only child, and Sir R[alph]'s estates, though dipped by electioneering, are considerable. Part of them are settled on her; but whether *that* will be *dowered* now, I do not know,—though, from what has been intimated to me, it probably will. The lawyers are to settle this among them, and I am getting my property into matrimonial array, and myself ready for the journey to Seaham, which I must make in a week or ten days.

I certainly did not dream that she was attached to me, which it seems she has been for some time. I also thought her of a very cold disposition, in which I was also mistaken—it is a long story, and I won't trouble you with it. As to her virtues, &c. &c. you will hear enough of them (for she is a kind of *pattern* in the north), without my running into a display on the subject. It is well that *one* of us is of such fame, since there is a sad deficit in the *morale* of that article upon my part,—all owing to my "bitch of a star," as Captain Tranchemont says of his planet.[1]

Don't think you have not said enough of me in your article on T * * [Thurlow]; what more could or need be said?[2]

* * * * * * * * * * * * * * * *

Your long-delayed and expected work[3]—I suppose you will take fright at "The Lord of the Isles" and Scott now. You must do as you like,—I have said my say. You ought to fear comparison with none, and any one would stare, who heard you were so tremulous,—though, after all, I believe it is the surest sign of talent. Good morning. I hope we shall meet soon, but I will write again, and perhaps you will meet me at Nottingham. Pray say so.

P.S.—If this union is productive, you shall name the first fruits.

[TO LEIGH HUNT]   *Octr. 15th. 1814*

My dear Hunt—I send you some game of which I beg your acceptance—I specify the quantity as a security against the porter—a hare—a pheasant—and two brace of partridges which I hope are fresh.—My stay in town has not been long and I am in all the agonies of quitting it again next week on business preparatory to a "change of condition" as it is called by the talkers on such matters—I am about to be married—and am of course in all the misery of a man in pursuit of happiness.—My intended is two hundred miles off—and the efforts I am making with lawyers &c. &c. to join my future connections—are for a personage of my single and inveterate habits—to say nothing of indolence—quite prodigious.——I sincerely hope you are better than

---

[1] Unidentified.

[2] In his review of Lord Thurlow's poems Moore made an obvious flattering reference to Byron: "We could name but one noble lord, among either the living or the dead, whose laurels are sufficiently abundant to keep the coronet totally out of sight." (*Edinburgh Review*, Vol. XXIII, p. 411.)

[3] Moore was reluctant to publish his *Lalla Rookh* in competition with Scott's *The Lord of the Isles*.

your paper intimated lately—and that your approaching Freedom will find you in full health to enjoy it.[1]

yrs. ever
Byron

[TO ANNABELLA MILBANKE]   *Octr. 16th. 1814*

In arranging papers I have found the first letter you ever wrote to me[1]—read it again—you will allow that mine appeared a very unpromising case—but I can forgive—that is not the word—I mean I can forget even the *reality* of your sentiments *then*—if you do not deceive yourself *now*.—It was this epistle to which I always recurred—which haunted me through all our future correspondence—and now farewell to it—and yet your friendship was dearer to me than any love—but your own.————I very well recollect recommending Lady C[aroline] to your regard—or rather to your care—but that was before I was acquainted with her real disposition—and she—no matter what—but I thought you might do her some good—& was very sure no principle in your mind could be shaken even by the guilty—far less the *giddy*—as I then conceived her to be——it is all very well—only do not take my recommendations for the future.—You would I think be amused or perhaps surprized if you knew how much of my late life I have passed alone—I began this on Saturday—and break off very abruptly—the rest of the letter merely referred to Mr. H's journey which I have touched upon in the other.—
    Monday Morn

[TO ANNABELLA MILBANKE]   *Octr. 17th. 1814*

In my last letter I mentioned Mr. Hanson's intention of meeting Mr. Hoar on Wednesday next—he has since gone into the country & writes to me that some indispensable business will delay him some days longer—but that after those he will make all possible haste in joining Mr. Hoar at Durham and forwarding our arrangements.—It is impossible for me to express how much I am disappointed by these

---

[1] Leigh Hunt was still in the prison where Byron had first visited him with Moore in May, 1813. He was not released until February 2, 1815.

[1] Her first letter was full of moral advice, and it ended: "Believe in the sincerity of a regard, which, though it never can change to love, deserves to be considered as more than worldly friendship." (Mayne, *Life of Lady Byron*, p. 59.)

procrastinations—but words are useless—and I must not add loss of temper to that of time—I have written to him by this post—and as he appeared & appears as sensible as myself of the importance of his commission to me—I am sure he will not willingly defer his journey. ———My own departure from London will take place about the same time—and I shall shorten my stay at Newstead—or pass it by altogether.——In your last you hinted that Lady Milbanke was still weakly—I had hoped that her strength was sufficiently reestablished since her visit to Elemore.[1]—If there were no other inducements for me to wish to leave London—the utter solitude of my situation with only my Maccaw to converse with—would be sufficient—though he is not the least rational of my acquaintance—I read—but very desultorily —and as to writing except to you—and Augusta—and where I must on duty or business—it is out of the question.——However—solitude is nothing new—nor even disagreeable to me—at least it was not till now—but I much question whether I shall ever be able to bear it again—I hope *not* to be put to the test—Write to me—if only a few words—and regard me as

unalterably yours
B

[TO JOHN HANSON]   *Octr. 17th. 1814*

Dear Sir/—It is a great pity that I should have written to Sir R[alph]'s—that you were to be at Durham on Wednesday—however —it is useless to say anything now—I hope you will make what haste you can—as independent of mere personal feelings on the subject— Miss M[ilbanke]'s interests & mine are so much at stake—& can gain nothing by delay.—I must wait here for your return—let me know the day & believe me

yrs. truly
BYRON

P.S.—Claughton's answer—have you heard from him?

[TO LADY MELBOURNE]   *Monday—Octr. 17th. 1814*

Dear Lady M[elbourn]e.—I have spared you for the last 3 or 4 days—but though I perceive by ye. papers & heard from Ld.

---

[1] Elemore Hall in the county of Durham where the Milbankes lived before moving to Seaham just after Annabella's birth.

M[elbourne] that you are at present monopolized by Royalty I can't help writing to you a few lines—to which I require no answer.—My agent was to have set off this day to meet Mr. Hoar (of whom you gave me some hints) at Durham—but he will be detained in the country or in town perhaps for this week—and then proceed to discuss with Sir R[alph]'s people upon the spot.—I shall not set off till a day or two after Hanson—and then I must take Newstead in my way but shall not remain there above 48 hours.—There have been several intimations to me from all quarters to proceed—which I am very willing to do—but as Lawyers are as essential in this business as clergymen & post-horses—I must wait for the former before I harness either of the latter.—May I trust that my answer to C[aroline] was satisfactory—and ask like King Claudius of Hamlet—how "was the argument—was there no offence in't?"—I am now quite alone with my books & my Maccaw—Douglas Kinnaird with whom I have mostly been—is gone to Brighton—and I miss him a good deal—on Friday— Lord K[innaird]—Douglas—*Kean* (*the Kean*) & myself dined together.——Kean is a wonderful compound—& excels in humour & mimicry—the last talent is rather dangerous—but one cannot help being amused with it:—in other respects—in private society—he appears diffident & of good address—on the stage he is all perfect in my eyes.— I am horribly low-spirited—a malady which don't often assail me—& for fear it should be infectious I may as well finish this epistle—which I don't well know why I began.—

ever yrs. most truly

B

P.S.—*Tuesday.*

I open my letter to tell you that ye. "Scotch Politician" (of whose scheme I believe I subsequently told you) has succeeded.—Howard has taken the *elder*—+'s friend[1]—it is not yet declared—because *his sire* is not yet apprized of the future Duchess—but settled in all other respects.—I suppose I am telling you what you have not yet heard— at least it is told me as a thing not known. Keep it so.—Does not all this amuse you?—at least *my* having told you how it was to be before hand:—I think I only want goodness to have made a tolerable Jesuit in the various plots & counter plots of which I am aware.

[1] Augusta's friend Lady Charlotte Leveson-Gower. The "Scotch Politician" is her mother, Lady Stafford. See Oct. 7, 1814, to Lady Melbourne (*a*).

My dear Hobhouse—If I have not answered your very kind letter immediately—do not impute it to neglect—I have expected you would be in town or near it—& waited to thank you in person.——— Believe me no change of time or circumstance short of insanity can make any difference in my feelings—and I hope in my conduct towards you—I have known you too long & tried you too deeply—a new mistress is nothing to an old friend—the latter can't be replaced in this world—nor—I very much fear—in the next—and neither in this nor the other could I meet with one so deserving of my respect & regard.—————Well—H.—I am engaged—& we wait only for settlements and all that to be married—my intended it seems has liked me very well for a long time—which I am sure her encouragement gave me no reason to suspect—but so it is according to her account—the circumstances which led to the renewal of my proposal I will acquaint you with when we meet—if you think such material concerns worth your enquiry.——Hanson is going down next week to Durham to confabulate with Sir R[alph]'s agents on the score of temporalities—& I suppose I must soon follow to my Sire in law's that is to be—I confess that the character of wooer in this regular way does not sit easy upon me—I wish I could wake some morning & find myself fairly married—I do hate (out of Turkey) all fuss & bustle—& ceremony so much and one can't be married according to what I hear without *some*.——I wish—whenever this same form is muttered over us—that you could make it convenient to be present—I will give you due notice—if you would but take a wife & be coupled then also like people electrified in company through the same chain—it would be still further comfort.—Good-Even—

ever yrs. most truly
B

My dear Hodgson.—I am truly sorry to trouble you, but my cousin G. Byron is in want of a loan—and if you could get the note now due cashed (of Mrs. Taylor's)[1] it would be very convenient. I enclose the

---

[1] Hodgson was engaged to a daughter of Mrs. Tayler. Another daughter had married the Rev. Henry Drury on Dec. 20, 1808. Mrs. Tayler may have been a widow when Byron in 1813 travelled all night in a stage coach to convince her that Hodgson would be free of debt and thus got her consent to the engagement with her daughter. According to Prothero (*LJ*, I, 197n) Drury's wife was daughter of Archdale Wilson Tayler, of Boreham Wood, Herts. The note for £150 must have been for a loan that Byron made to her.

note—excuse my haste and laconism—I am in town but for a few days and hurried with a thousand things—believe me

> ever yrs. most truly
> BYRON

Note for £150.0.0 enclosed.

[TO HENRY DRURY]   *Octr. 18th. 1814*

My dear Drury—Many thanks for your hitherto unacknowledged "anecdotes"[;] now for one of mine—I am going to be married—and have been engaged this month.————It is a long story—& therefore I can't tell it—an old—& (though I did not know it till lately)—a *mutual* attachment—the very sad life I have led since I was *your* pupil must partly account for the offs & ons in this now to be arranged business.——We are only waiting for the lawyers & settlements &c.—and next week or the week after—I shall go down to Seaham in the new character of regular suitor for a wife of mine own.—Do you remember the dialogue with that father of the girls who ran away with your best bound Tacitus last speechday?—Mr. I forget the name?—it is—or was—old enough—but no matter for that.——I hope Hodgson is in a fair way on the same voyage—I saw him & his idol at Hastings—I wish he would be married at the same time—I should like to make a party—like people electrified in a row by or rather—*through* the same chain—holding one another's hands, & all feeling the shock at once.—I have not yet apprized him of this—he makes such a serious matter of these things—and is so "melancholy & gentleman-like" that it is quite overcoming to us choice spirits—that never to be forgotten journey to Ox[for]d on his suitoring last year!—by the way it was about this time—do you recollect our ribaldry?—if you do—pray renew it.————They say one should not be married in a *black* coat—I won't have a blue one—that's flat—I hate it.—Jackson (the Pancratiast)[1] tells me he met with "two Mr. Drury's" to whom he sang several "*flash*"[2] dithyrambics with unbounded applause.—

> ever yrs Dear D. most amicably
> B

[1] In ancient Greece and Rome, a pancration (Latin, pancratium) was an athletic contest combining boxing and wrestling.

[2] "Flash" was a slang term for the language of thieves, sharpers, etc. Byron extended it to include the language of demi-monde characters he met in pugilistic circles.

P.S.—Your correspondent & my old amie Lady O[xfor]d hath gotten the King (& several of his subjects probably) of Naples as my successor—you may perhaps have heard this from Tu. Tayler[3]—the report is rife among the gossips.————

[TO ANNABELLA MILBANKE]   *Octr. 19th. 1814*

I return you Mrs. S[iddo]n's[1] very kind and—after all unaffected letter—her style to be sure is vastly poetical—and her epithets would be no worse for weeding than her periods for pruning—but then with her dramatic habits all this is but natural and you ought to be very thankful it was not in blank verse.———Our "incognito" enquirer— seems a little after the heroic mode also—who or what he is—or why he came there—I cannot conceive nor guess—all my intimates are sufficiently acquainted with your name and "most blest conditions" to render such queries useless—nor do I know one sufficiently interested about me to take the trouble on *my* account—and yet it could scarcely be a stranger—but be he who or what he may—it is odd enough—and of a piece with some of my past adventures which have occasionally been extravagant as those of a dull romance.———I once thought it might be Bruce[2]—but he is not in England or at least that part of it— it was like one of his high-flown experiments. I remember when I came down from Constantinople—meeting him & Lady Hester Stanhope at Athens:—some time after when they were embarking by night at the Piraeus—just as we parted he made me (for the first time of his life) a most "eternal" profession of friendship—after which he went upon the waters—and I mounted my horse and galloped back through the olives upon a steed as black as the "Giaours" and much on such an evening—since that time we never met.—————I am only waiting for Mr. Hanson's return to forward him—and set out myself to meet you.—We should find New[stea]d sufficiently spacious —indeed too much so—but not quite comfortable in its present state for a permanent residence—besides—we should certainly grow fond of it—and it would then be disagreeable to part with it—Augusta dotes on it—that is natural—but there is no reason why you should be encumbered with our family prejudices.—————I will take your

[3] Unidentified; perhaps a brother-in-law of Drury who had married a Miss Tayler.
[1] Mrs. Sarah Siddons, the famous actress, was a friend of the Milbankes.
[2] Michael Bruce, whom Byron met in Athens. See June 19, 1811, to Hobhouse (Vol. 2, p. 49).

word for the "world" and "it's kindness" without desiring to prove it's favours further—being only too much obliged to it for containing you.—

Ever—my Love—

most affectly yrs

B

P.S.—Assure Mrs. Siddons of my respect—and the pleasure I shall feel in improving my acquaintance with her—and give my *duty* to our Papa & Lady M,—and all our relations.——If you are fond of the drama you must see Kean—he is the triumph of mind over matter for he has nothing but countenance & expression—his figure is very little & even mean—but I never saw the Passions so expressed—on the stage at least—except by Mrs. Sid[don]s.——

[TO FRANCIS HODGSON]   *Octr. 19th. 1814*

My Dear Hodgson—She *is* to be Lady B. the moment the lawyers & settlers will let us.—It is a long story—and I must defer it—but I have misunderstood her—she has been attached to me for a considerable time—& the "previous attachment" turns out to have had no existence—we *both* thought that we were separated—and that obstacles since proved imaginary were between us—in the belief that I would never renew—she tried to make herself partial to another (this is her own account) but the delusion vanished on their meeting—and all *our* misapprehensions have arisen from the mutual reserve between persons so circumstanced as we supposed ourselves.——I have been accepted this month or more—but am here on business[;] the moment Mr. Hanson goes to Durham which will be in a week or less—I shall get ready—indeed *am* ready—to follow him—the father—mother—& all connections on both sides are most favourable—I love her—and hope she will be happy.————I shall stop at Augusta's in my way to Newstead & Seaham—Claughton gave up N[ewstead] & forfeited £25-000—out of £28-000—already paid—besides expenses of planting & improvements.—————I will try to come to Cambridge—indeed I must pass through it in my journey.—Hanson mentioned to me a wish that you could be prevailed on to undertake a domestic Chaplaincy for *Lord Portsmouth*—I think it would be a good thing for reasons I will explain when we meet.—At least it would enable you to marry—and you & your wife might live near Hurstbourne within a mile of the family mansion—however—more of this anon.—

ever yrs. most truly

B

P.S.—You might have young H[anson][1] as a pupil if you liked.—

[TO LADY MELBOURNE] *Octr. 19th. 1814*

My dear Lady M[elbourn]e.—I wrote to you with the same tidings yesterday.——She[1] hardly knew him—but seemed quite terrified at the idea of her dilemma—if it was proposed to her as had been intimated—and from that + released her at once—I hope + has burnt her letters—which she particularly desired—she behaved extremely well for malgré "the Politician" she wrote secretly (when the rest were at the Ld. races) a long explanatory epistle to + foretelling what has occurred—I think *him* in great luck.—Annabella is in all respects all I could wish & more than I deserve—my only regret is her having taken so long a period to decide upon a very simple proposi-:ion—when had she but said the same thing 2 years—even a year ago—what confusions and embarrassments good & bad might have been prevented—there are three or four which you know—and one or two you do not—now if she had even given me a *distinct* though distant hope—I would have acted with a view to it—as it was—in my pursuit of strong emotions & mental *drams* I found them to be sure and intoxicated myself accordingly—but now I am sobered my head aches & my heart too.—Next week I hope & intend to be at Seaham—Hanson *should* have been at Durham now but will set off in a few days—and I shall follow him with all speed.——I hear from Ann[abell]a very often—and the more I see of her—the more I find reason to congratulate myself,—& to thank *you*—for after all it could never have taken place but through your breaking the ice.—

ever yrs. most affectly.

B

[TO LADY MELBOURNE] *Octr. 20th. 1814*

My dear Lady M[elbourn]e.—Hanson is the Government solicitor of the stamp office—& was put in by Ld. Grenville[1]—I have known

---

[1] Newton Hanson later became Hodgson's pupil, through Byron's intervention.
[1] Lady Charlotte Leveson-Gower. See Oct. 7, 1814, to Lady Melbourne (Vol. 1, p. 113).
[1] See April 2, 1807, to Hanson.

him since I was a child—as to his integrity or ability I cannot speak—
I suppose as all men think "patrons capricious and mistresses fickle
but every one excepts *his own* mistress & *his own* patron" most people
except their own lawyer—perhaps the sale of News[tea]d and
Claughton's forfeiture (£25000) may be some proof of his talent—
for on all law points Hanson certainly beat him as the result proved
and the said Clau[ghto]n was also a lawyer.————All I can say is
he expressed himself extremely anxious & pleased about *the* match—
but a little more inquisitive than I have been about A[nnabella]'s
expectations——I expect him in town daily—the journey to Durham
was his own proposal—& he wrote to Hoar—who did not seem over-
pleased with Sir R[alph]'s letter calling him "agent" instead of
"Counsel" & God knows what mummery & jargon in the way of
technicals.—I only wait to forward Hanson and shall embark first for
New[stea]d for a day & so on to Seaham—I can assure you I find the
not being married exceedingly embarrassing & wish I had been so
these twelve hours.—————Of Lady Staff[ord][2]—"I tell the tale
as told to me" and I believe I was one of the first who knew of the
scheme—they were not certain *which* of the girls he would take—but
he was to have his choice by the account of one of them—now that he
has fixed on *her*—I wish it may go on—because she is the best little
creature on earth and anything but designing—or she would never
have betrayed this to + which was quite a work of supererogation.
+ has written to congratulate her—Oh—it is a delightful farce
altogether—and one of the scenes that reconcile one to existence for
if it were not for things of this kind and apple women tumbling down in
the street there would be nothing to laugh at.——"The opinions"
about A and B!—if she takes the least trouble I am the most manage-
able animal that was ever driven—and so her "eyes are like yours" a
little less mischievous I hope—though I believe you see without
them—at least you observe things that escape all other optics.
—————I am infinitely obliged by the wish for my society to replace
the P[rince] R[egent] & Ld. M[elbourne] but Lord Cow[pe]r will be a
much more lively proxy for both than I could hope to be—still I can't
conceive a more pleasant party if my intrusion did not spoil it.——But
alas! I can only send my sighs by the heavy coach and this letter by the
light one

ever yrs. most truly

B

2 Lady Stafford was the mother of Lady Charlotte Leveson-Gower.

P.S.—I enclose you a letter Hanson wrote to me after his daughter's marriage—the Devil's in it if he has not my interest at heart after that even by his own account.

[TO ANNABELLA MILBANKE]   *Octr. 20th. 1814*

I have been so much amused with your "extracts" though I had no idea what evil spirit I then appeared in your eyes—you were quite right however as far as *appearances*—but that was not my natural character—I was just returned from a far country where everything was different—& felt bewildered & not very happy in my own which I had left without regret & returned to without interest—I found myself I did not very well know why—an object of curiosity which I never wished to excite—and about a poem which I had no conception was to make such a fuss—my mind & my feelings were moreover occupied with considerations which had nothing in common with the circle where I was whirling—so that no wonder I was repulsive & cold—I never could conquer my disposition to be both in a crowd from which I was always wishing myself away.————Those who know me most intimately can tell you that I am if anything too *childish* with a greater turn for the ridiculous than anything serious—and—I could hope—not very illnatured *off the stage*—and if angry never *loud*—I can't say much for these qualifications—but I have such a regard for yours—that I am sure we shall be a very happy couple—I wish you had a greater passion for governing—for I don't shine in conducting myself—and am very docile with a gentle guide.—One of Augusta's friends writes to her & says she is so afraid—now I am to be married "that I shall become a good sort of man" an awful anticipation!—the P[rince] R[egent] has been at Brocket & talked on the subject to Ly. M[el-bourne] by no means ill-naturedly—as is his usual way—& might be excuseable enough as far as *I* am concerned—among other things he said "between her prose & his poetry what may we not expect"—as if—we were to do nothing else but make books—I am sure the employments the Morning Post found out for us would be much more useful & quite as entertaining—particularly the care of the poultry &c. &c.————I am only waiting for Mr. Hanson's return to set him off—& follow myself.—if—Dearest——these men of parchment can *settle* us—or put us in the way of being settled within a reasonable time—you will not long defer taking a name to which you will do more honour than has been conferred upon it since it's first inscription in "Domesday Boke" with the signature of my Progenitors

Erneis & *Ralph*—so you see your papa—& the papa of all my papas were synonimous.—ever my Love

yr. own

B

P.S.—Oh—I must tell you one of my present avocations.—D[ougla]s Kinnaird (a friend of mine brother to Lord Kd) applied to me to write words for a musical composer[1] who is going to publish the *real old undisputed Hebrew melodies* which are beautiful & to which David & the prophets actually sang the "songs of Zion"—& I have done nine or ten—on the sacred model—partly from Job &c. & partly my own imagination—but I hope a little better than Sternhold & Hopkins[2]—it is odd enough that this should fall to my lot—who have been abused as "an infidel"—Augusta says "they will call me a *Jew* next."

[TO JOHN HANSON]   *Octr. 21st. 1814*

Dear Sir/—I trust this will find you preparing to set out—as I rather think the *mines* can go on by themselves for the present—and am very sure—that this delay makes us all extremely uncomfortable. Do pray—dispatch—and don't forget that *I got up earlier* for one of your *marriages* than you seem disposed to allow me to do for my own.—

ever very truly yrs.

BYRON

P.S.—I have heard from Mr. Hodgson—who will take Newton when you please—if you like I will take him to Cambridge & settle him there in my way to N[ewstead] & S[eaham]—I wish however you would think of the *Chaplaincy* decidedly—I am certain *H[odgson]* is the *Man* of all others you want.—You see that *I* think of *your* concerns—I wish you would return the compliment.———

[TO JAMES CAWTHORN]   *Octr. 21st. 1814*

Sir—Some time ago I received your letter in the country but have been so much hurried that I hope you will excuse my not having answered it before.—If you can prove "the piracy"[1] & chuse to prose-

---

¹ Isaac Nathan. See [Oct. 1814?] to Nathan.
² See Sept. 15, 1814, to Moore (*b*), note 2.
¹ A piracy of *English Bards and Scotch Reviewers*, which Byron had suppressed in 1812.

cute I will pay the expences—it must undoubtedly be stopped—because independent of other considerations though the copyright was never parted with I should not permit others to publish what I refused you.—Of course my mind remains unaltered on the subject of publication—it must *not* proceed on any account—I can't conceive how the devil a temporary subject of that kind should still be sought after—unless it is the perversity of people—who want a thing because they can't have it.—

yrs. &c. &c.
BYRON

P.S.—Perhaps the best way would be to obtain an *injunction*—is not that the word?—

[TO ANNABELLA MILBANKE]   *Octr. 22d. 1814*

I fear that the letter which accompanied the enclosure[1] of your first contained something or other that has not quite pleased—but I judge merely from the tone of your answer rather than the words—indeed dearest—if so it was most unintentional—and any vexation which I bring on you must recoil tenfold on myself as is the case now.—You will not—I hope—wonder that I should seek to "forget" a delusion that had embittered my thoughts—and made me careless of my conduct—for so long a period—but I by no means wished to convey the slightest reflection on you—which would be equally selfish & ridiculous.———I did not like to destroy the letter because it was yours—and it was not too pleasant to retain it—because you are mine—and that letter says you never will be so.———Do you think—my love—that happiness depends upon similarities or differences in character?—I doubt it—I am rather inclined to lay more stress upon *intellect*—than is generally done—much upon temper—affection must do the rest.—When a sensible person is wrong—they must eventually perceive & own it without much struggle—but a fool is never to be convinced—and after all not worth convincing.———I shall only bewilder myself with metaphysical distinctions if I go on about *mind* and I am sure that of my own character I know nothing—nor could I if my existence were at stake tell what my "ruling passion" is—it takes it's colour I believe from the circumstances in which I am placed—there are few which at one period or other of my life have not affected me—but I could not fix on one which like "Aaron's serpent swallowed all

[1] See Oct. 16, 1814 to Annabella, note 1.

the rest".——"Happy with *you*" nay—if you doubt—at least do your-self justice—and reverse it—it is your happiness which is & ought to be chiefly consulted—mine is in the hope of not diminishing it—if I can add to it my own will proportionally increase.——I am as I have already said—waiting—& with encreased impatience for Mr. Hanson—at all events—I can not remain much longer here.———You ask me if Augusta is not "shy"—to excess—she is as I tell her—like a frightened hare—with new acquaintances—but I suppose has made a grand effort to overcome it in this instance.—She is now nursing—which will I fear prevent her accepting your father's very kind invitation—I wish with all my heart—she could.—"My thoughts" —I have written to you daily—& am only fearful of tiring you with words.—You do my "Maccaw" much honour—but are quite right to avail yourself of the only opportunity you could ever have of exerting the amiable passion of which you menace him with being the object.——

Ever thine
B

[TO JOHN HANSON]   *Octr. 22d. 1814*

Dear Sir/—When I tell you that your delay if prolonged will probably make a serious difference between the parties—I presume you will think that Mr. [Viney?] & his mines can perhaps condescend to let you go for a short time.[1]—I cannot add a word more—but am

very truly yours
BYRON

[TO JOHN COWELL]   *Octr. 22d. 1814*

My dear Cowell—Many & sincere thanks for your kind letter.——The bet or rather forfeit was one hundred to Hawke—and fifty to Hay—(nothing to Kelly) for a guinea received from each of the two former[1]—I shall feel much obliged by your setting me right if I err in this statement in any way——& have reasons for wishing you to

[1] Hanson had gone off suddenly to Ilfracombe, Devon, to see a client, when Byron was expecting him to go to Seaham to discuss the marriage settlement with Sir Ralph Milbanke's agent. See Oct. 24, 1814, to Hanson.

[1] When in Brighton in the summer of 1808 (the year he met John Cowell) Byron had made some wagers that he would not marry, and now those with whom he had bet were descending upon him.

recollect as much as possible of what passed and state it to Hodgson.—
My reason is this—some time ago—Mr. Hay required a bet of me
which I never made and of course refused to pay—& have heard no
more of it—to prevent similar mistakes is my object in wishing you to
remember well what passed—& to put Hodgson in possession of your
memory on the subject.—I hope to see you soon in my way through
Cambridge—remember me to H. and believe me ever & truly yrs.

BYRON

[TO JOHN HANSON]   *Oct. 24th. 1814*

Dear Sir—I am truly sorry to write to you in any terms but the
most friendly—but circumstances compel me.—It is now *five weeks*
since I announced to you Miss M[ilbanke]'s resolution & mine—&
since that period little or nothing has been done towards the object of
our wishes.—I should not be a very impartial judge doubtless in my
own case—but this is not my opinion so much as that of her connections & of mine—who have written to me—and when I state the
fact—that I am waiting for your return—they express their surprize
that in business of so much importance—so much time should be lost—
and delays as it were sought for—it looks like trifling on my part—
and on yours does not appear very attentive to me as a client or
friendly as a man.—I have written to you 3 times to press your
departure—but without an answer—I certainly did hope that on an
occasion not the least important with regard to my present as well as
future prospects & happiness there would not have been so much
necessity of urging you in behalf of yours very truly

BYRON

P.S.—A very little more delay will settle the business most
effectually—in which case I shall have reason to remember Mr.
[Viney?]¹—& your zeal in *his* cause—all the rest of my life.

[TO ANNABELLA MILBANKE]   *Octr. 25th. 1814*

It is with great regret that I shall miss meeting Lord Wentworth at
Seaham—but so it is—I could till now fix no precise day—and whatever appearance or consequences these delays may have or create—I
must bear them.———Hanson whom I have been expecting & urging

¹ See Oct. 22, 1814, to Hanson.

from day to day—now writes that he is ill—but will send his son—this will not do—it was his duty & is to be present and to meet Mr. Hoar in person—and he shall do so—or it shall be our last difference. Whether the man is mad—or only wishes to make me so—I know not—I have been acquainted with him since I was ten years old—which gives him a kind of claim upon what good-nature I possess—which he is pushing a little too far.—However—let that rest—I will set off on *Saturday*—and leave out Newstead & Newmarket on my way which I had at first intended to visit—if I can get away a day before—it shall not be lost—but I fear that I cannot remain at Seaham under the present circumstances above a few days—nothing would have made me deliberate so long—but the hope that when we did meet—the previous pause would render parting again unnecessary—but these things we can discuss in person.————If you can—convince your father—that he cannot be more vexed than—no wonder he is so—in short I can only say that I meant all this for the best—and my meaning turns out I think like one of those "good intentions" with which the Portuguese proverb tells us that a certain place (never to be mentioned by divines to "ears polite") is paved————I make all my apologies to your father rather than to *you*—for I am very sure *you* know me too well—not to understand my feelings on the subject without further explanation——The very circumstances that might appear tardy on my part—are in fact a proof of my impatience for it was to render all further interruptions & delays unnecessary that I submitted to these.—But enough of this—if I am alive I will set out on Saturday.—

ever most yrs.

B

P.S.—The oldest friend[1]—that is the earliest though not the kindest I ever had—is now lying between life and death a few streets from me—she was seized with a fever and delirium about a fortnight ago—I only heard of this within these few days—her husband (from whom she was separated) & her mother are now with her—her life has been a melancholy one though on her part blameless—I have not seen her for several years—and probably never may again—nor do I wish it—but I always wished her happy & to live while life could make her so.——You will think my letter—at least the postscript a collection of casualties and melancholy accidents—but—did you know Lady

_____

[1] Mary Chaworth-Musters.

Roseberry?[2] very young—very pretty—& very unwise it should seem—for the "on dit" is that she has gone off with Sir H. Mildmay (her sister was his late wife) I foresaw this in the summer—and all I can now say—is—that I hope it is *not* come to pass—and it is not unlikely to be false having been in the Newspapers.—If it turns out so —I ask her pardon—& yours at any rate for repeating such gossip.

————

[TO JOHN HANSON]   *Octr. 25th. 1814*

Dear Sir—Your illness is more than unfortunate—at least to me— had you but proceeded as at first intended you would probably have preserved your own health & saved me much misery.—It is useless to send Charles—take your own time—since it is so—but no one but yourself can confer at all satisfactorily with Sir R[alph]'s agents circumstanced as I now am.—In the mean time—I will tell you how your delay has situated *me*—Ld. W[entwort]h Miss M[ilbanke]'s uncle is leaving Seaham without seeing me as he particularly wished—her father & mother are very much displeased as are the rest of her connections—and herself very uneasy.—*Now*—my going without you—& without your conferring with Mr. ' Hoar—is out of the question—it would forward nothing—it would answer no purpose my solitary journey—except to attach Miss M[ilbanke] & myself more— without the prospect—at least the certainty of our marrying.——I need say little more—what to say to them I know not—after the delays already—they will merely look upon your illness as a new excuse—and perhaps of mine.—*I* of course can have no doubt of it— but—in short—this marriage will be broken off—& if so—whether intentional or accidental—I can't help it—but by God—I can never look upon anyone again as my friend who has even been the innocent cause of destroying my happiness.—

yrs. truly
BYRON

P.S.—It is of no use sending *Charles*—it is impossible he can give the explanations required—or that any but yourself should be sufficiently master of the subject.—

2 Lady Rosebery, wife of the 4th Earl of Rosebery, eloped with Sir Henry Mildmay. See Oct. 31, 1814, to Lady Melbourne.

My Love—Mr. Hanson is on his way from Devon at last—but if he does not arrive before Saturday—I shall not wait for him—Augusta wishes me so much to pass that way that I shall make "mine inn" at her abode for a short time and thence to our Papa's.—I console myself for not being in time to be presented to Ld. W[entwort]h with the thought —not very agreeable after all—that perhaps he would not have liked me—and though I prefer the old school & courtly deportment of the past generation—I can't flatter myself with the hope of recommending me to it's good graces—by a display of my own—if I may so quibble upon that important word in Ld. Chesterfield's dictionary.[1]——— You laugh at me—about your *serious* letter—which is very mischievous—it made me quite elegiac—not in words though—don't you think it a little odd—that I have not once "woefully balladed your eyebrow"?—one can't paint a storm upon deck though one may in port from recollection—neither could I—(almost a professed scribbler as I have been) ever rhyme or write upon any subject upon which my heart was set—till it was lost or won and some time had elapsed—and yet I have dealt less in *fiction*—than most bards—I will venture to say—than almost any of *the day.*————How sorry I am that Hobhouse is not in London—he would be so pleased with the prospect of seeing you—and yet I don't know—he is—when & where he likes—so very pleasing—that I think it may be as well not to present him till I can introduce you by our name———"Did Michael Cassio when you wooed my Lady—know of your love?"[2]—oh no—not at all—what a world of tragedy would have been saved could the Moor's ancient have received that response.—————As I do not know the distance—I cannot fix day & hour—but I shall probably arrive in an Evening—not late—at least too late—I bring no servant—except my valet—the others I shall leave—here or at Newstead.—A thousand thanks to you for calling me "Byron"—it sounds—(it never sounded so sweetly to me before) as if we had been married already—I hope Mr. Hoar will keep his promise of speed—I have been scolding Hanson till my rage is quite exhausted—& he seems (upon paper) in great haste and contrition.—The person I mentioned in my last—is better— but still very ill & weakly—her loving Lord has left London & her in

---

[1] Presumably the important word in Chesterfield's dictionary is "deportment".

[2] *Othello*, Act III, scene 3.

this state! and yet this very woman made his fortune—& brought him love & beauty besides. "These be your Christian husbands"

ever thine dearest—

B

P.S.—Don't forget me to your father and Lady M[ilbank]e—

[TO JOHN HANSON]   *Octr. 29th. 1814*

My dear Sir/—I am just setting out for Seaham—& beg you will come to Durham with all convenient speed.—Miss M[ilbanke] informs me that Ld. W[entworth] went to Durham on purpose to require a promise from Mr. Hoar that he would not delay a moment longer than the settlements actually required—so it becomes us to be at least as diligent.——I enclose you a letter from Mealey—with another paper on that eternal tax business—perhaps you can leave word with Mr. France or Charles to see to it.

ever yrs.

B

[on cover]: To be delivered on his arrival in London.—

[TO LADY MELBOURNE]   *Newark. Octr. 31st. 1814*

My dear Lady M[elbourn]e.—Your letter was delivered just as I was leaving town—or I do believe a day sooner would have stopped me—since I had much rather not have set out on my present expedition at this moment.—However I am thus far on my way to S[eaham]—on Saturday I got to +'s and stayed till late on Sunday— and here I am.—Last night I slept at the *inn* (Wansford) where it seems Sir Hal. [Mildmay] & the Countess Roseberry dined[1]—in very good spirits & quite at their ease—they slept at Eaton afterwards in the most decisive way—so that all appears quite regular.—Don't you think they are not much better than some people you may have heard of who had half a mind to *anticipate* their example—& don't yet know whether to be glad or sorry they have not?————I don't think *he*[2] much *admires* my marriage—he knows that I have made + my heiress—& though it is not a stupendous inheritance—yet as he sup-

---

[1] See Oct. 25, 1814, to Annabella Milbanke, note 2.
[2] Augusta's husband, Col. George Leigh.

227

poses the life a bad one &c. &c. I can see that he don't like any chance of my wife's being in his way—I remember when we met in town he advised me not to be in a hurry—& I know but one motive why he should say this—except a good one—& for that I never credit anybody—having no more *trust* in me than a turnpike-gate—though my Motto exacts it from every one else. Well—I am proceeding very slowly to S[eaham]—the last news I heard was that Ld. W[entworth] was leaving it—but had gone to D[urham] to direct Mr. Hoar most particularly to be as quick in the settling as possible—as *his* (Ld. W[entworth]'s) "whole heart was set upon the match"—all this is very fine—but it was very foolish dragging me out of town before my lawyer had arrived.——Ld. W[entworth] will be gone before I arrive—which I don't regret—but how the rest of us are to proceed I know not.—I shall not stay above a week—if I can help it—don't write till you hear from me *there*—for I am not sure I shall go now as Newstead is so near & I have something to do there.—Poor Mrs. Chaworth is mad in town—it came upon her at Hastings in the house where she succeeded A[ugusta] & me as tenant.——Chaw[ort]h went to her—but has since gone to Yorkshire to hunt—she is still ill—& I fear—dangerously as to sense—if not even life.——I am in very ill humour &

yours affectionately
B

[TO LADY MELBOURNE]   *Seaham. Novr. 4th. 1814*

My dear Lady M[elbourn]e.—I have been here these two days—but waited to observe before I imparted to you "my confidential Counsel" as Master Hoar would say—my remarks.——Your brother pleases me much—to be sure his stories are long—but I believe he has told most of them—& he is to my mind the perfect gentleman——but I don't like Lady Mil[bank]e at all—I can't tell why—for we don't differ—but so it is—she seems to be every thing here—which is all very well—and I am & mean to be very conformable & dutiful but nevertheless I wish she & mine aunt could change places as far as regards me & mine.—A[nnabella]'s meeting & mine made a kind of scene.—though there was no acting nor even speaking —but the pantomine was very expressive——she seems to have more feeling than we imagined—but is the most *silent* woman I ever encountered—which perplexes me extremely—I like them to talk—because then they *think* less—much cogitation will not be in my

228

favour—besides I can form my judgments better—since unless the countenance is flexible—it is difficult to steer by mere looks—I am studying her but I can't boast of my progress in getting at her disposition—and if the conversation is to be all on one side—I fear committing myself—& those who only listen—must have their thoughts so much about them—as to seize any weak point at once—however the die is cast—neither party can recede—the lawyers are here—mine & all—& I presume the parchment once scribbled I shall become Lord Annabella.———I can't yet tell whether we are to be happy or not—I have every disposition to do her all possible justice—but I fear she won't govern me—& if she don't it will not do at all—but perhaps she may mend of that fault.———I have always thought—first that she did not like me at all—& next—that her supposed after liking was *imagination*—this last I conceive that my presence would—perhaps has removed—if so—I shall soon discover it—but mean to take it with great philosophy—and to behave attentively & well—though I never could love but that which *loves*—& this I must say for myself—that my attachment always increases in due proportion to the return it meets with—& never changes in the presence of it's object—to be sure like Mrs. Damer I have "an opinion of absence."[1]———Pray write—I think you need not fear that the *answer* to *this* will run any of the risks you apprehend—It will be a great comfort to me in all events to call you Aunt & to know that you are sure of my being

ever yrs.
B

[TO LADY MELBOURNE] *Novr. 6th. 1814*

My dear Lady M[elbourn]e.—Annabella & I go on extremely well—we have been much together and if such details were not insipid to a third person it would not be difficult to prove that we appear much attached—& I hope permanently so.—She is as you know a perfectly good person—but I think not only her feelings and affections—but her *passions* stronger than we supposed—of these last I can't as yet positively judge—my observations lead me to guess as much however—she herself cannot be aware of this—nor could I except from a habit of attending minutely in such cases to their slightest indications & of course I don't let her participate in the discovery, in which after all I may be mistaken.—Our lawyers are in a fair train of concluding

---

[1] See May 1, 1814, to Lady Melbourne, note 3.

229

their parchment passports to matrimony—and I am happy to say—in the most amicable way without disputes—demurs—or more delays—when quite done—which may be in a fortnight—we are to marry *quietly*—& to set off by ourselves to Halnaby[1] for *the* Moon—and afterwards probably to a house (Farleigh)[2] which I have taken in Hampshire—a large & comfortably retired mansion which I know by having been there some years ago—& I think it will suit us very well.— Lady M[ilbanke] will probably have informed you of the settlements &c. I am making all the proposed arrangements about N[ewstead] & R[ochdale] and her present fortune is to be I think £20-000—which is all that is *certain*—I *would* not as you may suppose embarrass the old ones by boring them to bind themselves down about futurity—they say that Ld. W[entworth] has declared her by will his heiress—indeed he himself went over to Durham & told Hoar so in positive terms— but he best knows whether he will adhere to such intention—*I* wish to trust as little as possible to expectations—though even *hers* seem very sanguine—if realized it will all be very well—& if not—should she herself continue what I firmly believe her—I could bear—indeed I could hardly regret any posthumous disappointments—unless I thought that she suffered from her connection with me.—I am not— however—romantic nor indifferent to these—which are good things in themselves—but simply do not wish to set our hopes too high since their completion will not be the less pleasant because they were temperate—while their moderation in case of the contrary would save us any violent vexation.—————I think we all *improve*—& suit very well—I endeavour to conform to their habits which is not difficult —& I could hope that I am not a troublesome inmate—*they* are very kind—and A[nnabella] & I of course still kinder—I hope she will be happy—I am sure she can make & keep me so if she likes.—I wrote to you a day or two ago—& hope to sign myself soon—not more affectionately but more entirely

yours

B

P.S.—A[nnabella] showed me *your* remarks upon *her* requisites for a spouse—you can't think how sensible & amusing they are—I mean the *comments*.—I wish you would write to her—she seems to feel very kindly towards you—& I should love her were it only for that.—

---

[1] A country house of the Milbankes in Yorkshire.
[2] Hanson's country house in Hampshire.

My dear Lady Mel[bourn]e.—I delivered your letters—but have only mentioned ye receipt of your *last* to myself.————Do you know I have great doubts—if this will be a marriage now.—her disposition is the very reverse of *our* imaginings—she is overrun with fine feelings—scruples about herself & *her* disposition (I suppose in fact she means mine) and to crown all is taken ill once every 3 days with I know not what—but the day before and the day after she seems well—looks & eats well & is cheerful & confiding & in short like any other person in good health & spirits.—A few days ago she made one *scene*—not altogether out of C[aroline]'s style—it was too long & too trifling in fact for me to transcribe—but it did me no good——in the article of conversation however she has improved with a vengeance—but I don't much admire these same agitations upon slight occasions.—I don't know—but I think it by no means impossible you will see me in town soon—I can only interpret these things one way—& merely wait to be certain to make my obeisances and "exit singly." I hear of nothing but "feeling" from morning till night—except from Sir Ralph with whom I go on to admiration—Ly. M[ilbanke] too is pretty well—but I am never sure of A[nnabella]—for a moment—the least word—and you know I rattle on through thick & thin (always however avoiding anything I think can offend her favourite notions) if only to prevent me from yawning—the least word—or alteration of tone—has some inference drawn from it—sometimes we are too much alike—& then again too unlike—this comes of *system*—& squaring her notions to the Devil knows what—for my part I have lately had recourse to the eloquence of *action* (which Demosthenes calls the first part of oratory) & find it succeeds very well & makes her very quiet which gives me some hopes of the efficacy of the "calming process" so renowned in "*our* philosophy."—In fact and entre nous it is really amusing—she is like a child in that respect—and quite *caressable* into kindness and good humour—though I don't think her temper *bad* at any time—but very *self*-tormenting—and anxious—and romantic. ————In short—it is impossible to foresee how this will end *now*—anymore than 2 years ago—if there is a break—it shall be *her* doing not mine.—

ever yrs. most truly

B

[TO JOHN HANSON]   *Boroughbridge—Novr. 16th. 1814*

Dear Sir/—I am thus far on my way to town where we can confer on business—I thought it best to have a further personal conference with you.—I received yours with the enclosed from Clau[ghto]n—it looks well & will I hope turn out so.—Let me find a line from you in Albany—the post is just going

ever yrs.

B

[TO ANNABELLA MILBANKE]   *Boroughbridge—Novr. 16th. 1814*

My Heart—We are thus far separated—but after all one mile is as bad as a thousand—which is a great consolation to one who must travel six hundred before he meets you again.——If it will give you any satisfaction—I am as comfortless as a pilgrim with peas in his shoes—and as cold as Charity—Chastity or any other Virtue.—On my way to Castle Eden I waylaid the Post—& found letters from Hanson—which I annex for the amusement of Lady Milbanke who having a passion for business will be glad to see any thing that looks like it.—I expect to reach Newstead tomorrow & Augusta the day after.—Present to our parents as much of my love as you like to part with—& dispose of the rest as you please.—ever thine

ß

P.S.—I will begin my next with what I meant to be the postscript of this.—

[TO ANNABELLA MILBANKE]   *Novr. 20th. 1814*

Dearest A———My arrival at the other A's occurred yesterday at odds with the post-time so that I had not a moment to write to you.—Your two letters have been received with those to Augusta—who tells me that she has answered them.——As I am anxious to meet Hanson & hear further of our arrangements I shall not remain here beyond tomorrow; if Mr. Hoar has finished his part of the papers &c. I will take care that all the subsequent part is got over as soon as possible.——Do not tax yourself to write more frequently or at length than is perfectly agreeable—but address your next to Albany—where I hope to meet it.—How do you go on? is your health better?—and your spirits? I trust that your prescription for the reestablishment of the last has not failed in it's effect——Augusta & hers are all in good plight—I am trying to arrange so that she should meet us somewhere —soon after—or before our next interview.——————My popularity with "Hoar["] is a very unexpected pleasure—but I suppose it is a return in kind for the impression you made upon Hanson—I can assure you that any kind feeling on the part of our papa and mamma is most sincerely reciprocal.—To yourself Dearest if I were to write forever I could only come to one conclusion which I may as well make now & that is that I ever am most entirely & unalterably

your attached
B

P.S.—I don't ask you to consider this as a letter—but merely a memorandum that I am thinking of you now—& loving you ever— my wife.—A sends her hundred loves & regrets very much her absence from S.———

[TO ANNABELLA MILBANKE]   *Cambridge.—Novr. 22d. 1814*

My Love—I am detained here on my way to town to vote for a friend who is a candidate for a vacant medical professorship[1]—& shall not get away till tomorrow.—All your letters addressed to me at A's have been received—they are very kind and delightful—but I can't thank you for them properly with this horrible pen.—Thank your mother for hers also—and remember me to papa—I feel as if I had left home—and was gone to school again.—Opposite to me at this moment is a friend of mine—I believe—in the very act of writing to *his* spouse-elect—and complaining like me of his pen & paper to say nothing of absence & being obliged to scribble instead of speak. It gives me spirits to hear you have them—pray *keep* them now they are reappeared. "My last will have made you anxious to hear again—and indeed I am so myself" this is a sentence which I have borrowed by permission from my neighbouring suitor's epistle to his Ladye—I think it does very well in a dearth of periods of mine own.——Your mother talks of Hanson's coming to S. again—will that be necessary? —I have stolen another pen—but it is worse than the last—& am writing at an Inn—with noise "around above and underneath" with the worst & most intractable of implements—ink like water—& sand

---

[1] William Clark, anatomist, had planned to go abroad with Byron in 1813, but after many delays the project was given up. Clark did not win the professorship on this occasion, but in 1817 he became Professor of Anatomy at Cambridge.

like sawdust.—You shall hear from me tomorrow—and from town—where I shall not remain longer than you like—but I don't wish to hurry you—or to plague you with my assiduities—if I can help it.———Don't scold *yourself* any more—I told you before there was no occasion—you have not offended me.——I am as happy as Hope can make me—and as gay as Love will allow me to be till we meet and ever my Heart—thine

B

P.S.—Do write—and—never mind—I have several things to say of no great consequence—which I will postpone—in the mean time once more—Sweet Heart—Good morning.—————

[TO ANNABELLA MILBANKE] *Nov. 23d. 1814*

My Love—While I write this letter I have desired my very old & kind friend Mr. Hodgson to send you a note which I will enclose as it contains a piece of information that will come better from him than me—and yet not give you less pleasure.———I think of setting off for London tomorrow—where I will write again—I am quite confused & bewildered here with the voting & the fuss and the crowd—to say nothing of yesterday's dinner & meeting all one's old acquaintance the consequence of which is that infallible next-day's headache ever attendant upon sincere Friendship.—Here are Hobhouse and our cousin George Lamb—who called on me—& we have all voted the same way—but they say nevertheless our Man won't win—but have many votes howbeit.—Today I dine with Clarke the traveller[1]—one of the best & goodnatured of souls—and uniformly kind to me.—When we meet I think & hope I shall make you laugh at the scene I went through or rather which went through me—for I was quite unprepared and am not at the best of times sufficiently master of "the family shyness" to acquit myself otherwise than awkwardly on such an occasion.———Well but—sweet-Heart—do write & love me—and regard me as thine

ever & most
B

---

[1] Dr. Edward Daniel Clarke, Professor of Mineralogy at Cambridge, had travelled extensively in the Near East. He published an account of his travels in successive volumes, 1810–1823. He was much impressed by Byron's *Childe Harold.*

P.S.—Love to parents.———

P.S.—I have not—and am not to see H's note so I hope it is all very correct.²————

Dearest A—I sympathize with you on the original sin of your Suivante—it is a sad affair in a well regulated family—but I am glad it did not occur in *ours*—that is yours & mine that is to be—I would recommend the next to be as much in years and frightful as possible. There is a deal of confusion in Ld. Portsmouth's & Hanson's family— the brother of Ld P wants to lunatize him—or stultify him—and there is law & all kinds of squabble—which of course puts my taking Farleigh out of the question & I must look out for a residence else-where.——The settlements are arrived and in progress.————I have hardly yet recovered the bustle & bumpers of Cambridge—but am otherwise in tolerable plight—and quiet enough for London. ————On Saturday I saw Kean's Macbeth a fine but unequal performance—Miss O'Neill I have not seen.————I think Southey's Roderick¹ as near perfection as poetry can be—which con-sidering how I dislike that school I wonder at—however so it is—if he had never written anything else he might safely stake his fame upon the last of the Goths——Well—but you are returned to Seaham which I am glad to hear—all your epistles have been regularly received—and I hope that home and those hot luncheons of salubrious memory have quite reestablished you.—It is odd—while I am writing—in comes a clerical relation of mine²—& reminds me that he was the first person who ever mentioned *your* name to me—several years ago.—He tells me—that our Grandfathers were all in the same house at Westminster school &c. &c.--so you see our coming to-gether is quite in the course of events & vastly natural.—The man is talking on—and here is another visitor—so—Good morning—ma Mignonne—ever most entirely and affectionately thine

B

² Hodgson's note told Annabella that when Byron walked into the Senate House to vote for Dr. William Clark, the students burst out into spontaneous applause.

¹ Robert Southey's blank verse poem, *Roderick, the last of the Goths*, was pub-lished in 1814.

² R. C. Dallas first called Byron's attention to Miss Milbanke, but he was not a cleric (see Vol. 2, p. 80).

Dearest—Yesterday thine Unc. Ld. W[entworth] called—but I was seized with a fit of the *shys* and not at home—but I am going today to return his visit—which is the greatest bore in the world—but however as I ought I must—and there's an end.—I have forwarded your epistle to Mrs. Joanna[1]—I was very glad to see *not*—Southcote.

———I am very sorry for the dereliction of your handmaid—as I said before—but you could not act otherwise as the case appears—I hope your next solution will be more fortunate.—Your letters are very kind—my Love—as to the doubts—never mind, you see I have said nothing about them.—My naval cousin George[2] has just bore down—and his tongue is running nine knots an hour—so that I must for the present merely add

ever thine
B

P.S.—Love to Mamma & Sir R. with whom like his friend [Kion?] Long[3]—I hope "to smoke an amazing long pipe."——

[STATEMENT CONCERNING LORD PORTSMOUTH] [*Dec? 1814?*]

I have been acquainted with Mr. Hanson & his family for many years—he is my solicitor—about the beginning of March last—he sent to me to ask my opinion on the subject of Ld. Portsmouth[1] who as I understood from Mr. H[anson] was paying great attention to his eldest daughter. He stated to me that Mr. Newton Fellowes (with whom I have no personal acquaintance) was particularly desirous that Ld. Portsmouth should marry some elderly woman of his Mr. Fellowes's selection—by whom no issue could be reasonably expected —that the title and family estates might thereby eventually devolve on Mr. F[ellowes] or his children—but that Ld. P. had expressed a dislike to old women and a wish to choose for himself.—I told Mr. Hanson that if Miss Hanson's affections were not preengaged—& Lord Portsmouth appeared attached to her—there could be in my opinion no objection to the match.—I think—but cannot be positive— that I saw Lord Portsmouth at Mr. Hanson's two or three times

---

[1] Joanna Baillie, the poet and dramatist.
[2] George Anson Byron, who succeeded to the title as the 7th Baron Byron in 1824.
[3] Unidentified.
[1] See Sept. 28, 1814, to Hanson, note 1.

previous to the marriage—but I had no conversation with him upon it. The night before the ceremony I received an invitation from Mr. Hanson requesting me as a friend of the family to be present at the marriage which was to take place next morning.—I went next morning to Bloomsbury square where I found the parties.—Ly. Portsmouth with her brother & sister and another gentleman went in the carriage to St. George's Church. Ld. Portsmouth & myself walked—as the carriage was full—and the distance short. On our way Lord Portsmouth told me—that he had been partial to Miss Hanson from her childhood—and that since she grew up and more particularly subsequent to the decease of the late Lady P[ortsmouth] that the partiality had become attachment—that he thought her calculated to make him an excellent wife.—I was present at the ceremony—and gave away the bride.—Ld. Portsmouth's behaviour appeared to me— perfectly calm & rational on the occasion—he seemed particularly attentive to the priest and gave the responses audibly & very distinctly —I remarked this because in common conversation his Lordship has a hesitation in his speech.—After the ceremony we returned to Mr. Hanson's—whence I believe they went into the country where I did not accompany them.—Since their return I have occasionally seen Ld. & Lady Portsmouth in Bloomsbury Square—they appeared very happy.—I have never been very intimate with his Lordship and am therefore unqualified to give a decided opinion of his general conduct— but had I considered him insane—I should have advised Mr. Hanson when he consulted me on the subject *not* to permit the marriage.— his preference of a young woman to an old one—and of his own wishes to those of a younger brother—seemed to me neither irrational nor extraordinary.— — —

[TO FRANCIS FREELING?[1]]   *Six Mile Bottom nr. Newmarket.*
                                     [*December, 1814?*][2]

Sir,—It is with regret I trouble you with any complaints but in this case I have no other resource.—A letter addressed to me at this place (where a relative of mine resides and I sometimes visit) *has been charged*—I returned the cover and *wrote a short* but certainly not

---

1 Francis Freeling (1764–1836), postal reformer, was for many years secretary to the General Post Office. He was made a baronet in 1828.

2 Byron stopped twice at Six Mile Bottom on his way to Seaham before his marriage, once at the end of October, and again at Christmas time, 1814. This letter could have been written on either occasion.

uncivil note to the Postmaster at Newmarket regarding the charge to be returned—I have received *no answer whatever*.—Whether this person be in the right or wrong in the circumstance of the charge I feel assured that you will not approve of what I feel justified in terming the *insolence* of his conduct in withholding a reply.—Upon the subject of the letter itself I must state that *I* was not *here* & did not arrive for some time after the delivery of it—but I did not know that my absence authorized an exception from the usual privilege—for instance—Many letters are addressed to me at Newstead—or to London—while I am elsewhere without having been subjected to the same penalty.—If you will have the goodness to set the postmaster or me right and excuse this trouble you will much oblige

yr very obedt. humble Sert.

BYRON

P.S.—If you favour me with an answer address to—Seaham—Stockton on Tees—Durham.—

[TO ANNABELLA MILBANKE]   *Novr.—Decr. 1st. 1814*

Ld. Portsmouth and his brother have gone to Law about intellects—and it would be no proof of mine if I were to take Farleigh as a tenant until it is ascertained unto whom the brains and buildings actually belong.—Of course I must look round for another mansion.—Hanson hath gotten the papers—and is dealing upon them.—I have seen your uncle Ld. Wentworth—he called—and I returned his visitation.— — It would be difficult under these circumstances for me to fix any precise time for my return—as I wish to hear or see more of or from Claughton—and his intents about Newstead—and we have not heard from him since the letters I enclosed to you for Lady Milbanke.— — —I am asked to dine at Whitehall today[1]—but I fear I can't go—for there is a house and debate among the Lords this evening of some importance—which it may be as well to hear.—W[illiam] L[amb] and his moiety are not in town but all the rest I believe.— — —Hobhouse is in London & will probably return with me when the time is fixed. So—thou hast engaged a Cook for us—I will trust your taste.— — — —I will write tomorrow and if possible name the day or at least the week when we may meet—ever my Love

thine

B

P.S.—Love to our parents.— — —

[1] Melbourne House was in Whitehall.

My Love—The papers will require about ten days—and I hope also either to see or hear from Clau[ghton] in that time—the moment they are ready—I will set out—oh—by the way—I must not forget ye licence and all that—I will have it special—if you please—because I think it will be quieter to be married in a room—and mamma will lend us a cushion each to kneel upon.——I fear I must trouble your father to lend us Halnaby for a month—as this explosion among the senses of the Portsmouth family—has set me off about another house—as I would rather dwell among the reported sane.—And so—thou lovest me very much—we will love a great deal more yet though I hope.—I am glad you miss me—because *that* is not *my* fault—and I bear my own penance patiently in the malicious hope that you may wish that I had remained at S.—I told you in my last that I had seen your Unc. Ld. W[entworth] I thought he looked very well.—I am cut off from Melbourne House for the present—because that family firebrand—Ly. C[aroline]—has this day returned to Whitehall—and now I shan't see Ly. M[elbourne] again for some time which I regret.——————
Write—continue to love and to consider me as thine *most*

B

P.S.—Make all the duties & remembrances for me to all yours.——

Dearest A.—I am glad that Unc. was gracious—I said nothing to you about my fuss lest he should not—but it is all very well.—"the Cake"! I must try to be ready before it is baked—Hanson is urged & will be ready in ten days.——By the blessing of Hymen—his Godship has given up the white ribbon knots & fooleries which he was heretofore won't to inflict upon his votaries—or rather on their lacqueys—I am told that Nobody has them now—so don't let us be out of fashion—I am sure I wish we had been married these two years—but never mind—I have great hopes that we shall love each other all our lives as much as if we had never married at all.——I hear all our cousins are getting ready their presents C[aroline] amongst the rest—umph! "timeo Danaos et dona ferentes"[1] you know you are a blue—so I may quote Latin to you sans pedantry—and if you can't translate—I will

---

[1] Virgil, *Æneid*, II, 48: "I fear the Greeks, even when they offer presents."

in my next—I think I see your indignation at this disparaging proposition.————To amuse thee I send an extract from the M[ornin]g
Herald—you see they have not done with us yet—"two such interesting persons" (as Mrs. Locke[2]—do you know her? called us to
somebody the other day)—well—but I won't tell you all the conjectures &c. my journey has given rise to—Ly. M[elbourne] says it has
set all the talkers in tattle—and all is contradiction and mystery—*she*
did not half like my coming away—that was no fault of mine—but we
will make up for the past.—————

Ever thine—Mignonne—

most truly
B

[TO ANNABELLA MILBANKE]   *Dec. 7th. 1814*

Dearest—I yet hope to be ready before the overture has done being
played—and at any rate will only wait for the papers.—Of this
temporary separation I can only reecho your own words—with this
addition—that though perhaps of my deserving it was not of my
desiring.————Moore is in town—I was so glad to see him
again—that I am afraid I was rather too "exquisite in my drinking" at
dinner yesterday—for I find my head in a whirlwind and my fingers
bitten by my abominable parrot this morning—the latter accident I
did not discover when it happened—"I'faith I must have taken too
much Canaries" but I won't do so again—for I am never improved by
it.————"*The* Cake" dearest—I am in such agitation about it— if
it should be spoiled or mouldy—or—don't let them put too many eggs
& butter in it—or it will certainly circulate an indigestion amongst all
our acquaintance. I believe I told thee that I rejoiced in Unc's approbation—of which I rather desponded—but 'tis all very well.—I have
only time to scrawl myself in the midst of 50 interruptions—and
despite of them all

ever thine
B

[TO ANNABELLA MILBANKE]   *Decr. 8th. 1814*

Bella—my love—Clau[ghton]'s answer has at last arrived—and will
not do—his proposition is inadmissible as it not only involves reduction

2 Unidentified.

of price but delay in payment—I have ordered the flattest of all possible negatives in reply and there's an end.—One is at least out of suspense with him—but it is vexatious enough in our circumstances.— I shall have it sold to some other purchaser—from whom at all events —whether we obtain more or less I can have the whole sum paid down—he wanted me to take £92000—instead of 114-000 remaining after his present forfeiture—(I *will not*—)—and even that by slow degrees—the fact is I take it he has either not the money—or thinks me to be under such engagements as to give him an advantage— whether he is right or wrong—I have done with him.——————— Now dearest—I will not add one word as from myself or my own wishes—but leave it to you and yours to determine how far this may —will—or ought to cause any further delay in our marriage—I have lost no time in apprizing you of the circumstance—which I allow to be as disagreeable & inconvenient as could have been contrived or imagined.————"Your love is *not* but *half*-believed" it is too comfortable a creed for me to embrace by halves—I am convinced of it—as of my own.—————

ever thine
B

[TO ANNABELLA MILBANKE]   *Decr. 10th. 1814*

Dearest—I have only time to say that I intended to have written to thee this morning—and merely send this—but you should think it odd that I have not—the Post is impatient—and I have been interrupted all day.—

ever thine
B

[TO ANNABELLA MILBANKE]   *Decr. 12th. 1814*

Dearest A—I must needs say—that your Bells are in a pestilent hurry—a little like their prototypes of Bow—"turn again Whittington —Lord Mayor of London"[1] I am very glad however that I was out of hearing—deuce take them.————————The papers will I suppose be finished in this week or the next—undoubtedly my remaining in London will tend to hasten Hans[on]——I have not seen

[1] This was the refrain from the song "Bow Bells heard by Dick Whittington" (c. 1605). Richard Whittington, son of a London mercer, rose to be Lord Mayor of London three times before his death in 1423.

Lady Melbourne save at a distance—since the return of Medea & her dragons to Whitehall—but I found myself very unexpectedly opposite the whole party at Macbeth on Saturday night—however there was a "great gulph" the whole pit—between us—and a host of fiddlers—I believe she is going on very well—but know nothing about her.————I feel a little anxious about your answer to my last letter—& must conclude this—I shall probably write tomorrow if only to repeat how affectionately I ever am Dearest

thine

B

P.S.—I perceive in the M[ornin]g Chronicle report—that Sir H. Mildmay[2] in one of his amatory epistles compared himself to *Childe Harold*—conceive a *dandy* in despair moralizing or *im*-moralizing (like the melancholy Jaques) into such a similie.

[TO ANNABELLA MILBANKE]   *Decr. 14th. 1814*

Dearest—I waited an entire day and night in the hope or rather intention of sending thee a most heroic answer—but it won't do—the truth is my Love—you have made me vain enough to believe that you would marry me if I had not a "denier —" and I am very sure I would *you*—if you never *were* to have one.————The sale of N[ewstea]d would have liquidated all my debts and left us an immediate surplus sufficient for most of our present exigencies and even wishes—as it is "I am cabined—cribbed"—at least for the present—I should not have cared for the limitation of income—so much as the *debts*—they have however been lessened during the last year—and might perhaps have been done away—were it not that there were others whom—it was in some instances my duty—and in other my inclination—to assist—but even this would not have signified—had my purchaser kept to his bargain—though poor devil—I can't blame him—since his forfeiture is heavy enough.—————In short—you know pretty nearly as well as I do—how we are situated—things must come round in the end—for even if N[ewstead] & R[ochdale] are one or both sold at a loss—they will at least leave us clear—and your settlement secured into the bargain—well—"to marry or not" that's the question—or will you wait? perhaps the clouds may disperse in a month or two——do as you please.—————I scrawl in the greatest

---

[2] See Oct. 25, 1814, to Annabella Milbanke; and Oct. 31, 1814, to Lady Melbourne.

hurry—and half in the dark—and I am not sorry to quit this matter of fact terrestrial topic—but love me & regard me as from my heart of hearts truly thine

B

[TO THOMAS MOORE] *December 14, 1814*

My dearest Tom.—I will send the pattern[1] to-morrow, and since you don't go to our friend ("of the *keeping* part of the town")[2] this evening, I shall e'en sulk at home over a solitary potation. My self-opinion rises much by your eulogy of my social qualities. As my friend Scrope is pleased to say, I believe I am very well for a "holiday drinker." Where the devil are you? with Woolridge,[3] I conjecture—for which you deserve another abscess. Hoping that the American war will last for many years, and that all the prizes may be registered at Bermoothes,[4] believe me, &c.

P.S.—I have just been composing an epistle to the archbishop for an especial licence. Oons! it looks serious. Murray is impatient to see you, and would call, if you will give him audience. Your new coat!—I wonder you like the colour, and don't go about, like Dives, in purple.

[TO ANNABELLA MILBANKE] *Decr. 16th. 1814*

Dearest A—The parchments *are* ready which I did not know till yesterday—but I must also compose an epistle to his Grace of Canterbury for the license—I prefer it—because we can be married at any hour in any place without fuss or publicity—when I obtain it—I will write & fix the day of my arrival—which however can hardly take place before the end of next week or the beginning of the one after it.———I find that Claughton still wishes to treat although we have rejected his late proposition—but I have declined answering till I hear from another quarter where Hans[on] has been authorized to offer the purchase or sale or whatever it is or ought to be called.———It would undoubtedly have been better in many points of view to have had this arranged before our marriage—provided no very great delay

---

1 Moore had asked Byron for a pattern of his "olive-green coat, for I should like to wear the same livery." [*LJ*, III, 163n.]

2 Unidentified.

3 Dr. Stephen Woolriche was a surgeon who was a close friend of Moore.

4 Moore had been appointed Registrar of the Admiralty Court in Bermuda (Bermoothes—*Tempest*, Act I, scene 2) in 1803.

occurred in the discussion—but—be it as it is.———————I forwarded your letter to Lady Melbourne but have not seen her for some
time—ever most affectionately yours

B

[TO THE ARCHBISHOP OF CANTERBURY[1]] *Albany Decr. 16th. 1814*

My Lord—I have no adequate apology to offer to your Grace for
this intrusion—unless you will be pleased to accept as one—the
circumstance which compels me to take this liberty.——It has been
intimated to me that the proper and only method of obtaining the
favour which I am about to solicit—is by application to your Grace in
writing.—The request I venture to prefer is for a special licence to
unite in marriage Miss Anne Isabella Milbanke (the daughter of Sir
Ralph Milbanke) to him who has now the honour of addressing you.—
—If I have erred in the mode of application—I beg you to pardon my
ignorance or misinformation. I have the honour to be with the most
profound respect—my Lord—

your Grace's most obedt. very humble Servt.

BYRON

[TO JOHN HANSON] *Decr. 17th. 1814*

Dear Sir—Upon recollection I object to the word *"influence"* in the
affidavit[1] as I do not quite understand it—but I can speak to no
persuasion or *compulsion* as far as I saw.———I will be at one in
B[loomsbury] Square—

yrs. very truly
B

[TO ANNABELLA MILBANKE] *Decr. 18th. 1814*

My Love—I have written to the Archbishop and hope to set off on
Saturday next.—It is proper to add one thing—Ld. Portsmouth's
lunatic business comes on on Thursday—if the affair is in the first

[1] Dr. Charles Manners Sutton (1755–1828) had been Bishop of Norwich before
he was named Archbishop of Canterbury in 1805. He had opposed all concessions
to the Roman Catholics and may have been aware of Byron's speech in favour of
Catholic emancipation in the House of Lords in 1813.

[1] See [Dec. 1814?] (Byron's Statement Concerning Lord Portsmouth).

instance quashed (as is probable) by the Chancellor—there's an end—but if not—a further trial will come on next week in which my evidence will be required as I was present at his marriage —but let us hope that the first will decide on his Lordship's intellects.———However—even in case of my being subpoenaed to be in Court next week I will come down if you wish it—but I shall find it difficult to quit you again so soon after our marriage—which on obtaining his Grace's fiat may take place on any morning or evening in your drawing room—the papers are ready and I have desired Hans[on] to send them off to Hoar—and the signing & sealing may be settled as soon after my arrival as you please.———Dearest—all my anxieties have been principally on your account—but if you are satisfied it is enough—I shall have you and Hope—which are as much as mortal can require.———Clau[ghton] is very unwilling to relinquish all hopes of the purchase—but of this—more when we meet.——Ld. Melbourne called on me yesterday—but I have not seen Aunt M. for many days.———————"My wishes"—they are too like your own to bear repetition—believe me now and ever your most attached

B

[TO ANNABELLA MILBANKE]   *Decr. 20th. 1814*

Dearest Bella—There's the Archbishop's answer for you—and now we have only to get the license—and become *one* forthwith. I hope papa & Mamma will be kept in good humour by his Holiness's gratulation and am vastly sorry that you were scolded for my absence of which you are perfectly innocent—as you must recollect with what zeal you opposed my departure. As I must set out to settle divers concerns—and see after this same passport to our union—excuse my Laconism and believe me much more diffusely and attachedly ever thine

B

[TO ANNABELLA MILBANKE]   *Decr. 22d. 1814*

Dearest A—I am to have the license tomorrow—& am just returned from my first visit to Doctor's Commons (and my last too I presume) where I have been swearing my way to you.—The deeds are to be sent off to Hoar—and it will not be amiss if the said Hoar be ready at S[eaham] (or to arrive there) to get through the reading &

signing and sealing—& then we can be married on any afternoon—or morning if you prefer it—our passport comprehends all time and any place.———It is my hope to set off on Saturday [.] I believe Hobhouse accompanies me.—I have your letter sans date—with doubts in itself—and questions in the postscript—thereby approving the ancient adage that the important part of a Lady's epistle is generally comprized in that appendix.——"Any cause?" and "less confident?" a pretty pair of queries—"happiness" &c.—with regard to the last it would be presumptuous enough to feel too certain of uninterrupted felicity inasmuch as that depends not altogether on persons but things —and there are little incidents in the shape of disease—misfortune— and disappointment—which few grow old without encountering by way of episode.———I do not see any good purpose to which questions of this kind are to lead—nor can they be answered otherwise than by time and events.—You can still decide upon your own wishes and conduct before we meet—and apprize me of the result at our interview—only make sure of your own sentiments—mine are

yours ever

B

[TO ANNABELLA MILBANKE]   *Decr. 23d. 1814*

Dearest A—If we meet let it be to marry—had I remained at S[eaham] it had probably been over by this time—with regard to our being under the same roof and *not* married—I think past experience has shown us the awkwardness of that situation—I can conceive nothing above purgatory more uncomfortable.——If a postponement is determined upon—it had better have been decided at a distance—I shall however set out tomorrow—but stop one day at Newmarket.— ——Hobhouse I believe accompanies me—which I rejoice at—for if we don't marry I should not like a 2d. journey back quite alone—and remaining at S[eaham] might only revive a scene like the former and to that I confess myself unequal.——The profile—it is like—but I think more like the *Sphinx*—I am puzzling myself to imagine how you could have taken it unless opposite a mirror—or two mirrors—or—or —how?—

ever dearest A—

yrs

B

Decr. 23d, 1814

Dear Sir/—Pray write again to Mealey and peremptorily—for I suspect some *hitch* amongst them by his silence—I have written too—but I beg *you* will also and in case of any demur take proper steps to have the rent paid.

ever yrs.
BYRON

Decr. 23d. 1814

Dear Sir/—I forgot to ask if the N[ewstea]d rents were paid into *my* account and to *whom* at Nottingham? and how am I to draw for them?

yrs. ever
BYRON

Decr. 25th. 1814

Dearest A—I am thus. far on my way and as warm as Love can make one with the thermometer below God knows what—tomorrow I proceed Northward and if the Snow don't come down impossibly hope to reach S[eaham] in tolerable time—the license is in my portfolio—it is a very droll composition—but enables us to marry in the house—so pray let us [.] I am sure we shall catch cold kneeling any where else, to say nothing of being without a cushion.—Hobhouse is "bodkin" and takes up rather more room than "Happiness" who I believe wont join us till the last stage. We have heard of a treasure of a Maid for you—who is I believe past the usual age of indiscretion though there is no saying where that ends.—Col. L[eigh] is opposite to me making so many complaints of illness and calls for medicine—that my attention is called off and the rest of my letter will be like a prescription if I don't leave off.—A[ugusta] is looking very well—and just as usual—in every respect—so that better can't be in my estimation.—She writes to you with this—ever dearest

thine
B

P.S.—My love to Ly. M[ilbank]e & papa—I hope they will acquit me "of these my crimes supposed" since I went at last like Lord Grizzle "in hurry post haste for a license—in hurry ding-dong I come back"[1] with some apprehension of finding you like Huncamunca already "married to Tom Thumb."[2]—I wish you much merriment and minced pye—it is Xmas day.————

[TO JOHN HANSON]   *Decr. 31st. 1814*

Dear Sir/—I enclose you a damned twaddling cheating account from *Mealey*—so for Godsake send *down executions directly on all the defaulters*—there is no bearing this—and pray let me hear from you directly—how is Portsmouth?—but don't *quite forget* my various concerns

yrs. ever

B

[TO JOHN MURRAY]   *Decr. 31st. 1814*

Dear Sir/—A thousand thanks for *Gibbon*—all the additions are very great improvements.——At last I must be *most* peremptory with you —about the *print* from P[hillip]'s picture—it is pronounced on all hands the most stupid & disagreeable possible—so—do pray—have a new engraving & let me see it first—there really must be no more from the same plate—I don't much care myself—but every one I know torments me to death about it—and abuse it to a degree beyond repeating.————Now don't answer with excuses but for my sake —have it destroyed—I never shall have peace till it is.—I write in the greatest haste

ever yrs.

BYRON

P.S.—I have written this most illegibly but it is to beg you to destroy the print—and have another "by particular desire" it must be d————d bad to be sure since every body says so but the original— and he don't know what to say—but do *do* it—that is burn the plate— and employ a new *etcher* from the other picture—this is stupid & sulky.—

---

[1] In Fielding's *Tom Thumb, A Tragedy* (1730) Lord Grizzle is a comic character who kills Tom Thumb's ghost.
[2] Huncamunca, the daughter of King Arthur, married Tom Thumb in Fielding's burlesque tragedy.

[TO DOUGLAS KINNAIRD] *[January, 1815?]*

Dear D. K. Vede note on Number 2—I think that the best of the two[1]

Yrs.

B

[TO ISAAC NATHAN] *January 1815*

Dear Nathan—Murray being about to publish a complete edition of my *poetical effusions* has a wish to include the stanzas of the Hebrew Melodies—will you allow him that privilege without considering it an infringement on your copyright[?] I certainly wish to oblige the gentleman but you know Nathan it is against all good fashion to give and take back [.] I therefore cannot grant what is not at my disposal [;] let me hear from you on the subject [.][1]

Dear Nathan yrs truly
BYRON

[TO LADY MELBOURNE] *Halnaby, January 3d. 1815*

My dearest Aunt—We were married yesterday at ten upon ye. Clock—so there's an end of that matter and the beginning of many others.—Bell has gone through all the ceremonies with great fortitude —and I am much as usual and your dutiful nephew. All those who are disposed to make presents may as well send them forthwith and pray let them be handsome—and we wait your congrats. besides—as I am sure your benediction is very essential to all our undertakings.——Lady Mil[bank]e was a little hysterical and fine-feeling—and the kneeling was rather tedious—and the cushions hard—but upon the whole it did vastly well.—The drawing-room at Seaham was the scene of our conjunction—and thus we set off according to approved custom to be shut up by ourselves.——You would think we had been married these 50 years—Bell is fast asleep on a corner of the Sopha, and I am keeping myself awake with this epistle—she desires her love—and mine you have had ever since we were acquainted.—Pray —how many of our new relations (at least of mine) mean to own us?

[1] This, in Byron's hand, is at the top of "In the Valley of Waters" (one of the *Hebrew Melodies*) on a neat copy made by Lady Byron.
[1] Apparently Nathan did not consent, for his edition of the Hebrew Melodies with the musical accompaniment was published in April, and Murray some time after that published the poems in a separate edition without the music.

I reckon upon George & you and Lord M[elbourne] and the Countess and Count of the holy Roman empire[1]—as for *Caro*—and Caro-George[2]— and *William*[3] I don't know what to think do you?—I shall write to you again anon—at present receive this as an apology for that silence of which you were kind enough to complain—and believe me ever most affectionately thine

BYRON

P.S.—I enclose you an order for the box—it was not at liberty before—the week after next will be mine—and so on alternately.—I have lent it for the present week only to another person—the next is yours.—

[TO JOHN MURRAY (*a*)]   *Halnaby January sixth 1815*

Dear Sir—*The* marriage took place on the 2d. Inst. so pray make haste & congratulate away.—Thanks for the E[dinburgh] R[eview] and the abolition of the print.—Let the next be from the other of Philips' I mean (*not* the Albanian) but the original one in the exhibition —the last was from the copy—I should wish my sister & Lady B. to decide upon the next—as they found fault with the last—*I* have no opinions of my own upon the subject——Mr Kinnaird will I dare say have the goodness to furnish copies of the Melodies if you state my wish upon the subject—you may have them if you think them worth inserting.[1]—The vols. in their collected state must be inscribed to Mr. Hobhouse—but I have not yet mustered the expressions of my inscription—but will supply them in time.——With many thanks for your good wishes which have all been realized I remain

very truly yours,
BYRON

[TO JOHN MURRAY (*b*)]   *Halnaby, January 6th. 1815*

Dear Sir/—I send you another note to the Conclusion of "the

[1] The Melbournes' daughter married Peter, 5th Earl Cowper. Perhaps Byron gave them the fanciful title because of Earl Cowper's long pedigree.

[2] This was the nick-name of Mrs. George Lamb (Caroline Rosalie Adelaide St. Jules, married to the Melbournes' third son) to distinguish her from Caroline Lamb.

[3] William Lamb, Caroline Lamb's husband, was the second son and heir of Lord Melbourne after the death of the first son Peniston.

[1] But see January 1815, to Nathan, note 1.

Corsair" it is from Gibbon—a quotation[1]—and you will think it not mal apropos—I suppose it is not too late to add.—I answered yours yesterday and trust this will find you and all your family—literary and domestic in good plight & liking.—

yrs. ever truly
B

[TO JOHN HANSON]   *Halnaby, January 7th. 1815*

Dear Sir/—Mr. Hobhouse has a commission from me to talk to you on various subjects of my concerns—which I trust you will not think irrelevant or out of season—as they are of importance to me & mine.— I have been in hopes of hearing from you—but all in good time.—We have been married these five days—(on Monday last) you will be glad to hear that Lady Byron is very well—and that we agree admirably.—Pray let me hear soon—and believe me with many thanks for your good wishes

yours very truly
BYRON

P.S.—Lady B sends her compliments.—

[TO LADY MELBOURNE]   *January 7th. 1815*

Dearest Aunt—Bell sent you a few lines yesterday as an accompaniment to an answer of mine to an epistle of Caro's about her present—which of course she will be very glad to receive—I wonder C[aroline] should think it necessary to make such a preface—*we* are very well disposed *towards* her—and can't see why there should not be a peace with her as well as with America.——About this and every thing else I will do as you like—if you prefer that we should quarrel with that branch of the cousinhood—I shall have no objection—but I suppose George & Lord Cowper and I and our female appendages are not to be involved in the like bickering any more now than heretofore.—Bell & I go on extremely well so far without any other company than our own selves as yet—I got a wife and a cold on the same day—but have got rid of the last pretty speedily—I don't

[1] The note added at the end of *The Corsair* concerned the impression made on Alphonso III by the death of his wife Donna Isabella. "Alphonso retired into his chamber to bewail his irreparable loss, and to meditate on the vanity of human life." (Gibbon's *Miscellaneous Works*, 1837, p. 831.)

dislike this place—it is just the spot for a Moon—there is my only
want a *library*—and thus I can always amuse myself—even if alone—I
have great hopes this match will turn out well—I have found nothing
as yet that I could wish changed for the better—but Time does
wonders—so I won't be too hasty in my happiness.———I will tell
you all about the ceremony when we meet,—it went off very pleasantly
—all but the cushions—which were stuffed with Peach-stones I believe
—and made me make a face that passed for piety.—My love to all my
relatives—by the way what do they mean to give *me*? I will compromise
provided they let me choose what I will have instead of their presents
—nothing but what they could very well spare.—

ever Aunt thine dutifully

B

P.S.—Lady Byron sends her love—but has not seen this epistle—
recollect—*we* are to keep our secrets—& correspondence as heretofore
—mind that.—

[TO THOMAS MOORE]   *Halnaby, Darlington, January 10th, 1815*

I was married this day week. The parson has pronounced it—
Perry[1] has announced it—and the Morning Post, also, under the
head of "Lord Byron's Marriage"—as if it were a fabrication, or the
puff-direct of a new stay-maker.

Now for thine affairs. I have redde thee upon the Fathers,[2] and it is
excellent well. Positively, you must not leave off reviewing. You shine
in it—you kill in it; and this article has been taken for Sydney Smith's
(as I heard in town), which proves not only your proficiency in
parsonology, but that you have all the airs of a veteran critic at your
first onset. So, prithee, go on and prosper.

Scott's "Lord of the Isles" is out—"the mail-coach copy" I have,
by special licence of Murray.

* * * * * * * * * * * * * * *

Now is *your* time;—you will come upon them newly and freshly. It
is impossible to read what you have lately done (verse or prose)
without seeing that you have trained on tenfold. * * has floundered;
* * has foundered. *I* have tired the rascals (i.e. the public) with my

---

[1] James Perry, in his *Morning Chronicle* for Jan. 6, 1815, announced Byron's
marriage under the heading: "Marriage in High Life".

[2] Moore's article on Boyd's *Select Passages from the Writings of St. Chrysostom*
. . . appeared in the *Edinburgh Review*. Vol. XXIV, p. 58, Dec., 1814.

Harrys and Larrys, Pilgrims and Pirates. Nobody but S * * * y·
[Southey] has done any thing worth a slice of bookseller's pudding;
and *he* has not luck enough to be found out in doing a good thing.
Now, Tom, is thy time—"Oh joyful day!—I would not take a knight-
hood for thy fortune."[3] Let me hear from you soon, and believe me
ever, &c.

P.S.—Lady Byron is vastly well. How are Mrs. Moore and Joe
Atkinson's "Graces?"[4] We must present our women to one another.

[TO JOHN HANSON]   *Halnaby Darlington—January 11th. 1815*

Dear Sir/—I cannot help considering it as a little extraordinary—
firstly—that I have not heard one word from or of you since my last
letter—& 2ndly—that my friend Mr. Hobhouse who is particularly
charged by me to have some conversation with you on various subjects
of my affairs—should neither have been *admitted*—nor received any
answer to his letter!—I am naturally impatient to hear of Claughton—
and Mr. Hobhouse has much to say from me on the subject of Rochdale
&c. to which I must request your earliest attention and as speedy an
answer to this as suits your convenience.—

very truly yrs.
BYRON

P.S.—Lady Byron is very well & desires her Compliments.—

[TO JOHN CAM HOBHOUSE]   *January 11th. 1815*

My dear H.—You will much oblige me by insisting on an interview
with Signor Hanson—to whom I have *again* written with some anger
and much wonderment at his not seeing you—or writing to me.—I
will do what you like about it—only choose me a counsel, William
Adam[1] an' thou wilt.—The post presses—but more soon—Lady
Byron is well—& with me very

much yours
BYRON

[3] *Henry IV*, Part II, Act 5, scene 3.
[4] Joseph Atkinson, a Dublin friend of Moore, was living near him when he was
at Mayfield Cottage in Derbyshire.
[1] William Adam (1751–1839) had taken a leading part in the impeachment of
Warren Hastings in 1788. He was Attorney-General to the Prince of Wales and
Privy Councillor in 1815, and an intimate friend of Walter Scott.

Lady Melbourne has the box but I will write to her to transfer to you for any night or nights.

[TO JOHN HANSON]   *January 12th. 1815*

My dear Sir—Wyatt[1] may *possibly* be employed (as N[ewstea]d is a fine specimen of the mixed Gothic) by some personage disposed to lay out his superfluous thousands on the building itself—or he may be Clau[ghton]'s agent only—*you* have discernment enough to discover *that*—at any rate it may be as well to hear what he has to say—I approve of all you have hitherto done in answer &c. but am still anxious to have the estate sold—as you may easily suppose.——Your congratulations are very acceptable to Lady Byron & myself—and in return I wish you all possible success & happiness with you & yours—I shall hope soon to hear you have given Master Fellowes[2] his reward —and to find Ld. P[ortsmouth] triumphantly reinstated at Hurstbourne with Lady P[ortsmouth] to whom I beg my best remembrances in conjunction with Lady B's compliments—I hope soon to make them acquainted.——We must get what we can for N[ewstead]—I still think it upon the whole—much better to sell it—more particularly as I believe Lady B's title by heritage is older than mine (though that is ancient) and consequently our son (if we have one) would be Ld. *Noel* in the Senate.——Pray do something—and I shall be easily contented—so that the business is off my mind—believe me

yrs. very truly
BYRON

P.S.—Lady Byron sends her thanks & compliments.——

[TO JOHN HANSON]   *January 19th. 1815*

My dear Sir/—I find Mr. Hobhouse has written to you—but on one point he is mistaken—I *do* mean to *sell* Newstead and *that* as soon as possible—but that does not make me less anxious for an early arrangement (or sale it may be also) of Rochdale.—*Your* business with—or rather your son in law's—I see by the papers is not yet come on.—

---

[1] Benjamin Dean Wyatt (1775–1850?), was an architect of some distinction. Among his works was the new Drury Lane Theatre. He was surveyor of Westminster Abbey from 1813 to 1827.

[2] The Hon. Newton Fellowes, Lord Portsmouth's younger brother and next in line as heir, was trying to get a commission of lunacy granted against his brother to nullify Lord Portsmouth's marriage to Hanson's daughter.

Pray address your answer to this—to Seaham—Stockton on Tees—
where we go on Saturday—

ever truly yours
BYRON

P.S.—Pray let me hear soon what you have done with Claughton—
or Wyatt—or one—or both.—

[TO JOHN CAM HOBHOUSE] *January 19th. 1815*

My dear Hobhouse—I rejoice in the escape of your premises—*you*
did not set them a fire—did you?—You have made but one mistake in
your epistle to Spooney[1]—but that's a thumper—I *do* mean to sell
Newstead—and that the moment it can be sold—but that does not
prevent my being anxious about Rochdale—viz—to sell it too—
Newstead I won't keep if a fair price can be had for it.—I sent you a
box order—hast thou it—I wish to hear from Hans[on] before I fix upon
a Counsel—& then you shall hear—pray—when thou writest next
address to Seaham—where we go on Saturday.—Excuse this scrably
letter—all the ink's out.—

ever thine most truly
B

[TO THOMAS MOORE] *January 19th, 1815*

Egad! I don't think he is "down"; and my prophecy—like most
auguries, sacred and profane—is not annulled, but inverted

* * * * * * * * * * * * * * *

To your question about the "dog"[1]—Umph!—my "mother," I
won't say anything against—that is, about her; but how long a
"mistress" or friend may recollect paramours or competitors (lust
and thirst being the two great and only bonds between the amatory or
the amicable), I can't say,—or, rather, you know as well as I could
tell you. But as for canine recollections, as far as I could judge by a

1 Spooney was a cant term in "flash" language for a foolish pretending fellow.
Byron from this time used the appellation for Hanson in writing to Hobhouse,
particularly when he was irritated with his attorney and business agent.

1 Moore had asked Byron whether he as "friend of the dog" could say if it was
probable "that any dog (out of a melodrame) could recognize a master, whom
neither his own mother nor mistress was able to find out." The question arose from
his reading Southey's *Roderick* where such a situation is described.

cur of mine own (always bating Boatswain,[2] the dearest and, alas! the maddest of dogs), I had one (half a *wolf* by the she side) that doted on me at ten years old, and very nearly ate me at twenty. When I thought he was going to enact Argus, he bit away the backside of my breeches,[3] and never would consent to any kind of recognition, in despite of all kinds of bones which I offered him. So, let Southey blush and Homer too, as far as I can decide upon quadruped memories.

I humbly take it, the mother knows the son that pays her jointure— a mistress her mate, till he * * and refuses salary—a friend his fellow, till he loses cash and character, and a dog his master, till he changes him.

So you want to know about milady and me? But let me not, as Roderick Random says, "profane the chaste mysteries of Hymen"[4]— damn the word, I had nearly spelt it with a small *h*. I like Bell as well as you do (or did, you villain!) Bessy—and that is (or was) saying a great deal.

Address the next to Seaham, Stockton-on-Tees, where we are going on Saturday (a bore, by the way) to see father-in-law, Sir Jacob,[5] and my lady's lady-mother. Write—and write more at length —both to the public and

Yours ever most affectionately,

B

[TO JOHN HAY] *Halnaby Darlington January 19th. 1815*

Dear Sir/—Upon the subject of the marriage forfeit[1]—we shall not differ—I will enclose you a draft for the amount the moment I hear that Mr. Hawke has received his which I enclose by this post under cover to you—I would send yours by the same conveyance but as the post is not reckoned so secure in pecuniary conveyances as it was formerly—I wish to have the arrival of the one letter previously ascertained.—My reason for supposing the bet to be only *fifty* to you was this—the persons present said when I took Mr. Hawke's guinea

[2] Byron's favourite Newfoundland dog, who died in 1808. See Nov. 18, 1808, to Hodgson, note 1 (Vol. 1, p. 176).

[3] Byron made use of this episode in *Don Juan*, III, 23.

[4] *Roderick Random*, chapter 68.

[5] A character in Samuel Foote's comedy *The Mayor of Garratt* (1764) was called Sir Jacob Jollop. He was a pompous fool.

[1] In his reckless youth, when Byron was at Brighton with Scrope Davies and other gambling companions, he made a bet that he would never marry, and now they were asking for their forfeits.

that I risked too much—that it ought to be in a proportion of *fifty* to a thousand—which I offered to take of Capt. Kelly—this *he declined* & *no* bet passed between him & me—in consequence of these remarks I certainly did imagine that in my subsequent wager with you—if wager it may be called—I took one guinea to pay fifty—but as I have already stated—I shall not dispute that point—but am ready to pay the *hundred* on receiving the favour of an answer.—The Spanish bet—I cannot acknowledge—because I have not the most distant recollection of any such transaction except with Mr. Hawke—whom I duly paid— I asked Major Morgan in St. James's Street in company with Mr. Dalrymple—(the Major you will recollect was at that dinner at *Brighton*) and he gave it for me—I know that *he* is since dead—but Mr. Dalrymple will probably recollect the conversation as I begged him to attend to it—I would also refer to Mr. Davies who was of the party.—Most assuredly I had no recollection of such transaction—& could never have claimed the money of you in the event of a different result—& with Mr. Hawke I had a distinct remembrance of what passed between him & me—as the event proved.——The hundred I am ready to disburse—on receiving your answer—by the way—in my answer to you in 1811—I mentioned the marriage bet—and named *fifty* to you—so it is no *new* misconception of mine—but as I have before said—I *wave that*—because I cannot be certain as I am upon the other—and have no passion for being positive—unless I feel good grounds for being so—I wish Hawke joy—and enclose a letter for him in another cover—

yrs. truly
BYRON

P.S.—Many thanks for your Congrats.

[TO JOHN HANSON]   *January 21st. 1815*

Dear Sir/—No letter.—But I just trouble you with these few lines— to repeat that I am setting off for *Seaham* where I beg you will address your next to me.—In my last I mentioned that Mr. Hobhouse had made a mistake about Newstead—as it *is* my intention to sell it—and few things would give me more pleasure than to hear that it was *sold*— in your answer.—With Lady's [*sic*] B—compliments I remain

yours very truly
BYRON

Mine Aunt—This day completes my 27th. year of existence and (save a day) my "3 weeks after marriage"—I am 4 years and 3 months older than Bell who will be twenty three on May 17th.—I suppose this is a fair disproportion.——Yesterday I came here—somewhat anent my imperial will—but never mind—you know I am a very good natured fellow—and the more easily governed because not ashamed of being so—and so Bell has her own way—and no doubt means to keep it—for which reason I prodigiously applaud your having written 2 letters to her—and—only 3 to me—and one of them full of Lady Blarney (by way of emetic) &c. &c. which I presume you meant me to show—by the way—I cannot sufficiently admire your cautious style since I became chicken-pecked—but I love thee—ma Tante—and therefore forgive your doubts—*implied* but not expressed—which will last—till the next scrape I get into—and then we shall wax confidential again—and I shall have good advice—I look upon you as my Good Genius.—I am scribbling in my dressing room—and Bell is in bed—so you ought to think the length of this epistle a large effort of complaisance.—I sent C[aroline] an answer—which produced no rejoinder—thus—all is right—at least I hope so—we are all well—and Sir R[alph] is going on Tuesday to a County meeting—to oppose continuance of taxes.—I shall stay at home quietly with Mrs. Quotem.[1]——Love and health to all my new cousins—and particularly to Unc. M[elbourne]

> ever yours most truly
> B

Dear Sir/—I enclose you a paragraph from the Globe & M[ornin]g Post—which I can't help thinking to be of Claughton's invention—it is so like his damned tricks to prevent any other purchaser.—You know the forfeiture was £25-000 (not ten)—and that the cause of non-fulfilment was not the reluctance of the purchaser—but his not being to *time*—which occasioned the non completion.—I wish if you have a moment's leisure you will draw up and insert a paragraph contradictory of this—and stating the *real facts*—it will prevent the depreciation in some measure—and at any rate be the *real truth*.—I am very

---

[1] Caleb Quotem is a parish clerk in *The Review, or the Ways of Windsor* (1798), by Colman the Younger.

anxious to hear that you are victorious over Fellowes[1]—&c.—And
have much to hear & say on other subjects but am pressed for time[.]

yours ever

BYRON

Seaham—January 26th. 1815

My dear H[obhous]e—Your packet hath been perused and firstly I
am lost in wonder & obligation at your good nature in taking so much
trouble with Spooney[1] and my damnable concerns—I would leave to
your choice our "Counsellors at law" as Mrs. Heidelberg calls them—
a—Templeman[2]—I think stands first on your list—so prithee fix on
him—or whom you please—but do *you fix*—for you know *I* never
could.— N[ewstead] *must* be sold—without delay—and even at a loss—
out of *debt* must be my first object—and the sooner the better.—My
debts can hardly be less than thirty thousand—there is *six thousand*
charged on N[ewstead] to a Mr. Sawbridge—a *thousand*—to Mrs.
B[yron] at Nott[ingha]m—a *Jew debt* of which the interest must be
more than the principal—& of which H[anson] must get an amount
from *Thomas*—another Jew debt—six *hundred* prin[cipa]l—and no
interest (as I have kept that down) to a man in New Street—I forget
his name but shall know on half year's day—a good deal still before
majority—in which the "old women"[3] of former celebrity were
concerned—but *one* is defunct—and the debt itself may wait my
convenance—since it is not in my name—and indeed the interest has
pretty well paid principal & all being transcendantly usurious,—a
good deal of tradesmen &c. &c.—You know I have paid off *Scrope* that
is 6000 & more— nearly 3000 to *Hans.* Carnal[4]—then I lent rather
more than £1600 to Hodgson— £1000 to "bold" Webster—and
nearly 3000 to George L[eigh] or rather to Augusta—the *last* sums
I never *wish* to see again—and others I *may wish*—I have W[ebster]'s
bond which is worth a damn or two—but from Hodg[son] I neither
asked nor wanted security—but there was 150 lent at Hastings to the
same Hod[gson] which was punctually *promised* to be paid in six
weeks—and has been paid with the usual punctuality—viz—not at all.

[1] See Jan. 12, 1815, to Hanson, note 2.
[1] See Jan. 19. 1815, to Hobhouse, note 1.
[2] Giles Templeman, Solicitor.
[3] Mrs. Elizabeth Massingberd, Byron's landlady in London during his youth,
and her daughter acted for him as agents for securing loans from usurers.
[4] Reference unclear [?]

—I think I have now accounted for a good deal of Clau[ghton]'s disbursements—the rest was swallowed up by duns—necessities—luxuries—fooleries—jewelleries—"whores and fiddlers".—As for expectations, don't talk to me of "expects" (as Mr Lofty says to Croaker of "*sus*pects")[5] the Baronet is eternal—the Viscount immortal—and my Lady (*senior*) without end.—They grow more healthy every day and I verily believe Sir R[alph] Ly. M[ilbanke] and Lord W[entworth] are at this moment cutting a fresh set of teeth and unless they go off by the usual fever attendant on such children as don't use the "American soothing syrup" that they will live to have them all drawn again.—

[displaced sheet perhaps belonging here]

"The Melodies"—damn the melodies—I have other tunes—or rather tones—to think of—but—Murray *can't* have them, or *shan't*—or I shall have Kin[nair]d and Braham upon me.——Take the *box* any night or all nights week after *next*—only send to Lady Melbourne—to tell her of your intention for the night or nights—as I have long ago left her paramount during my absence.—

ever d[ea]r H. thine

B

[TO JOHN HAY]   *Seaham—Durham—January 26th. 1815*

Dear Hay—Enclosed is my draft for your hundred guineas on Messrs. Hoares *Fleet Street* (*not* Lombard Street where there is another synonymous cash-shop but not mine)—let me have an answer certifying safe receipt per post.——Hawke will tell you that the Spanish bet was *fifty*—betted & paid—saving and except twenty won of him by me at Manton's in two matches regularly deducted—thus I hope that our betting concerns are settled for the present to all our satisfaction.——I never repented the *poney* purchase—he was a Beauty—and I at last gave (for I would not have sold him) to a friend who died in Portugal—I believe he is now running free in Ld. Powerscourt's park in Ireland.——Pray tell me more—or as much as you like—of your cousin Mary[1]—I have some idea her family is related to my late mother's—I believe I told you our story some years ago—and thank you for recollecting it.—It is now nearly—I know not how

---

[5] In Goldsmith's *Good Natured Man* Lofty says to Croaker: ". . . and talk to me of suspects!"

[1] Mary Duff, Byron's distant cousin, seems to have been related to Hay as well. See Byron's journal of Nov. 26, 1813 (Vol. 3, pp. 221–223.)

many years—I was 27 a few days ago—and I have never seen her since we were children—and *young* children too—but I never forgot her nor ever can—if it was no impropriety in a "married man"—who may very possibly never see her again—and if he did—we are both out of harm's way—you would oblige me by presenting her with my best respects and all good wishes—she had a sister then in her cradle— *Helen* I think—is she married too?—it may seem ridiculous—but it is at any rate I hope not offensive to her nor hers—in me to pretend to recollect anything about her—at so early a period of both our lives— almost if not *quite* in our nurseries—but it was a pleasant dream which she must pardon me for remembering.—Is she pretty still?—I have the most perfect idea of her person as a child—but Time I suppose has played the devil with us both—but it is *time* also not to bore you further on the subject.——Since I saw you I have had a good deal of scramble at home and abroad—but am luckily anchored in the haven of matrimony. I rejoice to hear of Martin's promising prospects and can give him a very favourable account of marriage as far as my own experience has hitherto gone.—I should like to hear of his final settlement—and (I suppose I may ask *you*) what is become of *the Mrs. H.* to whom he was so inveterately constant in our time.—The bride I presume by your hint has had no lack of Madrigals—as when once the "Gods make a man poetical" the Devil generally keeps him so.—Good night— address your answer to this place—Sir Ralph Milbanke's—Seaham— Durham—and believe me

very truly yours
BYRON

[TO JOHN HANSON]　　　　　　　　　*Seaham—February 2d. 1815*

Dear Sir,—I have hitherto forbore troubling you further on my own business—since I left Halnaby—conceiving you to be fully occupied with your son in law's—of whose case I feel anxious to hear some information.——By a letter arrived from town today—I am told that it is supposed to run against his Lordship—which I should be truly sorry to hear confirmed—when you can spare time for a few lines—I shall be glad to receive them.—To revert for a minute to my own concerns—if Mr. Claughton is not disposed to accede to the terms proposed—it is at any rate high time that his *stocks* &c. should be removed from the premises—pray apprize him of this—and when you can spare a few minutes to attend to the subjects of Newstead & Rochdale—you will by so doing very much oblige

yours very truly

Byron

Seaham—Fy. 2d. 1815

My dear Aunt—Sans letter paper I have coopted awkwardly enough a sheet of foolscap whereupon to answer your epistle.—I cannot "laugh" at anything which gave you pain—and therefore will say nothing about your nervous headach except that I am glad that it is gone—one may see a "double face" without being delirious though—but I must cease talking of your complaint for fear of growing as sentimental as Bob Adair,[1] your larmoyant admirer.—Had you seen Lord Stair?[2]—if so the disorder as far as the *ach* (the face is too dull to be double) is accounted for.—It rejoices me to hear of Moore's success—he is an excellent companion as well as poet—though I cannot recollect that I "wept" at the song you mention—I ought to have done so—but whether I did nor not—it is one of the most beautiful and touching compositions that ever he penned—and much better than ever was compounded by any one else.———The *Moon* is over —but Bell & I are as lunatic as heretofore—she does as she likes— and don't bore me—and we may win the Dunmow flitch of bacon for anything I know—Mamma and Sir Ralph are also very good—but I wish the last would not speak his speech at the Durham meeting above once a week after it's first delivery.———I won't betray you if you will only write me something worth betraying.—I suppose your "C—noir" is +[3] but if + were a Raven or a Griffin I must still take my omens from her flight—I can't help *loving* her though—I have quite enough at home to prevent me from loving any one essentially for some time to come.—We have two visitors here—a Mrs. & Miss Somebody—the latter plain—and both hum-drum—they have made me so sleepy that I must [say] Goodnight

ever yours most nepotically

B

[1] Sir Robert Adair (1763–1855), diplomatist, was a close friend of Charles James Fox, and was sent on a number of diplomatic missions by him. He was British Ambassador in Constantinople while Byron was there.

[2] Byron considered Lord Stair a symbol of dullness. See Aug. 5, 1813, to Lady Melbourne, note 2 (Vol. 3, p. 85).

[3] The + stands for Augusta in Byron's letters to Lady Melbourne. The "C——noir" is "Corbeau-noir" ("Black crow"). See Lady Melbourne's letter to Byron of February 8, 1815 (*LBC*, I, 303).

I have heard from London that you have left Chatsworth[1] and all the women full of "entusymusy"[2] about you, personally and poetically; and, in particular, that "When first I met thee" has been quite overwhelming in its effect. I told you it was one of the best things you ever wrote, though that dog Power[3] wanted you to omit part of it. They are all regretting your absence at Chatsworth, according to my informant—"all the ladies quite, &c. &c. &c." Stap my vitals!

Well, now you have got home again—which I dare say is as agreeable as a "draught of cool small beer to the scorched palate of a waking sot"—now you have got home again, I say, probably I shall hear from you. Since I wrote last, I have been transferred to my father-in-law's, with my lady and my lady's maid, &c. &c. &c. and the treaclemoon is over, and I am awake, and find myself married. My spouse and I agree to—and in—admiration. Swift says "no *wise* man ever married;" but, for a fool, I think it the most ambrosial of all possible future states. I still think one ought to marry upon *lease*; but am very sure I should renew mine at the expiration, though next term were for ninety and nine years.

I wish you would respond, for I am here "oblitusque meorum obliviscendus et illis."[4] Pray tell me what is going on in the way of intriguery, and how the w——s and rogues of the upper Beggar's Opera go on—or rather off—in or after marriage; or who are going to break any particular commandment. Upon this dreary coast, we have nothing but county meetings and shipwrecks; and I have this day dined upon fish, which probably dined upon the crews of several colliers lost in the late gales. But I saw the sea once more in all the glories of surf and foam,—almost equal to the Bay of Biscay, and the interesting white squalls and short seas of Archipelago memory.

My Papa, Sir Ralpho, hath recently made a speech at a Durham tax-meeting; and not only at Durham, but here, several times since, after dinner. He is now, I believe, speaking it to himself (I left him in the middle) over various decanters, which can neither interrupt him

---

[1] Chatsworth, the Duke of Devonshire's mansion in Derbyshire not far from where Moore was living, was a gathering place of the Whig aristocracy. Caroline Lamb had spent much of her childhood there.

[2] John Braham, the tenor, a German Jew, so pronounced "enthusiasm". Byron used it to mock the emotion.

[3] James Power was the publisher of Moore's songs and national airs.

[4] Horace, *Epistle*, I, xi, 9. ". . . forgetting my friends and forgotten by them".

nor fall asleep,—as might possibly have been the case with some of his audience.

Ever thine,

B

I must go to tea—damn tea. I wish it was Kinnaird's brandy, and with you to lecture me about it.

[TO JOHN MURRAY] *Seaham—Stockton on Tees February 2d. 1815*

Dear Sir—You will oblige me very much by making an occasional enquiry in Albany at my chambers—whether my books &c. are kept in tolerable order—and how far my old woman continues in health and industry as keeper of my late den.———Your parcels have been duly received and perused—but I had hoped to receive "Guy Mannering" before this time.—I won't intrude further for the present on your avocations professional or pleasurable but am as usual

very truly yrs.

β

[TO JOHN HANSON] *Feby. 3d. 1815*

My dear Sir/—If Mr. Claughton will complete without further delay—I should have no great objection to give up the rents received for 1814—which by the way do not amount but to one *half years* paid to me—at least since I resumed the Estate. When he speaks of the advertisements or paragraphs—of which we know nothing except that I complained of them bitterly to you—in a late letter[1]—he forgets or seems to forget that they were obviously inserted to depreciate the *purchase* and not the purchaser—for which reason I still think they were inserted by himself notwithstanding the complaining tone in which he speaks of them.———There are one or two little points also of which he is not aware:—if Ld. W[entworth] who is going very unwell to Bath—were to die—an event which I am really far from wishing whatever pecuniary advantage might arise from his demise—as he has been most kind to me & mine both before & since the marriage—still

---

[1] See Jan 23, 1815, to Hanson.

I say—if such an occurrence intervened at present—or even the like accident to Sir Ralph—both being elderly and one of them at least in ill health—the plans & prospects about N[ewstead] might be so materially changed—to render the sale at least unnecessary—if not out of the question.—I am merely putting this as a possibility—but am willing to go on with Mr. Claughton's purchase—provided he be a little more prompt and payable than heretofore.——If he will meet and make the payments and securities good directly—I will wave the years rental.——But no more haggling—at least I hope not—for I will not sacrifice further.—I shall be most happy to hear of a favourable decision in Ld. Portsmouth's business[2]—it is really a most harsh and iniquitous business on F[ellowe]'s part—and the worst precedent possible—I should think so even if you and yours were out of the question.—

Believe me very truly yours
BYRON

P.S.—Enclosed is a letter from Mealey[3]—which how to answer?—do you take that upon you for I am not aware of the proper steps to be taken—or the merits of the case.—I shall write by this Post to Messrs Smith[4]—and you can draw for Sawbridge's annuity[5]—by the way—let *that* be redeemed the first thing from Clau[ghton]'s payment—if he makes one—and pray answer him soon—and settle the matter if possible—I mean—with Mr. C[laughto]n.—

[TO THOMAS MOORE]   *February 4, 1815*

I enclose you half a letter from * * [Hobhouse] which will explain itself—at least the latter part—the former refers to private business of mine own. If Jeffrey will take such an article, and you will undertake the revision, or, indeed, any portion of the article itself (for unless *you do*, by Phœbus, I will have nothing to do with it), we can cook up, between us three, as pretty a dish of sour-crout as ever tipped over the tongue of a bookmaker * * * *

You can, at any rate, try Jeffrey's inclination. Your late proposal

[2] See Jan. 12, 1815, to Hanson, note 2.
[3] Owen Mealey, steward of Newstead Abbey.
[4] Unidentified. Possibly creditors.
[5] Byron borrowed £6,000 from Sawbridge before going abroad in 1809.

from him made me hint this to * * [Hobhouse],[1] who is a much better proser and scholar than I am, and a very superior man indeed. Excuse haste—answer this.

Ever yours most,
B

P.S.—All is well at home. I wrote to you yesterday.

[TO JOHN CAM HOBHOUSE]   *February 5th, 1815*

My dear H[obhous]e—Will you call on Mr. Templeman[1] the barrister, and inform him that if his arrangements will permit, I request that he will have the goodness to undertake the examination and settlement of some affairs which require the opinion of counsel, and concerning which he may receive the requisite intelligence first from yourself and finally from Mr. Hanson, my solicitor.

Ever dear H., most truly yours,
BYRON

P.S.—I have this day written to Moore about your article and will send you his answer the moment I receive it or at least the substance thereof.

My debts I have informed you of as well as I can. Some of the tradesmen's are largish sums, but the coachmaker, tailor, and others have received a few hundreds which are receipted.

There is a damned dinner party, and I must dress. Again and again yours,

B

[TO LADY MELBOURNE]   *Fy. 5th. 1815*

My dear Aunt—Pray is there any foundation for a rumour which has reached me—that *les agneaux* (W[illiam] & C[aroline]) are about to separate?—If it is so—I hope that this time it is only on account of incompatability of temper—and that no more serious scenes have

---

[1] Jeffrey had written to Moore asking him to get Byron to write a review for the *Edinburgh*. The review of William Martin Leake's *Researches in Greece* was finally written by Hobhouse, and Byron, respecting Hobhouse's greater knowledge of factual details, added nothing to it. It appeared in the *Edinburgh Review* for February, 1815 (Vol. XXIV, pp. 353–369). Byron was here apparently suggesting another article in which he, Moore, and Hobhouse would collaborate.

[1] See Jan. 26, 1815, to Hobhouse.

occurred—in short I don't know what to wish—but no harm to any body—unless for the good of *our* family which she is always embroiling —pray tell me as much as your new code of confidence will permit—or what is still better—that this report (which came in a letter) is—as the person says it may be a "wicked scandal."—I answered you a few days ago—we have 3 or 4 visitors here—whom I wish gone again though very good people in their way—but alas in my *way* too—I did not know of their approach till their arrival—but I thought the cursed best liveries of the servants—and some old & ill-fashioned gold dessert-knives &c. boded me no good—as omens of preparation—& so it has turned out.——Bell is very well & looking so—but I have got a cold—it is going off however.—I have had a letter from Moore very laudatory of Lady Cowper in particular & the Chat[swort]h party in general.—Why did you call Lady S[usan] R[yder][1] *my* former "favourite" I never exchanged a word with her in my life after she came out—nor before—except at her mother's—& then because people seemed to treat her as a child & not talk to her at all:—I wish either she or any one else would get hold of that foolish piece of Nobility[2]—the Public have as much right to a Duchess of Devonshire as to the repeal of the property tax—and ought to petition for both.—

ever yours most truly

ℬ

[TO LADY MELBOURNE]   *Fy. 6th. 1815*

My dear Lady M[elbourn]e—I write to you upon mourning paper— all my Gilt (spell it with a *u* if you like) is gone—but it is really not malaprop.—for last night *was* nearly *my* last—as thus.—Thanks to my father in law & your worshiful brother's collieries & coals—my dressing room fire was so diabolically pregnant with charcoal—that I was taken almost to Lady like fainting—& if Bell had not in the nick of time postponed old Nick for the present—and sluiced me with Eau de Cologne and all sorts of waters besides—you might now have been repairing your latest suit of black to look like new for your loving nephew.—All this is true—upon the word of a man hardly resuscitated —& Bell herself has not been quite well since with her exertions—this is in favour of matrimony for had I been single—the lack of aid would

---

[1] Lady Susan Ryder was the daughter of the Earl of Harrowby and granddaughter (through her mother) of Granville Leveson-Gower, Marquess of Stafford. In 1817 she married Lord Obrington.

[2] The 6th Duke of Devonshire, who came to the title in 1811.

have left me suffocated—it was in bed that I was overwhelmed (though the Charcoal was in the next—my dressing room) and how her lungs withstood it I can't tell—but so it is—she is alive—and thanks to her so am I.——Our guests are gone—and I am very anxious to hear from you—you owe me a letter if not *two*—for this makes my third to your *one*.——News are none—except shipwrecks, and County meetings—the sea & the freeholders have been combustling about the Eastwind—& the property tax—and vessels have been lost—and speeches found in great plenty.—I am yawning hideously—because I can't hear your answer—instead of reading it—and this part of the night—the "Sweet of it" (as Falstaff says) in London—is the drowsiest here—so Good night

ever thine

B

[TO EDITOR OF THE *Poetical Register*¹]   *Seaham—Stockton on Tees Feby. 7th. 1815*

Sir—The translation from the Romaic is very much at your service —if you think it worth insertion.²——Some time ago I had some correspondence with Mr. Hogg on the subject of his proposed Miscellany—but I had not the most distant idea—nor from what I know of Mr. H[ogg] should I conceive it to be his intention to send forth his work in hostility to yours—neither can I suppose that a publication so well established & supported as the P[oetical] R[egister] will be shaken by any competition whatsoever of a rival nature.—— Mr. Hogg certainly requested me to contribute to his miscellany and to this I intended to accede—but many circumstances have since concurred to interrupt the composition of any piece which would have suited his purpose—and I am not at this moment in possession of any thing worth insertion or perusal—unless some short things meant to be songs (written for a set of Hebrew Melodies) should be thought better of than they deserve.—To three or four of these—yet unpublished—you shall be very welcome—but if they disappoint yourself and your readers—recollect that I hinted as much before hand— and do not hesitate to omit any one or all that may appear faulty or unsuitable.—I have the honour to be

your very obedt. humble Sert.

BYRON

¹ See Oct. 10, 1814, to Editor of the *Poetical Register*, note 1.
² This may have been the Romaic song "I wander near that fount of waters". See April 15, 1814, to Lady Sitwell, note 2.

My dear Thom,—Jeffrey has been so very kind about me and my damnable works, that I would not be indirect or equivocal with him, even for a friend. So, it may be as well to tell him that it is not mine; but that, if I did not firmly and truly believe it to be much better than I could offer, I would never have troubled him or you about it.[1] You can judge between you how far it is admissible, and reject it, if not the right sort. For my own part, I have no interest in the article one way or the other, further than to oblige * * [Hobhouse], and should the composition be a good one, it can hurt neither party,—nor, indeed, any one, saving and excepting Mr. * * * [Leake]

* * * * * * * * * * * * * * *

Curse catch me if I know what H[obhouse] means or meaned about the demonstrative pronoun, but I admire your fear of being inoculated with the same. Have you never found out that you have a particular style of your own, which is as distinct from all other people, as Hafiz of Shiraz from Hafiz of the Morning Post?[2]

So you allowed B * * and such like to hum and haw you, or, rather, Lady J * * [Jersey] out of her compliment, and *me* out of mine.[3] Sunburn me but this was pitiful-hearted. However, I will tell her all about it when I see her.

Bell desires me to say all kinds of civilities, and assure you of her recognition and high consideration. I will tell you of our movements south, which may be in about three weeks from this present writing. By the way, don't engage yourself in any travelling expedition, as I have a plan of travel into Italy, which we will discuss. And then, think of the poesy wherewithal we should overflow, from Venice to Vesuvius, to say nothing of Greece, through all which—God willing—we might perambulate in one twelve-months. If I take my wife, you can take yours; and if I leave mine, you may do the same. "Mind you stand by me, in either case, Brother Bruin."[4]

And believe me inveterately yours,

B

---

[1] See Feb. 4, 1815, to Moore, note 1.

[2] Robert Stott wrote under the name of Hafiz in the *Morning Post*.

[3] While at Chatsworth (the Duke of Devonshire's), Moore had written some verses to Lady Jersey (with a flattering allusion to Byron), which he told Byron he had later consigned to the flames.

[4] Foote's *Mayor of Garratt*, Act II, scene 2.

My dear Hobhouse—I give you full & unqualified authority to apply in my name & behalf to any Barrister of repute whom you think will undertake the business—surely this will be credential sufficient to show for the trouble you are taking on my account.——I am truly sorry to hear such things of H[anson]—and a little for myself—I suppose we shall have trouble enough with him—it is necessary that you should know that Clau[ghton] is about to complete as you will perceive by H[anson]'s last letter which I enclose—pray keep it carefully—I have transmitted to H[anson] the money for Sawbridge[1]— who—I presume has received it—& if possible see *H[anson]* & even *Clau[ghton]*—to whom when his *cash* is *ready*—it may be as *well* to *hint* about the instalments being paid to *me*.—Perhaps I had better come to town—I can in a few days—leaving Lady B[yron] with her father & Ly. M[ilbanke]—I write in haste—& you will perceive—seriously enough—nothing like *Self* to make a man in earnest—but I am ashamed of being such a wavering Stoic as to confess pain.—

ever dear H. your obliged & sincere
BYRON

P.S.—I enclose you a prologue copied out in another hand—alter— omit—but at any rate amend—it is untouched since written—& there is no time for me to improve it.——*Moore has written* to J[effrey] and I expect further tidings—perhaps your best way would be to send the packet to Moore—*Mayfield—Ashbourne—Derby*.——To return to my Ipecacuanha—I suppose Clau[ghton] won't be such a fool as to pay to Hanson till I have signed the new contract—preparatory—& in that case of course I will lay my digits upon the cash in person—the trustees for Lady B[yron] are only concerned for her settlement £60000—which will be secured on mortage of the estate—& the rest of course to me—& I propose to pay all debts—& pending these to lodge the superflux—but not in any *one* Banker's hands—but two or three—Hoares—Kinnairds—and Hammersleys—or any other worthy personages.——

My dear Drury—Many be the days of Byron Drury—for so let him be called—with many thanks on my part for the honour of my res-

---

[1] See Feb. 3, 1815, to Hanson, note 5.

ponsibility for his coming trespasses.—He is born—and I am married—I offer further thanks for your congratulations thereupon.—It is now six weeks and a day since I subsided into matrimony—since which period I have become duly domestic—and shall be happy to hear of the amputation of any further foxes—(particularly Hodgson's) tails in the same trap.———No doubt he was—as you describe—fulsome and osculatory—especially of an evening—as you are bounden to watch over the honour of that numerous family—I trust you kept—& keep an eye upon him for fear of anticipation.———You will also sympathize with me in your approbation of Lord Cranstoun's conduct at Staines—who hath recently pistolled his wife's paramour in the arm—and disqualified him from laying more than one hand upon his neighbour's moiety——Staines seems an unlucky spot—methinks they used to manage better at Salt Hill.[1]—I am now at my "father in law Sir Jacob's" (see "Mayor of Garrat") and we have had a visit from Ellison[2]—who looks married too—sooner or later it is what we all come to.—Health & Fraternity—

ever most truly yours
B

P.S.—My Half—(or three quarters) receives & returns your compliments—she is a woman of Learning—which I have great hopes she means to keep to herself—I never touch upon it for fear of quotation.——

[TO JOHN CAM HOBHOUSE]   *Fy. 17th. 1815*

My dear H.—Your packet shall go in a day or two[1]—but I wish first to hear once more from T[homas] M[oore] but I won't wait longer than tomorrow for that.———I enclose you another letter of Hanson's—which I have not yet answered but shall this day—*I am* disposed to give up—and not hold out with Clau[ghton] upon the present conditions.———I shall mention Winthrop[2]—but *do* see *Spooney* [Hanson] if you can.—Clau[ghton]'s address is Haydock

---

[1] Byron had been with the Oxfords at Salt Hill before they went abroad in 1813.
[2] Unidentified.

[1] Byron was holding Hobhouse's review of Leake which he had written for the *Edinburgh Review*, waiting for a final word from Moore before sending it. See Feb. 4, 1815, to Moore, note 1.
[2] The barrister employed by Hobhouse as counsel to look into Byron's financial affairs. Probably Benjamin Winthrop of Lincoln's Inn. Born 1767. M.A. University College, Oxford. Called to the Bar June 18, 1792.

Lodge—Warrington—Lancs.—It pleaseth me to hear that the prologue will save you any trouble—since you are taking a plaguy deal on my account.——I have had the cream of congratulations from *Scrope*—who has been *ill*—he says—I thought it had been his Uncle who was defunct—but I suppose Scrope is not yet sure which.— Excuse haste I will write more the morrow

ever thine

𝔅

P.S.—I like your review vastly—but it is long enough in itself— without any additions from me—I shall write to J[effrey] and do all I can about insertion—though I hope he will be *agreeable* (as folks say) without. If Mr. Claughton comes to town—he is generally at the Grecian Coffee House—and you can see him—& state from me that the payments must be made into such Bankers' in my name as I shall then direct.—

[TO JOHN HANSON]   *Fy. 17th. 1815*

My dear Sir,—I am not disposed to dispute further with Mr. Claughton—if he would be speedy in his payments and firm in his securities. Mr. Winthrop the Barrister is the gentleman appointed by me to look into my various concerns and I hope you will be prepared to give him the necessary information. Mr. Hobhouse has informed him on my part of what is required. It is my particular wish that no time should be lost in this—and you must be sensible how very important the adjustment of my affairs—at any rate some preparatory arrangement must now be.

It will give me great pleasure to hear of the reestablishment of Charles's[1] health—and I am not less eager to hear of the Chancellor's decision in favour of Lord Portsmouth.

Believe me, Very truly yours,

BYRON

[TO JOHN CAM HOBHOUSE]   *Fy. 18th. 1815*

My dear H.—I have written to Mr. *W*[*inthrop*]—referring him to you for more information—pray ask him if a *trustee can* or *cannot* be changed—& his advice about the receipt of the money—for the

---

[1] Son of John Hanson and partner in his law business.

trustees are only for the settlement I believe—the *sett[lement]s* were drawn up by Lady B[yron]'s people.— Claughton won't of course pay the money till *I* have signed—& sign I won't unless it is fairly deposited—for my use—in my name at my Bankers—as all except Lady B[yron]'s settlement is to be at my disposal.—Pray see Clau-[ghton]—when he sojourns at the Hellenic Coffee House Temple Bar (his usual Han[1] when in town) & if necessary let Mr. Winthrop see him—& do *you* say—do—& perpetrate all possible things to bring me fair & clear out of a thousand & one dilemmas.—"Tremble" if *you* tremble what must I?—I must be a little Earthquake.—See Hanson & talk to him—I have written to him stating Mr. Winthrop's appointment. I shall send off your review tomorrow but have had no further word from Moore

ever yours most truly

𝔅

[TO JOHN HANSON]   *Fy. 18th. 1815*

Dear Sir/—I wrote to you yesterday stating that in pursuance with the intention which Mr. Hobhouse had apprized you of on my part some time ago—it was my wish to appoint a Counsel to overlook the present arrangement of my affairs—and that Mr. Winthrop had accepted that appointment.—I now write again to request that every facility may be afforded to him—& that the business may be immediately entered into—as you must be fully aware of its importance. ——If Mr. Claughton arrives in town & is disposed to complete—it will be better that I should be there—and of course he will not make any payment—till the contract is signed by me.——I am a little surprized not to hear of the Chancellor's decision—& hope that it is or will be favourable to Lord P[ortsmouth].—

Believe me ever very truly yours
BYRON

[TO THOMAS MOORE]   *February 22d, 1815*

Yesterday I sent off the packet and letter to Edinburgh.[1] It consisted of forty-one pages, so that I have not added a line; but in my letter, I mentioned what passed between you and me in autumn, as my

---

[1] Hut (Albanian?).
[1] See Feb. 4, 1815, to Moore, and Feb. 17, 1815, to Hobhouse.

inducement for presuming to trouble him either with my own or * * [Hobhouse]'s lucubrations. I am any thing but sure that it will do; but I have told J[effrey] that if there is any decent raw material in it, he may cut it into what shape he pleases, and warp it to his liking.

So you *won't* go abroad, then with *me*,—but alone. I fully purpose starting much about the time you mention, and alone, too.

* * * * * * * * * * * * * * *

I hope J[effrey] won't think me very impudent in sending * * [Hobhouse] only; there was not room for a syllable. I have avowed * * [Hobhouse] as the author, and said that you thought or said, when I met you last, that he (J[effrey]) would not be angry at the coalition (though, alas! we have not coalesced), and so, if I have got into a scrape, I must get out of it—Heaven knows how.

Your Anacreon is come,[2] and with it I sealed (its first impression) the packet and epistle to our patron.

Curse the Melodies and the Tribes, to boot. Braham is to assist—or hath assisted—but will do no more good than a second physician. I merely interfered to oblige a whim of K[innaird]'s, and all I have got by it was "a speech" and a receipt for stewed oysters.

"Not meet"—pray don't say so. We must meet somewhere or somehow. Newstead is out of the question, being nearly sold again, or, if not, it is uninhabitable for my spouse. Pray write again. I will soon.

P.S.—Pray when do you come out? ever, or never? I hope I have made no blunder; but I certainly think you said to me (after W[ordswor]th, whom I first pondered upon, was given up) that * * [Hobhouse] and I might attempt * * * * [Leake?]. *His* length alone prevented me from trying my part, though I should have been less severe upon the Reviewée.

Your seal is the best and prettiest of my set, and I thank you very much therefor. I have just been—or, rather ought to be—very much shocked by the death of the Duke of Dorset.[3] We were at school together, and there I was passionately attached to him. Since, we have never met—but once, I think, since 1805—and it would be a paltry affectation to pretend that I had any feeling for him worth the name.

[2] Moore had sent Byron a seal with the head of Anacreon. Moore's earliest success as a poet had come with his translation of Anacreon, dedicated to the Prince of Wales, which was published in 1800.

[3] George John Frederick, 4th Duke of Dorset, born in 1793, had been one of Byron's younger favourites at Harrow. He was killed by a fall from his horse while hunting in Ireland, on February 14, 1815. Byron's poem to him had appeared in *Poems Original and Translated*, 1808.

But there was a time in my life when this event would have broken my heart; and all I can say for it now is that—it is not worth breaking.

Adieu—it is all a farce.

[TO JOHN CAM HOBHOUSE] *Fy. 24th. 1815*

My dear H—Your packet is forwarded to Dunedin—with a letter from me to the E[dito]r stating all about it—it was long enough without addenda.—I think you will see on a little reflection that it was much better for me to be silent altogether about your "Behemoth"—for obvious reasons—J[effrey] would have looked upon it as an attempt rather to review *you* than the philologer.—I have not yet had his answer.——I have a letter from Winthrop but none from Hans[on] in answer to 2 very decisive from me on the subject—you were right to "down him with the King of Prussia" about the question lying (*he* lies) in a small compass—it involves altogether N[ewstead] & R[ochdale] at the least more than £100000—& the law & his damned account will probably enlarge the question considerably—by the way— according to his own statement—that account may as well be narrowed to the question.—The £2040—he *borrowed* of me—& was to pay it again in a *month*—his first acknowledgement had the word *borrowed*— it was for a purchase in Essex—for which he wanted to make up the deposit—now why did he not say at once—let me have so much on account? instead of asking it as a loan—if his bill is to be so formidable —"ask him *that*—most thinking people—again & again I say—ask him that."——By the way ought not Winthrop to begin by being feeed—every man says Lawyer Scout in Joseph Andrews "ought to have a proper regard for his fee—no man can discommend him for attachment to his fee["]¹—let me be regular—enquire among the legal—& let me know the usual ways of your counsellors at law.——I see no prospect—or prospectus (as Murray would say) of the "golden days" you mention unless I were to buy in the lottery so called—or Clau[ghton] comes down with his Marks for the lands—

ever thine most truly

ß

[TO JOHN CAM HOBHOUSE] *Fy. 28th. 1815*

My dear H.—I was in *Chancery* to the last drop of my Wardship & minority—I am much mistaken if Hanson did not receive sums since

---

¹ Fielding, *Joseph Andrews*, Book IV, chapter 3.

my majority—at all events his accounts can only be from 1809—every thing passed through his hands—the sale of some farms in Norfolk— the sums lent by Sawbridge—&c. &c.—I have written to him again most peremptorily—I do not know who *passed* the *accounts*—but *ward* I was to my cost—for the Chancery was the plea of the savings being smaller than they would otherwise have been—though small enough in any case.——I fancy it must end in my coming up to town.——Your Review is accepted—but you will see I was right about "Behemoth" by these extracts from J[effrey]'s letter—which is remarkably kind & friendly.—"You seem to be aware that your learned Coadjutor stands perhaps too nearly in the character of a party concerned to be entirely trusted with the judicial function on the present occasion.—And I shall probably abridge the part in which he responds to Mr. L[eake] as the critic of his former publication." He then makes a few observations personally kind to me—about the additions which I told him were to have been made by me—but which I omitted to send on account of the length of the Article & goes [on] "The Article as it stands seems very smartly & pleasingly written and will require but a few retrenchments to suit it for our purposes—I am extremely obliged to Mr. H[obhouse] for the honour he has done us in trusting it in our hands—& beg you to make my best acknowledgements when you have occasion to write to him."—I shall set off from this place on Monday next furthest—and *solus*—any letters after that you had best address to Six Mile Bottom Newmarket—& if I come up to London—you will perhaps give me a bed and a book at Whitton—Lady B[yron] will remain here for the present.—

Ever dear H. yours most truly

𝔅

P.S.—Though I have written and decidedly to Mr. Hanson it may not be amiss to press him—I have shown my letters to Lady B[yron] who thinks it quite decisive and at the same time temperate.——

[TO JOHN HANSON]   *February 28th. 1815*

Dear Sir—To my great surprize I learn from London that no communication has been made on your part to Mr. Winthrop not-withstanding my two very pressing letters to you more than a week ago upon the subject.—I once more earnestly repeat that request—& beg leave to add that such omissions must lead to an end of all confidence and intercourse between us—being not only professionally negligent—but personally disrespectful.——Upon Mr. Claughton's business—I should feel disposed to wave the rents—though I think the corn bill & removal of property tax much more in favour of land——than circumstances appeared at the commencement of the treaty.— But the rents I would not hesitate to drop for an immediate & secure negociation.—The Rochdale question must be referred to Mr. Winthrop as counsel for an opinion without delay—he has been apprized of my intention—& I am at a loss to conjecture what can have prevented your immediate compliance with my request—if the affairs for which you are concerned on my part are not in your opinion of great magnitude—they at least involve the whole of my property— and in this respect require some attention.——I should also be glad of your account—which I will take the earliest opportunity in my power of settling. I am still with every inclination to remain

very truly yours
BYRON

[TO THOMAS MOORE]   *March 2d, 1815*

My dear Thom,—Jeffrey has sent me the most friendly of all possible letters, and has accepted * * [Hobhouse]'s article. He says he has long liked not only, &c. &c. but my "character." This must be *your* doing, you dog—ar'n't you ashamed of yourself, knowing me so well? This is what one gets for having you for a father confessor.

I feel merry enough to send you a sad song.[1] You once asked me for some words which you would set. Now you may set or not, as you like,—but there they are, in a legible hand, and not in mine,[2] but of my own scribbling; so you may say of them what you please. Why don't you write to me? I shall make you "a speech" if you don't respond quickly.

I am in such a state of sameness and stagnation, and so totally occupied in consuming the fruits—and sauntering—and playing dull games at cards—and yawning—and trying to read old Annual Registers and the daily papers—and gathering shells on the shore—

[1] These were the verses beginning, "There's not a joy the world can give like that it takes away." Moore gave them to his music publisher Power who published them set to music by Sir John Stevenson. The poem reflected Byron's feelings in contemplating the death of his Harrow friend the Duke of Dorset.

[2] Lady Byron had copied the poem for him as she had a number of the Hebrew Melodies.

and watching the growth of stunted gooseberry bushes in the garden—
that I have neither time nor sense to say more than

Yours ever,

B

P.S.—I open my letter again to put a question to you. What would
Lady C—k [Cork],[3] or any other fashionable Pidcock, give to collect
you and Jeffrey and me to *one* party? I have been answering his letter,
which suggested this dainty query. I can't help laughing at the thoughts
of your face and mine; and our anxiety to keep the Aristarch in good
humour during the *early* part of a compotation, till we got drunk
enough to make him "a speech." I think the critic would have much
the best of us—of one, at least—for I don't think diffidence (I mean
social) is a disease of yours.

[TO JOHN CAM HOBHOUSE]   *March 3d. 1815*

My dear Hobhouse—As I shall not perhaps set off as soon as I
expected—you may address your responses here as usual.——What
has happed between you and Lord J. T.[1]—I hear he has "lampooned
you & your friends"—so says Kinnaird—I hope I am included in the
number—but methinks that aged & venerable nobleman is meddling
with irascible men—men famous with the pen—& tolerable in accuracy with the pistol—how comes he into such a hornet's nest—
must we write or fight?—I am ready either as principal or second
against him and his whole generation.—In my last I told you J[effre]y
has accepted your composition.—I hope you are pleased with what he
says thereupon.—I have not heard from Hans[on] but have written to
him in a style worthy of Salmasius[2]—I have talked "professional
negligence and personal disrespect"—I have talked of "an end of all
confidence"—and still he answers nothing—"may he be damned like
the Glutton—a whoreson Achitophel."——I wish you would make
an inquest of the house of the D[uche]ss of Devonshire—now to be let

---

[3] The Hon. Mary Monckton, daughter of the 1st Viscount Galway, married the
7th Earl of Cork and Orrery in 1786. Before her marriage her liveliness had en-
chanted Dr. Johnson, according to Boswell. When Byron knew her she was a blue
stocking and a literary lion-hunter. In calling her a "fashionable Pidcock" Byron
referred to the keeper of the lions at Exeter 'Change.

[1] Unidentified.

[2] Claudius Salmasius (Claude de Saumaise) (1588–1653) was a French classical
scholar who had a high reputation in his day as a polemical writer. His defence of
Charles I was answered by Milton.

278

—& which if it suited I should be glad to take for the year.—In your observations therein—don't forget those *essentials* to happiness—as a dear deceased friend of ours used to call them—I mean the convenient position of the Κρεια[3]—or two—or more.———I am very comfortable here—listening to that monologue of my father in law which he is pleased to call conversation—he has lately played once upon the fiddle—to my great refreshment—we have had visitors—& they are gone—I have got K[innaird]'s receipt for the shellfish—but no shell fish for the Receipt—I hear Kean is coming to Sunderland—but probably not before my migration.—Well—now I want for nothing but an heir to my estate—and an estate for my heir.

ever yrs. most truly

𝔅

[TO JOHN HANSON]   *March 4th. 1815*

Dear Sir—When the interest is considered—and that my total loss will be—(including the £5000) better than 13000—if the interest be 8000—I do not see how Mr. C[laughton] will press for the rents—if he really means to purchase.—You should also have given him—or give him a hint of the difference of times—since he prepared to renew—for certainly—the repeal of the property tax—and the corn bill (if carried & continued) must make in favour of land—this he ought to consider.———I could wish that it were concluded one way or the other—for this state of suspense is intolerable.———Nothing will give me more pleasure than to hear of Ld. P[ortsmouth]'s success—and Charles's recovery—Lady B[yron] sends her compliments & I remain

very truly yours

BYRON

[TO THOMAS MOORE]   *March 8th, 1815*

An event—the death of poor Dorset—and the recollection of what I once felt, and ought to have felt now, but could not—set me pondering, and finally into the train of thought which you have in your hands. I am very glad you like them, for I flatter myself they will pass as an imitation of your style. If I could imitate it well, I should have

[3] χρεια—necessity, i.e., toilet or W.C.

no great ambition of originality—I wish I could make you exclaim with Dennis, "That's my thunder, by G–d!"[1] I wrote them with a view to your setting them, and as a present to Power, if he would accept the words, and *you* did not think yourself degraded, for once in a way, by marrying them to music.

Sunburn N[athan]!—why do you always twit me with his vile Ebrew nasalities? Have I not told you it was all K[innaird]'s doing, and my own exquisite facility of temper? But thou wilt be a wag, Thomas; and see what you get for it. Now for my revenge.

Depend—and perpend—upon it that your opinion of * * [Scott]'s Poem will travel through one or other of the quintuple correspondents, till it reaches the ear and the liver of the author. Your adventure, however, is truly laughable—but how could you be such a potatoe? You, "a brother" (of the quill) too, "near the throne," to confide to a man's *own publisher* (who has "bought," or rather sold, "golden opinions" about him) such a damnatory parenthesis! "Between you and me,"[2] quotha—it reminds me of a passage in the Heir at Law— "Tête-à-tête with Lady Duberly, I suppose"—"No—tête-à-tête with *five hundred people*;"[3] and your confidential communication will doubtless be in circulation to that amount, in a short time, with several additions, and in several letters, all signed L.H.R.O.B., &c. &c. &c.

We leave this place to-morrow, and shall stop on our way to town (in the interval of taking a house there) at Col. Leigh's, near Newmarket, where any epistle of yours will find its welcome way.

I have been very comfortable here,—listening to that d–d monologue, which elderly gentlemen call conversation, and in which my pious father-in-law repeats himself every evening—save one, when he played upon the fiddle. However, they have been very kind and hospitable, and I like them and the place vastly, and I hope they will live many happy months. Bell is in health, and unvaried good-humour and behaviour. But we are all in the agonies of packing and parting; and I suppose by this time to-morrow I shall be stuck in the chariot with my chin upon a band-box. I have prepared, however, another carriage for

[1] John Dennis introduced a new device for making thunder upon the stage. It was used in his tragedy *Appius and Virginia*. The tragedy failed but the managers continued to use his method of making thunder. When he saw it used in *Macbeth*, he exclaimed "See how the fellows use me; they have silenced my tragedy, and they roar out my thunder."

[2] Moore had written confidentially to his publisher Mr. Longman: "Between *you and me*, I don't much like Scott's poem [*The Lord of the Isles*]." And he got a reply from the whole firm, Longman, Hurst, Orme, Rees, Brown.

[3] George Colman the Younger, *The Heir-at-Law*, Act I, scene 1.

the abigail, and all the trumpery which our wives drag along with them.

Ever thine, most affectionately,
B

[TO JOHN HANSON (*a*)]   *March 9th. 1815*

Dear Sir/—I send this to request you will favour me with Claughton's answer to Col. Leigh's Six Mile Bottom nr. Newmarket.—I write this in my way to my [*sic*] London—but shall stop at my sister's a day or two

yrs. truly
BYRON

P.S.—I have received yours with Clau[ghton]'s last—but am anxious to hear of the result of his interview with "a gentleman on the 6th"—

[TO JOHN HANSON (*b*)]   *Boroughbridge—March 9th. 1815*

Dear Sir/—I received yrs. with Mr. C[laughton]'s enclosed on my way to town this day—I send this on the chance of finding you at *York*—(from which I hope you will soon return) to request that you will forward his next letter either to *Mrs. Leigh's near Newmarket*— or if it arrives late in the *next* week to me at Albany London

yrs. truly
B

[TO JOHN HANSON]   *March 12th. 1815*

My dear Sir/—Enclosed is Clau[ghton]'s letter—what is to be done?—I will conclude *no treaty* till the *money* is *ready*—& I think— he had better move his things off the premises—& there let it end— this is merely the old story over again—

yrs. truly
B

P.S.—Pretty stuff—to talk of recontracting before the money is paid!—That is out of the question.

Dear Sir—I have heard from Mr. Claughton & have answered him in general terms but have postponed any decision till I heard further from you.—You had better write to him now—& if he *can* make his means tangible—& his securities eligible—let us go on—can he give us good bills for the £32·000 payable in May?—in course I must have mortgage for the rest of the purchase money.—I wish Mr. Winthrop to be consulted also as to the nature of the security & how far it is eligible—but of that when we conclude.———The Corn bill is passed—the property tax repealed—& the purchaser of land has now no bad bargain.—Indeed if the strange events in France go on & end in favour of Bonaparte—land will be where it was—& all Mr. C[laughton]'s fine reasonings about its depreciation become null & void.———I write this on the supposition that you are now in London—& shall be glad of a few lines in answer—I hope you are about to attend to the other business already mentioned.—

ever yours truly
B

P.S.—I told him I could not give up the rents—in the mean time—I would suggest that if he cannot be quick—we must try another purchaser—for I am tired of all this off & on.—

[TO THOMAS CLAUGHTON]   *March 26th. 1815*

Dear Sir,—I think it proper to inform you that I have this day received from town proposals from a highly reputable quarter to treat for Newstead—To my last letter I have received no answer—and in your last you did not seem prepared for immediate payments—without which I cannot be expected to renew any contract. Mr. Hanson (for whose opinion I stated in the conclusion of my last letter that I reserved myself) has answered to the purpose that the estate is still on sale—& open to purchase. Upon these circumstances you will form your own judgement—with mine you have been some time acquainted —I had and have every disposition to give you the preference—but the delays and demurs in treaty and payment—justify me in giving attention to other offers.—I shall be in town on Tuesday—where Mr.

Hanson now is—who will be glad to hear from you. I have the
honour to be

Yours very truly,
BYRON

[TO JOHN CAM HOBHOUSE]   *March 26th. 1815*

My dear H[obhous]e—I am full of wonder & regret at your
migratory project[1]—which I yet hope may be interrupted—wishing
you nevertheless all possible success & divertiment if you *will* go.—
We expect to be in town on Tuesday—Lady B[yron] is very well &
very thankful for the Prince de Ligne's autograph.[2]——Buonaparte!!!
—I marvel what next.—I have written to nobody & am as lazy &
stupefied as can be.—Your intention of travelling again puts all the
things I meant to say in abeyance till you come back—& I shall only
add sincerest good wishes and regards of

yours ever most affectly.
B

[TO JOHN HANSON]   *March 26th. 1815*

My dear Sir—I think it will be but proper to intimate to Mr.
Claughton that we have other offers for N[ewstead]—I told him I was
willing to treat but reserved myself for your opinion.——The best
bidder shall have it.——I expect to be in town on Tuesday—where I
hope to hear from or see you well.—

yrs. ever truly
B

P.S.—Our home is in Piccadilly—the Duchess of Devon's.——

1 Napoleon had just escaped from Elba and landed in France. Hobhouse, eager
to get near the centre of action, planned to go to Paris, but did not leave before
Byron arrived in London, having delayed his journey in order to see his friend.
After calling on Byron at 13 Piccadilly Terrace, the Duchess of Devonshire's house
which he had leased for a year, Hobhouse recorded in his diary: ". . . he advises
me not to marry though he has the best of wives."

2 Hobhouse had sent Lady Byron an autograph of the Prince de Ligne, a famous
literary man as well a General. It was he who said of the Congress of Vienna:
"Le Congrès danse mais ne marche pas."

I meaned to write to you before on the subject of your loss;[1] but the recollection of the uselessness and worthlessness of any observations on such events prevented me. I shall only now add, that I rejoice to see you bear it so well, and that I trust time will enable Mrs. M[oore] to sustain it better. Every thing should be done to divert and occupy her with other thoughts and cares, and I am sure all that can be done will.

Now to your letter. Napoleon—but the papers will have told you all.[2] I quite think with you upon the subject, and for my *real* thoughts this time last year, I would refer you to the last pages of the Journal I gave you. I can forgive the rogue for utterly falsifying every line of mine Ode—which I take to be the last and uttermost stretch of human magnanimity. Do you remember the story of a certain abbé, who wrote a Treatise on the Swedish Constitution, and proved it indissoluble and eternal? Just as he had corrected the last sheet, news came that Gustavus III had destroyed this immortal government. "Sir," quoth the abbé, "the King of Sweden may overthrow the *constitution*, but not *my book*!!"[3] I think *of* the abbé, but not *with* him.

Making every allowance for talent and the most consummate daring, there is, after all, a good deal in luck or destiny. He might have been stopped by our frigates—or wrecked in the Gulf of Lyons, which is particularly tempestuous—or—a thousand things. But he is certainly Fortune's favourite, and

> Once fairly set out on his party of pleasure,
> Taking towns at his liking and crowns at his leisure,
> From Elba to Lyons and Paris he goes,
> Making *balls for* the ladies, and *bows to* his foes.

You must have seen the account of his driving into the middle of the royal army, and the immediate effect of his pretty speeches. And now, if he don't drub the allies, there is "no purchase in money."[4] If he can take France by himself, the devil's in't if he don't repulse the invaders, when backed by those celebrated sworders—those boys of the blade, the Imperial Guard, and the old and new army. It is impossible not to be dazzled and overwhelmed by his character and career. Nothing

[1] The death of Olivia Byron Moore, Moore's daughter of whom Byron was the god-father.

[2] Napoleon escaped from Elba on February 26, and entered Paris on March 20.

[3] Byron probably read this story in Grimm's *Correspondance* (ed. 1813), Partie III, tome iv, pp. 668–669.

[4] *Henry IV*, Part I, Act. III, scene 3.

ever so disappointed me as his abdication, and nothing could have reconciled me to him but some such revival as his recent exploit; though no one could anticipate such a complete and brilliant renovation.

To your question, I can only answer that there have been some symptoms which look a little gestatory. It is a subject upon which I am not particularly anxious, except that I think it would please her uncle, Lord Wentworth, and her father and mother. The former (Lord W[entworth]) is now in town, and in very indifferent health. You perhaps know that his property, amounting to seven or eight thousand a year, will eventually devolve upon Bell. But the old gentleman has been so very kind to her and me, that I hardly know how to wish him in heaven, if he can be comfortable on earth. Her father is still in the country.

We mean to metropolize to-morrow, and you will address your next to Piccadilly. We have got the Duchess of Devon's house there, she being in France.

I don't care what Power says to secure the property of the Song, so that it is *not* complimentary to me, nor any thing about "condescending" or "*noble* author"—both "vile phrases," as Polonius says.

* * * * * * * * * * * * * * *

Pray, let me hear from you, and when you mean to be in town. Your continental scheme is impracticable for the present. I have to thank you for a longer letter than usual, which I hope will induce you to tax my gratitude still further in the same way.

You never told me about "Longman" and "next winter," and I am *not* a "mile-stone."[5]

[TO SAMUEL TAYLOR COLERIDGE]   *Piccadilly, March 31st, 1815*

Dear Sir,—It will give me great pleasure to comply with your request,[1] though I hope there is still taste enough left amongst us to

---

[5] Moore explains this as follows: "I had informed him of my intention to publish with the Messrs. Longman in the ensuing winter, and added that, in giving him this information, I found I had been—to use an elegant Irish metaphor—'whistling jigs to a mile-stone'." (Moore, I, 612.)

[1] Byron had been an admirer of Coleridge's "Rime of the Ancient Mariner" and other poems, but he had ridiculed his "To a Young Ass" in *English Bards and Scotch Reviewers*. This letter is in reply to Coleridge's request that Byron use his influence to get a publisher for a volume of his poems. It was at Byron's urging that Murray published in 1816 "Christabel", "Kubla Khan", and other poems. And when he became a member of the sub-committee of management of Drury Lane soon after this, Byron tried to get Coleridge to write a tragedy for that theatre, but Coleridge's promise was never fulfilled.

render it almost unnecessary, sordid and interested as, it must be admitted, many of "the trade" are, where circumstances give them an advantage. I trust you do not permit yourself to be depressed by the temporary partiality of what is called "the public" for the favourites of the moment; all experience is against the permanency of such impressions. You must have lived to see many of these pass away, and will survive many more—I mean personally, for *poetically*, I would not insult you by a comparison.

If I may be permitted, I would suggest that there never was such an opening for tragedy. In Kean, there is an actor worthy of expressing the thoughts of the characters which you have every power of imbodying; and I cannot but regret that the part of Ordonio[2] was disposed of before his appearance at Drury-lane. We have had nothing to be mentioned in the same breath with "Remorse" for very many years; and I should think that the reception of that play was sufficient to encourage the highest hopes of author and audience. It is to be hoped that you are proceeding in a career which could not but be successful. With my best respects to Mr. Bowles, I have the honour to be

Your obliged and very obedient servant,

BYRON

P.S.—You mention my "Satire," lampoon, or whatever you or others please to call it, I can only say, that it was written when I was very young and very angry, and has been a thorn in my side ever since; more particularly as almost all the persons animadverted upon became subsequently my acquaintances, and some of them my friends, which is "heaping fire upon an enemy's head," and forgiving me too readily to permit me to forgive myself. The part applied to you is pert, and petulant, and shallow enough;[3] but, although I have long done every thing in my power to suppress the circulation of the whole thing, I shall always regret the wantonness or generality of many of its attempted attacks.

---

[2] It was through Byron's influence that Coleridge's tragedy *Remorse* had been produced successfully at Drury Lane in January, 1813. Alexander Rae had taken the part of Ordonio in that production.

[3] Byron was thinking of his lines (262–64) in *English Bards*:

"The bard who soars to elegise an ass
So well the subject suits his noble mind,
He brays, the laureat of the long-ear'd kind."

[TO JOHN MURRAY]   [*April, 1815?*]

Perhaps the enclosed from Paris may amaze Mr. Hammond[1] or
some of *your* knowing ones—let me have it again this Evening—
                                                    ever yrs.
                                                        B

[TO JOHN MURRAY]   *April 4th. 1815*

Dear Sir—I wish to see you tomorrow if you can call conveniently
any time between 12 & two.——Do not forget to bring or send the
plate of the print[1]—which I must have given up—& nothing will ever
convince me it is given up till I have it here.—If tomorrow is inconvenient for you to call here any other morning will do.—
                                                    ever yrs. very truly
                                                        B

[TO JOHN MURRAY]   *April 9th. 1815*

Dear Sir—Thanks for ye. books—I have one great objection to your
proposition about inscribing the vase—which is that it would appear
ostentatious on my part—& of course I must send it as it is without any
alteration.[1]—
                                                    yrs. very truly
                                                        B

[TO LADY BYRON]   [*April 13–14? 1815*]

Dearest—Now your mother is come I won't have you worried any
longer—more particularly in your present situation which is rendered

---

[1] Perhaps George Hammond (1763–1853), diplomatist, who had been in
various embassies, Under Secretary for Foreign Affairs, an intimate of Grenville
and Canning, and joint-editor of the *Anti-Jacobin*. The enclosure was probably a
letter from Hobhouse who had gone to Paris shortly after Napoleon entered the
city.
[1] Byron had asked Murray to destroy the print made from an engraving of his
portrait by Phillips. See Jan. 6, 1815, to Murray.
[1] Two days before this letter was written, on April 7, Byron had been introduced to Walter Scott by John Murray, and they took an instant liking to each
other. Scott had sent Byron a Turkish dagger, and he responded by sending to
Scott a large sepulchral vase of silver.

very precarious by what you have already gone through. Pray—come home[1]—

ever thine
B

[TO JOHN HANSON] *April 15th. 1815*

Dear Sir/—I send you the enclosed which I have settled—at least given a draft for it.—I cannot but think it very odd after what I told you that I should not have heard from you that Randall[1] had brought his action—and I think it no less extraordinary as as a piece of conduct in him to take such a step without giving me notice.—

yrs. truly
BYRON

[TO SIR JAMES BLAND BURGES[1]] *April 22d. 1815*

My dear Sir James—It has been intimated to me that several erronious statements of the disposition of Lord Wentworth's property have appeared in the papers[2]—and Lady Byron agrees with me in suggesting that if Lady M[ilbanke] & you had no objection—& there is no impropriety in the request—it would not be amiss if Mr. Long or any other person acquainted with the facts were to insert a contradictory paragraph stating simply & shortly the heads & truth of Ld. W[entworth]'s testament.——I take it these foolish fellows N. & B. have something to do with any falsity which may have gone forth on the subject—but whether or not—it might I think prevent unpleasant feelings & misrepresentation to state the real circumstances.—

I am much & truly yr. obliged Sert.
BYRON

P.S.—I believe one statement went so far as to say that Lady B[yron] was *not* in the entail!—

[1] Lord Wentworth, Lady Byron's uncle, was seriously ill in London and she had gone to stay with him until her mother could come from Seaham.

[1] Unidentified. Probably one of Byron's many creditors.

[1] Sir James Bland Burges had married the Hon. Elizabeth Noel, sister of Lady Milbanke. It was as one of the executors of Lord Wentworth's estate that Byron addressed him.

[2] Lady Byron's uncle Lord Wentworth had died on April 17. The bulk of his property went to his sister Lady Milbanke. Henceforth she and Sir Ralph Milbanke took the name of Noel by the terms of the will.

Dear Aunt—I have not seen the tragedy—nor knew that Murray had it—if I had—you would have received it without delay—was not you at the play on Thursday?—I thought you were visible but obscurely in Ld. E[gremont]'s[1] box.——Bell has got a sad cold—but I hope will be better soon.—Ld. W[entworth]'s will is what was expected—but his property more considerable—the executors tell me that the estates entailed on Lady M[ilbanke] & Bell &c. are or may be made nearly eight thousand a year—& there is a good deal of Personalty besides & money &—God knows what—which will come in *half* to Lady Mil[banke] now Noel—The Tamworths[2] have the other half of the personals only.—These consist of partly Lady W[entworth]'s fortune—& twenty thousand in the 3 per cents—There are separate estates left for sale—firstly to pay all debts—& then to divide the residue between the two natural children.—I hope we shall meet soon—Bell is pronounced in a certain way—but I fear the present state of her health will materially interfere with that prospect for the present.—I will however hope better.—

yrs ever truly
B

Lord Wentworth died last week. The bulk of his property (from seven to eight thousand per ann.) is entailed on Lady Milbanke and Lady Byron. The first is gone to take possession in Leicestershire, and attend the funeral, &c. this day.

* * * * * * * * * * * * * * *

I have mentioned the facts of the settlement of Lord W[entworth]'s property, because the newspapers, with their usual accuracy, have been making all kinds of blunders in their statement. His will is just as expected—the principal part settled on Lady Milbanke (now Noel) and Bell, and a separate estate left for sale to pay debts (which are not great) and legacies to his natural son and daughter.

---

[1] For Lady Melbourne's relations with Lord Egremont see [1813?], to M. G. Lewis, note 1 (Vol. 3, page 4).

[2] Lady Milbanke's sister's child, Sophy Curzon, had married Lord Tamworth.

Mrs. ⁎ ⁎ [Wilmot]'s tragedy[1] was last night damned. They may bring it on again, and probably will; but damned it was,—not a word of the last act audible. I went (*malgré* that I ought to have staid at home in sackcloth for unc., but I could not resist the *first* night of any thing) to a private and quiet nook of my private box, and witnessed the whole process. The first three acts, with transient gushes of applause, oozed patiently but heavily on. I must say it was badly acted, particularly by ⁎ ⁎ [Kean], who was groaned upon in the third act,—something about "horror—such a horror" was the cause. Well, the fourth act became as muddy and turbid as need be; but the fifth—what Garrick used to call (like a fool) the *concoction*[2] of a play—the fifth act stuck fast at the King's prayer. You know he says "he never went to bed without saying them, and did not like to omit them now." But he was no sooner upon his knees, than the audience got upon their legs—the damnable pit—and roared, and groaned, and hissed, and whistled. Well that was choked a little; but the ruffian-scene—the penitent peasantry—and killing the Bishop and the Princess—oh, it was all over. The curtain fell upon unheard actors, and the announcement attempted by Kean for Monday was equally ineffectual. Mrs. Bartley[3] was so frightened, that, though the people were tolerably quiet, the Epilogue was quite inaudible to half the house. In short,—you know all. I clapped till my hands were skinless, and so did Sir James Mackintosh, who was with me in the box. All the world were in the house, from the Jerseys, Greys, &c. &c. downwards. But it would not do. It is, after all, not an *acting* play; good language, but no power. ⁎ ⁎ ⁎ ⁎ ⁎ ⁎ ⁎

Women (saving Joanna Baillie) cannot write tragedy; they have not seen enough nor felt enough of life for it. I think Semiramis or Catherine II. might have written (could they have been unqueened) a rare play.

⁎ ⁎ ⁎ ⁎ ⁎ ⁎ ⁎ ⁎ ⁎ ⁎ ⁎ ⁎ ⁎ ⁎ ⁎

It is, however, a good warning not to risk or write tragedies. I

---

[1] Mrs. Wilmot, later Lady Dacre, wrote a tragedy called *Ian*, which was produced at Drury Lane, April 22, 1815. The prologue was written by William Lamb, and the epilogue by Moore, but that did not save it. It was the beauty of Mrs. Wilmot in her spangled dress that inspired Byron to write his lyric "She walks in beauty like the night" in 1814.

[2] According to Boswell, Garrick had used the word in connection with a tragedy, saying that it was "wrong in the first concoction". (See Boswell's *Life of Johnson*, Birkbeck Hill, ed., Vol. III, p. 259).

[3] Mrs. Bartley (formerly Miss Smith) took the place of Mrs. Siddons, when the latter retired, as a leading actress.

never had much bent that way; but, if I had, this would have cured me.

Ever, carissime Thom.,

thine, B

[TO JOHN HANSON]   *April 25th. 1815*

Dear Sir/—I have no interest nor time to make any.——Neither *today*—nor *yesterday*—have any advertisements whatever respecting the sale of N[ewstead] appeared in my two papers—M[orning] C[hronicle] or M[orning] P[ost].—Do have this enquired into.—I can only say if we do not hear from N[ewstead] tomorrow—I have no chance or prospect of avoiding Thomas's[1] demands.—I shall call today sometime.

yrs. truly

B

[TO FRANCIS HODGSON]

13, *Piccadilly Terrace Saturday Ev[eni]ng Ap. 29* [*1815*]
Dear Mr. Hodgson—I am desired by B[yron] to write you a few lines of *recommendation* for your new Pupil to convey to you—I cannot exactly make out what I am to say except that Mr. Hanson was desirous B. should write to recommend him to you—& that he is as usual *lazy*, & wishes me to tell you he would have written but that Ly. B[yron] has been unwell & her Uncle died last week——I am sure you will be glad to hear that I think her better, & that B[yron] is very well—Now for the Pupil—to the best of B's knowledge & belief he is excessively clever, but rather behind hand for a long vacation of 14 months—he is to be brought up to the Bar—& nobody can bring him there so soon as you—B. says—

Yrs. very sincerely

Augusta Leigh

I am allowed to add a P.S. to excuse myself for writing such a stupid letter it being B's dictation
one word of common sense
B. desires me to add, Ly B[yron]—is in the Family Way—& that Ld. Wentworth has left all to her mother & then to Ly B. & children— but B is (*he says*) a "very miserable Dog" for all that!

---

[1] Thomas was one of the most pressing of the usurers from whom Byron borrowed considerable sums while he was a minor.

[TO JOHN HANSON]   *May 5th. 1815*

Dear Sir—I have but just got home (eleven o'clock) when it is too late to visit or receive visits, but tomorrow I am at your service.— What is the matter?—not a quarrel with Fellowes[1]—I hope?— Pray send a word in answer.—

                                                      yrs. truly
                                                           B

[TO JOHN HANSON]   *May 18th. 1815*

Dear Sir—I have called day after day in the vain expectation of your return to London.—In the mean time—all my concerns are going on as ill as delay can make them—the advertisements of the sales never inserted—and no arrangements made for the tenants payments—or the mortgages &c &c.—I really think that occupied as you are with your own business—mine is not forwarded as it should be—and with that persuasion I only wait for the conclusion of the sales—& your account —to transfer the dispatch of it to other hands, which would be a relief to you as well as myself.—I wish an earlier day could be fixed for the auction of the estates—I see no great use in waiting till so late a day in June—pray let me hear from you when you arrive

                                                    yrs. &c. &c.
                                                          Bn

[TO JOHN MURRAY]   *May 21st. 1815*

Dear Sir/—You must have thought it very odd not to say ungrateful —that I made no mention of the drawings &c.[1] when I had the pleasure of seeing you this morning.—The fact is—that till this moment—I had not seen them—nor heard of their arrival—they were carried up into the library where I have not been till just now—& no intimation given to me of their coming.—The present is so very magnificent—that—in short—I leave Lady B[yron] to thank you for that herself—and merely send this to apologize for a piece of apparent & unintentional neglect on my own part.

                                                    yrs very truly
                                                         BYRON

---

[1] The Hon. Newton Fellowes was persisting in his effort to get his brother, Lord Portsmouth, who had married Hanson's daughter, declared insane so that he could inherit the title and estate.

[1] Murray had given Lady Byron twelve drawings, by Stothard, done as illustrations for Byron's poems.

292

[TO JOHN HANSON]   *May 22d. 1815*

Dear Sir/—Enclosed is a letter from Mealey—which requires attention—some immediate step must be taken to compel the remaining tenants to pay their rents—and I do not think what is paid—is the full amount due from Bendall &c.—I hope & request that this may be done directly.—Perhaps Smith[1] had better remit to Messrs Hoares the payments already made.

                                                    yrs. truly
                                                    BYRON

[TO WILLIAM HOAR[1]]   *May 23, 1815*

Lord and Lady Byron request Mr. Hoar's acceptance of the "Hebrew Melodies" as a trifling acknowledgement of their obligations to his friendship—

[TO JOHN HERMAN MERIVALE]   *May 28, 1815*

Dear Merivale—I have been stupid enough to postpone ordering my Travelling Carriage till it is too late to have it—it being shut up at the Coachmakers—and all their people out on Sunday—so that I can't . . . now go to Harrow . . . I must beg you to make my apology to Drury.

[TO GEORGE BARTLEY[1]]   *Piccadilly Terrace May 30th.* [*1815*]

Ld. Byron presents his compliments to Mr. Bartley & would be obliged if Mr. B. would inform him if he received a note yesterday from Ld. B. containing a request for some tickets & five guineas in payment for the same.—As Ld. B. retained his box—the tickets were of no consequence—but Ld. B. would be glad to hear that Mr. Bartley received the enclosure safely—as Ld. B. understands from his servant that Mr. B. was not at home when the note arrived.—

---

[1] Bendall and Smith were Newstead tenants, and Mealey was steward of the estate.

[1] William Hoar was the business agent and friend of Lady Byron's family, who with Hanson had worked out the marriage settlement. The note is in Lady Byron's hand.

[1] George Bartley was an actor at Drury Lane. He had married Miss Smith, who was also in the repertory.

Dear Sir—I am most truly concerned to find, from the paper this morning, that you was in serious danger the other day. I hope nothing more occurred than what was stated, and that you did not *personally* suffer.[1] Those lonely fields are at all times dangerous. I trust you will be more cautious in future how you venture to traverse them.

Believe me yours, etc.
BYRON

[TO LEIGH HUNT]   *13 Piccadilly Terrace. May–June 1st. 1815*

My dear Hunt—I am as glad to hear from as I shall to be see you.[1] —We came to town what is called late in the season—& since that time—the death of Lady Byron's uncle (in the first place) and her own delicate state of health have prevented either of us from going out much—however she is now better—& in a fair way of going creditably through the whole process of beginning a family.—I have the alternate weeks of a private box at D[rur]y Lane Th[eatr]e—this is my week—& I send you an admission to it—for Kean's nights—friday —& saturday next—in case you should like to see him quietly—it is close to the stage—the entrance by the private box door—& you can go without the bore of crowding—jostling—or dressing.—I also enclose you a parcel of recent letters from Paris[2]—perhaps you may find some extracts that may amuse yourself or your readers—I have only to beg you will prevent your copyist—or printer—from mixing up any of the *English* names—or *private* matter contained therein— which might lead to a discovery of the writer—and as the Examiner is sure to travel back to Paris—might get him into a scrape—to say nothing of his correspondent at home.——At any rate I hope & think the perusal will amuse you.——Whenever you come this way—I shall be happy to make you acquainted with Lady B—whom you will

---

[1] While returning at night from Stoke Newington across the fields, Murray was knocked down and robbed of all his money by two robbers (he had only 3s. 6d. and a few coppers, and they failed to take his watch). Byron referred to the incident in a letter to Moore on June 12, 1815. (Smiles, *A Publisher and His Friends*, I, 268.)

[1] Leigh Hunt had been released from prison on February 2, 1815, after two years incarceration for "libelling" the Prince Regent, and was then living at Maida Vale.

[2] The letters were from Hobhouse, who had gone to Paris early in April to observe events after the return of Napoleon.

find any thing but a fine Lady—a species of animal which you probably do not affect more than myself.——Thanks for ye. Mask[3]—there is not only poetry and thought in the body—but much research & good old reading in your prefatory matter.—I hope you have not given up your narrative poem[4]—of which I heard you speak as in progress.— It rejoices me to hear of the well doing and regeneration of "the Feast"[5] setting aside my own selfish reasons for wishing it success.— —I fear you stand almost single in your liking of "Lara"—it is natural that *I* should—as being my last & most unpopular effervescence —passing by it's other sins—it is too little narrative—and too metaphysical to please the greater number of readers—I have however much consolation in the exception with which you furnish me. From Moore I have not heard very lately—I fear he is a little humourous because I am a lazy correspondent—but that shall be mended.—

ever your obliged & very sincere friend
BYRON

P.S.—"*Politics!*"—The barking of the wardogs for their carrion has sickened me of them for the present.—

[TO LEIGH HUNT]   [*June, 1815?*]

[In Hunt's hand: Dear Byron, Shall I keep this couplet?] why not? unless you can make it better—& this will not be done easily.—With the whole since my last pencil marks in the first pages—I have no fault to find—but many more beauties truly [than] there is time & place to express here.[1]—

[TO MATTHEW GREGORY LEWIS]   *June 6th. 1815*

Dear Luigi—I will take you down—(but *name* your *hour*) & shall be very glad to meet *Rogers* & G[eorge] Lamb.

ever yrs.
B

---

[3] Hunt's *The Descent of Liberty, a Masque* was published in 1815.
[4] Hunt's narrative poem, on which he had been working while in jail, was *The Story of Rimini*. It was published in 1816 by Murray.
[5] The second edition of Hunt's *The Feast of the Poets* (first published in 1814) came out in 1815 with a long passage devoted to Byron, kindly critical but mostly laudatory.
[1] Byron had written some pencilled comments on the manuscript of *The Story of Rimini* which Hunt had submitted to him.

. . . The Editor of the publication to which you allude is not perhaps aware that something of the kind appeared in another periodical work some time ago. I believe Mr. Dallas (of Weston) furnished the few particulars annexed to the print, which was taken from a picture by Westall. I have no picture in my own possession at present nor am I aware of any person who could give the required information. . . .

[TO THOMAS MOORE]   *13, Piccadilly Terrace, June 12th. 1815*

I have nothing to offer in behalf of my late silence, except the most inveterate and ineffable laziness; but I am too supine to invent a lie, or I *certainly* should, being ashamed of the truth. K * * [Kinnaird], I hope, has appeased your magnanimous indignation at his blunders. I wished and wish you were in the Committee, with all my heart.[1] It seems so hopeless a business, that the company of a friend would be quite consoling,—but more of this when we meet. In the mean time, you are entreated to prevail upon Mrs. Esterre[2] to engage herself. I believe she has been written to, but your influence, in person, or proxy, would probably go father than our proposals. What they are, I know not; all *my* new function consists in listening to the despair of Cavendish Bradshaw,[3] the hopes of Kinnaird, the wishes of Lord Essex,[4] the complaints of Whitbread,[5] and the calculations of Peter Moore,[6]—all of which, and whom, seem totally at variance. C. Bradshaw wants to light the theatre with *gas*,[7] which may, perhaps

[1] Byron had just become a member of the sub-committee of management of Drury Lane Theatre and was eager to have Moore on the committee as well, but Kinnaird's invitation apparently was worded so as to imply that it was not desirable to have too many poets on the committee, and Moore was mildly offended that he was asked and then put off.

[2] Since Moore was in Dublin, Byron suggested as a joke, that Mrs. Esterre, widow of a man killed in a duel with the Irish leader Dan O'Connell, should be invited to appear on the stage as an attraction.

[3] The Hon. Augustus Cavendish Bradshaw, who was something of a dandy, was connected with the management of Drury Lane.

[4] George, 5th Earl of Essex, was on the sub-committee with Byron.

[5] Samuel Whitbread, son of a wealthy brewer, had married a daughter of Earl Grey and took an active part in Whig politics. As Manager of Drury Lane Theatre he did much to put it on its feet.

[6] Peter Moore, another wealthy member of the committee, was an intimate friend of Sheridan, whom he assisted in rebuilding Drury Lane Theatre.

[7] Gas was just coming into use for lighting. The Lyceum Theatre was first lighted by gas in 1803.

(if the vulgar be believed) poison half the audience, and all the *Dramatis Personae*. Essex has endeavoured to persuade K * * [Kinnaird] not to get drunk, the consequence of which is, that he has never been sober since. Kinnaird, with equal success, would have convinced Raymond[8] that he, the said Raymond, had too much salary. Whitbread wants us to assess the pit another sixpence,—a d——d insidious proposition—which will end in an O. P. combustion.[9] To crown all, R * * [Robins],[10] the auctioneer, has the impudence to be displeased, because he has no dividend. The villain is a proprietor of shares, and a long-lunged orator in the meetings. I hear he has prophesied our incapacity,—"a foregone conclusion," whereof I hope to give him signal proofs before we are done.

Will you give us an Opera? no, I'll be sworn, but I wish you would. * * * * * * * *

* * * * * * * * * * * * * * * *

To go on with the poetical world, Walter Scott has gone back to Scotland. Murray, the bookseller, has been cruelly cudgelled of misbegotten knaves, "in Kendal green," at Newington Butts, in his way home from a purlieu dinner—and robbed,[11]—would you believe it?—of three or four bonds of forty pound apiece, and a seal-ring of his grandfather's, worth a million! This is his version,—but others opine that D'Israeli, with whom he dined, knocked him down with his last publication, "the Quarrels of Authors," in a dispute about copyright. Be that as it may, the newspapers have teemed with his "injuria formae," and he has been embrocated and invisible to all but the apothecary ever since.

Lady B[yron] is better than three months advanced in her progress towards maternity, and, we hope, likely to go well through with it. We have been very little out this season, as I wish to keep her quiet in her present situation. Her father and mother have changed their names to Noel, in compliance with Lord Wentworth's will, and in complaisance to the property bequeathed by him.

I hear that you have been gloriously received by the Irish,—and so you ought. But don't let them kill you with claret and kindness at the

8 Stage manager at Drury Lane.
9 An attempt to raise the prices of seats at Covent Garden in 1809 caused riots in the theatre and cries of "O.P." ("Old Prices"). Kemble, the manager, finally gave way and restored the former prices of admission.
10 George Henry Robins, the famous auctioneer, had a financial interest in Drury Lane Theatre. He was a friend of Sheridan, Colman, Kinnaird, Kemble, and others interested in the theatre.
11 See [June, 1815?] to Murray, note 1.

national dinner in your honour, which, I hear and hope, is in contemplation. If you will tell me the day, I'll get drunk myself on this side of the water, and waft you an applauding hiccup over the Channel.

Of politics, we have nothing but the yell for war; and C * *h [Castlereagh] is preparing his head for the pike, on which we shall see it carried before he has done. The loan has made every body sulky.[12] I hear often from Paris, but in direct contradiction to the home statements of our hirelings. Of domestic doings, there has been nothing since Lady D * *. Not a divorce stirring,—but a good many in embryo, in the shape of marriages.

I enclose you an epistle received this morning from I know not whom; but I think it will amuse you.[13] The writer must be a rare fellow.

P.S.—A gentleman named D'Alton (not your Dalton) has sent me a National Poem called "Dermid."[14] The same cause which prevented my writing to you operated against my wish to write to him an epistle of thanks. If you see him, will you make all kinds of fine speeches for me, and tell him that I am the laziest and most ungrateful of mortals?

A word more;—don't let Sir John Stevenson[15] (as an evidence on trials for copyright, &c.) talk about the price of your next Poem, or they will come upon you for the *Property Tax* for it. I am serious, and have heard a long story of the rascally tax-men making Scott pay for his. So, take care. Three hundred is a devil of a deduction out of three thousand.

[TO JOHN HANSON] *June 16th. 1815*

Dear Sir—I have called to beg you to get on with the *will*[1]—& to

[12] On May 26, Castlereagh, the Foreign Minister, had pushed through the House of Commons approval for a loan of £5,000,000, to "be granted to His Majesty to make good the arrangements entered into with the Emperors of Austria and Russia and the King of Prussia."
[13] The letter was from a Mr. J. R. upbraiding Byron for the sentiments expressed in his "Ode to Napoleon Buonaparte" in view of Napoleon's return. "Let not Englishmen talk of the stretch of tyrants, while the torrents of blood shed in the East Indies cry aloud to Heaven for retaliation."
[14] John D'Alton, an Irish lawyer, published in 1815 *Dermid, or Erin in the Days of Brian Boru, a Poem*. It was a large quarto in twelve cantos, offered at 45s.
[15] Sir John Stevenson (1762–1833) was the musical composer who wrote accompaniments for Moore's *Irish Melodies*.
[1] This was Byron's final will, signed on July 29, 1815, which provided that the income from the residue of his estate, after the £60,000 of Lady Byron's marriage settlement was paid, should go to his sister and her children. Hobhouse and Hanson were to be the executors.

ask whether Smith has transferred the rents already paid to Hoares—
or no—I wish you would enquire.—Pray what day have you fixed for
New[stea]d?—and is Fairbrother's[2] agent gone?

yrs. ever
B

[TO ALI PASHA]   *London—June 25th. 1815*

Vezir—I was honoured by your Highness's letter conveyed to me
by Dr. Holland.—It rejoices me to hear of your health and prosperity
—may they continue for many years.—An American Gentleman (Mr.
Ticknor)[1] has promised to deliver from me to your Highness a
curious pistol (the properties and management of which he will
explain) which I shall feel honoured by your accepting.—I yet hope
one day to revisit Albania—a country—which the recollection of your
kindness to Strangers must ever endear to me.—I am with the most
profound respect

yr. obliged Sert.
BYRON

[TO MONSIEUR————]   *Londres 25me. de Juin—1815*

Monsieur—Si je puis me flatter de conserver encore une place dans
votre souvenir vous me feriez grand plaisir en le temoignant par
quelques politesses envers Mr. Ticknor, qui aura l'honneur de vous
présenter cette lettre—Permettez, Monsieur, que je repète combien je
suis reconnaissant pour toutes celles dont vous m'avez comblé
pendant mon sejour à Athènes. J'ai l'honneur d'être

Votre très humble et très obligé Sert.[1]
BYRON

---

2 Fairbrother was the auctioneer who offered Newstead Abbey for sale on
August 14, 1812. Insufficient offers caused it to be bid in by the seller, and it was
after that that Claughton made his offer and signed a contract which he never
completed and finally gave up with a forfeit of £25,000. Byron was urging
Hanson to prepare for another auction.

1 George Ticknor, a young American, introduced by Gifford, visited Byron
several times before leaving for a continental tour. Ticknor was later to become a
distinguished historian.

1 The letter is in Lady Byron's hand, but signed by Byron. It may have been
addressed to M. Fauvel, French Consul at Athens when Byron was there.

My dear Lady Jersey—I really cannot thank you sufficiently for your very magnificent present—and shall therefore only say that you could not have bestowed it on one more sensible of ye. obligation.— We were not aware that you were accessible on evenings or I should certainly not have omitted to pay my respects to those whom I never saw without pleasure or left without regret.——I can however safely say that I have been more frequently your guest than any other person's with whom I am acquainted—and am but too glad to find that I have not been so too often.—Upon "the revolutions" I can say nothing—except that Providence appears to have taken a particular fancy to Lord Castlereagh—for the same reason perhaps that the Irishman's most bitter imprecation is said to be *"God* bless you" meaning thereby that nobody else will.—

ever yr. obliged & faithful &c.
BYRON

[TO JOHN HANSON] *Tuesday—[June 27, 1815]*

I shall call tomorrow at three o clock in the expectation of your return—and I wish much to fix a day for ye. departure for N[ewstead] if convenient.

yrs. very truly
BYRON

[TO JOHN HANSON] *June 29th. 1815*

Dear Sir—I cannot help regretting very much that you cannot come to town where every thing is standing still on account of your absence—two or three persons have called respecting Newstead & Rochdale to whom no answer can be given—& the rents remain unpaid—& my will in no state of forwardness—I have called day after day in expectation of seeing you—and hearing that you had fixed sure time for proceeding to N[ewstead]—I wish also to know if Mr. Wharton[1] has been furnished with the required papers and many other points—which I cannot discuss upon paper—unless at a length which

[1] Sir Ralph Noel had transferred his business affairs from William Hoar to Gerard Blisson Wharton, senior partner in Wharton & Ford. An attempt was being made by the Noels to raise some money for the Byrons, as part payment of Annabella's marriage settlement of £20,000, none of which had yet been paid. (See Elwin, page 320.)

would exceed the limits of a letter.—I enclose you a card left for you about Newstead—do you know the person? Pray let me know when I am to expect you as I am tired of dancing attendance daily.—

ever yrs. very truly
BYRON

P.S.—Have you had any answer from Brown & Henshaw?[2] it is surely necessary to ascertain the point of extent.—

[TO JOHN HERMAN MERIVALE]   *July 1st. 1815*

My dear Merivale—I had no such meaning—on the contrary—I have great hopes that you intend to go on—it is my wish to begin with Henry 6th.—and as to the comedy we will see what is to be done with it next season—I have some doubts of it—but none of your part therein.——If you feel disposed to try a separate flight of your own—I will present it with very great pleasure[1]—we are really in want of opera & comedy—particularly the former which when successful draws more than 50 *Shakespeares*—excuse the blasphemy—but it is really the case—our committee are going on very amicably—and if I could but once see you a *staple* dramatist—I should think myself conferring much good on the concern.—But on this matter we must talk more at large.

ever yrs.
B

[TO THOMAS MOORE]   *July 7th, 1815*

"Grata superveniet,"[1] &c. &c. I had written to you again, but burnt the letter, because I began to think you seriously hurt at my indolence, and did not know how the buffoonery it contained might be taken. In the mean time, I have yours, and all is well.

I had given over all hopes of yours. By the by, my "grata superveniet" should be in the present tense; for I perceive it looks now as if it

---

2 Unidentified.

1 John Herman Merivale was a friend of Hodgson and Henry Drury, whose sister he married. He had literary ambitions and apparently had submitted something to Byron for the consideration of the sub-committee of management of Drury Lane, of which Byron became a member through the influence of Douglas Kinnaird. Byron was eagerly seeking new talent for Drury Lane.

1 "Grata superveniet, quae non sperabitur, hora", Horace, *Epistle* I, iv, 14. ("The hour that is not hoped for will be delightful when it arrives.")

applied to this present scrawl reaching you, whereas it is to the receipt of thy Kilkenny epistle that I have tacked that venerable sentiment.

Poor Whitbread [2] died yesterday morning,—a sudden and severe loss. His health had been wavering, but so fatal an attack was not apprehended. He dropped down and, I believe, never spoke afterwards. I perceive Perry attributes his death to Drury-lane,—a consolatory encouragement to the new Committee. I have no doubt that * * , who is of a plethoric habit, will be bled immediately; and as I have, since my marriage, lost much of my paleness, and,—"horresco referens" [3] (for I hate even *moderate* fat)—that happy slenderness, to which, when I first knew you, I had attained, I by no means sit easy under this dispensation of the Morning Chronicle. Every one must regret the loss of Whitbread; he was surely a great and very good man.

Paris is taken for the second time. I presume it, for the future, will have an anniversary capture. In the late battles, like all the world, I have lost a connexion,—poor Frederick Howard,[4] the best of his race. I had little intercourse, of late years, with his family, but I never saw or heard but good of him. Hobhouse's brother is killed. In short, the havoc has not left a family out of its tender mercies.

Every hope of a republic is over, and we must go on under the old system. But I am sick at heart of politics and slaughters; and the luck which Providence is pleased to lavish on Lord * * [Castlereagh] is only a proof of the little value the gods set upon prosperity, when they permit such * * *s as he and that drunken corporal, old Blucher, to bully their betters. From this, however, Wellington should be excepted. He *is* a man,[5]—and the Scipio of our Hannibal. However, he may thank the Russian frosts, which destroyed the *real élite* of the French army, for the successes of Waterloo.

La! Moore—how you blasphemes about "Parnassus" and "Moses!" I am ashamed for you. Won't you do any thing for the drama? We beseech an Opera.[6] Kinnaird's blunder was partly mine.[7] I wanted you of all things in the Committee, and so did he. But we are now glad you were wiser; for it is, I doubt, a bitter business.

When shall we see you in England? Sir Ralph Noel (*late* Milbanke—he don't promise to be *late* Noel in a hurry) finding that one

---

[2] See June 12, 1815, to Moore, note 5.

[3] Virgil, *Aeneid*, I, 204. ("I shudder at the recollection.")

[4] The Hon. Frederick Howard, third son of Lord Carlisle, was killed at the battle of Waterloo. Byron left a tribute to him in *Childe Harold*, III, 29–30.

[5] For Byron's later opinion of Wellington, see *Don Juan*, 9:1–5.

[6] See July 1, 1815, to Merivale, note 1.

[7] See June 12, 1815, to Moore, note 1.

man can't inhabit two houses, has given his place in the north to me for a habitation; and there Lady B[yron] threatens to be brought to bed in November. Sir R. and my Lady Mother are to quarter at Kir[k]by— Lord Wentworth's that was. Perhaps you and Mrs. Moore will pay us a visit at Seaham in the course of the autumn. If so, you and I (*without our wives*) will take a *lark* to Edinburgh and embrace Jeffrey. It is not much above one hundred miles from us. But all this, and other high matters, we will discuss at our meeting, which I hope will be on your return. We don't leave town till August.

Ever, &c.

[To ?] *July 10th. 1815*

Sir—I believe that the committee have already decided upon the Management—and I regret that your proposition did not arrive earlier as I should have very willingly submitted it to their consideration.—It is now I fear too late—but I will mention the subject—and if any change should take place—will apprize you of it—I have the honour to be

yr very obedt. Sert.
[Signature cut out]

[TO JOHN HANSON] *July 11th. 1815*

Dear Sir—I have called about my *Will*[1]—which I hope is nearly ready.—I also wish to have the robes and sword sent up to my house— and the *Pedigree*[2] this last must be looked for immediately—I recollect perfectly seeing it at your house—and trust that it is not lost nor mislaid—as it is not only a document of importance but beautiful and valuable as a piece of work from the inlaid engravings upon it.—Pray let it be looked for *immediately* I am very anxious about it.—

yrs. truly
BYRON

---

[1] See June 16, 1815, to Hanson, note 1.

[2] This Pedigree, perhaps the very one Byron referred to, with inset engravings of the various Byrons, is now in the possession of the heir apparent of the Byron title, Col. Geoffrey Byron, a descendant of Byron's cousin, George Anson Byron who inherited the title after his death.

My dear Sir,—A Volume of Poems of which I have the pleasure of congratulating you as the author, was yesterday put into my hands, by the Bookseller—the satisfaction I experienced from the perusal, made me anxious for the immediate acquaintance and society of the Gentleman, who has so kindly favoured the world with the production of his leisure hours. As the first efforts of an aspiring muse they merit the warmest approbation. The works of the most experienced in the art, are not however void of defect, and be you not therefore surprised, if the eye of greater experience, though not of superior genius, to yourself may have discovered some redundancies of style—some points capable of correction, in the Volume before us.

I hope I shall not offend by offering my opinion, and soliciting your company to Breakfast, on Friday Morning next for that purpose. To be allowed to guide your poetic flight to fame and to usher to the world your future labours is the earnest wish of

My dear sir, your faithful friend and warm admirer,

BYRON

[TO THOMAS DIBDIN (*a*)]   [*July? 1815*]

Dear Sir,—You will oblige me with a couple of pit orders for this night, particularly if prohibited.[1]

Yours very truly,
BYRON

P.S.—I mean two orders for one each—single admission.

[TO THOMAS DIBDIN (*b*)]   [*July? 1815*]

Dear Sir,—Is not part of the dialogue in the new piece a little too double, if not too broad, now and then? for instance, the word "ravish" occurs in the way of question, as well as a remark, some half dozen times in the course of one scene, thereby meaning, not raptures, but rape. With regard to the probable effect of the piece, you are the best judge; it seems to me better and worse than many others of the same

---

[1] Prothero took the text of this letter from a copy in Lady Byron's handwriting, signed by Byron. The copy has since disappeared.

[1] Dibdin says that this note was written after a meeting of the Committee at which it was decided that no free admissions should be issued.

kind.[1] I hope you got home at last, and that Miss——has recovered from the eloquence of my colleague, which, if it convinced, it is the first time,—I do not mean the first time his eloquence had that effect,—but that a woman could be convinced she was not fit for any thing on any stage.

Yours truly,
BYRON

[TO JOHN TAYLOR[1]]   *13 Piccadilly Terrace July 23rd. 1815*

Dear Sir—I have to thank you for a volume in the good old style of our elders and our betters—which I am very glad to see not yet extinct.—Your good opinion does me great honour though I am about to risk it's loss by the return I make for your valuable present.—With many acknowledgements for your good wishes—and a sincere sense of your kindness believe me

yr. obliged & faithful Sert.
BYRON

P.S.—I ought to tell you that there are many errors of the press in this Edition of Murray's which are disgraceful to him & me—but it is the best I have and as such I offer it.—

[TO JAMES CAZENOVE[1]]   *13 Piccadilly Terrace July 23rd. 1815*

Dear Sir—On receiving your letter I immediately mentioned Miss M. to the Managers & the Committee—but I am sorry to say that according to the present arrangements for the season there will be no vacant engagement.——I hope this early answer is at least a proof that I have attended to your recommendation—I can assure you it is not my fault that it was not more effectual.—

ever yrs. very truly
BYRON

---

[1] After the death of Whitbread, Thomas Dibdin and Alexander Rae were appointed joint managers of Drury Lane Theatre. Dibdin, himself a prolific playwright, did a good deal of adapting of plays accepted for performance.

[1] John Taylor (c. 1757–1832), editor and poetaster, met Byron at Drury Lane and became a great admirer. He was later editor of the *Morning Post*. For more details see *LJ*, III, 213–14n.

[1] James Cazenove was one of two brothers who had been captured by Napoleon and imprisoned for eight years. They escaped through Bosnia and came to Greece while Byron was there. He gave them financial assistance to return to England. See March 5, 1811, to Hobhouse, note 1 (Vol. 2, p. 41).

P.S.—Your old friend *"Jack"*[2] has made a devil of a finish—you have now got him prisoner of war in turn.———

[TO JOHN WILLIAM WARD]   *13 Piccadilly Terrace—July 26th. 1815*

D[ea]r Sir—I have received a letter from a Mrs. Scott written in very great apparent distress at the dismission of her daughters in ye course of our late retrenchments.—Her case seems a hard one—as by her account there was a promise from Mr. Whitbread to apply for their continuance—and as their salaries & situations are probably not above the *Chorus*—perhaps they would do as well as others whom we must employ in their place.—Of this person and her family I know nothing except from her letter—nor have I any motive in this application in their favour—beyond what is already stated.—I wish them to be replaced if it can be done without much inconvenience—and is not contrary to the will of my colleagues and the opinions of Mr. Rae and Mr. Didbin whom—you will oblige me—by consulting upon the subject—& acquainting me with the result.— I am

yr. very obedt. humble Sert.

BYRON

To Mr. Ward Secretary &c. &c. &c.[1]

[TO JOHN HANSON]   *July 26th 1815*

Dear Sir—I will be with you at your hour punctually tomorrow.—

yrs. very truly

B

P.S. Many thanks for the Venison which is excellent—I shall write to thank Lord & Lady P[ortsmouth] tomorrow.

[TO LEIGH HUNT]   *July 28th. 1815*

My dear Hunt—If you have done with Mr. Hobhouse's letters[1]— you will oblige me by returning them by the bearer.—I send you a scrawl in rhyme which—if you use it—I would wish to be inserted

---

[2] A name used by English prisoners in France to refer to Napoleon.

[1] The Hon. John William Ward (afterward Lord Dudley) was secretary of the Drury Lane sub-committee.

[1] See June 1, 1815, to Hunt, note 2.

306

anonymously[2]—it certainly does not contain your political sentiments nor indeed my own altogether—but I have endeavoured to adapt them to the person speaking or *singing*—if he can ever be supposed to do so simple a thing as *ye last*.—A perpetual harrass of different kinds has prevented me from calling on you lately but I am always & truly

yrs.

BYRON

[TO JOHN HANSON] *August 8th. 1815*

Dear Sir—Col. Leigh delivers this.—His father is dead & has left his affairs in confusion—I wish you would see his Attorney—whose report of them *I* don't altogether believe—& enquire into the real nature of the property & the claims upon it—he advises the Col. not to administer—an advice which I would not have adopted hastily till we see why—his name is Fallofield Scott—& was concerned for the late General L[eigh].—

ever yrs.

BYRON

[TO FRANCIS FREELING[1]] *13 Piccadilly Terrace August 15th. 1815*

Lord Byron presents his compliments to Mr. Freeling & would be glad to know if the letter of which he encloses the cover was not over-charged upon the pretext stated on the address by the postman.—The charge was thirteen pence halfpenny.—

[TO JOHN MURRAY?] *[August 16, 1815]*

Dear Sir/—I return your book with many thanks.———Do you happen to know or to have the means of knowing whether Mr. Jeffrey was in town during any part of the late London winter—that is since April to this present August?—perhaps Mr. P.[1] could inform you—I want to know for a particular reason.—

yrs truly, &c.

B

---

[2] This was Byron's "Napoleon's Farewell" ("From the French"), which was published anonymously in *The Examiner,* July 30, 1815. The manuscript is dated by Lady Byron, "July 25, 1815". The verses were of course not a translation but Byron's own.

[1] See [Dec. 1814?], to Freeling, notes 1 and 2.

[1] Unidentified. Possibly James Perry of the *Morning Chronicle.*

[TO JOHN CAM HOBHOUSE]   *Aug[u]st 22nd. 1815*

My dear H.—I find that I can't come tomorrow which I regret much
& hope this will arrive betimes to prevent any trouble to your house-
maids—Don't swear & make a face at

yrs. very truly
B

[TO JOHN MURRAY]   *August 26th. 1815*

In reading the 4th. vol of yr. last Edition of ye. poems published in
my name—I perceive that piece *12*—page *55*—is made nonsense of
(that is greater nonsense than usual) by dividing it into stanzas 1 2 &c.
&c. in which form it was not written—& not printed in the octavo
Editions—the poem in question is one continued piece—& not divided
into sections as you may very easily perceive by the pointing and as
such I request that in future (when opportunity occurs) it may be
printed

yrs. truly
B

P.S. The poem begins "Without a stone &c.["]¹ I send it as it was
& ought to be.—

[TO LADY BYRON]   *Epping. August 31st. 1815*

Dearest Pip—The learned Fletcher with his wonted accuracy having
forgotten something I must beg you to forward it.———On my dressing
table *two phials labelled "drops"* containing certain liquids of I know not
what pharmacopoly—(*but white* & clear so you can't mistake I hope)
one of these I want in my materia medica.—Pray send it carefully
packed to me at Goose's per coach on receiving this—and believe me

ever most lovingly thine—
B (not *Frac.*)¹

¹ This is the poem "To Thyrza", written October 11, 1811, on his hearing of the
death of John Edleston, the Cambridge choirboy, and first published with *Childe
Harold*, 1812.
¹ Apparently this means that he is not now in a "fractious" mood as he was before
he left Piccadilly. Lady Byron had already written to say how much she missed him:
"*nau* [naughty] B—— is a thousand times better than *no* B." Byron was on his way
to see his sister. Her father-in-law had just died and his will was being contested,
while her husband, George Leigh, "that very helpless gentleman", seemed unable
to do anything about it and Byron wanted to help her.

Dearest Pip—I am very glad that Sir James[1] has at last found his way back—he may now transfer his attention from his son's leg to your Mother's leg-acy—which seemed in some peril of amputation also in his absence.—Goose left a mousetrap in the apartment allotted to me the consequence of which is that from the very convenient place of it's application I have nearly lost a toe.———The parcel came & contained also a billet from Roody[2] to my Valet—from which I infer that she is better in one sense & worse in another.—All the children here look shockingly—quite *green*—& Goose being as *red* as ever you have no idea what a piece of patchwork might be made of the family faces.———Has Hanson marched for N[ewstead]?—Goose is taking a quill from her wing to scribble to you so

yrs. alway most conjugally

B

A—da—

Dear Mrs. George[1]—We intend to be inveterately impartial no doubt—& your request is in direct opposition to our intentions—I shall therefore do all I can to forward it.—I return to town tomorrow but will write to the committee before I set off that no time may be lost: you say that you shall "try to *soften* Kinnaird & George"[2] I beg leave to say that I expect to be *softened* as well as another & desire you will set about that process immediately & begin with me first as the most obdurate of the party.———I believe the person on whose behalf you have applied to be the same recommended by Lady Bessborough a great point in her favour particularly with me.———You "*wish—beg—and entreat*"—I presume that these expressions are to be allotted one apiece to George—Kinnaird & me—pray in future let me have the *first* only—& I shall consider it as a command.—I have been staying at

---

1 Sir James Bland Burges, Lady Noel's brother-in-law and Annabella's uncle, was one of the executors of Lord Wentworth's will.

2 Ann Rood, Lady Byron's maid, later (in 1816) married Byron's valet Fletcher.

1 Caroline Rosalie Adelaide St. Jules, supposed "adopted" (actually illegitimate) daughter of Elizabeth, second Duchess of Devonshire, married George Lamb, third son of the Melbournes. She was frequently referred to as Mrs. George or Caroline George to distinguish her from Caroline, wife of William Lamb.

2 Kinnaird and George Lamb were members with Byron of the sub-committee of management of Drury Lane Theatre.

Mrs. Leigh's since Wednesday—which prevented me from receiving your note till this Morning—Bell [Annabella] is in town & very well. —Will you give my love to Aunt M[elbourne] & believe me very truly yrs.

BYRON

[TO JAMES WEDDERBURN WEBSTER]

Piccadilly Terrace.—Sept. 4th. 1815

My dear W.—Certainly—if Lady Frances [Webster] has no objection—& you are disposed to be so complimentary—I cannot but be accordant with your wish;—I give you joy of the event & hope the name will be fortunate.[1]—Lady B. is very well & expects to lie in in December.—I wish a boy of course—they are less trouble in every point of view—both in education & after life.—

You are misinformed—I am writing nothing—nor even dreaming of repeating that folly—& as to Lady B. she has too much good sense to be a scribbler—your informant is therefore more facetious than accurate.————

A word to you of Lady [Caroline[2]][Lamb]—I speak from experience—*keep clear of her*—(I do not mean as a woman—that is all fair) she is a villainous intriguante—in every sense of the word——mad & malignant—capable of all & every mischief—above all—guard your *connections* from her society——with all her apparent absurdity there is an indefatigable & active spirit of meanness & destruction about her—which delights & often succeeds in inflicting misery— once more—I tell you keep her from all that you value—as for *your- self*—do as you please—no human being but myself knows the thorough baseness of that wretched woman—& now I have done.———

I believe I can guess the "important subject" on which you wish to write—but I would rather decline hearing or speaking of it—for many reasons—the most obvious & proper of which is that however false—it is too delicate for discussion even with your most intimate friends—to copy your own words I "believe nothing I hear" on this point—& advise you to follow the example.———

[1] Apparently Webster asked permission to name an expected child after Byron. See Vol. 3, p. 106, note 1.

[2] On the original MS there is an attempt to obliterate, by another hand, the name which appears on the MS copy of this letter. The copy indicates that this letter was addressed to Place Vendôme, Paris.

I write in the greatest hurry—just returned to London——if you answer I will write again—in the interim

Yrs ever
B

[TO JOHN HANSON] *Sept. 6th. 1815*

Dear Sir—I have to request that you will immediately take legal measures to prevent the Revd.——Hurt of [Linby?] from sporting on Newstead Manor—which he is in the habit of doing constantly without permission & in spite of repeated warning.—I have no objection to the man's shooting provided he do it in a gentlemanly manner—but his conduct has been the reverse—& pray see to it immediately—as he is likely to be troublesome.—The tenants must discharge him from their grounds I believe—but whatever the mode is pray let it be done.—

yrs. ever
Byron

[TO WILLIAM SOTHEBY[1]] *Septr. 15th. 1815. 13. Piccadilly Terrace*

Dear Sir—"Ivan"[2] is accepted & will be put in progress on Kean's arrival.—The Theatrical gentlemen have a confident hope of its success—I know not that any alterations for the stage will be necessary —if any they will be trifling & you shall be duly apprized.——I would suggest that you should not attend any except the latter re-hearsals—the performers have a great objection and attribute much mischief to Mrs. Wilmot's[3] too constant attendance on those oc-casions—the managers have requested me to state this to you—you can see them—viz—Dibdin & Rae[4]—whenever you please—& I will do any thing you wish to be done—on your suggestion—in the mean time.—Mrs. Mardyn[5] is not yet out—& nothing can be determined till she has made her appearance—I mean as to her capacity for the part

---

1 William Sotheby (1757–1833) had gained some reputation as a miscellaneous writer and translator (of Wieland's *Oberon* and Virgil's *Georgics*), and later wrote a number of unsuccessful tragedies. Byron later ridiculed him in *Beppo* as a "bustling Botherby".

2 Sotheby's tragedy *Ivan* was eventually declined by Drury Lane.

3 See April 23, 1815, to Moore, note 1.

4 Managers of Drury Lane Theatre.

5 Mrs. Mardyn, the Irish actress, made her first appearance at Drury Lane on Sept. 26, 1815, in *Lover's Vows*, a piece adapted for the stage by Mrs. Inchbald.

you mention which I take it for granted is not in Ivan—as I think Ivan may be performed very well without her—but of that hereafter.—

ever yrs very truly
BYRON

P.S. You will be glad to hear that the Season has begun uncommonly well—great & constant houses—the performers in much harmony with the Committee & one another—& as much good humour as can be preserved in such complicated & extensive interests as the D[rury] L[ane] Proprietory.—

[TO JAMES WEDDERBURN WEBSTER]

13 Terrace Pic[cadill]y Sept. 18th 1815

My dear W.—Your letter of the 10th is before me.—Since your last I received a note from Lady Frances [Webster] containing a repetition of your request—which was already answered in my reply to you—I am obliged by her politeness & regret that she should have taken the trouble of which I presume *you* were the occasion.————

With regard to Lady C.[aroline] L.[amb]———I wrote rather hurriedly & probably said more than I intended or than she deserved—but I fear the main points are correct—she is such a mixture of good & bad—of talent and absurdity—in short—an exaggerated woman—that—that—in fact I have no right to abuse her—and did love her very well—till she took abundant pains to cure me of it—& there's an end—You will deliver her the enclosed note from me—if you please—it contains my thanks for a cross of the "Legion of Honour" which she sent me some time ago from Waterloo—I never received it till yesterday.[1]————You may have seen "much" but not enough to know her thoroughly in this time—she is a good study for a couple of years at least.—I will give you one bit of advice which may be of use—she is most *dangerous* when *humblest*—like a Centipede she *crawls & stings.*———

As for *"him"* [William Lamb]—we have not spoken these three years—so that I can hardly answer your question—but he is a handsome man as you see—and a clever man as you may see—of his temper I know nothing—I never heard of any prominent faults that he possesses—and indeed she has enough for both————In short his good qualities are his own—and his misfortune is having her—if the

[1] The Websters and the Lambs were in Paris where the English fashionable world had flocked after the Peace. Lady Caroline and Lady Frances both flirted with the military officers, including Wellington. And Webster, a notorious philanderer, apparently made advances to Lady Caroline.

woman was quiet & like the rest of the amatory world it would not so much signify—but no—everything she says—does—or imagines—must be public—which is exceedingly inconvenient in the end however piquant at the beginning.————

And now to the serious part of your epistle—Humph—what the devil can I say?——as your mind is so divided upon the subject—I wonder you should ask me to say anything—it is thrusting poor dear innocent me into the part of Iago—from whom however I shall only take one sentence—

"Long live she so—& long live you to think so!"—

I must repeat however that it is not a topic for discussion——you must know & judge for yourself—and as to the "real opinion of the World" which you wish to hear—you may surely discover that without my turning it's speaking trumpet—one thing you may be sure of—if there is any thing bad you will always as Sheridan says "find some damned good natured friend or other to tell it you"———

Pray are the Rawdons in Paris?—if they are—I wish you could remember me to Miss R—& tell her that Lady B. has not heard from her since she wrote from Rome.————

If you come to England—you will easily find me—probably in London—

ever yrs. most truly
B

[TO MISS CATHERINE LEVY[1]]   *13, Piccadilly Terrace*
Sept. 23–29, 1815

. . . I hope you are aware of the difficulties which exist, & the qualities which are requisite in the profession you wish to assume . . .

[TO WILLIAM SOTHEBY]   *Septr. 24th. 1815*

Dear Sir—I think it would be advisable for you to see the acting managers when convenient—as there must be points on which you will want to confer: the objection I stated was merely on the part of the performers—and is *general* & not *particular* to this instance—I thought it as well to mention it at once—and some of the rehearsals you will doubtless see notwithstanding.——Rae I rather think has his eye on Naritzen[1] for himself—he is a more popular performer than Bartley[2]

---

[1] According to the Sotheby catalogue, there were two letters to Miss Levy, concerning her wish to be an actress, but no indication as to whether the quotation is from that of Sept. 23 or the one of Sept. 29.

[1] Alexander Rae was an actor as well as manager. He had taken the part of Ordonio in Coleridge's *Remorse* in 1813.

[2] George Bartley played the part of Falstaff at Drury Lane in 1815.

and certainly the *cast* will be stronger with him in it—besides he is one of the managers and will feel doubly interested if he can *act* in both capacities,——Mrs. Bartley[3] will be Petrowna—as to the Empress—I know not what to say or think—the truth is we are not amply furnished with tragic women—but must make the best of those we have—you can take your choice of them.—We have all great hopes of the success —on which—setting aside other considerations—we are particularly anxious as being the first tragedy to be brought out since the old Committee.——By the way—I have a charge against you—as the Great Mr. Dennis roared out on a similar occasion "By G-d *that* is *my* thunder" so do I exclaim "*This* is *my* Lightning."[4]—I allude to a speech of Ivan's in the scene with Petrowna & the Empress—where the thought and almost expression are similar to Conrad's in the 3d. Ca[nt]o of "the Corsair."—I however do not say this to accuse you— but to exempt myself from suspicion:—as there is a priority of six months publication on my part between the appearance of that composition & of your tragedies.——George Lamb meant to write to you —if you don't like to confer with the managers at present—I will attend to your wishes—so state them.—

yrs very truly
BYRON

[TO JOHN TAYLOR]   *13 Terrace Piccadilly Septr. 25th. 1815*

Dear Sir—I am sorry you should feel uneasy at what has by no means troubled me[1]—if your Editor—his correspondents & readers are amused I have no objection to be the theme of all the ballads he can find room for—provided his lucubrations are confined to *me* only.—It is a long time since things of the kind have ceased to "fright me from my propriety"[2] nor do I know any similar attack which would induce me to turn again unless it involved those connected with me whose qualities I hope are such as to exempt them even in the eyes of those who bear no good will to myself.——In such a case—supposing it to occur—to *reverse* the saying of Dr. Johnson—"what the law could not

[3] See April 23, 1815, to Moore, note 3.
[4] See March 8, 1815, to Moore, note 1.
[1] See July 23, 1815, to Taylor, note 1. As part proprietor of the *Sun* Taylor had written to apologize for some satiric verses his editor had inserted beginning "When my Lord came wooing to Miss Ann Thrope,/He was just a *Childe* from School."
[2] *Othello*, Act II, scene 3.

do for me—I would do for myself"[3] be the consequences what they might.—I return you with many thanks—Colman & the letters—the poems I hope you intended me to keep—at least I shall do so—till I hear the contrary.—

very truly yours
BYRON

[TO JOHN MURRAY]   *Septr. 25th. 1815*

Dear Sir—Will you publish the Drury Lane Magpye?[1] or what is more will you give fifty or even forty pounds for the Copyright of the said?—I have undertaken to ask you this question on behalf of the translator—and wish you would—we can't get so much for him by ten pounds from any body else—& I knowing your magnificence—would be glad of an answer.—

ever yrs.
B

[TO JOHN MURRAY]   *Septr. 27th. 1815*

Dear Sir—That's right—& splendid & becoming a publisher of high degree—Mr. Concanen (the translator) will be delighted—& pay his washerwoman—& in reward for your bountiful behaviour in this instance—I won't ask you to publish any more for D[rury] L[ane] or any Lane whatever again.——You will have no tragedy or anything else from me I assure you—and may think yourself lucky in having got rid of me for good without more damage—but I'll tell you what we will do for you—act Sotheby's Ivan—which will succeed—& then your present & next impression of the dramas of that dramatic gentleman will be expedited to your heart's content[1]—& if there is anything very good—you shall have the refusal—but you shan't have any more requests.———Sotheby has got a thought—and almost the words from the 3d. C[an]to of the Corsair—which you know was published six months before his Tragedy—it is from the storm in Conrad's cell—I have written to Mr. S[otheby] to claim it—& as Dennis roared out of

---

[3] Byron refers to Johnson's letter to Macpherson, following his exposure of the *Ossian* pretensions: "Any violence offered me I shall do my best to repel; and what I cannot do for myself, the law shall do for me." (Boswell, ed. Hill, Vol. II, p. 298.)

[1] *The Magpie, or Maid of Palaiseau*, a French melodrama (*La Pie Voleuse*), translated by Concanen, was produced at Drury Lane Sept. 12, 1815. Dibdin was unsuccessful in getting it published, but Byron persuaded Murray to take it.

[1] Murray had published Sotheby's *Five Tragedies* in 1814.

the pit "by God *that's my* thunder" so do I & will I exclaim—"by God that's *my lightning*" that electrical fluid being in fact the subject of the said passage.——You will have a print of Fanny Kelly in the Maid[2]— to prefix—which is honestly worth twice the money you have given for the M.S.—pray—what did you do with the note I gave you about Mungo Park?[3]—

ever yrs. truly

BYRON

[TO THOMAS DIBDIN]   *13 Pi[ccadilly] Terrace. Septr. 27th. 1815*

Dear Sir—I enclose Mr. Murray's bill (£40) for the Magpye— which is ten or twenty more than Whittingham's offer[1]—he wishes the M.S. to be sent to Mr. Dove printer—whose address he don't mention—the print of Miss Kelly should go with it—& any little memoir of the story would do to set off the preface—I suppose we have done all for Concanen—which we could & have got him a decent price.——You should have Mr. Sotheby's tragedy in hand[2]—it is I think in the Committee Room—but I have let loose the Author upon you—so now shift for yourself.——When will Kean be out? I think he should be announced—I have great hopes of Dowton's Shylock[3]—and Iago if he will take the latter.

yrs. truly

Bn

P.S. Murray is not in town—but at Chichester—his draft is however dated London which I suppose will make no difference.——

[TO LEIGH HUNT]   *13 Terrace—Pic[cadill]y Octr. 7th. 1815*

My dear Hunt—I had written a long answer to your last which I put into the fire—partly—because it was a repetition of what I have already said—& next because I considered what my opinions are worth before I made you pay double postage—-as your proximity lays you

---

[2] Fanny Kelly played the part of Annette in *The Magpie*.

[3] Mungo Park (1771–1806), African explorer, who was killed on his second expedition to the Niger. Murray published, in 1815, *The Journal of a Mission to the Interior of Africa in the* Year *1805* by Mungo Park.

[1] See Sept. 25, 1815, to Murray, note 1. Dibdin had offered *The Magpie* to his publishers, Whittinham and Arliss.

[2] See Sept. 15, 1815, to Sotheby.

[3] William Dowton (1764–1851) was chiefly known as a comic actor. He played Shylock at Drury Lane Oct. 5, 1815, without much success.

within the jaws of the tremendous "twopenny" & beyond the verge of Franking—the only parliamentary privilege (saving one other) of much avail in these "Costermonger days"—Pray don't make me an exception to the "Long live King Richard" of your bards in "the feast"[1]—I do allow him to be "prince of the bards of his time"[2] upon the judgment of those who must judge more impartially than I probably do.—I acknowledge him as I acknowledge the Houses of Hanover & Bourbon the—not the "one eye'd Monarch of the blind" but the blind Monarch of the one-eyed. I merely take the liberty of a free subject to vituperate certain of his edicts—& that only in private.——I shall be very glad to see you—or your remaining canto[3]—if both together so much the better.——I am interrupted——

[TO JOHN HANSON]   *Octr. 9th. 1815*

Dear Sir—I enclose you a letter from Nottingham—& wish to know what I am to do—& to apprize you that I may have the proper steps taken to defend the action for the amount—can they bring it without serving me or my solicitor with the process?—perhaps you had better write and direct an [appea]rance to be made for me—in order to gain the time—as you know present payment is not in my power.——Mealey has I understand been doing every thing to impede & discourage the sale of Newstead—I desire therefore that he may have his discharge as tenant immediately.——He shall not remain on that property—while it is mine.—Col. [Dalbiack's?] money is I hear to be had in a few days[1]—I hope you have our papers ready—that it may be received—& that nothing is wanting from Hoar or you—as you must be sensible how important it is to me that you should have all in readiness—I want to see you—& at any rate must hear from you.

yrs. ever truly
BYRON

[1] Hunt's *Feast of the Poets*, of which he was preparing a second edition.

[2] Byron had already indicated to Hunt that he had some reservations about the merits of Wordsworth, who to Hunt was the "King Richard" of the bards, but he did not want to be set down in *The Feast* as one who did not pay some homage to him. See Oct. 30, 1815, to Hunt.

[3] The last canto of Hunt's *Story of Rimini*.

[1] This was a time when Byron's debtors were closing in on him, and there were threatened executions. Sir Ralph Noel, in an effort to help the Byrons, had sold some of the farms on the Seaham estate to a Col. Dalbiac for £7,350, but "the law's delay" was such that no relief came in time and Byron was forced to sell his books and bailiffs were in the house just before Lady Byron's lying-in. See Elwin, *Lord Byron's Wife*, p. 320.

P.S. My best respects to Lord & Lady P[ortsmouth].——Lady Byron being in her eighth month will render it difficult for her to be absent from home at this time.—

[TO JOHN HANSON]   *10th. Oct. 1815*

Dear Sir—At half past *two* tomorrow I will wait upon you—if that hour don't suit—send up in the morning & *fix* a time.

                                                                yrs. ever
                                                                    B

[TO LEIGH HUNT]   *Octr. 18th. 1815*

Dear Hunt—I send you a thing whose greatest value is it's present rarity[1]—the present copy contains some M.S. corrections previous to an Edition which was printed but not published—and in short all that is in the suppressed Edition the 5th.—except twenty lines in addition for which there was not room in the copy before me.———There are in it *many* opinions I have altered—& some which I retain—upon the whole I wish that it had never been written—though my sending you this copy (the only one in my possession unless one of Lady B[yron]'s be excepted) may seem at variance with this statement—but my reason for this is very different—it is however the only gift I have made of the kind this many a day—

P.S. You probably know that it is not in print for sale—nor ever will be—(if I can help it)—again.——

[TO SAMUEL TAYLOR COLERIDGE]
                                          13—Terrace Piccadilly—Oct. 18th. 1815

Dear Sir—Your letter I have just received.—I will willingly do whatever you direct about the volumes in question—the sooner the better—it shall not be for want of endeavour on my part—as a Negociator with the "Trade" (to talk technically) that you are not enabled to do yourself justice.—Last Spring I saw W[alte]r Scott—he repeated to me a considerable portion of an unpublished poem of yours[1]—the wildest &

---

[1] This was a copy of *English Bards and Scotch Reviewers*, with Byron's manuscript corrections and alterations for the suppressed 5th edition.
[1] *Christabel.*

finest I ever heard in that kind of composition—the title he did not mention—but I think the heroine's name was Geraldine—at all events —the "toothless mastiff bitch"—& the "witch Lady"—the descriptions of the hall—the lamp suspended from the image—& more particularly of the *Girl* herself as she went forth in the evening—all took a hold on my imagination which I never shall wish to shake off.—I mention this—not for the sake of boring you with compliments—but as a prelude to the hope that this poem is or is to be in the volumes you are now about to publish.—I do not know that even "Love" or the "Ancient Mariner" are so impressive—& to me there are few things in our tongue beyond these two productions.———W[alte]r Scott is a staunch & sturdy admirer of yours—& with a just appreciation of your capacity—deplored to me the want of inclination & exertion which prevented you from giving full scope to your mind.—I will answer your question as to the "Beggar's [Bush?]" [2]—tomorrow—or next day—I shall see Rae & Dibdin (the acting M[anage]rs) tonight for that purpose.—Oh—your tragedy—I do not wish to hurry you—but I am indeed very anxious to have it under consideration—it is a field in which there are none living to contend against you & in which I should take a pride & pleasure in seeing you compared with the dead— I say this *not* disinterestly but as a *Committee* man—we have nothing even tolerable—except a tragedy of Sotheby's—which shall not interfere with yours—when ready—you can have no idea what trash there is in the four hundred *fallow* dramas now lying on the shelves of D[rury] L[ane]. I never thought so highly of good writers as lately— since I have had an opportunity of comparing them with the bad.—

ever yrs. truly
BYRON

[TO LEIGH HUNT]   *Octr. 22d. 1815*

My dear Hunt—You have excelled yourself—if not all your Contemporaries in the Canto which I have just finished[1]—I think it above the former books—but that is as it should be—it rises with the subject —the conception appears to me perfect—and the execution perhaps as nearly so—as verse will admit.———There is more originality than I recollect to have seen elsewhere within the same compass—and fre-

---

2 The *Beggar's Bush* was the title of a tragi-comedy by John Fletcher and Philip Massinger.

1 The third canto of *The Story of Rimini*.

quent & great happiness of expression—in short—I must turn to the faults—or what appear such to me—there are not many—nor such as may not be easily altered being almost all *verbal*:—and of the same kind as those I pretended to point out in the former cantos—viz—occasional quaintness—& obscurity—& a kind of harsh & yet colloquial compounding of epithets—as if to avoid saying common things in the common way—"difficile est proprié communia dicere"[2] seems at times to have met with in you a literal translator.—I have made a few & but a few pencil marks in the M.S.—which you can follow or not as you please.——The poem as a whole will give you a very high station—but where is the Conclusion?—don't let it cool in the composition?—you can always delay as long as you like revising—though I am not sure—in the very face of Horace—that the "nonum &c."[3] is attended with advantage unless we read "months" for "years." I am glad the book sent reached you[4]—I forgot to tell you the story of it's suppression—which shan't be longer than I can make it.—My motive for writing that poem was I fear not so fair as you are willing to believe it—I was angry—& determined to be witty—& fighting in a crowd dealt about my blows against all alike without distinction or discernment.—When I came home from the East—among other new acquaintances & friends—politics & the state of the Notts rioters—(of which county I am a landholder—& Ld. Holland Recorder of the town) led me by the good offices of Mr. Rogers into the society of Ld. Holland—who with Lady H[olland] were particularly kind to me:— about March[5] 1812—this introduction took place—when I made my first speech on the Frame bill—in the same debate in which Ld. H[olland] spoke.——Soon after this I was correcting the 5th. E[ditio]n of E[nglish] B[ards] for the press—when Rogers represented to me that he knew Ld & Lady H[olland] would not be sorry if I suppressed any further publication of that poem—& I immediately acquiesced: & with great pleasure—for I had attacked them upon a fancied & false provocation with many others—& neither was nor am sorry to have done what I could to stifle that ferocious rhapsody.—This was

[2] Horace, *De Arte Poetica*, line 128. "It is difficult to treat of common things in an appropriate manner [in an un-hackneyed way]". Byron used the phrase as a motto when he published the first two cantos of *Don Juan*.

[3] Horace, *De Arte Poetica*, line 388: Nonumque prematur in anum . . . "Let (your compositions) rest in the cupboard for nine years."

[4] *English Bards and Scotch Reviewers*. See Oct. 18, 1815, to Hunt, note 1.

[5] It was in February that Byron first became acquainted with Lord Holland, whom he consulted before making his maiden speech in the House of Lords on February 27, 1812.

subsequent to my acquaintance with Lord H[olland] & was neither
expressed nor understood as a *condition* of that acquaintance—Rogers
told me he thought I ought to suppress it—I thought so too—& did it
as far as I could—& that's all.——I sent you my copy—because I
consider your having it much the same—as having it myself—Lady
B[yron] has one—I desire not to have any other and sent it only as a
curiosity and a memento.—

[TO SAMUEL TAYLOR COLERIDGE]   *Octr. 27th. 1815*

Dear Sir—I have "the Christabelle" safe—& am glad to see it in
such progress—surely a little effort would complete the poem.—On
your question with W[alter] Scott—I know not how to speak—he is a
friend of mine—and though I cannot contradict your statement I must
look to the most favourable part of it—all I have ever seen of him has
been frank—fair & warm in regard towards you—and when he repeated this very production it was with such mention as it deserves and
that could not be faint praise.—But I am partly in the same scrape myself as you will see by the enclosed extract from an unpublished poem
which I assure you was written before (not seeing your "Christabelle"
for that you know I never did till this day) but before I heard Mr.
S[cott] *repeat* it—which he did in June last[1]—and this thing was begun
in January & more than half written before the Summer—the coincidence is only in this particular passage and if you will allow me—in
publishing it (which I shall perhaps do *quietly* in Murray's collected
Edition of my rhymes—though not *separately*) I will give the extract
from you—and state that the original thought & expression have been
many years in the Christabelle. The stories—scenes—&c. are in
general quite different—mine is the siege of Corinth in 1715—when
the Turks retook the Morea from the Venetians——the Ground is

---

[1] Coleridge had written the first part of *Christabel* in 1798. A friend, John
Stoddart, later Chief Justice of Malta, had read the manuscript and repeated some of
the lines to Walter Scott in 1802, when he was planning to write *The Lay of the
Last Minstrel*. Scott later acknowledged that the poem's cadences haunted him and
that he owed something of Gilpin Horner to Coleridge. He also borrowed a few
phrases. Then in 1815 Scott recited to Byron some lines he remembered from
Coleridge's poem. Byron had already written some lines in *The Siege of Corinth* that
seemed to reflect the tone and manner of *Christabel*, though not closely the words.
To guard himself against the charge of plagiarism he wrote this letter to Coleridge
and added a note to the poem when it was published in 1816, acknowledging the
resemblance but giving the circumstances that would absolve him of intentional
imitation. (See *Poetry*, III, 471.) *Christabel*, through Byron's influence with Murray,
was published later the same year.

quite familiar to me—for I have passed the Isthmus *six*—I think—
eight times—in my way to & fro——the hero—is a renegade—& the
night before the storm of the City—he is supposed to have an apparition or wraith of his mistress—to warn him of his destiny—as he sits
among the ruins of an old temple.—I write to you in the greatest
hurry——I know not what you may think of this:—if you like I will
cut out the passage—& do as well as I can without—or what you
please.—

ever yrs.
BYRON

P.S. Pray write soon—I will answer the other points of your letter
immediately.——

[TO JOHN TAYLOR]   *October 27th. 1815*

P.S. Your best way will be to publish no more eulogies, except upon
the "elect"; or if you do, let him (the editor) have a previous copy, so
that the compliment and the attack may appear together, which would,
I think, have a good effect.

[TO THOMAS MOORE]   *13, Terrace, Piccadilly, October 28, 1815*

You are, it seems, in England again, as I am to hear from every body
but yourself; and I suppose you punctilious, because I did not answer
your last Irish letter. When did you leave the "swate country?" Never
mind, I forgive you;—a strong proof of—I know not what—to give
the lie to—
"He never pardons who hath done the wrong."
You have written to **. You have written to Perry, who intimates
hope of an Opera from you. Coleridge has promised a Tragedy.[1] Now,
if you keep Perry's word, and Coleridge keeps his own, Drury-lane
will be set up;—and, sooth to say, it is in grievous want of such a lift.
We began at speed, and are blown already. When I say "we." I mean
Kinnaird, who is the "all in all sufficient."[2] and can count, which none
of the rest of the Committee can.
It is really very good fun, as far as the daily and nightly stir of these

---

[1] Coleridge had written to Byron on Oct. 17, 1815, that he was composing a
tragedy which he hoped to submit to the Drury Lane committee before the third
week in December, but of course it was never finished.
[2] *Othello*, Act IV, scene 1.

strutters and fretters go; and, if the concern could be brought to pay a shilling in the pound, would do much credit to the management. Mr.———[Sotheby] has an accepted tragedy, * * * * [*Ivan*], whose first scene is in his sleep (I don't mean the author's). It was forwarded to us as a prodigious favourite of Kean's; but the said Kean, upon interrogation, denies his eulogy, and protests against his part. How it will end, I know not.

I say so much about the theatre, because there is nothing else alive in London at this season. All the world are out of it, except us, who remain to lie in,—in December, or perhaps earlier. Lady B[yron] is very ponderous and prosperous, apparently, and I wish it well over.

There is a play before me from a personage who signs himself "Hibernicus." The hero is Malachi, the Irishman and king; and the villain and usurper, Turgesius, the Dane. The conclusion is fine. Turgesius is chained by the leg (*vide* stage direction) to a pillar on the stage; and King Malachi makes him a speech, not unlike Lord Castlereagh's about the balance of power and the lawfulness of legitimacy, which puts Turgesius into a frenzy—as Castlereagh's would, if his audience was chained by the leg. He draws a dagger and rushes at the orator; but, finding himself at the end of his tether, he sticks it into his own carcass, and dies, saying, he has fulfilled a prophecy.

Now, this is *serious, downright matter of fact*, and the gravest part of a tragedy which is not intended for burlesque. I tell it you for the honour of Ireland. The writer hopes it will be represented:—but what is Hope? nothing but the paint on the face of Existence; the least touch of truth rubs it off, and then we see what a hollow-cheeked harlot we have got hold of. I am not sure that I have not said this last superfine reflection before. But never mind;—it will do for the the tragedy of Turgesius, to which I can append it.

Well, but how dost thou do? thou bard, not of a thousand, but three thousand![3] I wish your friend, Sir John Piano-forte,[4] had kept that to himself, and not made it public at the trial of the song-seller in Dublin. I tell you why; it is a liberal thing for Longman to do, and honourable for you to obtain; but it will set all the "hungry and dinnerless, lank-jawed judges" upon the fortunate author. But they be d————d!—the "Jeffrey and the Moore together are confident against the world in

---

[3] Moore's publisher Longman had agreed to pay £3,000 for *Lalla Rookh*, without having seen the manuscript.

[4] Sir John Stevenson, who made the musical arrangements for Moore's songs.

ink."[5] By the way, if C ∗ ∗ e [Coleridge]—who is a man of wonderful talent, and in distress, and about to publish two vols. of Poesy and Biography, and who has been worse used by the critics than ever we were—will you, if he comes out, promise me to review him favourably in the E[dinburgh] R[eview]? Praise him, I think you must, but you will also praise him *well*,—of all things the most difficult. It will be the making of him.

This must be a secret between you and me, as Jeffrey might not like such a project;—nor, indeed, might C[oleridge] himself like it. But I do think he only wants a pioneer and a sparkle or two to explode most gloriously.

Ever yours most affectionately,

B

P.S.—This is a sad scribbler's letter; but the next shall be "more of this world."

[TO LEIGH HUNT]   *13 Terrace Piccadilly Septr.—Octr. 30th. 1815*

My dear Hunt—Many thanks for your books of which you already know my opinion.[1]—Their external splendour should not disturb you as inappropriate—they have still more within than without.——I take leave to differ from you on Wordsworth[2] as freely as I once agreed with you—at that time I gave him credit for promise which is unfulfilled—I still think his capacity warrants all you say of *it* only—but that his performances since "Lyrical Ballads"—are miserably inadequate to the ability which lurks within him:—there is undoubtedly much natural talent spilt over "the Excursion" but it is rain upon rocks where it stands & stagnates—or rain upon sands where it falls without fertilizing—who can understand him?—let those who do make him intelligible.—Jacob Behman—Swedenborg—& Joanna Southcote are mere types of this Arch-Apostle of mystery & mysticism—but I have done:—no I have not done—for I have two petty & perhaps unworthy objections in small matters to make to him—which with his pretension to accurate observation & fury against Pope's false translation of the

---

[5] This is an example of how Byron used Shakespearean quotations for his own purposes. See *Henry IV*, Part I, Act V, scene 1: "The Douglas and the Hotspur both together/Are confident against the world in arms."

[1] The revised edition of Hunt's *The Feast of the Poets*.

[2] In note 20 Hunt discussed and praised Wordsworth.

"Moonlight scene in Homer"[3] I wonder he should have fallen into—
these be they.—He says of Greece in the body of his book—that it is a
land of

> "*rivers—fertile* plains—& *sounding* shores
> Under a cope of *variegated* sky"[4]

The rivers are dry half the year—the plains are barren—and the
shores *still* & *tideless* as the Mediterranean can make them—the Sky is
anything but variegated—being for months & months—but "darkly—
deeply—beautifully blue."—The next is in his notes—where he talks
of our "Monuments crowded together in the busy &c. of a large
town"—as compared with the "still seclusion of a Turkish cemetery in
some *remote* place"[5]—this is pure stuff—for *one* monument in our
Churchyards—there are *ten* in the Turkish—& so crowded that you
cannot walk between them—they are always close to the walks of the
towns—that is—merely divided by a path or road—and as to "*remote*
places"—men never take the trouble in a barbarous country to carry
their dead very far—they must have lived near to where they are
buried—there are no cemeteries in "remote places"—except such as
have the cypress & the tombstone still left when the olive & the
habitation of the living have perished.——These things I was struck
with as coming peculiarly in my own way—and in both of these he is
wrong—yet I should have noticed neither but for his attack on Pope for
a like blunder—and a peevish affectation about him of despising a
popularity which he will never obtain.—I write in great haste—& I
doubt—*not* much to the purpose—but you have it hot & hot—just as it
comes—& so let it go.——By the way—both he & you go too far
against Pope's "so when the Moon &c." it is no translation I know—
but it is not such *false* description as asserted—I have read it on the
spot—there is a burst—and a lightness—and a glow—about the night
in the Troad—which makes the "planets vivid"—& the "pole glow-
ing" the moon is—at least the sky is clearness itself—and I know no
more appropriate expression for the expansion of such a heaven—over
the scene—the plain—the sea—the sky—Ida—the Hellespont—

[3] In the "Essay Supplementary to the Preface" in the 1815 edition of his
Poems Wordsworth criticised Pope's "translation of the celebrated moonlight scene
in the *Iliad*."

[4] *Excursion*, Book IV (first edition, 1814).

[5] In an "Essay upon Epitaphs" added to the notes in the first edition of *The
Excursion* (page 437), Wordsworth says: "Let a man only compare in imagination
the unsightly manner in which our Monuments are crowded together in the busy,
noisy, unclean, and almost grassless Church-yard of a large Town, with the still
seclusion of a Turkish Cemetery, in some remote place. . . ."

Simois—Scamander—and the isles—than that of a "flood of Glory."
——I am getting horribly lengthy—& must stop—to the whole of
your letter I say "ditto to Mr. Burke" as the Bristol Candidate cried
by way of Electioneering harangue:[6]—you need not speak of morbid
feelings—& vexations to me—I have plenty—for which I must blame
partly the times—& chiefly myself: but let us forget them—*I* shall be
very apt to do so—when I see you next—will you come to the theatre
& see our new Management?—you shall cut it up to your heart's content root & branch afterwards if you like—but come & see it?—if not I
must come & see you.—

ever yrs very truly & affectly.
BYRON

P.S.—Not a word from Moore for these 2 months.—Pray let me
have the rest of "Rimini["] you have 2 excellent points in that poem—
originality—& Italianism—I will back you as a bard against half the
fellows on whom you throw away much good criticism & eulogy—but
don't let your bookseller publish in *Quarto* it is the worst size possible
for circulation—I say this on Bibliopolical authority—

again—yours ever

ß

[TO THOMAS MOORE]   *Terrace, Piccadilly, October 31, 1815*

I have not been able to ascertain precisely the time of duration of the
stock market; but I believe it is a good time for selling out, and I hope
so. First, because I shall see you; and, next, because I shall receive
certain monies on behalf of Lady B[yron], the which will materially
conduce to my comfort,—I wanting (as the duns say) "to make up a
sum."

Yesterday, I dined out with a largeish party, where were Sheridan
and Colman, Harry Harris of C[ovent] G[arden][1] and his brother, Sir
Gilbert Heathcote, D[ougla]s Kinnaird, and others, of note and notoriety. Like other parties of the kind, it was first silent, then talky, then
argumentative, then disputatious, then unintelligible, then altogethery,

---

[6] Henry Cruger, seeking a seat with Burke at Bristol, spoke those words on
the hustings, according to Burke's biographers. Apparently they were effective,
for both were returned to Parliament.

[1] Unidentified. Thomas Harris (d. 1820) had been proprietor and manager of
Covent Garden in the eighteenth century. He had a violent dispute over management with Colman the elder. He was later stage-manager.

then inarticulate, and then drunk. When we had reached the last step of this glorious ladder, it was difficult to get down again without stumbling;—and, to crown all, Kinnaird and I had to conduct Sheridan down a d————d corkscrew staircase, which had certainly been constructed before the discovery of fermented liquors, and to which no legs, however crooked, could possibly accommodate themselves. We deposited him safe at home, where his man, evidently used to the business, waited to receive him in the hall.

Both he and Colman were, as usual, very good; but I carried away much wine, and the wine had previously carried away my memory; so that all was hiccup and happiness for the last hour or so, and I am not impregnated with any of the conversation. Perhaps you heard of a late answer of Sheridan to the watchman who found him bereft of that "divine particle of air," called reason, * * * * * * * * * * He, the watchman, found Sherry in the street, fuddled and bewildered, and almost insensible. "Who are you, sir?"—no answer. "What's your name?"—a hiccup. "What's your name?"—Answer, in a slow, deliberate, and impassive tone—"Wilberforce!!!"[2] Is not that Sherry all over?—and, to my mind, excellent. Poor fellow, *his* very dregs are better than the "first sprightly runnings" of others.

My paper is full, and I have a grievous headache.

P.S.—Lady B[yron] is in full progress. Next month will bring to light (with the aid of "Juno Lucina, *fer opem*," or rather *opes*,[3] for the last are most wanted), the tenth wonder of the world—Gil Blas being the eighth, and he (my son's father) the ninth.

[TO SIR JAMES BLAND BURGES (*a*)]   *Octr. 31st. 1815*

Dear Sir James—It has been intimated to me that a demur has arisen on your part to the signature of certain papers requisite to complete the purchase of Col. Dolbiac from Sir R[alph] Noel[1]—by the advice of certain most sagacious Counsel—because of the probability that Lady Noel will have another child.——The certificate of the Curate—& an extract from the Parish Register—which I understand states her Ladyship to be sixty four years of age—may perhaps after mature delibera-

---

[2] William Wilberforce (1759–1833), chiefly noted as an anti-slavery advocate, became a strict Evangelical, one of the "Clapham Sect", and was a teetotaller.

[3] According to mythological tradition, Juno Lucina presided over child-birth, and newly born babies were under her protection. ferre opem = to bring aid; opes = means, wealth.

[1] See Oct. 9, 1815, to Hanson, note 1.

tion & a few further references to Lawyers & physicians of approved skill & practice—induce you to incur the hazard of this responsibility.—In the mean time—as Lady Byron has at present a little preceded her mother in the promise of increasing the family—and the advance of that part of the settlement upon her—would be a great convenience to me—I hope it will not be deemed intrusive—if I request (after these important points have been sufficiently canvassed) that you will have the goodness to annex your name in conjunction with the remaining parties—to the deeds in question. Believe me to be with great truth & respect

your obliged & affect. Sert.

BYRON

[TO SIR JAMES BLAND BURGES (*b*)]   *Octr. 31st. 1815*

Dear Sir James—Though Mr. Sugden[1] must not only be an excellent lawyer but a profound natural philosopher—I am happy to hear that Mr. *Long*[2] has sanctioned *your opinion* by his coincidence—& thereby permitted us all to exert our understandings & judge of common things in the common way—without putting in a parenthesis for miracles.—Howbeit I have no objection to give the security you mention—& will have a deed executed by my lawyer for the purpose—stating the facts—the age of Lady N[oel]—&c. &c. & give you ample satisfaction.——To be serious—it appears to me—that No lawyer—nor man of common sense could have started such an objection—unless for the purposes of impediment & vexation to the parties concerned—if Lady Noel's age be indeed 64 & can be proved so.——I shall be very glad of your drama[3]—& think Mr. Sugden may furnish you with a very novel & comic incident for it.——When finished I shall be happy to receive it—the theatre is much in want of something of the kind.

ever truly yrs.

BYRON

[TO SIR JAMES BLAND BURGES]   *Novr. 1st. 1815*

Dear Sir—I thank you for the copy of the will.—My reasons for believing in Mr. Long's intentional impertinence were—because I have

[1] Unidentified.

[2] Unidentified.

[3] A barrister who held various posts and who served in Parliament, Burges also wrote poems, plays, and epigrams. And he apparently tried to enlist Byron's interest at Drury Lane to get his play produced.

the authority of the professional for saying his conduct was unprofessional—of gentlemen for saying it was ungentlemanly—and of the unprovoked (for I would not trust my own judgment feeling as I did) for pronouncing it an unprovoked & gratuitous insult.——I applied to the Executors firstly—because—it is usual when the servant is rude to appeal to the Master—& secondly because insolent as I knew him to be—& bad as I have many reasons to believe him—I could hardly think he would venture so to conduct himself without the hope of protection of his employers.——It cannot be viewed as a transaction between Mr. H[anson?] & Mr. L[ong]:—the application was made as from me at my request—& in compliance with that I understood to be a promised courtesy from the Executors.—As to the thing itself—surely there cannot be two opinions on the *manner* or the *intention*. You ask me why "I should suppose an intention to offend me on the part of Mr. Long"—to which I can answer best by another question—viz—can there be a doubt on the part of any connection of Lady or Sir R[alp]h Noel of Mr. Long's "intentions" towards her & every branch of her family?——I say nothing to you which I do not wish to be stated to that person—Mr. L—& which I will not myself say to him still more explicitly—taking the responsibility personal or otherwise on myself.——And now having said so much upon one of those beings —who seem sent into the world to make mischief among their betters:—one word from myself to you—I have looked upon you with respect & esteem which has encreased with our acquaintance—and to hurt your feelings would be to injure my own—whatever has passed in the present instance is the result of your situation & the conduct of the man to whom my last & present note referred—& not from any want of personal regard or respect on the part of

yrs. very truly
BYRON

[TO THOMAS MOORE]   *November 4th, 1815*

Had you not bewildered my head with the "stocks," your letter would have been answered directly. Hadn't I to go to the city? and hadn't I to remember what to ask when I got there? and hadn't I forgotten it?

I should be undoubtedly delighted to see you; but I don't like to urge against your reasons my own inclinations. Come you must soon, for stay you *won't.* I know you of old;—you have been too much leavened with London to keep long out of it.

329

Lewis is going to Jamaica to suck his sugar-canes. He sails in two days; I enclose you his farewell note. I saw him last night at D[rury] L[ane] T[heatre] for the last time previous to his voyage. Poor fellow! he is really a good man—an excellent man—he left me his walking-stick and a pot of preserved ginger. I shall never eat the last without tears in my eyes, it is so *hot*. We have had a devil of a row among our ballerinas: Miss Smith[1] has been wronged about a hornpipe. The Committee have interfered, but Byrne, the d————d ballet-master, won't budge a step. *I* am furious, so is George Lamb. Kinnaird is very glad, because—he don't know why; and I am very sorry, for the same reason. To-day I dine with K[innair]d—we are to have Sheridan and Colman again; and tomorrow, once more, at Sir Gilbert Heathcote's.[2]

* * * * * * * * * * * * * * *

Leigh Hunt has written a *real good* and *very original Poem*,[3] which I think will be a great hit. You can have no notion how very well it is written, nor should I, had I not redde it. As to us, Tom—eh, when art thou out? If you think the verses worth it,[4] I would rather they were embalmed in the Irish Melodies, than scattered abroad in a separate song—much rather. But when are thy great things out? I mean the Po[em] of Po[em]s—thy Shah Nameh.[5] It is very kind in Jeffrey to like the Hebrew Melodies.[6] Some of the fellows here preferred Sternhold and Hopkins,[7] and said so;—"the fiend receive their souls therefor!"

I must go and dress for dinner. Poor, dear Murat,[8] what an end!

---

[1] Of Miss Smith, who married the ballet-master Oscar Byrne, Byron said elsewhere ("Detached Thoughts", No. 68): "I used to protect Miss Smith, because she was like Lady Jane Harley in the face."

[2] It was at Lady Heathcote's ball that Caroline Lamb made a dramatic scene on account of Byron in 1813. (See July 6, 1813, to Lady Melbourne, (*a*) and (*b*), Vol. 3, pp. 71–72.)

[3] *The Story of Rimini.*

[4] These were the stanzas beginning "There's not a joy the world can give like that it takes away" which he had sent to Moore. They were eventually set to music by Sir John Stevenson and published by James Power, publisher of Moore's *Irish Melodies*.

[5] The *Shah Námeh* is a rhymed history of Persia. Byron uses the name as a synonym for Moore's eastern tale *Lalla Rookh*.

[6] Jeffrey had written June 11, 1815, to Moore, who passed the compliment on to Byron: "I have just got a set of Lord Byron's works, and read his *Hebrew Melodies* for the first time. There is rather a monotony in the subjects, but a sweetness of versification to which I know but one parallel, and a depth and force of feeling which, though indicated only by short sobs and glances, is here as marked and peculiar as in his greater pieces." (Moore, *Memoirs*, II, 79.)

[7] Sixteenth-century versifiers of the Psalms.

[8] Joachim Murat had been proclaimed King of Naples and the Two Sicilies in 1808, and on Napoleon's return he attempted a campaign against the Austrians but was defeated and captured and condemned to death on October 13, 1815.

You know, I suppose, that his white plume used to be a rallying point in battle, like Henry Fourth's. He refused a confessor and a bandage;— so would neither suffer his soul or body to be bandaged. You shall have more to-morrow or next day.

Ever, &c.

[TO JOHN MURRAY (*a*)]   *Nov. 4th. 1815*

Dr. Sr.—I will attend to the remarks when I have the proofs—of which there is no hurry.—I send you a vol. of the Turkish History— with the page (151) & paragraph marked—on which the story is founded—& which we must extract as a short advertisement[1]—I suppose you mean it to be the 1st. part of the 4th vol. of the po[em]s.— —I also want to make a short extract from Christabelle in a note about Coleridge which I shall insert.

Yours tr[ul]y

ß

[TO JOHN MURRAY (*b*)]   *Novr. 4th. 1815*

Dr. Sr.—When you have been enabled to form an opinion on Mr. Coleridge's M.S. you will oblige me by returning it—as in fact I have no authority to let it out of my hands.—I think most highly of it—& feel anxious that you should be ye. publisher[1]—but if you are not—I do not despair of finding those who will.——I have written to Mr. L[eig]h Hunt stating your willingness to treat with him[2]—which when I saw you—I understood you to be——terms & time I leave to his pleasure & your discernment—but this I will say—that I think it the *safest* thing you ever engaged in—I speak to you—as a man of business—were I to talk as a reader or a Critic—I should say it was a very wonderful & beautiful performance—with just enough of fault to make its beauties more remarked & remarkable.—And now to the last—my own—which I feel ashamed of after the others—publish or not as you like I don't care *one damn*—if *you* don't—no one else shall—

---

1 This was for *The Siege of Corinth*, which Byron still expected Murray to publish with the collected edition of his poems. It was published separately with *Parisina* in 1816.

1 Murray published *Christabel*, with other poems of Coleridge, in 1816.

2 Murray followed Byron's advice and published Hunt's *The Story of Rimini* in 1816.

& I never thought or dreamed of it except as one in the collection—if it is worth being in the 4th vol. put it there & nowhere else—& if not put it in the fire.—

yrs.

𝕭

[TO LEIGH HUNT] [*Nov. 4–6, 1815?*]

[First part of letter missing] . . . of any in his way:——With regard to the E[nglish] B[ards]—I have no concealments—nor desire to have any from you or yours—the suppression occurred (I am as sure as I can be of anything) in the manner stated—I have never regretted that— but very often the composition—that is the *humeur* of a great deal in it:——as to the quotation you allude to I have no right—nor indeed desire to prevent it[1]—but on the contrary in common with all other writers—I do & ought to take it as a compliment.——The paper on the Methodists[2] was sure to raise the bristles of the godly—I redde it and agree with the writer on one point in which you & he perhaps differ—that an addiction to poetry is very generally the result of "an uneasy mind in an uneasy body" disease or deformity have been the attendants of many of our best—Collins mad—Chatterton *I* think— mad—Cowper mad—Pope crooked—Milton blind—Gray—(I have heard the last was afflicted by an incurable & very grievous distemper— though not generally known) & others——I have somewhere redde however that poets *rarely* go *mad*—I suppose the writer means that their insanity effervesces & evaporates in verse—may be so.—I have not time nor paper to *attack* your *system*—which ought to be done— were it only because it is a *system*—so by & bye—have at you.—

yrs. ever
BYRON

[1] In an article in the *Examiner* (Nov. 5, 1815) Hunt quoted from Byron's note on Henry Kirke White in *English Bards and Scotch Reviewers* (note to line 831).
[2] The paper on the Methodists had appeared in the *Examiner* of Oct. 22, 1815. The writer had taken the view that poets and artists had an "original poverty of spirit and weakness of constitution". Hunt refuted this, quoting Byron on Kirke White, but Byron tended to agree with the writer of the article.

[TO JOHN HANSON] *Novr. 8th. 1815*

Dear Sir/—Thorogood on my giving bills for the demands of two of the annuitants withdrew the executions[1]—& promised me that the rest should stand over for the present—(till I received this forthcoming money) he said the other *two* would not be enforced—he had authority to say so.—Notwithstanding this—I enclose one just come in—not through *him* however but from an Attorney (*Rhodes* on the part of Baxter)[2]—I wish you to send to Thorogood & ask him how he came to deceive me so completely—because I see no purpose it could answer whatever.——I should also be glad to know what you think I had best do.——

yrs. truly
BYRON

[TO JOHN MURRAY] *Novr. 14th. 1815*

Dear Sir/—I return you your bills—not accepted—but certainly not *unhonoured*.[1]—Your present offer is a favour which I would accept from you if I accepted such from any man:—had such been my intention I can assure you I would have asked you fairly and as freely as you would give—& I cannot say more of my confidence or your conduct.——The circumstances which induce me to part with my books—though sufficiently—are not *immediately* pressing—I have made up my mind to them—& there's an end.—Had I been disposed to tresspass on your kindness in this way;—it would have been before now—but I am not sorry to have an opportunity of declining it—as it sets my opinion of you—& indeed of human Nature in a different light from that in which I have been accustomed to consider it.——Believe me very truly

yr. obliged & humble Sert.
BYRON

[TO ALEXANDER RAE] *Novr. 19th. 1815*

Dear Sir—I have the recollection—(though not a very distinct one through the medium of a severe headache the consequence of Mr.

---

[1] After the death of Lord Wentworth, Byron's debtors supposed that he had come into money and closed in on him.

[2] Baxter was the coachmaker.

[1] Hearing of Byron's intention to sell his books because of his financial difficulties, Murray sent him a cheque for £1,500, saying that he could give him as much more in a few weeks, and offering to sell his copyrights for his benefit. (Smiles, *A Publisher and His Friends*, I, 353.)

Kinnaird's hospitality) of having expressed myself last night harshly in the matter of "Sotheby versus Kean" with regard to the latter of those gentlemen.—This was wrong—in the *manner*—first because he was not present—secondly—because I was heated with wine—but I was irritated & carried away by the progress of the discussion—& used stronger language than was warranted by the occasion which I regret.—I do not think—at least I hope—that I am not apt to sin in this sort—& as I have been very anxious to keep up the courtesies of our new Connections—I cannot swerve from them myself without feeling quite as much—upon reflection—if not more—than if I saw them infringed by others.————With regard to the *matter* of *fact* however—which was in question—I retain my opinion that Mr. Sotheby has made out his Statement.————Mr. Kinnaird knows nothing of this letter—but I have no objection to his seeing it—as also Mr. Lambe [,] Mr. Dibdin & Mr. Kean.————I have no hesitation in saying—explicitly—& certainly spontaneously—& not from the suggestion of any person—that I regret having spoken of Mr. Kean in harsh & hasty terms—the *strength* of which I can only account for—by that of the wine I had taken—& the turn which the discussion took.— Having said this—I must still repeat—that this regret extends only to the *expression*—as improper:—on the main point of Mr. Sotheby's assertion being correct—I retain my beliefs.—

I am very truly yr. obliged & obedt. Sert.

BYRON

[TO————————]   *13 Terrace Piccadilly Novr. 28th. 1815*

Sir—I feel great regret in the apprehension that my delay in return-ing your M.S. may have occasioned any inconvenience—your letter had been mixed with others—& as there was no date nor name to the poem—I was at a loss where to address ye Author.——I am sorry to say that I know of no situation in D[rury] L[ane] T[heatre] or else-where—where my recommendation would be of service—the difficul-ties in which that property is involved being such as to render the strictest economy unavoidable—many of the offices have been done away with or retrenched—& the rest were filled up at the beginning of the Season.—I must also set you right on one point—I am *not* "Chair-man" of the Committee—neither do I possess greater influence there —than the remaining members.———Upon your poem I have no pretensions to pass an opinion—the title is poetical—& the subject affords the most extensive field for the Imagination;—I have no doubt that you have treated it as it deserves:—with good wishes for it's success I have the honour to be

yr. very obedt. humble Sert.
BYRON

[TO THOMAS DIBDIN]   *13 Piccadilly Terrace Decr. 1st.* [1815]

Dear Sir—I send you two things one of which called "the Family likeness" is I think very good—of the other I can say nothing but desire an early answer on the subject of both—particularly the former—they were sent to me yesterday.

Yours truly
BYRON

[TO CHARLES HANSON]   *Decr. 13th. 1815*

Dear Charles—I have seen your father once since your letter—& since I met Lady P[ortsmouth][1] at his house.——He still presses an immediate decision on your part:—I could only repeat your wishes on that subject as far as it was safe so to do—but I do not think that any representation from my quarter will alter his determination on that point.[2]—I told him as you desired me—that you would return—only requesting not to be pressed upon the subject—on which condition you would engage not to marry without his knowledge—I hope I have not misstated your request. His answer was still the same—& really feeling as I do upon the whole business—more particularly as he himself told me what had passed about Mr. T. H. & Eliza—I found it very difficult to urge him further.—I do not presume to advise you—I only wish with all my heart—that—but I suppose it is of no use—& I may as well hold my tongue.—

ever yrs. very truly
BYRON

P.S.—If I can be of any use—command me—I forgot to say—that your father said—he would receive you with the greatest joy provided this were given up.

[1] Hanson's daughter Mary Anne had married Lord Portsmouth.
[2] Charles Hanson had set his heart on marrying a girl of whom his father disapproved, and Byron was trying to act as intermediary between him and his father.

Decr. 17th. 1815

Dear Sir/—Pray get on as quick as you can—I shall expect your checks with the deeds about *one* tomorrow—which had better at any rate be got forward—These cursed delays of these fellows—(Sir R[alph]'s people, Ld. M &c.) are beyond all provocation unnecessary —I have sent a note to Ld. Melbourne desiring him to forward it—

ever yrs.

BYRON

[TO THE REV. CHARLES ROBERT MATURIN[1]] *Terrace Piccadilly.—*
Decr. 21st. 1815

Sir—Mr. Lamb—(one of my colleagues in the S[ub] Committee) & myself have read your tragedy: [2]—he agrees with me in thinking it a very extraordinary production—of great & singular merit as a composition & capable—we hope—with some alterations & omissions— of being adapted even to the *present* state of the Stage—which is not the most encouraging to men of talent.—What it seems to want for this purpose is *lowering* (in some of the Scenes)—& this for the sake of the physical powers of the actor—as well as to relieve the attention of an audience—no performer could support the tone & effort of continual & sustained passion through five acts—the "dark Knight" must also be got rid of—and another catastrophe substituted—which might be done with no great difficulty.—Perhaps you would allow my friend G. Lamb—(who is a man of great good sense & considerable powers) to attempt the adaptation—as you are not upon the spot yourself—for my own part—I would willingly—did I not conceive that it would be better done by him:—it is besides a responsibility which I could only undertake in a case—where I felt indifferent as to the result—which I need hardly add would not be so here.——I talk to you of all this—in the *hope* that it may be brought forward—but not in the certainty— Lamb & I are but two in *5*—& it is difficult to say what obstacles may not arise in the jarring interests of a theatre to prevent the representation of any piece whatever:—I have been *vainly*—since my connection with it—endeavouring to obtain a trial of the revival of "*De Mont-*

---

[1] Charles Robert Maturin (1782–1824) was a writer of terror or mystery novels, of which *Melmoth, the Wanderer* is the best known.

[2] The tragedy was *Bertram*, which on the recommendation of Scott and Byron was produced at Drury Lane in May, 1816, with great success.

fort."[3]——Kean would be Bertram—but I know no woman for [Imogine?]—but Mrs. Siddons—however—we must do the best we can for the part—supposing the play to be accepted.—At any rate—if our people will not—I shall feel it a duty to you—to offer it to Covent Garden—& will obtain what I can for you from the Booksellers—for the copyright—with your permission.—I am sorry to hear—[you] have been unfortunate in this "best of all possible worlds" but who has not?—Enclosed is a draft on my Banker (Messrs Hoares *Fleet Street—not* the Lombard St. H[oare]'s) for fifty pounds—will you excuse my taking so great a liberty as to offer you a loan—you can repay it at your own time & leisure.—I am Sir

yr. very obedt. humble Sert.

BYRON

[TO JOHN HANSON] *Decr 23d. 1815*

Dear Sir—I intended to call this evening but feeling a little indisposed will postpone it for a day or so:—I see no reason for being in a *hurry* to decide on Mr. Davison's[1] proposition—but if there is any thing particular which you wish me to answer let me know it.—Pray—do not forget to obtain Sir Ralph's endorsement to Col. Dolbiac's[2] note as soon as possible—as he & Lady Noel leave town *early* next week—

ever yrs.

BYRON

P.S.—I wish you also to send immediately to the annuitants—Thomas &c. & treat with them for the adjustment of the principal.——

[TO JOHN MURRAY] *Decr. 25th. 1815*

Dear Sir/—I send you some lines—written some time ago—& intended as an opening to the "Siege of Corinth"[1]—I had forgotten

---

[3] *De Montfort* was the most popular of Joanna Baillie's "Plays of the Passions", this one displaying the passion of hate.

[1] Unidentified.

[2] See Oct. 9, 1815, to Hanson, note 1.

[1] These were the 45 lines beginning "In the year since Jesus died for men", and ending "And sit with me on Acro-Corinth's brow?" They were not prefixed to *The Siege of Corinth* during Byron's lifetime, and were first published by Moore (I, 638–39).

them—& am not sure that they had not better be left out now—on that you & your Synod can determine[.]

yrs. &c.
Bɴ

[ᴛᴏ ᴛʜᴇ ʀᴇᴠ. ᴅʀ. ᴇ. ᴅ. ᴄʟᴀʀᴋᴇ]   [*December 28, 1815*]

With Ld. B's best remembrances to Dr. C[larke] & in a devil of a hurry.—

[ᴛᴏ ʟᴀᴅʏ ʜᴏʟʟᴀɴᴅ]   [*December 29, 1815*]

I shall have great pleasure in waiting upon you tomorrow. Lady Byron is much obliged by your enquiries and both she and the little girl are going on as well as possible. . . .

Ever yours,
Bʏʀᴏɴ

Appendix I

LIST OF LETTERS AND SOURCES

VOLUME 4

Date	Recipient	Source of Text	Page
		1814	
[1814]	[R. C. Dallas?]	MS. Murray	11
[1814?]	[?]	MS. Myers and Co. Cat. No. 5, Spring, 1965	11
[1814?]	John Murray	MS. Murray	11
[Jan.?]	[John Murray (*a*)]	Text: Myers and Co. Cat. No. 304, Spring, 1935	11
[Jan.?]	John Murray (*b*)	MS. Stark Library, University of Texas	11
[Jan.]	J. H. Merivale	MS. Carl H. Pforzheimer Library	12
Jan. 2	Thomas Moore	MS. Murray	12
Jan. 2	John Murray	MS. Murray	14
[Jan. 3?]	John Murray	MS. Murray	14
[Jan. 4]	John Murray	MS. Murray	15
Jan. 5	Thomas Ashe	MS. Murray	15
[Jan. 6?]	John Murray	MS. Murray	16
Jan. 6	Thomas Moore	Text: Moore, I, 515–16	16
[Jan. 7]	Augusta Leigh	MS. The Earl of Lytton	17
[Jan. 7]	John Murray (*a*)	MS. Murray	17
[Jan. 7]	John Murray (*b*)	MS. Murray	18
Jan. 7	Thomas Moore	Text: Moore, I, 517	18
Jan. 8	Thomas Moore	Text: Moore, I, 517–18	18
Jan. 8	Lady Melbourne	MS. Murray	19
[Jan. 8]	John Murray	Robert H. Taylor Coll. Princeton University Library	20
Jan. 10	Lady Melbourne	MS. Murray	21
[Jan. 10–11?]	John Murray	Text: *Poetry*, III, 294–295n.	22
Jan. 11	Lady Melbourne	MS. Murray	23

Date	Recipient	Source of Text	Page
	1814 (continued)		
[Jan. 11]	John Hanson	MS. Murray	24
[Jan. 11]	John Murray	MS. Murray	24
Jan. 12	Augusta Leigh	MS. The Earl of Lytton	25
[Jan.?]	Augusta Leigh	MS. British Museum (Add. 31037)	25
Jan. 12	Lady Melbourne	MS. Murray	26
Jan. 13	Lady Melbourne	MS. Murray	27
Jan. 13	Thomas Moore	Text: Moore, I, 518–19	30
Jan. 13	John Hanson	MS. Murray	30
Jan. 14	[?]	Text: S. J. Davey Cat. 30 (1889)	30
Jan. 14	John Hanson	MS. Murray	31
Jan. 15	Lady Melbourne	MS. Murray	31
[Jan. 15]	John Murray	MS. Murray	32
Jan. 16	John Murray	MS. Murray	33
Jan. 16	Lady Melbourne	MS. Murray	33
Jan. 18	J. Wedderburn Webster	MS. Murray	35
Jan. 22	John Murray	MS. Murray	36
Jan. 24	John Hanson	MS. Murray	38
Jan. 29	Lady Melbourne	MS. Murray	39
Jan. 31	John Hanson	MS. Murray	40
[Feb.?]	John Murray	MS. Murray	41
[Feb.?]	Answer to *Courier*	MS. Murray	41
Feb. 1	John Hanson	MS. Murray	43
Feb. 4	John Murray	MS. Murray	44
Feb. 5	John Murray	MS. Murray	46
Feb. 6	John Murray	MS. Murray	47
Feb. 6	Lady Melbourne	MS. Murray	47
Feb. 7	John Murray	MS. Murray	48
[Feb. 8]	John Murray	MS. Murray	49
Feb. 9	Leigh Hunt	MS. Victoria and Albert Museum, (John Forster Coll.)	49
Feb. 10	Thomas Moore	Text: Moore, I, 526–27	51
[Feb. 10]	John Murray (*a*)	MS. Murray	52
[Feb. 10]	John Murray (*b*)	MS. Murray	52
Feb. 11	Lady Melbourne	MS. Murray	53
Feb. 12	Annabella Milbanke	MS. The Earl of Lytton	54
Feb. 12	John Murray (*a*)	MS. Murray	57

Date	Recipient	Source of Text	Page
		1814 (continued)	
Feb. 12	John Murray (*b*)	MS. Murray	57
[Feb. 12?]	[Lady Holland?]	MS. Beinecke Library, Yale University	57
Feb. 14	[?]	MS. Mrs. Aristotle Onassis	58
[Feb. 14]	John Murray (*a*)	MS. Murray	58
[Feb. 14]	John Murray (*b*)	MS. Murray	59
Feb. 15	Lord Holland	MS. British Museum (Add. 51639)	59
Feb. 15	Annabella Milbanke	MS. The Earl of Lytton	60
Feb. 16	Samuel Rogers (*a*)	MS. Watson Library, University College London	61
Feb. 16	Samuel Rogers (*b*)	Text: *LJ*, III, 38	61
Feb. 16	Thomas Moore	Text: Moore, I, 530–31	62
Feb. 17	R. C. Dallas	MS. Henry E. Huntington Library	63
Feb. 17	John Murray	MS. Murray	64
Feb. 18	R. C. Dallas	MS. Stark Library, University of Texas	64
Feb. 18	Lady Melbourne	MS. Murray	64
[Feb. 18]	John Murray	MS. Murray	65
Feb. 19	Annabella Milbanke	MS. The Earl of Lytton	65
Feb. 20	J. Wedderburn Webster	MS. Historical Society of Pennsylvania	67
Feb. 20	[John Hamilton Reynolds]	Text: *The Athenaeum*, Dec. 31, 1831	68
Feb. 21	Lady Melbourne	MS. Murray	69
Feb. 25	John Murray	MS. Murray	70
Feb. 25	Annabella Milbanke	MS. The Earl of Lytton	71
Feb. 26	John Murray	MS. Murray	71
Feb. 26	Thomas Moore	Text: Moore, I, 533–34	72
Feb. 26	Samuel Rogers	MS. John Rylands University Library, Manchester	73
[Feb. 27?]	Samuel Rogers	MS. Beinecke Library, Yale University	74
Feb. 28	Francis Hodgson	Text: Moore, I, 525–26	74

Date	Recipient	Source of Text	Page
	1814 (continued)		
Feb. 28	J. Wedderburn Webster	MS. Stark Library, University of Texas	75
[March?]	Lady Melbourne	MS. Murray	75
March 1	John Murray	MS. Murray	76
March 2	John Murray	MS. Murray	76
March 3	Thomas Moore	MS. Moore, I, 535–37	76
March 3	Annabella Milbanke	MS. The Earl of Lytton	78
March 6	[Thomas Phillips?]	MS. Pierpont Morgan Library	79
March 12	Thomas Moore	Text: Moore, I, 537–38	79
March 12	John Murray	MS. Murray	81
March 15	Annabella Milbanke	MS. The Earl of Lytton	82
March 19	John Murray	MS. Murray	83
March 21	J. Wedderburn Webster	MS. Henry E. Huntington Library	83
March 24	James Hogg	Text: Printed copy, National Library of Scotland	84
March 26	Scrope Berdmore Davies	MS. William L. Clements Library, University of Michigan	86
March 30	Lady Melbourne	MS. Murray	86
March 30	Charles Hanson	MS. Murray	87
[Mar. 30– Apr. 6?]	J. Wedderburn Webster	MS. Carl H. Pforzheimer Library	88
[April?]	Harriette Wilson	Text: Harriette Wilson's *Memoirs*, 1929, p. 248	88
April 2	John Murray	MS. Murray	89
April 3	—————France	MS. Murray	89
April 8	Lady Melbourne	MS. Murray	90
April 9	John Murray	MS. Murray	91
April 9	Thomas Moore	Text: Moore, I, 540–42	91
April 10	John Murray (*a*)	MS. Murray	94
April 10	John Murray (*b*)	MS. Murray	94
April 11	John Murray	MS. Murray	94
April 12	John Murray (*a*)	MS. Murray	95
April 12	John Murray (*b*)	MS. Murray	95
April 12	John Murray (*c*)	MS. Murray	95
April 12	John Murray (*d*)	MS. Murray	96

Date	Recipient	Source of Text	Page
	1814 (continued)		
April 12	John Murray (e)	MS. Murray	96
April 12	John Cam Hobhouse	MS. Murray	96
April 15	Martin Archer Shee	MS. Carl H. Pforzheimer Library	96
April 15	Lady Sitwell	MS. Beinecke Library, Yale University	97
April 16	Bernard Barton	MS. University of Leeds Library	97
[April 16]	John Murray	MS. Murray	98
[April 17–18?]	John Murray	MS. Murray	98
April 18	[?]	MS. Stark Library, University of Texas	98
April 18	Lady Melbourne	MS. Murray	99
April 19	Dr. William Clark	MS. Trinity College Library, Cambridge	99
April 20	Thomas Moore	Text: Moore, I, 543–44	100
April 20	Annabella Milbanke	MS. The Earl of Lytton	101
April 21	John Murray	MS. Murray	102
April 22	John Murray	MS. Murray	102
[April 23]	John Murray	MS. Murray	103
April 24	Lady Melbourne	MS. Murray	103
April 25	John Murray	MS. Murray	103
April 25	Lady Melbourne	MS. Murray	104
April 26	[Sir William Gell?]	MS. John S. Mayfield Coll. Syracuse University Library	105
April 26	Charles Hanson	MS. Murray	106
April 26	John Murray (a)	MS. Murray	106
April 26	John Murray (b)	MS. Murray	106
April 29	Lady Charleville	MS. University of Nottingham Library	107
April 29	John Murray	MS. Murray	107
April 29	Charles Hanson	MS. Murray	108
April 29	Lady Melbourne	MS. Murray	108
April 30	Lady Melbourne	MS. Murray	110
May 1	Lady Melbourne	MS. Murray	111
May 1	John Murray	MS. Murray	112
May 3	Miss Mercer Elphinstone	MS. The Marquess of Lansdowne	112

Date	Recipient	Source of Text	Page
		1814 (continued)	
May 4	Thomas Moore (*a*)	Text: Moore, I, 553–44	113
May 4	Thomas Moore (*b*)	Text: Moore, I, 554	114
May 5	Thomas Moore	Text: Moore, I, 556	114
[May?]	Thomas Moore	Text: Moore, I, 555	115
[May 8?]	Thomas Moore	Text: Moore, I, 556	115
May 9	Augusta Leigh	MS. Murray	115
May 16	Lady Melbourne	MS. Murray	116
May 18	Thomas Moore	Text: Moore, I, 557	117
May 23	Thomas Moore	Text: Moore, I, 558	117
May 24	John Murray	Text: Copy in Murray MSS.	117
[May 26?]	Thomas Moore	Text: Moore, I, 555	118
May 27	John Hanson	MS. Murray	118
May 27	William Sotheby	MS. Henry E. Huntington Library	118
May 28	Lady Melbourne	MS. Murray	119
May 29	Lady Jersey	MS. The Earl of Jersey	120
May 31	Thomas Moore	Text: Moore, I, 560–61	120
June 6	John Hanson	MS. Murray	121
[June 7?]	Samuel Rogers	MS. Watson Library, University College London	121
June 8	Henrietta D'Ussières	MS. Murray	122
June 10	Lady Melbourne	MS. Murray	123
June 11	J. Wedderburn Webster	MS. Murray	124
June 12	Charles Hanson	MS. Murray	125
June 14	Thomas Moore	Text: Moore, I, 561–62	125
June 14	John Murray	MS. Murray	126
June 18	Augusta Leigh	MS. Murray	126
June 19	Samuel Rogers	MS. H. F. Oppenheimer	128
June 21	Lady Melbourne	MS. Murray	129
June 21	John Murray	MS. Murray	129
June 21	Annabella Milbanke	MS. The Earl of Lytton	130
June 24	Augusta Leigh	MS. Murray	130
June 24	John Murray (*a*)	MS. Murray	132
June 24	John Murray (*b*)	MS. Murray	132
June 26	Lady Melbourne	MS. Murray	132
June 27	Samuel Rogers	Text: *LJ*, III, 101–02	133
June 27	John Murray (*a*)	MS. Murray	134

Date	Recipient	Source of Text	Page
		1814 (continued)	
June 27	John Murray (b)	MS. Berg Coll., New York Public Library	134
June 28	Lady Melbourne	MS. Murray	134
June 29	[?]	MS. Pierpont Morgan Library	135
July 2	Lady Melbourne (a)	MS. Murray	135
July 2	Lady Melbourne (b)	MS. Murray	137
July 8	Francis Hodgson	MS. John S. Mayfield Coll., Syracuse University Library	137
July 8	Thomas Moore	Text: Moore, I, 566–67	138
[July]	Thomas Moore	Text: Moore, I, 567	138
July 11	Francis Hodgson	MS. John S. Mayfield Coll., Syracuse University Library	139
July 11	Charles Hanson	MS. Murray	140
July 11	John Murray	MS. Murray	140
July 12	John Murray	MS. Murray	140
July 13	Charles Hanson	MS. Murray	141
July 15	Charles Hanson	MS. Murray	141
July 17	John Hanson	MS. Murray	142
July 18	John Murray	MS. Murray	142
July 18	Francis Hodgson	Text: Sotheby Catalogue July 4, 1917	142
July 19	John Hanson	MS. Murray	143
July 23	John Cam Hobhouse	MS. Murray	143
July 23	John Murray	MS. Murray	144
July 23–24?]	John Murray	MS. Murray	145
July 24	John Hanson	MS. Murray	145
July 24	John Murray	MS. Murray	145
July 28	John Murray	MS. Murray	146
July 29	[John Murray] (a)	MS. Pierpont Morgan Library	146
July 29	John Murray (b)	MS. Murray	147
July 29	John Hanson	MS. Murray	147
July 31	John Murray	MS. Murray	147
[Aug.]	Charles Hanson	MS. Murray	148
Aug. 1	Annabella Milbanke	MS. The Earl of Lytton	148
Aug. 2	John Murray	MS. Murray	149

347

Date	Recipient	Source of Text	Page
		1814 (continued)	
[Dec.?]	[Francis Freeling?]	MS. Stark Library, University of Texas	237
Dec. 1	Annabella Milbanke	MS. The Earl of Lytton	238
Dec. 3	Annabella Milbanke	MS. The Earl of Lytton	239
Dec. 5	Annabella Milbanke	MS. The Earl of Lytton	239
Dec. 7	Annabella Milbanke	MS. The Earl of Lytton	240
Dec. 8	Annabella Milbanke	MS. The Earl of Lytton	240
Dec. 10	Annabella Milbanke	MS. The Earl of Lytton	241
Dec. 12	Annabella Milbanke	MS. The Earl of Lytton	241
Dec. 14	Annabella Milbanke	MS. The Earl of Lytton	242
Dec. 14	Thomas Moore	Text: Moore, I, 597–98	243
Dec. 16	Annabella Milbanke	MS. The Earl of Lytton	243
Dec. 16	Archbishop of Canterbury	MS. Rosenbach Museum	244
Dec. 17	John Hanson	MS. Murray	244
Dec. 18	Annabella Milbanke	MS. The Earl of Lytton	244
Dec. 20	Annabella Milbanke	MS. The Earl of Lytton	245
Dec. 22	Annabella Milbanke	MS. The Earl of Lytton	245
Dec. 23	Annabella Milbanke	MS. The Earl of Lytton	246
Dec. 23	John Hanson (a)	MS. Murray	247
Dec. 23	John Hanson (b)	MS. Murray	247
Dec. 25	Annabella Milbanke	MS. The Earl of Lytton	247
Dec. 31	John Hanson	MS. Murray	248
Dec. 31	John Murray	MS. Murray	248
		1815	
[Jan.?]	Douglas Kinnaird	MS. Houghton Library Harvard University	249
Jan.?	Isaac Nathan	MS. Facsimile, Nathan, *Fugitive Pieces*, pp 144–45	249
Jan. 3	Lady Melbourne	MS. Murray	249
Jan. 6	John Murray (a)	MS. Murray	250
Janı 6	John Murray (b)	MS. Murray	250
Jan. 7	John Hanson	MS. Murray	251
Jan. 7	Lady Melbourne	MS. Murray	251
Jan. 10	Thomas Moore	Text: Moore, I, 601	252
Jan. 11	John Hanson	MS. Murray	253

Date	Recipient	Source of Text	Page
		1815 (continued)	
March 3	John Cam Hobhouse	MS. Murray	278
March 4	John Hanson	MS. Murray	279
March 8	Thomas Moore	Text: Moore, I, 609–10	279
March 9	John Hanson (a)	MS. Murray	281
March 9	John Hanson (b)	MS. Murray	281
March 12	John Hanson	MS. Murray	282
March 22	John Hanson	MS. Murray	282
March 26	Thomas Claughton	MS. Biblioteca Nazionale Centrale, Florence	282
March 26	John Cam Hobhouse	MS. Clark Library, University of California, Los Angeles	283
March 26	John Hanson	MS. Murray	283
March 27	Thomas Moore	Text: Moore, I, 611–12	284
March 31	Samuel Taylor Coleridge	Text: Moore, I, 613–14	285
[April?]	John Murray	MS. Murray	287
April 4	John Murray	MS. Murray	287
April 9	John Murray	MS. Murray	287
[April 13–14?]	Lady Byron	MS. The Earl of Lytton	287
April 15	John Hanson	MS. Murray	288
April 22	Sir James Bland Burges	MS. Roe-Byron Coll., Newstead Abbey	288
April 22	Lady Melbourne	MS. Murray	289
April 23	Thomas Moore	Text: Moore, I, 619–20	289
April 25	John Hanson	MS. Murray	291
April 29	Francis Hodgson	MS. Roe-Byron Coll., Newstead Abbey	291
May 5	John Hanson	MS. Murray	292
May 18	John Hanson	MS. Murray	292
May 21	John Murray	MS. Murray	292
May 22	John Hanson	MS. Murray	293
May 23	William Hoar	MS. Carl H. Pforzheimer Library	293
May 28	John Herman Merivale	Text: Sotheby Catalogue, March 17, 1930	293
May 30	Mr. Bartley	MS. Carl H. Pforzheimer Library	293
[June?]	John Murray	Text: LJ, III, 199	294

Date	Recipient	Source of Text	Page

Date	Recipient	Source of Text	Page
		1815 (continued)	
Aug. 8	John Hanson	MS. Stark Library, University of Texas	307
Aug. 15	Francis Freeling	MS. Francis Lewis Randolph	307
[Aug. 16]	[John Murray?]	MS. Stark Library, Univeristy of Texas	307
Aug. 22	John Cam Hobhouse	MS. Murray	308
Aug. 26	John Murray	MS. Murray	308
Aug. 31	Lady Byron	MS. The Earl of Lytton	308
Sept. 1	Lady Byron	MS. The Earl of Lytton	309
Sept. 3	Mrs. George Lamb	MS. Stark Library, University of Texas	309
Sept. 4	J. Wedderburn Webster	MS. Art Gallery, Museums, and Royal Pavilion, Brighton	310
Sept. 6	John Hanson	MS. Murray	311
Sept. 15	William Sotheby	MS. Henry E. Huntington Library	311
Sept. 18	J Wedderburn Webster	MS. Art Gallery, Museums, and Royal Pavilion, Brighton	312
Sept. 23–29	Miss Catherine Levy	Text: Sotheby Catalogue, July 8, 1959	313
Sept. 24	William Sotheby	MS. Henry E. Huntington Library	313
Sept. 25	John Taylor	MS. Haverford College Library	314
Sept. 25	John Murray	MS. Murray	315
Sept. 27	John Murray	MS. Murray	315
Sept. 27	Thomas Dibdin	MS. Pierpont Morgan Library	316
Oct. 7	Leigh Hunt	MS. Victoria and Albert Museum (John Forster Collection)	316
Oct. 9	John Hanson	MS. Murray	317
Oct. 10	John Hanson	MS. Murray	318

Date	Recipient	Source of Text	Page
		1815 (continued)	
Oct. 18	Leigh Hunt	MS. Victoria and Albert Museum (John Forster Collection)	318
Oct. 18	Samuel Taylor Coleridge	MS. Beinecke Library, Yale University	318
Oct. 22	Leigh Hunt	MS. Victoria and Albert Museum (John Forster Collection)	319
Oct. 27	Samuel Taylor Coleridge	MS. Murray	321
Oct. 27	John Taylor	Text: W. P. Courtney, *Eight Friends of the Great* (1910) p. 86; Taylor, *Records*, II, 353	322
Oct. 28	Thomas Moore	Text: Moore, I, 629–31	322
Oct. 30	Leigh Hunt	MS. Victoria and Albert Museum (John Forster Collection)	324
Oct. 31	Thomas Moore	Text: Moore, I, 634–35	326
Oct. 31	Sir James Bland Burges (*a*)	MS. Roe-Byron Coll., Newstead Abbey	327
Oct. 31	Sir James Bland Burges (*b*)	MS. Stark Library, University of Texas	328
Nov. 1	Sir James Bland Burges	MS. Stark Library, University of Texas	328
Nov. 4	Thomas Moore	Text: Moore, I, 635–36	329
Nov. 4	John Murray (*a*)	MS. Murray	331
Nov. 4	John Murray (*b*)	MS. Murray	331
[Nov. 4–6?]	Leigh Hunt	MS. Victoria and Albert Museum (John Forster Collection)	332
Nov. 8	John Hanson	MS. Murray	333
Nov. 14	John Murray	MS. Murray	333
Nov. 19	Alexander Rae	MS. Beinecke Library, Yale University	333
Nov. 28	[?]	MS. Robert H. Taylor Coll., Princeton University Library	334

FORGERIES OF BYRON'S LETTERS

[1814?]: To ["My dear Mac"] Signed "N. Byron". MS. Rosenbach Museum

[1814?]: To John Hanson. MS. Stark Library, University of Texas.

April 29, 1814: To Mr. Kean. Schultess-Young, III, pp. 158–59.

July 29, 1814: To Miss Berry. Cited by Ehrsam, p. 205. No source given.

Aug. 3, 1814: To W. Webster. Schultess-Young, Letter III, pp. 158–59.

Dec. 19, 1814: To "Dear Sir". MS. Murray.

March, 1815. Thor's Day. To Sir James Mackintosh. Schultess-Young, Letter VIII, pp. 166–67.

April 3, 1815. To [?]. MS. Morgan Library.

[June–Oct.?, 1815.] Monday Morning, Piccadilly Terrace: To W. Webster. Schultess-Young, Letter V, pp. 161–62.

1815, Sept. 23 [28?] To Thomas Dibdin. MS. Roe-Byron Collection, Newstead Abbey.

Nov. 1, 1815: To Matthew Gregory Lewis. MS. La Trobe Library, State Library of Victoria, Melbourne, Australia.

Appendix III

BIBLIOGRAPHY FOR VOLUME 4

(Principal short title or abbreviated references)

Astarte—Lovelace, Ralph Milbanke, Earl of: *Astarte: A Fragment of Truth Concerning George Gordon Byron, Sixth Lord Byron*. Recorded by his grandson. New Edition by Mary Countess of Lovelace, London, 1921; New York, 1921.

Dictionary of National Biography.

Elwin, Malcolm: *Lord Byron's Wife*, London, 1962; New York, 1963. Reissue London, 1974.

Fox, Sir John: *The Byron Mystery*, London, 1924.

LBC—*Lord Byron's Correspondence*, ed. John Murray, 2 vols., London, 1922.

LJ—*The Works of Lord Byron. A New, Revised and Enlarged Edition. Letters and Journals*, ed. Rowland E. Prothero, 6 vols., London, 1898–1901.

Marchand, Leslie A.: *Byron: A Biography*, 3 vols., New York, 1957; London, 1958.

Mayne, Ethel Colburn: *The Life and Letters of Anne Isabella Lady Noel Byron*, London, 1929; New York, 1929.

Moore, Thomas: *Letters and Journals of Lord Byron: with Notices of His Life*, 2 vols., London, 1830.

Poetry—*The Works of Lord Byron. A New, Revised and Enlarged Edition. Poetry*, ed. Ernest Hartley Coleridge, 7 vols., London, 1898–1904.

Smiles, Samuel: *A Publisher and His Friends: Memoir and Correspondence of the Late John Murray . . .* , 2 vols., London, 1891.

BIOGRAPHICAL SKETCH

(See also Sketches in earlier volumes.)

Sir Walter Scott

Byron had little personal contact with Walter Scott, having met him only a few times at John Murray's and elsewhere during Scott's visits to London in 1815. Born in 1771, Scott was seventeen years older, had established a high reputation for his poetry, and had published *Waverley* (anonymous and unacknowledged) before they met. Although Byron had made some unkind remarks about Scott's romantic poetry in *English Bards and Scotch Reviewers,* he soon repented, and after their first meeting at 50 Albemarle Street their relationship was warm and cordial on both sides. Their correspondence was not extensive but Byron never forgot Scott's kind and understanding critique of the third canto of *Childe Harold* in the *Quarterly Review,* even though it was tempered with much censure of the pessimism and despair in the poem and of the author's unconventional political and moral attitudes. On his side, Byron gave expression in his letters and journals to his unbounded admiration and enthusiasm for Scott's novels, and for him as a man. Fundamentally their views of life were quite different. Scott's mild and gentle Toryism and his conventional outlook removed him far from Byron's world of passion and iconoclastic speculation. But Scott sensed, as did few of his contemporaries of like conservative minds, the essential "sincerity and strength" of Byron's character. It is a measure of his own character that he did not flinch when Byron dedicated *Cain,* his most daring drama, "To Sir Walter Scott", inscribing himself proudly "his obliged friend". Scott's comment on the poem was: "He has certainly matched Milton on his own ground". Byron had put Scott at the top of his "Gradus ad Parnassum" in his journal of 1813, and he continued to value him as a writer with no critical reservations to the very end, claiming that he had read Scott's novels fifty times.

INDEX OF PROPER NAMES

Page numbers in italics indicate main references and Biographical Sketches in the Appendix. Such main biographical references in earlier volumes are included in this index and are in square brackets.

364

COLLEGE OF MARIN

3 2555 00102702 3

DATE DUE

Demco, Inc. 38-293